Digital Computer
System Principles

McGRAW-HILL COMPUTER SCIENCE SERIES

RICHARD W. HAMMING
Bell Telephone Laboratories

EDWARD A. FEIGENBAUM
Stanford University

Bell and Newell *Computer Structures: Readings and Examples*
Cole *Introduction to Computing*
Donovan *Systems Programming*
Gear *Computer Organization and Programming*
Givone *Introduction to Switching Circuit Theory*
Hamming *Computers and Society*
Hamming *Introduction to Applied Numerical Analysis*
Hellerman *Digital Computer System Principles*
Kain *Automata Theory: Machines and Languages*
Kohavi *Switching and Finite Automata Theory*
Liu *Introduction to Combinatorial Mathematics*
Newman and Sproull *Principles of Interactive Computer Graphics*
Nilsson *Artificial Intelligence*
Ralston *Introduction to Programming and Computer Science*
Rosen *Programming Systems and Languages*
Salton *Automatic Information Organization and Retrieval*
Stone *Introduction to Computer Organization and Data Structures*
Watson *Timesharing System Design Concepts*
Wegner *Programming Languages, Information Structures, and
Machine Organization*

SECOND EDITION

Digital Computer System Principles

Herbert Hellerman

School of Advanced Technology
State University of New York at Binghamton

McGRAW-HILL BOOK COMPANY

New York   St. Louis   San Francisco   Düsseldorf
Johannesburg   Kuala Lumpur   London   Mexico   Montreal   New Delhi
Panama   Rio de Janeiro   Singapore   Sydney   Toronto

Digital Computer System Principles

1 2 3 4 5 6 7 8 9 0   K P K P   7 9 8 7 6 5 4 3

This book was set in Press Roman by Scripta Technica, Inc.
The editors were Richard F. Dojny and Annette Hall;
the designer was J. E. O'Connor;
and the production supervisor was Joe Campanella.
The drawings were done by Vantage Art, Inc.
The printer and binder was Kingsport Press, Inc.

Library of Congress Cataloging in Publication Data

Hellerman, Herbert, 1927–
    Digital computer system principles.

    (McGraw-Hill computer science series)
    1. Electronic digital computers. I. Title.
QA76.5.H448 1973   001.6'4'044   72-5530
ISBN 0-07-028073-8

To my wife Elaine

Contents

x *Contents*

Preface

The rapid progress in the design and application of general-purpose digital computers has tended to outdistance systematic treatment of the field as a whole. A major step in this treatment is to recognize information processing as a subject in its own right and not as just a tool for other disciplines. This recognition is justified by the large and growing body of techniques and knowledge derived from the many designs and widespread use of computer systems, as well as the influence of such systems on our way of thinking about problems.

This second edition is an extensively revised version of the first edition, but it has the same basic purpose: to give a college-level treatment of the important principles of digital computer systems. The viewpoint is primarily tutorial rather than encyclopedic in that it is intended to impart skills and to encourage a critical and analytic spirit. Much attention is given to those ideas that are common to many aspects of computer systems so that the reader may not only learn specific practices, but also learn *how* to learn about them to develop the awareness and confidence needed to tackle new problems. To help accomplish this, categories of structure, alternative considerations, and summary information are highlighted in charts which constitute many of the figures. Also, no opportunity is lost to repeat unifying techniques and ideas (like space-time trade-offs and the finite-state-machine model) in several different contexts.

Major changes from the first edition include: use of the APL language rather than its predecessor, the Iverson language; more emphasis on statistics and string processing in programming examples; expanded treatment of program translation; extensive revision of the chapter on finite-state and Turing machine models; statements on the principles and rationale of microprogramming; and inclusion of architectural features of the IBM system/370 as well as some detail of the buffer store organization of the Model 155.

The reader is assumed to be comfortable with mathematics through college algebra. In a few cases, higher mathematics is used, but these are infrequent and may be skipped without losing continuity. Although the text is self-contained and hence suitable to novices, it is likely to be best appreciated by those who are not encountering the subject of programming for the very first time. Those with some computer experience may also welcome a systematic coverage of material they may have acquired only piecemeal.

A key notion in all of computer science is the sequential process. Examples include methods of solving linear equations, evaluating formulas, or determining the internal switching operations to implement a single computer instruction. Programming in this broad sense is a major theme of this book. Topics in logical design, machine description, numerical analysis, and program translation are discussed from this viewpoint.

Chapter 1 gives a brief historical perspective and an informal overview of important ideas of machine organization and programming.

Chapter 2 introduces the APL programming language used throughout the book. Most of the examples and exercises in this chapter are taken from elementary numerical mathematics, statistics, and string processing.

Chapter 3 discusses several topics of language description and translation, including techniques used in compilers and interpreters.

Chapter 4 is an introductory treatment of storage organization, including descriptions of selected devices and algorithms for list maintenance, sorting, and searching.

Chapters 5, 6, and 7 are hardware-oriented and treat combinational circuits, bussing and magnetic-core storage, and sequential circuits, respectively.

Chapter 8 is concerned with the detailed representation and manipulation of information and includes arithmetic operations and coding schemes.

Chapter 9 is concerned with the architecture of computer equipment, i.e., the alternatiaves available to designers in selecting addressing, instruction sequencing, input/output control, and privileged-mode features. It also includes a detailed discussion of the rationale and technique of microprogramming and a simple machine example.

Chapter 10 is a description of the architecture of the IBM system /360 and system/370. Although the emphasis is on the appearance of the system to its machine-language users, some implementation topics are also included, especially the buffer-storage organization of the Model 155.

Chapter 11 is an introduction to reliability theory and some of its elementary applications to computer systems.

As indicated earlier, programming forms a major theme of the book. The APL language was selected to meet the need of a single comprehensive method of describing sequential processes as programs. It was chosen because its extensive set of operators and its ability to directly specify operations on arrays permit concise descriptions without requiring unessential detail. Algorithms for internal machine operations, programming systems, and problem solutions are presented as programs or statements in a single notation. Most programs are augmented by word descriptions (sometimes line-by-line). Since the first edition of this book, which used the Iverson language (an early form of APL), machine implementations of APL have become available on several computers. For those readers with access to such a system, the programs in the text may be entered and run from timesharing terminals. If an APL system is not available, the programs may still be used as a powerful means of description and may also be transcribed to other machine-executable languages. For convenience in reference and to encourage self-study, most of the APL operators (including examples of use) are summarized in a few charts.

To highlight general applicability of results and techniques, topics are often treated abstractly, but are illustrated with concrete examples. These are taken from several systems, especially IBM systems. This is due in part to my own experience but also to the fact that most of the world's computers are manufactured by IBM. Of course many features of IBM systems originated in equipment of other manufacturers or in research groups and also appear elsewhere.

Like the first edition, this book is intended for colleges and college-level courses in industry as well as for self-study. A one-semester introductory course at the senior-first-year graduate level in electrical engineering may use most of Chapters 1, 2, 5, 6, 7, and 8. A course in programming, using APL as the major language, can use Chapters 1, 2, 3, 4, etc., to introduce a simple Assembler language using part of Chapter 9. A two-semester course in introductory computer science or computer engineering could use the book in cover-to-cover fashion.

I am indebted to Mr. John McPherson and Dr. Frank Beckman of the IBM Systems Research Institute for the encouragement that led to the first edition. Others who contributed with valuable criticisms include Mr. C. L. Gold, Mr. John McKeehan, Miss Barbara White, and Dr. G. M. Weinberg. My indebtedness to Dr. K. E. Iverson, the principal architect of the APL language, is indicated by the use of the language throughout the text. The diligent work of Mr. Gary Rogers of the State University of New York, Binghamton, in checking out several of the APL programs and reading proof was most valuable. Finally, thanks are due to Mrs. Shanna McGoff for her help in typing the manuscript.

Herbert Hellerman

1

Automatic Computer Systems

The modern general-purpose digital computer system, which is the subject of this book, is the most versatile and complex creation of mankind. Its versatility follows from its applicability to a very wide range of problems, limited only by human ability to give definite directions for solving a problem. A *program* gives such directions in the form of a precise, highly stylized sequence of statements detailing a problem-solution procedure. A computer system's job is to reliably and rapidly execute programs. Present speeds are indicated by the rates of arithmetic operations such as addition, subtraction, and comparison, which lie in the range of about 100,000 to 10,000,000 instructions per second, depending on the size and cost of the machine. In only a few hours, a modern large computer can do more information processing than was done by all of mankind before the electronic age, which began about 1950! It is no wonder that this tremendous amplification of human information-processing capability is precipitating a new revolution.

To most people, the words "computer" and "computer system" are probably synonymous and refer to the physical equipment, such as the Central Processing Unit, console, tapes, disks, card reader, and printers visible to anyone visiting a computer room. Although these devices are essential, they make up only the visible "tip of the iceberg." As soon as we start to use a modern computer system, we are confronted not by the machine directly but by sets of rules called *programming languages* in which we must express whatever it is we want to do. The central importance of programming language is indicated by the fact that even the physical computer may be understood as a hardware interpreter of one particular language called the *machine language.* Machine languages are designed for machine efficiency, which is somewhat dichotomous with human convenience. Most users are shielded from the inconveniences of the machine by one or more languages designed for good man-machine communication. The versatility of the computer is illustrated by the fact that it can execute translator programs (called generically *compilers* or *interpreters*) to transform programs from user-oriented languages into machine-language form.

It should be clear from the discussion thus far that a computer system consists of a computer machine, which is a collection of physical equipment, and also programs, including those that translate user programs from any of several languages into machine language. Most of this book is devoted to examining in some detail theories and practices in the two great themes of computer systems: equipment (hardware) and programming (software). It is appropriate to begin, in the next section, by establishing a historical perspective.

1.1 HISTORICAL PERSPECTIVE

Mechanical aids to counting and calculating were known in antiquity. One of many ancient devices, the abacus, survives today as a simple practical tool in many parts of the world, especially the East, for business and even scientific calculations. (A form of the abacus was probably used by the ancient Egyptians, and it was known in China as early as the sixth century B.C.) In the hands of a skilled operator, the abacus can be a powerful adjunct to hand calculations. There are several forms of abacus; they all depend upon a positional notation for representing numbers and an arrangement of movable beads, or similar simple objects, to represent each digit. By moving beads, numbers are entered, added, and subtracted to produce an updated result. Multiplication and division are done by sequences of additions and subtractions.

Although the need to mechanize the arithmetic operations received most of the attention in early devices, storage of intermediate results was at least as important. Most devices, like the abacus, stored only the simple current result. Other storage was usually of the same type as used for any written material, e.g., clay tablets and later paper. As long as the speed of operations was modest and the use of storage also slow, there was little impetus to seek mechanization of the *control* of sequences of operations. Yet forerunners of such control did appear in somewhat different contexts, e.g., the Jacquard loom exhibited in 1801 used perforated (punched) cards to control patterns for weaving.

Charles Babbage (1792–1871) was probably the first to conceive of the essence of the general-purpose computer. Although he was very versatile, accomplished both as a mathematician and as an engineer, his lifework was his computing machines. It is worth noting that Babbage was first stimulated in this direction because of the unreliability of manual computation, *not* by its slow speed. In particular, he found several errors in certain astronomy tables. In determining the causes, he became convinced that error-free tables could be produced only by a machine that would accept a description of the computation by a human being but, once set up, would compute the tables and print them—all without human intervention. Babbage's culminating idea, which he proposed in great detail, was his Analytic Engine, which would have been the first general-purpose computer. It was not completed because he was unable to obtain sufficient financial support.

As Western industrial civilization developed, the need for mechanized computation grew. As the 1890 census approached in the United States, it became clear that if new processes were not developed, the reduction of the data from one census would not be complete before it was time for the next one. Dr. Herman Hollerith applied punched cards and simple machines for processing them in the 1890 census. Thereafter, punched-card machines gained wide acceptance in business and government.

The first third of the twentieth century saw the gradual development and use of many calculating devices. A highly significant contribution was made by the mathematician Alan Turing in 1937, when he published a clear and profound theory of the nature of a general-purpose computing scheme. His results were expressed in terms of a hypothetical "machine" of remarkable simplicity, which he indicated had all the necessary attributes of a general-purpose computer. Although Turing's machine was only a theoretical construct and was never seriously considered as economically feasible (it would be intolerably slow), it drew the attention of several talented people to the feasibility of a general-purpose computer.

World War II gave great stimulus to improvement and invention of computing devices and the technologies necessary to them. Howard Aiken and an IBM team completed the Harvard Mark I electric computer (using relay logic) in 1944. J. P. Eckert and J. W. Mauchly developed ENIAC, an electronic computer using vacuum tubes in 1946. Both these machines were developed with scientific calculations in mind. The first generation of computer technology began to be mass-produced with the appearance of the UNIVAC I in 1951. The term "first generation" is associated with the use of vacuum tubes as the major component of logical circuitry, but it included a large variety of memory devices such as mercury delay lines, storage tubes, drums, and magnetic cores, to name a few.

The second generation of hardware featured the transistor (invented in 1948) in place of the vacuum tube. The solid-state transistor is far more efficient than the vacuum tube partly because it requires no energy for heating a source of electrons. Just as important, the transistor, unlike the vacuum tube, has almost unlimited life and reliability and can be manufactured at much lower cost. Second-generation equipment, which appeared about 1960, saw the widespread installation and use of general-purpose computers. The third and fourth generations of computer technology (about 1964 and 1970) mark the increasing use of integrated fabrication techniques, moving to the goal of manufacturing most of a computer in one automatic continuous process without manual intervention. Although this goal is not quite met even by existing fourth-generation technology, costs are sharply down, reliability has increased, and miniaturization improved. Miniaturization is essential for high speed because electric signals must travel from point to point within the computer. Since the maximum propagation speed is limited to the speed of light, minimum delays require the shortest possible path lengths, obtainable by fabricating circuit components and their interconnections as small as possible.

Hardware developments were roughly paralleled by progress in programming, which is, however, more difficult to document. An early important development, usually credited to Grace Hopper, is the symbolic machine language which relieves the programmer from many exceedingly tedious and error-prone tasks. Another milestone was FORTRAN (about 1955), the first widely used *high-level language*, which included many elements of algebraic notation, like indexed variables and mathematical expressions of arbitrary extent. Since FORTRAN was developed by IBM, whose machines were most numerous, FORTRAN quickly became pervasive and, after several versions, remains today a very widely used language.

Other languages were invented to satisfy the needs of different classes of computer use. Among the most important are COBOL, for business-oriented data processing; ALGOL, probably the most widely accepted language in the international community, particularly among mathematicians and scientists; and PL/I developed by IBM and introduced in 1965 as a single language capable of satisfying the needs of scientific, commercial, and system programming. Finally, in this brief and incomplete listing we must mention APL, the language developed chiefly by K. E. Iverson, which is used throughout this book. APL is in many ways the most sophisticated of existing languages and first became widely available in 1966.

Along with the introduction and improvements of computer languages, there was a corresponding development of programming technology, i.e., the methods of producing the compiler and interpreter translators and other aids for the programmer. A very significant idea that has undergone intensive development is the *operating system*, which is a collection of programs responsible for monitoring and allocating all systems resources in response to user requests in a way that reflects certain efficiency objectives. By 1966 or so, almost all medium to large computers ran under an operating system. Jobs were typically submitted by users as decks of punched cards, either to the computer room or by *remote-job-entry* (RJE) terminals, i.e., card reader and printer equipment connected by telephone lines to the computer. In either case, once a job was received by the computer, the operating system made almost all the scheduling decisions. A large computer could run several hundred or even thousands of jobs per 24-hour day with only one or two professional operators in the machine room.

The 1960s saw a great intensification of the symbiosis of the computer and the telephone system (*teleprocessing*). Much of this was RJE and routine non-general-purpose use, such as airline reservation systems. Considerable success was also achieved in bringing the generality and excitement of a general-purpose computer system to individual people through the use of *timesharing* systems. Here, an appropriate operating-system program interleaves the requests of several human users who may be remotely located and communicating over telephone lines using such devices as a teletype or typewriter terminal. Because of high computer speed relative to human "think" time, a single system could comfortably service 50 to 100 (or more) users, with each having the "feel" of his own private computer. The timesharing system, by bringing people closest to the computer, seems to have very great potential, as yet largely unexplored, for amplifying human creativity.

1.2 A CLASSIFICATION OF AUTOMATIC COMPUTERS

Automatic computers may be broadly classified as analog or digital (Fig. 1.2.1). Analog computers make use of the analogy between the values assumed by some physical quantity, such as shaft rotation, distance, or electric voltage, and a variable in the problem of interest. Digital computers in principle manipulate numbers directly. In a sense all computers have an analog quality since a physical representation must be used for the abstraction that is a number. In the digital computer, the analogy is minimal, while the analog computer exploits it to a very great extent.

Both analog and digital computers include a subclass of rather simple machines that mechanize only specific simple operations. For example, the slide rule is an analog computer that represents numbers as distances on a logarithmic scale. Multiplication, division, finding roots of numbers, and other operations are done by adding and subtracting lengths. Examples of operation-only machines of the digital type include adding machines and desk calculators.

A second class, more sophisticated than operation-only machines, may be termed *problem-setup* machines. In addition to performing arithmetic operations they can accept a description of a procedure to link operations in sequence to solve a problem. The specification of the procedure may be built into the machine's controls, as in certain special-purpose machines, or a plugboard arrangement may be supplied for specifying the desired sequence of operations. The main idea is that the problem-solution procedure is entered in one distinct operation, and thereafter the entire execution of the work on the problem is automatic.

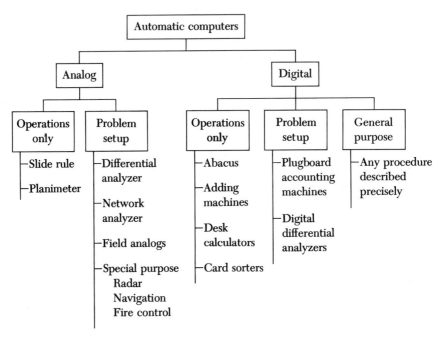

Fig. 1.2.1 A classification of computers.

The electronic differential analyzer that emerged in the late 1940s is the most general form of *analog* computer. It is constructed from a few types of carefully engineered precision circuits (integrators, summing amplifiers, precision potentiometers, and capacitors) each capable of a single operation. The problem is usually set up on the machine by plugboard. Since there is usually no provision for storing results internally, the output is generally sent directly to a curve plotter. Precision, limited by drift and noise, is typically no higher than 1 part in 1000 of full scale. Compared with general-purpose digital computers, analog computers suffer from lack of generality of the problems that can be handled, low precision, difficulty in performing complex operations (including multiplication and division at high speed), inability to store large amounts of information effectively, and equipment requirements that must grow directly with problem size. However, for the jobs to which it is suited, particularly mathematical or simulation problems involving differential equations, the analog computer can often give high speed, if required, at lower cost than a digital computer. The high speed of the analog computer is the result of its highly parallel operation; i.e., all its parts are working concurrently on separate parts of the same problem.

A most important theoretical question that can be asked of a problem-setup machine is: What is the range of problems solvable by this machine? As a practical matter, this question is rarely asked in this form because plugboard machines are usually designed for specifically stated kinds of problems. Nevertheless, the question of ultimate logical power, i.e., the range of problems solvable by a given machine, is fundamental. In 1937 Turing made a direct contribution to this subject when he defined a remarkably simple hypothetical"machine" (since named a universal Turing machine) and proved, in effect, that any solution procedure can be expressed as a procedure for this machine (see Chap. 7). By implication, any machine that can be made to simulate a universal Turing machine also has its generality. The class of such machines is called *general purpose.* Most commercially available electronic digital computers are, for practical purposes, general-purpose machines. They differ in speed, cost, reliability, amount of storage, and ease of communication with other devices or people, but not in their ultimate logical capabilities.

1.3 THE NATURE OF A COMPUTER SYSTEM

A computer system is best considered as a collection of *resources* that are accessible to its users by programs written according to the rules of the system's programming languages. The resources are of two major classes with a wide variety of components in each:

1. Equipment (hardware)
  a. Storages To hold both programs and data
  b. Processing Logic Implementing arithmetic, logical manipulation of infor- mation
  c. Control Logic Concerned with movement of information and sequencing of events
  d. Transducers Devices for translating information from one physical form to another, e.g., a printer that converts electric signals to printed characters on paper
2. Programs (software)
  a. Application Programs Programs written to satisfy some need of com- puter users outside the operation of the computer system itself, e.g., scientific, payroll, and inventory-control programs—in fact most of the work computers do
  b. System Programs Programs concerned with the means by which the system provides certain conveniences to its users and manages its own resources, e.g., language translators and operating-system programs

1.4 PRINCIPLES OF HARDWARE ORGANIZATION

From now on we shall use the word *computer* to mean only the *hardware* part of a general-purpose computing system.

All computers have certain qualitative similarities, which will now be described. The reader will readily appreciate, however, the lack of precision in listing these common properties—our objective at present is to describe these in such a way that the essential nature of the machine, and the basis of its generality, can be intuitively understood.

From the viewpoint of the user, the machine manipulates two basic types of information: (1) operands, or data, and (2) instructions, each of which usually specifies a single arithmetic or control operation (e.g., ADD, SUBTRACT), and one or more operands which are the objects of the operation.

Within the machine, both instructions and data are represented as integers expressed in the binary number system or in some form of binary coding. This is done because the "atom" of information is then a two-state signal (called 0 or 1) which requires only the simplest and most reliable operation of electronic devices. Although the binary representation of instructions and data must appear within the machine for processing to take place, most users of computers may use the common decimal representation of numbers and alphabetic names of operations and data. Translator programs (usually supplied by the computer manufacturer) executed by the machine translate these convenient representations into the internal binary form. In other words, the binary representation of information inside the computer is important for reasons of electronic technology but is *not* an essential principle of the general-purpose computer.

The following is a list of attributes common to general-purpose digital computers:

1. The machine is capable of storing a large amount of information (both data and instructions). For economy reasons, there are usually at least three levels of storage speed and capacity. The amount of storage is a fundamental limiting factor in the range of problems that can be handled.
2. The repertoire of instructions is typically small (from about 16 to 256 types) but is judiciously chosen to cover the requirements for any procedure.
3. Operands are referenced by name; the names of operands can be processed by instructions.
4. Instructions are accessed from storage and executed automatically. Normally, the location in storage of the next instruction is held in an instruction (or program) counter. This *pointer* is most often stepped in value (increased by 1) to specify the location of the next instruction, but certain instructions specifically modify the program counter to contain a value that depends on the outcome of comparisons between specified operands. This gives the

program the ability to *branch* to alternative parts of the program, i.e., alternative instruction sequences.

The general organization of a typical computer is shown in Fig. 1.4.1. The heart of the system is the Central Processing Unit (CPU), shown as comprising a main storage, which holds both program and data, an Arithmetic-logic Unit (ALU), which contains processing circuitry such as an adder, shifter, and a few fast *registers* for holding the operands, and the instruction currently being processed. The program counter would also be included in the ALU, although in some diagrams the program control facilities are shown as a distinct function. One part of the CPU is a set of routing circuits which provide paths between storage and the ALU and input/output controllers or channels. In the type of system illustrated, many storage or input/output devices may be wired to one channel; but only one device per channel can be transmitting information from or to main storage at any one time. This is, of course, a restriction on the number of devices that can operate concurrently. It is imposed because of the economy of sharing common paths to main storage and simplicity in controlling movement of information between the devices and storage.

The major parts of a computer may be described as follows:

1. Storage   Means for storing a rather large volume of information and a simple economical access mechanism for routing an element of information to/from storage from/to a single point (register). Storage is usually available in several

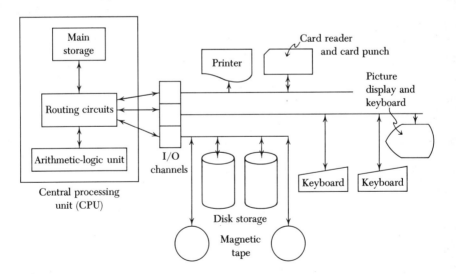

Fig. 1.4.1   General organization of a typical digital computer.

versions, even in the same system; these vary in access time, capacity, and cost.

2. *Data Flow* The switching networks that provide paths for routing information from one part of the computer to another.

3. *Transformation* The circuits for arithmetic and other data manipulation. This function is usually concentrated in a single Arithmetic-logic Unit (ALU). The centralization provides economy since a single set of fast expensive circuits is used in time sequence for all operations. Transformation circuits operate on information obtained from storage by control of the data-flow switching. As will be seen later, many of the more complex transformations such as subtraction, multiplication, and division can be obtained economically by control of sequences of very elementary operations such as addition, shifting, etc.

4. *Control* This is a general term that includes the important function of performing time sequences of routings of information through the data flow. The control function appears on many levels in a computer. Usually the control is organized as a set of time sequences, or *cycles*. Each cycle period is commonly (but not always) divided into equally spaced time units called *clock intervals*. The term "cycle" refers to a specific type of sequence for selections on the data flow performed in a succession of clock intervals. For example, there is an *instruction fetch cycle* during which an instruction containing information about a transformation is brought from storage to an ALU register. At each clock interval within the cycle, an elementary operation is performed such as routing the storage location of the instruction to the storage-access mechanism, signaling for storage access, or routing of the instruction obtained to an ALU register.

5. *Input/Output* Since information in the processor and storage of the computer are represented by electric signals, devices are provided to convert information from human-generated to machine-readable form on input, and in the opposite direction on output. A very common scheme for performing this transducer function uses a punched card. An operator reads the information from handwritten or typed documents and enters the information on a keyboard, much like a typewriter keyboard, of a keypunch machine. This machine translates the key strokes into holes on the card (see Fig. 1.4.2). The cards are then sent to the card reader, which contains the necessary equipment to READ the cards, i.e., sense the hole positions and translate them into the internal electric-signal representation. The punched card stores information in a nonvolatile form and can be read by human beings (by reading either the hole configurations or the printed characters at the top of card). A card-punch machine may be controlled by the computer to produce punched-card output of the results of processing.

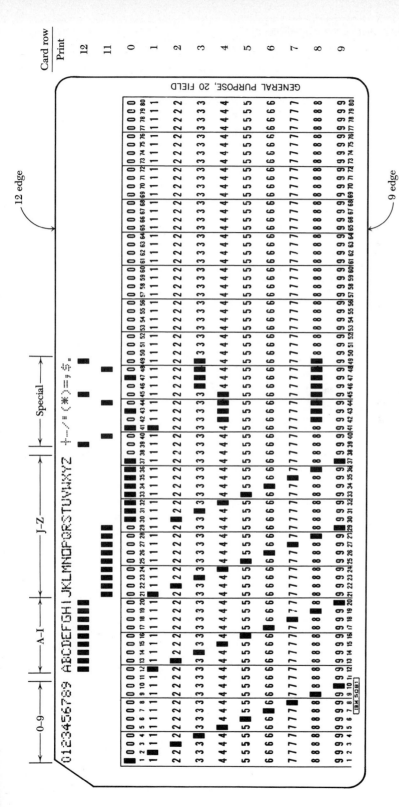

Representation of Data: Each of the 80 columns may contain one or more holes (small dark rectangles) representing an alphanumeric character. The card shown was punched to show the representations of the 10 decimal digits, 26 letters of the alphabet, and 12 special symbols (including blank) of a common symbol set.

Fig. 1.4.2 An 80-column IBM card showing row-column numbering and holes punched for the 48-character set used by the FORTRAN language.

The punched card and its associated machines are examples of input/output devices. Other devices available include typewriters, punched paper tape, printers, cathode-ray-tube displays, analog-digital converters.

There is no sharp distinction between the storage function and the input/output function (the punched card was seen to contain both). However, a useful distinction can be made based on whether the output is directly machine-readable. On this basis, printers, typewriters, cathode-ray displays are input/output devices; punched cards, punched tape, magnetic tape are storage devices.

A very common terminology classifies all devices and machines not a part of the Central Processing Unit and its directly accessible storage as input/output.

1.5 CONVENTIONS ON USE OF STORAGE

Certain conventions are almost universally assumed in using computer storage. These are independent of the physical nature of the device constituting storage—whether it uses magnetic tape, magnetic disks, transistors, etc. Two fundamental operations, viewed from the storage unit are:

1. *READ* (copy) Copies the contents of some specified portion of the storage and sends it to some standard place. Note that the copy operation is, to the user, *nondestructive;* i.e., information in storage is not modified by reading it out.
2. *WRITE* (replace) Results in *replacement* of the present contents of a specified portion of storage from some standard place.

Sometimes the technology of a storage device naturally tends to violate these conventions. In such a case it is engineered with additional circuits to provide the same functional appearance to the user as described above.

1.6 ELEMENTS OF PROGRAMMING

For our present purposes, storage is assumed to consist of an array of cells which may be visualized as a long row of pigeonholes. Each cell contains information called an *operand* which may be likened to a number written on a piece of paper contained in the cell. *Each cell is given a name—the information in the cell is referenced only by the name of the cell it occupies, not by its content.* The operand referenced is then used for computation. The machine hardware usually has a wired-in name scheme whereby the cell names are the integers 0, 1, 2, etc. The user may, however, choose different names such as X, Y, Z, I, etc., for the cells. The translation of user names to machine names is a simple routine process since each user name is simply assigned to one machine name. This justifies our use of mnemonic symbols for names of operands.

Unless otherwise specified, numbers will denote operands, letters the *names* of operands. For example

(1) $X \leftarrow 5$

is read "5 specifies X," which means the operand or usual number 5 replaces the contents of the cell named X. As another example consider the statement

(2) $Y \leftarrow 1 + X$

which means "the contents (operand) of the cell whose name is X is added to 1 and the result replaces the contents of the cell named Y." For brevity, we usually read this statement as "X plus 1 specifies Y." It is important to note that although the statement generally results in a change in the contents of Y, the contents of X remain unchanged. A simple program consists of a sequence of statements like the ones illustrated above. Although detailed rules of writing statements (symbols allowed, punctuation required, etc.) vary widely from program language to program language, many of the principles of programming can be illustrated adequately using a single language (APL in our case).

Since a computer normally handles large volumes of information, a key notion is designation and processing of *arrays* of information. A one-dimensional array of cells will be called a *vector*. An example of a vector is

(3) $X \equiv 3,29,47.4,82,^-977.6$

An *element* or *component* of a vector will be denoted by a two-part designation. One part is the name of the entire vector; the other, written between brackets, gives the *position* of the element being referenced. In the above example

(4) $X[2] \equiv 29$

(assuming element position numbers in X start at 1 from the left).

Note also the meaning of a variable index. For example,

(5) $Y \leftarrow X[I]$

means "the content of cell I is used as a position number in X, and the content of the cell so designated in X replaces the content of Y."

For example, if X is the vector specified in (3), the sequence

$I \leftarrow 3$
$Y \leftarrow X[I]$

results in Y being respecified by the number 47.4.

A variable such as

$X[I]$ or $X[3]$

is said to be subscripted or indexed—the variable I is called an index variable. Index operations are extremely important because they allow us in effect to systematically compute cell names from other cell names or constants.

Why is it important to be able to compute names? One reason is that without this facility, it would be necessary to specify each cell *explicitly* by a unique name. Generating thousands of names would be tedious, and sooner or later we would probably devise a systematic naming procedure similar or identical to the indexed-variable idea. A second reason for the power of indexed variables is that the calculation of names can be included in the program for processing the data, thus greatly shortening the statement of the program but lengthening the time to execute it. For example, assume that 100 numbers have been entered into storage and called vector X. Two programs are shown in Fig. 1.6.1 to do the same job: compute S, the sum of the numbers.

Figure 1.6.1*a* is easy to understand immediately; it is a straight-line program consisting of all 100 executed steps written explicitly. Figure 1.6.1*b* is a much shorter program because it contains a *loop*. Looping is a very profound programming concept which will be discussed in great detail in Chap. 2. For now, note that in Fig. 1.6.1*b*, the "guts" of the program is statement 4, which adds the value in the I position of X and S, to produce the new S. This statement

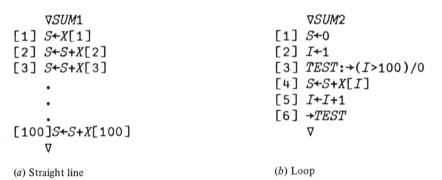

```
    ∇SUM1                          ∇SUM2
[1] S←X[1]                    [1] S←0
[2] S←S+X[2]                  [2] I←1
[3] S←S+X[3]                  [3] TEST:→(I>100)/0
     •                        [4] S←S+X[I]
     •                        [5] I←I+1
     •                        [6] →TEST
[100]S←S+X[100]                    ∇
     ∇
```

(*a*) Straight line   (*b*) Loop

Fig. 1.6.1   Straight-line and loop programming to sum 100 numbers X.

will be executed repetitively as we shall now see, each time with a new value of
I. Certainly, line 5 increases I by 1, and line 6 directs the program to line 3 since
this is where the statement labeled *TEST* is found. Line 3 says: "Compare I for
greater than 100; if so, branch to line 0, which by convention means *exit* from
the program. Otherwise, continue to the next statement (line 4)." With these
rules, it is seen that for the case at hand, lines 4, 5, and 6 will each be executed
100 times and line 3 will be executed 101 times; in other words lines 3 to 6
constitute a program loop. Comparing the straight-line and loop programs of Fig.
1.6.1, we find that the number of written statements is 100 in the first case and
only 6 in the second. This advantage of a short *written* program is somewhat
offset by the fact that the loop program requires 403 *executed* statements
compared to only 100 for the straight-line program. The additional executed
statements in the loop program are required for index updating and testing.

In this section we have only introduced some basic ideas of programming. For
a more comprehensive treatment, see Chaps. 2 and 3.

1.7 SOME FACTS OF COMPUTER TECHNOLOGY

Modern digital computers are constructed from large numbers of a few types of
components. Complex operations are performed by rapidly executing time
sequences of rather simple operations. Because of the large number of
components (even a medium-sized computer may have a million parts),
reliability of the mode of operation is a necessity. For this reason, most parts are
only required to distinguish between two states of operation—the minimum
number possible.

The function which requires the greatest number of logical elements is storage.
Providing reliable and economical storage structures is a central objective of
computer design. Generally speaking, technologies which yield low cost per unit
of information stored also yield relatively slow access to the information. To
realize the potential speed of fast electronic switching devices such as transistors
and diodes, storage is usually designed in a hierarchy of size and speed.
Highest-speed storage is constructed of the same components as the data-flow
and transformation circuits; a few *registers* of this type are included in the
Central Processing Unit for holding the immediate data and instruction being
processed. Next in the hierarchy is usually the *processor,* or *main* storage,
typically constructed at present from tiny donut-shaped magnetic cores wired
into an array. Processor storage ranges in capacity (at present) from about
50,000 to 10 million bits.

Storage in amounts larger than about 100 million bits can be economically
realized at present only on surfaces that require mechanical motion for access.

Technology	Random access, μsec	Start/stop, μsec	Capacity, 10^6 bits	Flow rate, kilobits/sec	Price/bit, cents	Medium cost 10^{-3} cent/bit
Transistor (monolithic)	.2	N.A.	5	256,000	9†	N.A.
Magnetic core	2	N.A.	10	64,000	5.6	N.A.
Magnetic disk per drive	30,000	N.A.	800	6,400	.005‡	.13
Magnetic tape per drive	N.A.	2,000	414	2,560	.007‡	.0023
Punched cards	N.A.	N.A.	N.A.	.019	N.A.	.09

Note: All prices are commercial prices in 1972; N.A. means not applicable.
  † Monolithic memory units with price per bit of 0.1 cent were found.
  ‡ Prices of drives and control unit per bit on-line. Does not include media prices (see last column).

Fig. 1.7.1 **Rough comparison of representative storages.**

A summary of the cost, size, and speed for several technologies is given in Fig. 1.7.1.

1.8 PRINCIPLES OF THE SPACE-TIME RELATIONSHIP

The computer designer or user must be aware of some rather fundamental notions of how a computer and a problem can be organized to "trade" space and time. The word "space" will roughly correspond to "amount of equipment."

One simple example of this trade-off idea in the case of machine parts will now be discussed. Two ways of obtaining the same function are shown in Fig. 1.8.1; the function is the appearance of six signals—each of these can be either ON (= 1) or OFF (= 0). The circuit outputs are to appear as 0, except at *timing* or *clock intervals* when the signals appear at the output point(s). To ensure that the output appears only at clock intervals, each signal and a clock pulse are fed into an AND circuit which gives a 1 output only when the signal line and clock line are both 1; at other times the output is 0.

In part (*a*) of Fig. 1.8.1 we see one representation of our set of six signals. Each signal uses its own line; the output appears on six output lines (and requires six AND circuits). In part (*b*) we see a second possibility—the six signals circulate as pulses in a delay-line structure—the delay is in this case six clock times. Here the signals appear in *time sequence* on a single wire.

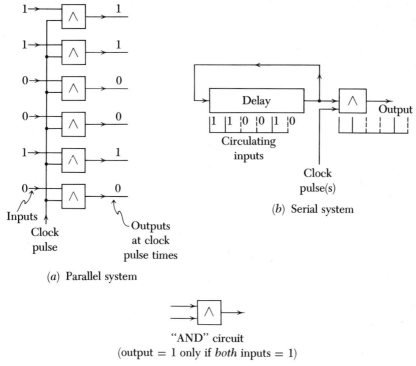

(a) Parallel system

(b) Serial system

"AND" circuit
(output = 1 only if *both* inputs = 1)

Fig. 1.8.1 Parallel and serial representations of ON-OFF signals.

The first circuit is extensive (and expensive) in space but concise (inexpensive-fast) in time. The second circuit has exactly dual properties. Notice also that as the number of signals grows, the parallel circuit grows proportionately but the time to receive all the signals remains the same. The serial circuit on the other hand requires no more lines (or AND circuits) to handle more signals, although the delay must increase proportionately.

Many of the desirable properties of a computer, especially its reliability, result from its use of simple components in a simple manner. Complex structures and operations are built up by using many simple components and intricate time sequences of the signals they generate or modify.

Because of the many devices for processing, control, and particularly storage, great efforts are exerted to obtain economical structures. The time-space relationship discussed above provides one method of reducing cost at the expense of time. This is an example of the idea of *time sharing,* i.e., using the same equipment (such as the adder circuit) successively in time by routing to it the numbers to be added in time sequence. The routing of information from place to place within the computer is therefore a fundamental operation. The paths provided for routing determine the *data-flow* structure of the machine—a most important characteristic of any computer.

The time-space relationship may also be illustrated by programming organization. Recall that in the procedures for summing a list of numbers, one can program *straight-line,* thereby obtaining an expensive space (storage) program but a fast-execution-time program. An alternative is to program the problem utilizing a loop; this results in great storage savings but longer execution time. In most cases, the loop program usually gains space by a much greater factor than it loses speed; it is the preferred method for all but the shortest lists.

The major point of the above discussions on time-space relationships is a fundamental property of data processing; in any task to be done, there is usually a choice of several solutions, which can be compared, to a first order, by the extent to which they trade space and time.

From the brief introduction given in this chapter, some broad properties of computer systems should be discernible. First, a general-purpose computer is one that can accept a precise stylized description of a procedure, called a *program,* for solving any problem solvable in a finite number of steps and can then execute the program automatically to process data made available to the machine. It follows that professional users of systems must understand how to write precise procedure descriptions, and it is therefore appropriate to begin the detailed study of computer systems with programming principles (see Chap. 2).

The algorithm, or program, is important not only to the users of a computer but also, for two reasons, to its designers. (1) Product designers can perform intelligently only if they understand how the products will be used, i.e., programmed. (2) The sequences of internal switching operations necessary to implement arithmetic and other operations are also algorithms—these are the algorithms which must be specified and implemented by the logical designer.

A modern computer has been likened to a grand piano, on which the user can play Beethoven or "Chopsticks." Achieving the most value for an investment in equipment and manpower is a problem in optimizing resources that has some of the properties of combinatorial mathematics; i.e., a "slight" change in specifications or the criterion of optimization can make a very great difference in performance. The general-purpose nature of the computer rarely raises doubt that "answers" to a well-defined problem can be obtained one way or another. The central question is usually how to obtain the answers in a way that optimizes user convenience, problem-solution time, storage space, reliability, or some combination of such parameters. Needless to say, all these factors are interdependent, and some can be improved only at the expense of others. This has already been illustrated in the case of space versus time in the examples given earlier in this chapter. Some fairly general, but as yet undiscovered, "conservation" laws may relate these parameters; but at this time, the general interrelations can only be discussed qualitatively, although quantitative analysis of trade-offs are readily possible and should be done in specific cases.

PROBLEMS

1.1 Discuss in your own words the relationship between a physical computer and a programming language.

1.2 What are the principal advantages of transistors over vacuum tubes?

1.3 Why is circuit miniaturization important in computers?

1.4 Explain briefly the nature of an operating system.

1.5 List some major properties of a timesharing system.

1.6 What is the significant difference between a problem-setup and a general-purpose computer?

1.7 List and discuss briefly three disadvantages and one advantage of analog computers compared to general-purpose digital computers.

1.8 *a)* What is the maximum number of hole configurations on an entire IBM card?
b) If at most two holes per column are permitted, how many different characters can be represented in a single card column (see Appendix B for a review of combinational analysis)?

1.9 A certain computer's card code has 256 possible characters; each card column must be able to represent any character by some hole–no-hole configuration. If at most k holes are to be permitted per column, what is the minimum value of k?

1.10 Consider the statement sequence

```
[1] A←5
[2] B←7
[3] C←A+B
[4] B←C+2×A
```

What are the values of A, B, and C after execution of this sequence?

1.11 Storage in a computer system is usually structured into a hierarchy of various types of devices. Give some examples. What is the reason for the hierarchy rather than a single storage type throughout?

1.12 *a*) Write a loop program for S, the weighted sum of the 100 numbers X where $X[I]$ is weighted (multiplied) by $W[I]$. Assume that X,W numbers are available to the program (neglect input and output).
b) How many statements are written to compute S?
c) How many statements are executed to compute S?

1.13 Repeat Prob. 1.12, only now assume that *two* weighted sums of X values $S1$ and $S2$ must be computed with the two weight vectors $W1$ and $W2$. Use a single loop to compute both sums. Compare counts of parts (*b*) and (*c*) with those of Prob. 1.12.

REFERENCES

1. Ashby, W. R.: "Design for a Brain," John Wiley & Sons, Inc., New York, 1960.
2. Bowden, B. V. (ed.): "Faster than Thought," Sir Isaac Pitman & Sons, Ltd., London, 1953.
3. Brennan, R. D., and H. Sano: PACTOLUS: A Digital Analog Simulator for the IBM 1620, *AFIPS Proc. Fall Jt. Comput. Conf.,* October 1964, pp. 229–311.
4. Brooks, F. P., Jr., and K. E. Iverson: "Automatic Data Processing," John Wiley & Sons, Inc., New York, 1963.
5. Davis, M. (ed.): The Undecidable, in "Basic Papers on Undecidable Propositions, Unsolvable Problems and Computable Functions," Raven Press, New York, 1965.
6. Feigenbaum, E., and J. Feldman (eds.): "Computers and Thought," McGraw-Hill Book Company, New York, 1963.
7. Goode H. H., and R. E. Machol: "System Engineering," McGraw-Hill Book Company, New York, 1957.
8. Huskey, H. D., and G. A. Korn: "Computer Handbook," McGraw-Hill Book Company, New York, 1962.
9. Johnson, C. L.: "Analog Computer Techniques," 2d ed., McGraw-Hill Book Company, New York, 1963.
10. Karplus, W. J., and W. J. Soroka: "Analog Methods," 2d ed., McGraw-Hill Book Company, New York, 1959.
11. Morrison, P., and E. Morrison (eds.): "Charles Babbage and His Calculating Engines," Dover Publications, Inc., New York, 1961.
12. Neumann, J. von: The General and Logical Theory of Automata, in J. R. Newman (ed.), "The World of Mathematics," vol. iv, pt. 19, Simon and Schuster, Inc., New York, 1956.

2

Programming

The word "program" has come to have several connotations in computer system terminology. A rather abstract definition states that a program is a precise specification of a procedure by a string of symbols, each belonging to a definite prespecified alphabet; the string and its substrings obey a definite syntax, or rules of allowable formation. There is also a set of semantic rules by which the symbol strings are given operational meaning. The symbol alphabet, rules of syntax, and operational rules for interpreting combinations of symbols comprise a *programming language.* A particular symbol string constituting a program specifies transformation on symbol strings called *input* or *intermediate* data, to produce output data.

According to this definition there is no direct connection between a program and a computing machine. This is an important point; a program may be executed by any mechanism, including human beings, capable of recognizing symbols and following prespecified rules defining their operational meaning. Viewed in this light, each computing machine represents one specific language, called the *machine language,* whose symbols, syntax, and operations are built into the circuitry of the arithmetic and control parts of the machine. In any given computer, these are of course fixed once and for all. For reasons of economy in the construction of the machines, machine languages are usually primitive and inconvenient for direct human use. Fortunately, it is entirely feasible, as well as widespread practice, to define programming languages that are much better suited to human expression than the machine language and then translate programs expressed in this more convenient form into machine language. The task of translation may be done automatically by any general-purpose machine supplied with a *translator* program, i.e., a program that can treat the user's program as data and transform it into a machine-executable program. Notice that the same machine may process programs in several languages provided a translator program is supplied for each.

Once it is understood that the language which the programmer uses need not be, and usually is not, the machine language, it is best to avoid unessential detail by deferring until later certain aspects of machine operation such as handling binary numbers rather than the more familiar decimal numbers. On the other hand, it is important to note at once certain other properties of the structure of the machine. For example, as mentioned in Chap. 1, most computer systems, for economy reasons, include a variety of storage devices. These divide roughly into two classes which may be described briefly as fast-access small-size and slow-access large-size. The former, typified by magnetic-core memories, are usually called *main* or *processor* storage, while the latter, typified by magnetic drums, disks, or tape devices, are called *auxiliary* or *input/output* storage devices. Since most machines can execute programs only from processor (main) storage, an important aspect of programming is the control of movement of information between auxiliary storage and processor storage. Perhaps the simplest case is illustrated in Fig. 2.0.1*a,* which shows that information (containing the program and data) is first entered, the program is then executed, and finally the results are delivered, say to a printing device. This approach is feasible only if the processor storage is large enough to contain the entire program and data. A slightly more complex case is illustrated in Fig. 2.0.1*b,* where the entire problem will not fit into processor storage. Here, the program takes a "gulp" of input, then computes, then delivers a "gulp" of output, and then repeats the cycle. The input may include new programs as well as data. This case is still simple from the control viewpoint because auxiliary storage is not required for intermediate results. The more general case is shown in Fig. 2.0.1*c,* where processor storage is too small to contain the entire problem program and intermediate results. The planning of efficient accesses to portions of data and program on auxiliary storage can be complex. For this type of problem, very much a part of practical programming, the property of the program as a symbol string, although still important, is somewhat overshadowed by the scheduling and storage allocation functions.

This chapter will neglect the storage management and input/output problems and hence the discussion will be directly applicable to the system of Fig. 2.0.1*a,* although the results are partially applicable to the other cases as well. Some of the underlying principles of programming will be discussed—although a single programming language is used in detailed examples, the description includes considerations common to many languages. The particular language used throughout this book is APL, which will be presented in some detail.

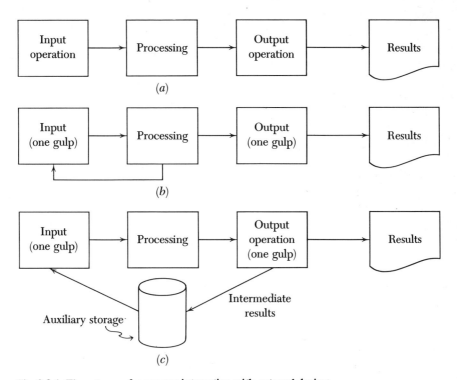

Fig. 2.0.1 Three types of processor interaction with external devices.

Operational skill in any language can be gained only by applying it to descriptions of specific sequential processes. This chapter illustrates use of the APL language with examples drawn from numerical mathematics, statistics, and nonnumerical processing. Many of the programs are selected not only to show how various features of APL may be used but also to understand the algorithms, which in many cases are of interest in their own right.

2.1   APL: THE PROGRAMMING LANGUAGE USED IN THIS BOOK

In this book we shall use one programming language, called APL, to precisely describe most of the algorithms and sequential processes. APL is an acronymn for A Programming Language, the name of a book published by K. E. Iverson in 1962. There, an elegant and powerful programming language was presented and used for a variety of algorithms. The language evolved through the years 1962 to 1966 primarily through paper use since it was not machine-executable. About 1966, a computer implementation completed at the IBM

Research Center made the language available in a *timesharing* mode. This means that each user can enter and store programs and data from a typewriterlike device called a *terminal,* which is connected to a computer via telephone lines. The computer can respond to user messages very quickly (1 sec or less per line of input for most inputs). The interactions between each user and the computer alternate: first the user types a line, then the computer responds, then the user types again, etc. This polite alternation at human reaction times is called *conversational* interaction. Because of the high speed of the computer and relatively slow human typing and "thinking" times, the computer can satisfy each request in most cases in a very short "time slice" of processing. The computer can then carry on several conversations which appear to the people at the terminals to be happening at the same time. Thus, the single computer is being *timeshared* by several users, but the sharing is interleaved at such high speeds that each user at his terminal feels as if he had his own private APL machine.

Although the timesharing aspects of APL are not essential to the language itself, it will often be helpful in learning the language to imagine oneself at an APL terminal (if one is available, all the better).

The primary advantages of APL over most other computer languages are its large set of built-in operators and its ability to apply these simply and consistently to entire arrays of numbers, bits, and character data. The operators include the familiar *arithmetic* ones, like add, subtract, multiply, divide, and exponentiation $(+ \ - \ \times \ \div \ *)$, as well as *logical* (Boolean) operators (AND, OR, etc.) and *relational* operators that result in 1 or 0 (meaning yes or no) as some stated comparison condition is or is not satisfied. Other operators *select* or can *reorder* elements of an array. Single operators and variables may be combined to form expressions.

In the next few sections, all the above ideas (and some others) will be described and illustrated in specific detail for the APL language. However, although the major objective will be to discuss APL, we shall also keep in mind the need to learn something about *how to learn* programming languages, i.e., the principles and categories common to many languages, not only APL. A few such considerations are:

1. *Alphabet* (or character set)   The atoms for constructing *symbol strings* which form the substance of all computer work
2. *Syntax*   Rules for forming legal *strings* designating:
   a. Operands (data)
   b. Variables (names)
   c. Statements
   d. Programs
3. *Semantics*   Rules specifying what various symbol strings *mean,* i.e., what they tell the computer to do

2.2 ALPHABET (CHARACTER SET), OPERANDS, AND VARIABLES

The alphabet of APL, showing all its atomic symbols as they appear on the terminal keyboard, is illustrated in Fig. 2.2.1.† The following ideas help explain the character positions on the keyboard. Readers who will not be using an APL terminal may skip the four points below.

1. The alphabetic letters and digits appear in their normal (typewriter) positions except that 1 is a distinct symbol (*not* the letter L).
2. The lower symbol on each key is obtained by normal keying; the upper symbol by depressing SHIFT and the key together. Note that the shifted letters do *not* result in capital letters but in special symbols.
3. The characters on the same key (or adjacent keys) are arranged to help us remember their relationship. Thus, E and ϵ share the same key, as do I and ι (the latter is Greek iota). Another example is Q and *?*, which is helpful in remembering the location of *?*.
4. Certain keys do not print but still have meaning (and in APL operation, send signals to the computer). Examples are space (or blank), which we shall sometimes write as $\not b$, back space, and carrier return.

Operands are the symbol *strings* that designate numbers, characters, or other data units to be processed or that result from processing. APL recognizes three types of operands:

1. Number
2. Bit
3. Character

†IBM typing element (golf ball) no. 1167987 or 1167988 supplies these symbols; no. 1167987 is for correspondence-code terminals and ordinary IBM Selectric typewriters.

Fig. 2.2.1   APL/360 keyboard.

Most modern programming languages permit numbers to be written by the user in much the same way as with pencil and paper. However, there is always a restriction to some maximum number of significant digits because most computers can *directly* represent numbers of only a definite limited range; direct computer arithmetic is finite-precision arithmetic. (However, any precision can be programmed on any general-purpose machine at the expense of programming effort, storage efficiency, and speed.) In APL, 10 significant digits are normally used (at least in printouts).

Because most computers use a different internal representation for integers and for mixed numbers (see Chap. 8), some programming systems require the user to signal the program translator (compiler) about the operand type. For example, in the FORTRAN language, numbers that are to use the *internal-integer* representation are written without a decimal point, other numbers (*floating-point*) with a decimal point. There is a trend toward removing these restrictions as programming technology develops. However, such conveniences are often at the expense of machine efficiency. In any case, the reader is cautioned to read the fine print on data representation in learning a computer language.

APL is quite permissive about the forms of number representation as typified by the following legal examples:

(1) $39 \equiv 39.0 \equiv +39.0$

(2) $.0039 \equiv .39E^{-}2$

(3) $X \leftarrow {}^{-}39.4$

Equation (1) shows that the decimal point for an integer is optional. Equation (2) illustrates the use of the letter E in a number to designate a power of 10 multiplier (in this case 10^{-2} is the multiplier). This permits very large and very small numbers to be conveniently represented although of course only a limited number of significant digits are available no matter what the magnitude of the number. Equation (3) illustrates the simple assignment or specification statement. It is read "the value ${}^{-}39.4$ specifies X" or "the value ${}^{-}39.4$ replaces the contents of the cell named X." In the particular specification of Eq. (3) [and also Eq. (2)] note the upper minus sign (${}^{-}$) which is used only as part of a negative operand value; the usual negative operator symbol (-) applies to variables (and operands).

A *bit* data value can be only a 0 or 1 and can be used exactly in the usual sense with arithmetic operations. However, some operators (like $\wedge, \vee, \sim$, signifying AND, OR, NOT) apply *only* to bit data (or else a DOMAIN ERROR results). Also, bit data use storage very efficiently since several bits are "packed" into one computer word. Conversion between bit and number form of data, when required, is done automatically by APL without any specification from the user.

Character data consist of alphabetic characters which have no inherent numerical value in APL (although such values can be easily assigned through programming). When used in statements, character data must start and end with quote marks; thus

$$X \leftarrow {}'J\,'$$

means that the *character* J specifies (is placed in the cell named) X. The quote marks are *not* part of the data but are essential to denote the *character J* as distinct from the *name J* (if the quotes were omitted). As a more subtle example consider the statement

$$X \leftarrow 3 + 2$$

as opposed to

$$X \leftarrow 3 + {}'2\,'$$

The first statement means the usual "2 is added to 3 and the result is placed in the cell named X." The second statement attempts to add the *character* 2 to the *number 3*, which is illegal since *character* 2 does *not* have a value.† Although APL character data do not have values, they can still be manipulated by (1) selection of some characters from a string, (2) forming new strings from old ones by catenation (one string following another), and (3) by testing for equality (sameness). Also, a single APL statement can easily associate a number value to each character of a string.

Thus far we have considered the syntax of numbers, bit, and character data. We now turn to the syntax of *names*. In APL, as in most languages, a name must begin with an alphabetic character and be followed by either alphabetic or digit characters. Thus, some legal names are

$$X \qquad JOE \qquad J1 \qquad JOE1 \qquad P1E5$$

The distinction between an operand and a variable is the difference between an object and its name. This important idea lies at the heart of mathematics as well as computing. One of the most fundamental advantages of use of names is where a given expression must be referenced repeatedly, as illustrated in Fig. 2.2.2. The convenience is even more evident in the case where a change must be made in one or more operands. In Fig. 2.2.2 the operand-only program requires 20 symbol changes if a, b, c values are all changed, while the program using names requires only 3 changes.

---

†In some computers and languages, each character of the system alphabet is assigned an integer value. The alphabet listed in increasing order of these integers is called the collating sequence.

```
[1] Z←3+5-4
[2] X←(3+5-4)×(3+5-4)+(3+5-4)
[3] Y←(3+5)×(3+5-4)×(3+5-4)
```

(*a*) Literal Program (23 variable–literal symbols)

```
[1] A←3
[2] B←5
[3] C←4
[4] D←A+B
[5] Z←D-C
[6] X←Z×Z+Z
[7] Y←D×Z×Z
```

(*b*) Symbolic program (23 variable–literal symbols)

Fig. 2.2.2   Reference by literal and by variable contrasted.

In some programming systems, classes of names are used to require the programmer to pass certain characteristics of the operands to the language translator (compiler). Thus in FORTRAN and PL/I, names starting with letters I, J, K, L, M, or N denote integers (unless declared otherwise). Names beginning with other letters denote numbers that are represented internally by floating-point words (unless declared otherwise).

Variables name *data collections* as well as single values. In APL, simple assignment statements illustrating this are

(4) $X←3,4,5,8,9.6$

(5) $X←3\ 4\ 5\ 8\ 9.6$

(6) $X←'CAT\ AND\ MOUSE'$

(7) $X←'DON''T'$

The first two statements each show that the variable X names a *vector* of five numbers; in the first case the numbers (elements) are separated by commas, in the second by blanks (both separators are equivalent). Equation (6) shows a character string, or vector, specifying X; X then has 13 elements. Elements of a character vector follow each other directly; blanks or commas are *not* used as separators and hence they can be used as data. Equation (7) also shows a character string specifying X, but we now see a special case since the character vector is to contain a quote symbol (in *don't*) and quote symbols are used to delimit the string. In this case, APL requires a double-quote to represent a data quote character (as shown).

2.3 A SIMPLE PROGRAM

We shall shortly resume our systematic presentation of APL principles, but since this is somewhat tedious, we digress to consider a complete simple program as shown in Fig. 2.3.1*a*. This program, which we have chosen to name $SIMP$, requests the user to enter a vector of numbers and then computes and prints the number of numbers, their mean, and standard deviation. Since Fig. 2.3.1 includes a line-by-line comment, we shall only remark on some general ideas here. First, there are two phases involved:

1. Function definition
2. Function execution

		Remarks
	$\nabla SIMP$	Header giving program name
	[1] $'ENTER\ NUMBERS'$	Print heading (characters between quotes)
	[2] $X\leftarrow\square$	Input awaited to specify X
	[3] $N\leftarrow\rho X$	No. of elements of X specifies N
(a)	[4] $M\leftarrow(+/X)\div N$	M (=mean) is sum over X divided by N
	[5] $S\leftarrow((+/(X-M)\star 2)\div N)\star 0.5$	S is the standard deviation
	[6] $'NO.\ OF\ NUMBERS='; N$	Print heading, then N value
	[7] $'MEAN=';M;'\ STD.\ DEV.=';S$	Print headings and M and S values
	∇	End-of-program symbol
	$SIMP$	Call of function $SIMP$ to execution†
	$ENTER\ NUMBERS$	Execution of line 1
(b)	$\square:$	A cue symbol (by APL) for data input
	$\quad 3\ 8\ 9\ 12$	User-typed data (execution of line 2)
	$NO.\ OF\ NUMBERS=4$	Execution of line 6
	$MEAN=8\quad STD.\ DEV.=3.24$	Execution of line 7

†*Note:* APL system typing starts at far left of line; user typing
          is always indented to the right.

Fig. 2.3.1   A concise program for mean and standard deviation of data vector X.

Function definition means the written form of the function. All modern programming languages permit the user to specify a program (APL calls this a function) which is stored in the machine's memory. Since several programs may be stored, each must be identified by a *name* which in this example is $SIMP$. *An APL function definition always starts and ends with the symbol* ∇.

In APL, any variable or operand that appears without a specification (or branch) is interpreted as a request for printout. Using this rule, we can readily see that when the program is executed, lines 1, 6, and 7 will result in printouts (see Fig. 2.3.1*b*).

A program requests *input data* for (say) vector X by the statement

$$X \leftarrow \square$$

The number of elements (values) in a vector X is obtainable by the ρ operator. Thus N is specified as this number by line 3

$$N \leftarrow \rho X$$

The sum of *all* elements of vector X is easily specified in APL by

$$+/X$$

Readers familiar with other programming languages like FORTRAN or ALGOL will take special note of the fact that Fig. 2.3.1 contains no loops. APL programs which have a minimum number of loops and branches are said to be *concise*. A program written in the more conventional style and therefore containing loops and branches is said to be *detailed*. Figure 2.3.2 shows a detailed program for the mean. This program contains a loop (statements 6 and 7, plus the initialization statements 4 and 5). Also of interest is the indexed variable $X[I]$, which denotes "the Ith element of X." Principles of indexing and looping will be discussed in more detail later.

Remarks

$\nabla DETM$	Header giving program name
[1] `'ENTER NUMBERS'`	Print message
[2] $X \leftarrow \square$	Input awaited to specify X
[3] $N \leftarrow \rho X$	No. of elements of X specifies N
[4] $M \leftarrow 0$	Initialize M to 0
[5] $I \leftarrow 1$	Initialize I to 1
[6] $ADD: M \leftarrow M + X[I]$	Add next $X[I]$ to M
[7] $\rightarrow (N \geq I \leftarrow I+1)/ADD$	Increment I by 1; branch to ADD if $N \geq I$
[8] $M \leftarrow M \div N$	M (=mean) specified by $M \div N$
[9] `'MEAN='`$;M$	Print header then M
∇	End-of-program symbol

Fig. 2.3.2 Detailed program for mean of data vector X.

2.4 EXPRESSIONS: RIGHT-TO-LEFT RULE

Most languages permit expressions of essentially arbitrary extent to be formed with specified operators. The ability to write expressions (rather than being restricted to one-operator statements) eliminates the need for much "scratch-pad" storage and the variables needed to name it. The resulting simplification reduces programming errors and permits problem statements to more closely resemble familiar algebraic expressions.

The formation of expressions in any language is governed by certain rules for forming legal symbol strings. The set of all such rules for a given language is called its *syntax*. For example, a common syntax rule is that the number of left and right parentheses must be the same in any expression.

Algebra permits expressions including the operators $+, -, \times, \div$ to any degree of complexity. Multiplication and division are performed first, then addition and subtraction; the process proceeds from left to right, subject to the precedence rules. Left and right parentheses are used to denote subexpressions. A subexpression may be of any length and may include other subexpressions. All operations included between each parenthesis pair are performed to produce a single value, which only then is subject to the operators outside the parenthesis pair according to the precedence and left-to-right rules. A further common convention allows the multiplication sign to be elided (omitted). This can be done only if every name is restricted to be a single letter; otherwise there would be confusion between the product of two variables and a single multilettered variable.

Many computer languages based on algebra follow similar rules. For example, in the FORTRAN language, all the above rules apply except that FORTRAN permits multiple-character names and hence forbids eliding the multiplication symbol. APL requires a multiplication symbol for the same reason.

In order to understand a language thoroughly it must be possible to *imitate* the program translator, i.e., to scan each expression as a symbol string and interpret each symbol and substring encountered. In APL this is done in *strict right-to-left order* with no precedence given to any operator over any other. In the following examples, redundant parentheses are used as an exposition device to clearly show APL's order of processing an expression with several operators.

EXAMPLES:

APL	APL fully parenthesized	Result value
3+4×3	3+(4×3)	15
4×3+3	4×(3+3)	24
4×5-3	4×(5-3)	8
4+5-7+6+2	4+(5-(7+(6+2)))	¯6
4+5+(-7)+6+2	4+(5+((-7)+(6+2)))	10

The right-left rule is certainly a departure from the conventions of algebra. The reason for this bold step is elegance and simplicity since now there is only one rule to remember. Also, precedence rules tied to operators (like multiplication before addition) become very cumbersome when there are many operator types, as there are in a rich language like APL. It is consistent with the right-to-left scan rule to read operations verbally as follows, for example:

> 3-2   "2 subtracted from 3"
> 3÷2   "2 divided into 3"
> 3*2   "the 2 power of 3" (which is 9)

APL's use of strict right-left scan of statements is somewhat controversial. It is easy to learn since it is so simple and consistent, but also easy to forget, especially since we have been trained in the scan rules of arithmetic and algebra. Of course, one can always insert parentheses to force any order of evaluation. Thus

$$4 \times 3 + 2 \equiv 20 \quad \text{but} \quad (4 \times 3) + 2 \equiv 14$$

It might be thought that in complex expressions APL will require more use of parenthesizing. However, this is not entirely clear. We now give one interesting counterexample. Consider finding the value of the polynomial

$$P = 5y^3 + 2y^2 + 7y + 9$$

By "brute force" and using only addition and multiplication operations, we might write

$$P \leftarrow (5 \times Y \times Y \times Y) + (2 \times Y \times Y) + (7 \times Y) + 9$$

The well-known technique of *nesting* reduces the number of multiplications and storage references. This may be written

$$P \leftarrow 9 + Y \times (7 + Y \times (2 + Y \times (5)))$$

This form is similar to what would be written in any programming language and requires only three multiplications for a polynomial of degree 3 (or N multiplications for degree N). In APL, the right-to-left scan rule permits *all* the parentheses of the nested form to be dropped

$$P \leftarrow 9 + Y \times 7 + Y \times 2 + Y \times 5$$

2.5 BASE VALUE AND REPRESENTATION (INVERSE BASE VALUE)

Before leaving the subject of polynomials, it is appropriate to point out that a number is usually represented by a digit string; the problem of obtaining the number from the digit string is one of evaluating a polynomial. This will be illustrated presently; but first, let it be understood that the *natural numbers,* zero and the positive integers, have an existence and meaning apart from any particular representation of them. Thus the number "seventeen" could be expressed as a series of seventeen strokes, as the symbols 17, the symbols XVII, and in many other ways. The usual manner of denoting a number will be adopted as standard for referring to the number value; e.g., seventeen will be written as 17.

Most common systems of representing numbers use strings of integers called *digits* to represent a number. Each digit is restricted to a definite range from zero to some limit $R-1$; i.e., only zero and the first $R-1$ integers are permitted to appear in any position of the string representing the number. The number R is called the *radix* of the number system. Our familiar number system uses a radix of 10. The function that gives the number X from a specification of the radix R and a digit string D is called the *base-value* operator. In general,

(1) $X \leftarrow R \bot D$

means that X is specified as the value obtained by treating the elements of the vector D as digits in the number system of radix R. For example,

(2) $347 \equiv 10 \bot 3,4,7$

The base-value operation permits the distinction to be made between a number and its representation as a digit string in a system of any specified radix. The next question is, how does one actually derive a number value from a digit string? Here it is helpful to start with a specific familiar example and then generalize. The number 347 may be written in the following ways (among many possible ways):

(3) $347 \equiv 10 \bot 3,4,7 \equiv 3 \times 10^2 + 4 \times 10^1 + 7 \times 10^0$

(4) $347 \equiv 8 \bot 5,3,3 \equiv 5 \times 8^2 + 3 \times 8^1 + 3 \times 8^0$

In general, for $N \equiv \rho D$

(5) $X \equiv R \bot D \equiv (D[1] \times R * N-1) + (D[2] \times R * N-2) + \ldots D[N]$

The digit string 3,4,7 in the radix-10, or decimal-radix, system represents 347; the digit string 5,3,3 in the radix-8, or octal, system represents 347. Equation (5) shows the general case of radix R and digit string D. The base-value operator is seen to be the evaluation of a polynomial. Equation (1) or (5) therefore serves to designate any polynomial. For the special case of the number value from a digit string, the digits are the *coefficients* and the radix is the quantity raised to successive powers. The *weight* of the high-order (leftmost) digit is the radix raised to a power 1 less than the number of digits being represented; the exponents of the weights of the digits decrease by 1 as one progresses to the right.

Since obtaining the number corresponding to a digit string is a polynomial evaluation, the method of nesting is a good technique for actual computation.

EXAMPLE: Find the number X whose base-2 representation is

$$D \equiv 1,1,0,1,0,1$$

SOLUTION:

$$X \equiv 1+2\times(0+2\times(1+2\times(0+2\times(1+2\times(1)))))$$

Evaluation "inside-out":

$$X \equiv 1+2\times(2\times(1+2\times(2\times3)))$$
$$\equiv 1+2\times(2\times(1+12))$$
$$\equiv 1+2\times(26)$$
$$\equiv 53 \quad \text{(ans.)}$$

An alternative method, valuable for a representation consisting of only a few digits, is to first list the weights of the digits, then place each digit under its weight. Each digit is then multiplied by its weight, and then the products are added.

EXAMPLE: Find the number X whose base-2 representation is $1,1,0,1,0,1$

SOLUTION:

Weights	32	16	8	4	2	1
Digits	1	1	0	1	0	1
Products	32	16	0	4	0	1

Sum of products $\equiv 53$ (ans.)

In some other systems of notation $10 \perp 3,4,7$, is written

$$(347)_{10}$$

or $8 \perp 5,3,3$ is written

$$(533)_8$$

The base-value operator operates on a radix and a digit string and produces a number. It is important to have a way of specifying the inverse to this operation. Appropriately enough, the inverted base symbol is used for this purpose. The general form is

(6) $D \leftarrow (N\rho R)\top X$

Here the arguments are the radix R, the number of digits N desired in the representation, and the value to be represented X. The result is the N-digit string D, a vector which is the representation of the positive integer X or 0 in base R.

EXAMPLE: Give the three-digit representation of 347, base 8.

SOLUTION:

$D \equiv 5,3,3 \equiv (3\rho 8)\top 347$

Thus far only notation for inverse base value has been discussed. Notice that D, the result of the operation, can be checked by applying the base-value operator to it and comparing the number obtained with X. However, we have not yet given a procedure for performing the inverse-base-value operation. Such a procedure may be easily derived from the polynomial nature of the radix representation of a number. The procedure is not given here; it is included in a more detailed treatment of number representation in Chap. 8.

2.6 PRIMITIVE SCALAR OPERATORS, ELEMENT-BY-ELEMENT RULE

The class of primitive scalar operators may apply to single operands, in which case they are said to be *monadic,* or else to a *pair* of operands, in which case they are termed *dyadic.* The dyadic operators include the familiar $+,-,\times,\div$, and * (the latter for exponentiation). Monadic operators include magnitude (= absolute value), the logical *NOT*, and monadic use of many dyadic operator symbols.

Figure 2.6.1 defines and illustrates all of APL's scalar operators. In most cases, each operator symbol is defined in both a monadic and a dyadic sense, often with quite different meanings. For example, the operator symbol L in its monadic sense rounds down, but in the dyadic sense means minimum:

Monadic: $\lfloor 3.45 \equiv 3 \equiv$ nearest integer equal or less than 3.45
Dyadic: $8\lfloor 5 \equiv 5 \equiv$ minimum of 8,5

Since the figure shows all scalar operators, we limit ourselves to discussing only those that are a bit unusual or of special interest. The *signum* is a monadic operator that takes on one of three values, $^-1$ or 0 or 1, as its argument is negative, zero, or positive. Thus

$\times 5 \equiv 1$ and $\times^- 9 \equiv ^- 1$ and $\times 0 \equiv 0$

Monadic form $f\,B$		f	Dyadic form $A\,f\,B$	
Definition or example	Name		Name	Definition or example
$+B \leftrightarrow 0+B$	Plus	+	Plus	$2+3.2 \leftrightarrow 5.2$
$-B \leftrightarrow 0-B$	Negative	-	Minus	$2-3.2 \leftrightarrow {}^{-}1.2$
$\times B \leftrightarrow (B>0)-(B<0)$	Signum	×	Times	$2\times3.2 \leftrightarrow 6.4$
$\div B \leftrightarrow 1\div B$	Reciprocal	÷	Divide	$2\div3.2 \leftrightarrow 0.625$
(see table below)	Ceiling	⌈	Maximum	$3\lceil7 \leftrightarrow 7$
	Floor	⌊	Minimum	$3\lfloor7 \leftrightarrow 3$
$\star B \leftrightarrow (2.71828\dots)\star B$	Exponential	⋆	Power	$2\star3 \leftrightarrow 8$
$\circledast\star N \leftrightarrow N \leftrightarrow \star\circledast N$	Natural logarithm	⊛	Logarithm	$A\circledast B \leftrightarrow \log B$ base A $A\circledast B \leftrightarrow (\circledast B)\div\circledast A$
$|{}^{-}3.14 \leftrightarrow 3.14$	Magnitude	|	Residue	(see table below)
$!0 \leftrightarrow 1$ $!B \leftrightarrow B\times!B-1$ or $!B \leftrightarrow$ gamma $(B+1)$	Factorial	!	Binomial coefficient	$A!B \leftrightarrow (!B)\div(!A)\times!B-A$ $2!5 \leftrightarrow 10 \quad 3!5 \leftrightarrow 10$
$?B \leftrightarrow$ random choice from ιB	Roll	?	Deal	A mixed function (see Fig. 2.18.2)
$\circ B \leftrightarrow B\times3.14159\dots$	Pi times	○	Circular	See table at left
$\sim1 \leftrightarrow 0 \quad \sim0 \leftrightarrow 1$	NOT	~		

Ceiling / Floor:

B	$\lceil B$	$\lfloor B$
3.14	4	3
${}^{-}3.14$	${}^{-}3$	${}^{-}4$

Residue:

Case	$A\|B$
$A\neq0$	$B-(|A)\times\lfloor B\div|A$
$A=0,B\geq0$	B
$A=0,B<0$	DOMAIN ERROR

Logical functions:

f	Name						
∧	AND	A	B	$A\wedge B$	$A\vee B$	$A\barwedge B$	$A\veebar B$
∨	OR	0	0	0	0	1	1
⍲	NAND	0	1	0	1	1	0
⍱	NOR	1	0	0	1	1	0
		1	1	1	1	0	0

Relations. Result is 1 if the relation holds, 0 if it does not:

f	Name
<	Less
≤	Not greater
=	Equal
≥	Not less
>	Greater
≠	Not Equal

$3\leq7 \leftrightarrow 1$

$7\leq3 \leftrightarrow 0$

Table of dyadic ○ functions

$(-A)\circ B$	A	$A\circ B$
$(1-B\star2)\star.5$	0	$(1-B\star2)\star.5$
Arcsin B	1	Sine B
Arccos B	2	Cosine B
Arctan B	3	Tangent B
$({}^{-}1+B\star2)\star.5$	4	$(1+B\star2)\star.5$
Arcsinh B	5	Sinh B
Arccosh B	6	Cosh B
Arctanh B	7	Tanh B

Fig. 2.6.1 Primitive scalar functions (operators).

For most other arithmetic and logical operators, the monadic use of an operator symbol is seen to be closely related to the dyadic use.

As one example of the use of scalar operators, consider an expression to round the number X to, say, three decimal places. We reason as follows: Multiply X by $1000\,(\equiv 10*3)$, add $.5$, then round down to the nearest integer. Finally divide by $10*3$. Thus

$$(\lfloor.5+X\times 10*3\,)\div 10*3$$

Many physical counters, including automobile odometers, count cyclically; i.e., after some upper count is reached, the counter starts over with 0 count. This property is closely related to an operation in number theory called the *residue*.

The number K, called the residue of the number N modulo M, is written

(1) $K \leftarrow M \mid N$

Here, K, M, N, Q are integers which satisfy the relations

(2) $0 \leq K < M$

(3) $N \equiv K + M \times Q$

In these expressions, N and Q may be negative. If N is positive, then K is seen to be the remainder when N is divided by M. If N is positive and smaller than M, then K will be equal to N. If N is negative, then

(4) $M \mid -(\mid N) \equiv M \mid (M - M \mid \mid N)$

EXAMPLES:

1. The residue of 12 modulo 16 is $K \equiv 16 \mid 12 \equiv 12$.
2. The residue of 19 modulo 16 is $K \equiv 16 \mid 19 \equiv 3$.
3. The residue of $^-19$ modulo 16 is $K \equiv 16 \mid {}^-19 \equiv 16 \mid (16 - 16 \mid 19) \equiv 13$

Among the most interesting and powerful of the dyadic operators are the six *relationals*. Each specifies a *condition* to be tested on its two arguments; if the condition *is* satisfied, the result is 1, otherwise the result is 0. For example

$$3 > 5 \equiv 0 \quad \text{also} \quad 3 \geq 3 \equiv 1 \quad \text{also} \quad {}^-2 > 1 \equiv 0$$

Thus relational operators provide a way to *compare* values and record the outcome as data to be manipulated later. The relationals are equivalent to certain logical expressions when their arguments are bits (see Fig. 2.6.2).

Relational operator	Equivalent for bit operands
$U \leftarrow X < Y$	$U \leftarrow (\sim X) \wedge Y$
$U \leftarrow X \leq Y$	$U \leftarrow (\sim X) \vee Y$
$U \leftarrow X = Y$	$U \leftarrow (X \wedge Y) \vee ((\sim X) \wedge (\sim Y))$
$U \leftarrow X \geq Y$	$U \leftarrow X \vee \sim Y$
$U \leftarrow X > Y$	$U \leftarrow X \wedge \sim Y$
$U \leftarrow X \neq Y$	$U \leftarrow (X \wedge \sim Y) \vee ((\sim X) \wedge Y)$

Fig. 2.6.2   Relational operators and their Boolean equivalents.

Thus far, the scalar operators each apply to single scalars or a pair of scalars. We now state a simple but powerful principle that extends all these operators to vectors and higher-order arrays such as matrices.

ELEMENT-BY-ELEMENT RULE: All scalar monadic and dyadic operators apply to vectors in the element-by-element sense. For dyadic operators, the two argument vectors (or arrays) must be of the same dimension(s) except that one may be a scalar and the other an array, in which case the scalar is used repetitively with *every* element of the array.

EXAMPLES: Use the data

$$X \leftarrow 3 \ 4 \ 5 \ 2$$
$$Y \leftarrow 1 \ ^-5 \ 2 \ 9$$

Then

$$X + Y \equiv 4 \ ^-1 \ 7 \ 11$$
$$X + 1 \equiv 4 \ 5 \ 6 \ 3$$
$$X \lceil Y \equiv 3 \ 4 \ 5 \ 9$$
$$2 \mid X \equiv 1 \ 0 \ 1 \ 0$$

2.7   BRANCHING, LOOPING, AND TRACING

A program is a named written sequence of statements. When a program is called into execution, the first written statement is the first to be executed; this is followed by the next in written sequence and so forth until a *branch*-type statement is reached. A branch forces the strict sequence to be broken and sequencing to resume at some other point in the program. Branching is an essential operation, provided in some form or another in every programming language. However, the way it is specified varies considerably from language to language. In this section, APL's branching statements will be described.

Before discussing branching, it is necessary to observe how a statement may be given a name. In APL this is done by starting the statement with its desired name (the usual syntax for names applies) and terminating it with a *colon* character which is a separator from the body of the statement. For example NXT is the name of the following statement

[9] $NXT:J\leftarrow J+1$

Since a branch says in effect "if some condition is satisfied, branch to a specified statement and continue from there," every branch statement specifies the name of a statement and most branches also specify a *condition* to be tested. Branching in APL is typified by the forms shown in Fig. 2.7.1. All forms include the right-pointing arrow, which may be read GO TO. The form with a slash most often specifies a condition by a relational operator connecting two data values to be compared. If the relation is satisfied, the result of the relation is 1, this selects the branch name (following the slash). Otherwise, the relation results in 0, which as a selector results in a null; a branch to null is interpreted as no branch, i.e., continue to next statement. A somewhat different way to specify a branch in APL is similar to FORTRAN's "computed GO TO," i.e., a list of branch locations is given followed by an index; the index chooses one of these as the location of the branch.

Consider now the very simple problem of summing all elements of vector X. This may be done in APL without branching, but we shall use this simple example to illustrate branching and loop-control principles. Our program first requires a name for the sum, say S. Then we plan for S to be computed by adding to its current value the next value from vector X. Thus, the "inner core" of the program will be the statement

$S\leftarrow S+X[I]$

This statement is to be executed N times, each time with a new value of I to pick up the next element of X. Figure 2.7.2 shows a few different programs for the same problem. For simplicity these programs do *not* show input or output statements. In all cases, I is incremented by 1 and a test is made for I larger than N, in which case there is an exit from the program. The programs differ in the position of the exit-test or index-update statements. In (*a*), called the technique of *leading decisions,* the exit test is made at the *start* of the loop; so this program works properly even if X is empty ($N=0$) while the other programs will always pass through the loop at least once (since the test is at the end of the loop). In all programs, the variables S and I are initialized (to 0 and 1 respectively) *before* the first statement within the loop.

Example statement	Meaning
→0	Exit from program
→REP	Branch to (statement named) REP
→ null	No branch; null can be obtained in several ways
→($N \geq I$)/0	If $N \geq I$, exit from program, otherwise continue
→($N \geq I$)/REP	If $N \geq I$, branch to REP, otherwise continue
→(REP,TEP,MEP)[J]	Branch to REP or TEP or MEP as J=1 or 2 or 3

Fig. 2.7.1   APL branching statements.

```
      ∇  SUM1                        ∇  SUM2
[1]      N←ρX                 [1]      N←ρX
[2]      S←0                  [2]      S←0
[3]      I←1                  [3]      I←1
[4]      TST:→(N<I)/0         [4]      REP:S←S+X[I]
[5]      S←S+X[I]             [5]      I←I+1
[6]      I←I+1                [6]      →(N≥I)/REP
[7]      →TST                      ∇
      ∇
           (a)                           (b)
```

```
           ∇  SUM3
      [1]      N←ρX
      [2]      S←0
      [3]      I←1
      [4]      REP:S←S+X[I]
      [5]      →(N≥I←I+1)/REP
           ∇
```

(c)

Fig. 2.7.2   Some branching styles: (a) leading decision, (b) trailing decision, and (c) combining index update and branch.

The procedure for understanding or validating a program is, in principle, very simple. One simply interprets each statement and follows exactly the operations specified. Any practical program must after all be a finite sequential process; by following all steps with all possible data, the entire procedure and all the results specified by the program will be exposed. Of course such complete *tracing* of the program would be impractical and rather foolish since the purpose of a program is to avoid such exhaustive execution by the writer. On the other hand, every program must be checked out or "debugged," and this means that the programmer must be prepared with examples whose results are known. If the objective is to check out or understand the workings of a program, then a procedure called a *trace* can be most valuable.

A trace is a listing of the values of selected variables (sometimes all of them) with special attention to *changes* in values. A trace is illustrated by Fig. 2.7.3 for the program for summing four numbers (X). The trace array is obtained by the process of interpreting each step of the program, recording the values of the traced variables, and then proceeding to the next step. Branches are executed as indicated.

The trace list consists of rows of numbers; each row gives the values of certain variables *after* execution of the step whose number is given as the leftmost entry. Each row of a trace is therefore a "snapshot" of certain storage locations (variable values) after a particular step has been completed. Although all variables could be listed after each step, to reduce tedium it is common practice to choose variables of special interest especially in the control of the program. These include index variables and others appearing in tests for program branches as well as the result variable.

Note that in the particular trace shown after step 0 the value of I has not yet been specified; a? is therefore entered. Also, values of a variable not changed in any specific step are not copied in the list—this makes the list somewhat easier to read. Thus the value of S after the second execution of step 4 is 12 since this is the last previous recorded entry for S.

Tracing by hand is tedious but sometimes necessary to produce a working program. Some programming systems permit the user to specify trace options, e.g., printout of selected statements and variables each time the statement or variable is executed.

In APL, to trace statements (say) 4 and 5 of function *SUM2* the user types the command

$T \Delta SUM2 \leftarrow 4, 5$

Thereafter, whenever *SUM2* is called into execution, the result after every execution of lines 4 and 5 will be printed. The trace is turned *off* by the command

$T \Delta SUM2 \leftarrow 0$

```
      ∇SUM3
[1]  N←ρX
[2]  S←0
[3]  I←1
[4]  REP:S←S+X[I]
[5]  →(N≥I←I+1)/REP
      ∇
```

Index *I*≡1 2 3   4
Data   *X*≡3 9 ⁻14 8

After line	S	I
1	?	?
2	0	?
3		1
4	3	
5		2
4	12	
5		3
4	⁻2	
5		4
4	6	
5		5

Fig. 2.7.3   **Program to sum four numbers and trace.**

2.8 PRINCIPLES OF LOOPING SUMMARIZED

A loop may be used whenever a given sequence of operations is to be repeated several times. Results identical to those obtained by using the loop can always be obtained by straight-line programming, a sequence of instructions without a loop. In fact a straight-line program requires fewer *executed* instructions than a loop to do the same job. However, the loop usually requires far fewer instructions to be *written,* thus saving programming effort and storage required for the program. The loop and straight-line methods may sometimes be combined in a single scheme.

To summarize, the advantages and disadvantages of a loop (over straight-line programming) are:

Advantages:
1. Number of instructions written is independent of the number of times the loop is executed. This allows easy change of the number of executions by change of a parameter.
2. Fewer instructions written and stored if the number of times the loop is executed is large.

Disadvantages:
1. Programming is more difficult, so care must be taken in loop control.
2. The number of instructions executed is larger than in the straight-line program. The excess due to those required for loop control increase program execution time.

A program loop can usually be considered as composed of four parts:

1. *Initialization*   Initial setting of variables
2. *Execution*   Operations on data performed in each loop pass
3. *Modification of Control Parameter*   Required in each loop pass
4. *Exit Test and Branch*   Required in each loop pass

The number of errors that can be made in programming loops (as well as other sections of a program) usually amaze novice programmers. Aside from syntactic errors in specifying loop control in the particular language being used, common errors include:

1. Specifying one more or one less traversal of the loop than is really intended
2. Failure to properly initialize the index parameter to other variables which appear in the loop

An important notion in programming (really more general than loop control) is *self-initialization.* This means that it is good practice to include explicit statements for specifying initial values for variables in the program itself. This helps ensure that starting values of variables will be under specific program control each time the program or a program part such as a loop is executed anew.

To illustrate the provisions for branching and looping in another language, Fig. 2.8.1 shows the possibilities in the FORTRAN language. In FORTRAN, statement names must be integers. Each FORTRAN statement is described in an equivalent statement or statement sequence in our language. The first two examples are specified by the FORTRAN key words GO TO and correspond directly to types already described. The key-word IF denotes a comparison of a

FORTRAN	*APL equivalent*
GO TO 4	$\rightarrow S4$
GO TO (19,6,10),I	$\rightarrow(S19,S6,S10)[I]$
IF(X−Y)12,10,17	$\rightarrow(S12,S10,S17)[1+(X\geq Y)+X>Y]$

DO 37 I=1,14,3	$I\leftarrow 1$
Statement	REP: Statement
Statement	Statement
37 Statement	Statement
Statement	$\rightarrow(14\geq I\leftarrow I+3)/REP$
.	Statement
.	.
etc.	etc.

Fig. 2.8.1   FORTRAN and APL branching statements.

parenthesized variable or expression with zero and a choice of one of three successor statements as the comparand is less than, is equal to, or is greater than zero. In the example, the programmer wanted to compare X and Y, so the comparand is the expression X − Y. The third type of branch designation is the DO statement intended to simplify the initialization, update, and test operations required in the control of program loops. The DO statement specifies a range of statements to be included in the loop; the range extends from the statement immediately following the DO to the statement whose label is specified immediately after the word DO. There follows specification of the variable used to control loop execution (I), an initial value for this variable, followed by the largest value of this variable, followed by the increment to be made in the variable each time the loop is traversed. The increment is placed in the last position since then it is permitted to omit writing it in the event its value is 1. Analysis of the description shows that the three statements in the DO loop would be executed five times, the successive values of I being 1, 4, 7, 10, and 13, respectively. The first time through the loop any reference to I finds the value 1, the next traversal finds I $\equiv$ 4, etc. The value of I (tentatively) after the last pass is 16, which, because it is greater than the limit value of 14 specified in the DO statement, results in exit from the DO loop. With certain not-too-severe restrictions, FORTRAN permits DO statements within the range of other DO statements; for details see any FORTRAN manual.

2.9 ARRAYS AND INDEXING: RAVEL AND RESHAPE

APL, like most languages, permits the user to give a name to a collection or array of data values. Also, selected elements of an array may be specified by indexing.

A linear collection of values, each in a definite position, is called a *vector* (in mathematics this is also called an *n*-tuple). The term "vector" is analogous to the use of the same word to designate the two or three numbers that specify coordinate values of a point in a plane or three-dimensional space. The APL notation pertinent to vectors is illustrated by

(1) $\rho X \equiv$ no. of elements of X

(2) $X[3] \equiv$ element in position 3 of X

(3) $X[I] \equiv$ element in position I of X

APL permits the user a choice of how to assign index values: 0-origin or 1-origin. On the computer, the user declares this choice with a special command:)ORIGIN 0 or)ORIGIN 1. In the 0-origin scheme, the possible index values are 0, 1, 2, etc. While in the 1-origin scheme, they are 1, 2, etc. Unless otherwise stated, 1-origin indexing will be assumed.

A vector may be indexed by a vector of index values with the following meaning:

$$X[3,9,1] \equiv X[3],X[9],X[1]$$

As another example; if

$$X \leftarrow 1,3,8,4,9$$

then

$$X[2,3,4,2] \equiv 3,8,4,3$$

Two-dimensional rectangular arrays are called *matrices*. Some pertinent notation for matrix X:

$$
\begin{aligned}
\rho X &\equiv \text{ a two-element vector} \\
(\rho X)[1] &\equiv \text{ no. of rows of } X \\
(\rho X)[2] &\equiv \text{ no. of columns of } X \\
X[I;] &\equiv \text{ row(s) } I \text{ of matrix } X \\
X[;J] &\equiv \text{ column(s) } J \text{ of matrix } X \\
X[I;J] &\equiv \text{ element in row } I \text{ and column } J \text{ of } X
\end{aligned}
$$

A matrix may be strung out row by row to form a vector by the *ravel* operator (,). Thus if

$$X \equiv \begin{matrix} 3 & 1 & 2 \\ 4 & 7 & 6 \end{matrix}$$

then

$$,X \equiv 3\ 1\ 2\ 4\ 7\ 6$$

Ravel will also convert a scalar into a vector of one element, so that

$$\rho,2 \equiv 1$$

The inverse to ravel is *reshape* (ρ)

$$(2,3)\rho(3,1,2,4,7,6) \equiv \begin{array}{ccc} 3 & 1 & 2 \\ 4 & 7 & 6 \end{array}$$

The reshape operator is thus seen to take two arguments (one to the left, one to the right of ρ). The left argument specifies the structuring information, the right argument the data to be restructured.

Data to specify a matrix X of say 3 rows and 5 columns may be requested from the terminal by

$$X \leftarrow (3\ 5)\rho X \leftarrow \square$$

The input requested by the $\square$ should be the matrix elements in row order, i.e., the first row followed by the second, etc. For this particular statement, the $\square$ will prompt the user to enter data. He should then enter 15 numbers for matrix X as a row-list vector. The statement is seen to reshape this data into a 3-row 5-column matrix. If he wishes to enter the data in column order, he may use the transpose operator $\lozenge$

$$X \leftarrow \lozenge(3\ 5)\rho X \leftarrow \square$$

Since reshaping alters the dimensionality of an array, it is important to understand the dimension information which is obtainable by the monadic ρ operator. This is shown in Fig. 2.9.1. The dimension of a scalar is seen to be a null (empty) vector, and its rank is zero. The dimension of a vector is equal to the number of its elements, and its rank is 1. The dimensions of a matrix are the two numbers giving the numbers of rows and columns, and the rank is then 2. Note that the dimension of an array is always a vector (*not* a scalar even in the case of a scalar or vector).

In APL, it is quite possible and useful to have null variables denoting empty arrays. One way to specify a null vector is to use the reshape operator with 0 as the left (shaping) argument

$$X \leftarrow 0 \rho 0$$

Another way is

$$X \leftarrow \iota 0$$

Data entry of numbers requires the statement

$$X \leftarrow \square$$

Since statement-end is signaled when the user presses the *RETURN* key, only one line of data may be entered. The following program fragment will permit

Type of array	Dimension ρA	Rank $\rho\rho A$	$\rho\rho\rho A$
Scalar	null	$1\rho0$	$1\rho0$
Vector	$1\rho N$	$1\rho1$	$1\rho1$
Matrix	M,N	$1\rho2$	$1\rho1$
Three-dimensional	L,M,N	$1\rho3$	$1\rho1$

Fig. 2.9.1 Dimension and rank relationships.

entry of *any number* of numbers on any number of lines until the line $\iota 0$ is typed, which terminates the input:

```
X←ι0
REPX:X←X,B←□
→(0≠ρB)/REPX
```

Although the data entered represent the vector X, they can be restructured into a matrix using the reshape operator.

2.10 DATA GENERATOR OPERATORS

Data are the raw material processed by programs. Data may be supplied to an APL program in at least the following ways:

1. Input statement typified by

```
X←□     for numeric or bit data or variable names or expressions
X←⍞     for character data
```

Although the values as typed are in strict linear order, i.e., a vector, they can be structured as a matrix or higher-order array by the reshape operator discussed earlier.

2. Literal statements in the program such as

```
X←1 3 14.7 ¯19
```
or
```
X←'THE BIG CAT'
```

3. Literal values combined with the reshape operator

```
7ρ1 2≡1 2 1 2 1 2 1
```

4. Data generation operators

The data generator operators can specify either single values or whole arrays of values in simple and convenient ways. Such data are useful for quickly obtaining values for testing a program and a rich variety of other circumstances.

The dense integer sequence from 1 to N is generated by the statement typified by

$$X \leftarrow \iota N$$

Thus for example

$$\iota 6 \equiv 1 \ 2 \ 3 \ 4 \ 5 \ 6$$

Since the argument N specifies the number of elements generated, if N is 0, a *null* vector is specified.

One important use of this operator is to specify an index list. Thus, the first five elements of vector X are obtained by

$$X[\iota 5] \equiv X[1,2,3,4,5]$$

Also, the five elements of X starting with (say) the third element are

$$X[2+\iota 5] \equiv X[2+1,2,3,4,5] \equiv X[3,4,5,6,7]$$

In many statistical and simulation studies, a source of *random numbers* is required. APL can supply random integers by means of the two operators called *roll* and *deal*. Appropriately enough, the operator symbol is the question mark, which is indicative of the uncertainty of predicting a particular random number.

The *roll* operator is typified by the statement

$$X \leftarrow ?10$$

The result is an integer in the range from 1 to 10 drawn from a flat distribution. To specify, say, 100 such random numbers, we apply the roll operator element by element to 100 copies of the value 10 thus:

$$X \leftarrow ?100\rho 10$$

A second type of random-number generator, called *deal,* generates N random numbers each in the range from 1 to M with the added proviso that they are all *distinct* (no duplicate values):

$$X \leftarrow N?M$$

2.11 REDUCTION OPERATIONS: INNER AND OUTER PRODUCT

We have already encountered the extremely convenient APL notation for the *sum* of all elements of vector X

(1) $Y \leftarrow +/X$

meaning

$$(2) \qquad Y \equiv \sum_{i \equiv 1}^{\rho X} X_i$$

Equation (1) is called a sum (or +) *reduction* because the result is reduced in dimension from the argument. Note that Eq. (1) or (2) is shorthand for

$$(3) \qquad Y \leftarrow X[1] + X[2] + \ldots X[\rho X]$$

APL generalizes this idea to permit *any* scalar dyadic operator to be used in reduction, i.e., in the same way as + is used above. Thus if f is any scalar dyadic operator, the f reduction of vector X is equivalent to applying f to the "strung-out" elements of X.

$$(4) \qquad f/X \equiv X[1] f X[2] f \ldots f X[\rho X]$$

In interpreting Eq. (4), we scan from right-to-left as usual in APL.

EXAMPLES: Use as data

$$X \leftarrow 1 \ 3 \ 4 \ 2$$

Then

$$+/X \equiv 1+3+4+2 \equiv 10$$
$$\times/X \equiv 1 \times 3 \times 4 \times 2 \equiv 24$$
$$-/X \equiv 1-3-4-2 \equiv 1-(3-(4-2)) \equiv 0$$
$$\lceil/X \equiv 1 \lceil 3 \lceil 4 \lceil 2 \equiv 4$$

In the last case, the *maximum reduction* results in the *largest* element of the vector.

In the case of a matrix, we have the option of reduction over all values of the row index or over all values of the column index. These are designated by a bracketed integer following the slash (see Fig. 2.11.1).

There are particularly potent uses of the reduction operators combined with the the relationals.

EXAMPLE: Compute N, the number of negative values of vector X,

$$N \leftarrow +/X < 0$$

In matrix mathematics, the *inner product* of two vectors X and Y having the same number of elements is defined by†

---

†The remainder of this section may be skipped without losing essential continuity. Examples of inner and outer products may be found in the chart of Fig. 2.11.1.

Reduction:

1. General form for vectors (f is any scalar dyadic operator):

$$f/X \equiv X[1] \ f \ X[2]... f \ X[\rho X]$$

Note: The right side is interpreted in usual APL right-to-left scan.

Examples:

```
+/3,5,8,10≡3+5+8+10≡3+(5+(8+10))≡26
-/3,5,8,10≡3-5-8-10≡3-(5-(8-10))≡¯4
```

2. General form for matrices:

$f/[I]$ apply $f/$ to the vectors formed by stepping coordinate I.
If I is omitted, it is understood as the *last* coordinate.

Examples:

```
    1 3 8
    2 4 7        Then +/[1]X≡5,11,22≡ column sums
X≡1 1 2          (sums obtained by stepping coordinate 1or rows)
    1 3 5        Also +/[2]X≡+/X≡12,13,4,9≡ row sums
```

Inner product:

1. General form for vectors (f, g any two scalar dyadic operators):

$$X f.g Y \equiv f/X g Y$$

Examples:

```
X≡3,5,2,10          Y≡1,2,4,3
X+.×Y≡+/X×Y≡+/3,10,8,30≡51
X+.≥Y≡+/X≥Y≡+/1,1,0,1≡3
```

2. If X is a matrix of M rows, and Y is a vector, the result is a vector Z

$$Z[I] \equiv X[I;] f.g \ Y \quad \text{for } 1 \le I \le M$$

3. If Y is also a matrix but with N rows and K columns, Z is a matrix

$$Z[I;J] \equiv X[I;] f.g \ Y[;J] \quad \begin{matrix} 1 \le I \le M \\ 1 \le J \le K \end{matrix}$$

Outer product:

All possible pairs of each element of X and each of Y combined with operator f. Result is matrix $Z \equiv X \circ . f Y$ where

$$Z[I;] \equiv X[I]fY \quad \text{for} \quad 1 \le I \le \rho X$$

Example:

```
X≡3,5,2,10   and    Y≡1,2,4,3

          0 0 0 1
          0 0 0 0
X∘.=Y≡0 1 0 0
          0 0 0 0
```

Fig. 2.11.1 Reduction, inner and outer products.

(5) $Z \equiv \sum\limits_{I \equiv 1}^{\rho X} X\,[I] \times Y\,[I]$

In APL we write

(6) $Z \leftarrow X + . \times Y$

However, APL generalizes this result so that *any* two scalar dyadic operators, say *f* and *g,* may be applied in a similar manner. Thus

(7) $Z \leftarrow X f . g Y$

means

(8) $Z \leftarrow f / X g Y$

The operator *g* (any dyadic operator) is first applied in the element-by-element sense to X and Y and then the operator *f* (any dyadic operator) is applied to the result in reduction.

If X is a matrix and Y a vector, the above "product" is equivalent to the usual matrix-vector product. Thus, for example,

(9) $Z \leftarrow X + . \times Y$

is legal only if Y has as many elements as X has columns and then means

$Z[I] \equiv X[I;\,]+.\times Y \quad I \equiv 1,2,\ldots(\rho X)[1]$

If X and Y are matrices and they are conformable, i.e., the number of columns of X equals the number of rows of Y, then, for example,

(10) $Z \leftarrow X + . \times Y$

means the I row of X is taken in reduction with the J column of Y to produce the I, J result of Z:

(11) $Z[I;J] \leftarrow X[I;\,]+.\times Y[\,;J]$

The *outer product* of vector X with vector Y is written

(12) $Z \leftarrow X \circ . + Y$

where Z is a *matrix* such that

$$Z[I;]\equiv X[I]+Y \quad I\equiv 1,2,\ldots \rho X$$

That is, the Ith element of X is taken with *every* element of Y, thus generating row I of the result.

2.12 GENERATION OF SIMILARITY MATRIX*

A problem of increasing importance in information retrieval, medical diagnosis, and other applications is the determination of similarity or *distance* between sets of data. One such class of problem will now be described.

Assume a set of n objects, each of which can be described in terms of m properties. Each object will in general contain a different amount of each property. For example, in a medical diagnosis problem the "objects" may be patients and the "properties" the results of laboratory tests.

The problem is to obtain a similarity matrix which gives the "closeness" of each object to any other one based on *all* the properties. There is no unique measure of closeness. One simple and useful measure is based on a geometric picture whereby any *row* of the object-property matrix P is interpreted as a point and hence a vector in multidimensional space (of dimension M). The geometric *distance* between two points is a measure of similarity of the two vectors (and hence the data of the two rows). The square of the distance between two points in a space is obtained by taking the sum of the squares of the differences between corresponding coordinates. An example and program is shown in Fig. 2.12.1.

2.13 SOLUTION OF LINEAR EQUATIONS AND MATRIX INVERSION*

Systems of linear equations arise in problems in electric networks, linear programming, and heat flow, just to name a few.

In the first part of this section, conventional matrix notation and terminology will be used in discussing mathematical properties rather than our programming language. The term "matrix multiplication" will be used for the inner-product operation described in Sec. 2.11 and will be specified by omitting operator symbols between the variables. Vectors and matrices will be denoted by lowercase and uppercase boldface type.

*Starred sections cover specialized topics and may be omitted without loss of continuity.

Properties

	0	1	2	3
0	1	4	3	1
1	2	1	3	5
2	1	1	4	1
3	3	8	2	4
4	2	3	3	2
5	0	2	4	2

Objects (rows)

Object-property
matrix P

Objects

	0	1	2	3	4	5
0	0	26	10	30	3	7
1	26	0	18	52	13	15
2	10	18	0	66	7	3
3	30	52	66	0	31	53
4	3	13	7	31	0	6
5	7	15	3	53	6	0

Objects (rows)

Distance matrix D
(distance squared)

```
      ∇ DISTANCE
[1]    N←(ρP)[1]
[2]    D←(N,N)ρ0
[3]    J←1
[4]  B1:I←1
[5]  B2:D[I;J]←(P[I;]-P[J;])+.×(P[I;]-P[J;])
[6]    →(N≥I←I+1)/B2
[7]    →(N≥J←J+1)/B1
[8]    'DISTANCE SQUARED MATRIX:'
[9]    D
      ∇
```

Legend

0-origin indexing	
P	Object-property matrix
D	Distance-squared matrix

Fig. 2.12.1 Computation of distance-squared matrix.

With these conventions, a set of m linear equations in n variables x is written:

(1) $Ax \equiv b$

where $m \equiv$ number of equations $\equiv$ number of rows of A $\equiv$ number of components of b

$n \equiv$ number of variables $\equiv$ number of components of x $\equiv$ number of columns of A

We also assume the case of *inhomogeneous* equations, which means that at least one component of b is nonzero.

Any vector x that satisfies Eq. (1) is called a *solution vector* or simply a *solution*. Depending on the values of components of A as well as the relation between m, n, there may be a unique solution, no solution, or an infinity of solutions.

In order to better understand the later discussion we list the following rules of matrix algebra.

Addition is commutative

(2) $A + B \equiv B + A$

Addition is associative

(3) $A + (B + C) \equiv (A + B) + C$

Multiplication is associative

(4) $A(BC) \equiv (AB)C$

Multiplication is in general *not* commutative, i.e.,

(5) $AB \neq BA$ in general

In ordinary algebra, division may be expressed as the dividend multiplied by the reciprocal of the divisor. The reciprocal of any nonzero number q is implicity defined as that number, denoted by the symbol q^{-1}, that satisfies

(6) $qq^{-1} \equiv 1$

Here the 1 is the identity value for multiplication (since it is the only number whose product with any number gives the number itself). Analogous reasoning may be used to first identify an identity matrix ϑ, which by the rules for matrix multiplication is easily verified to be

(7) $\vartheta_j{}^i \equiv \begin{matrix} 0 & \text{for} & i \neq j \\ 1 & \text{for} & i = j \end{matrix}$

The matrix, called symbolically A^{-1}, that satisfies

(8) $A^{-1}A \equiv \vartheta$

is called the *inverse* of matrix A. It may be shown that A^{-1} exists if and only if the determinant of A is nonzero.

Assume A^{-1} exists; then using it as a premultiplier on both sides of Eq. (1),

(9) $A^{-1}Ax \equiv A^{-1}b$

using the associative law on the left and Eq. (8)

(10) $\vartheta x \equiv A^{-1}b$

The identity nature of ϑ means that Eq. (10) becomes

(11) $x \equiv A^{-1}b$

Thus, a solution of a set of linear equations may be obtained by multiplying the inverse of the coefficient matrix by the vector of right-side constants. This technique is particularly valuable if several x vectors are to be computed for different b vectors but with the same A matrix.

Procedures for solving systems of n equations in n unknowns and for inverting an $n \times n$ matrix are quite similar. There are two classes of methods, called *direct* and *indirect*.

Direct methods can produce the inverse, if it exists, in a definite number of steps which, for n fairly large, is on the order of n^3 times the number of operations in the inner loop of the program. The time for inner-loop operations depends upon the program and the machine, but a rough rule of thumb gives it as two to three times the sum of the machine's multiplication and addition times.

An indirect method starts with an initial approximate solution (which can be quite poor or even a guess) and successively improves it. The improvements in the approximate solution continue until some terminating condition is met such as Eq. (1) being satisfied to within some prespecified *residual* vector.

A general direct method and an indirect method are described in the following paragraphs. However, it must be pointed out that these rather general methods may not be the most efficient ones for many common problems. For example, sparse matrices, i.e., those with many 0s, are often encountered. Special methods for this case not only can be faster than a general algorithm, they can also save storage space by not requiring storage of the 0 components.

The Gauss-Jordan method of matrix inversion is a commonly used direct method. In the article by A. Orden it is used as the underlying principle for a program, described there in some detail, which can compute any of the following:

1. The solution of a set of linear equations
2. The inverse of a matrix
3. The determinant of a matrix
4. The rank of a matrix, i.e., the maximum number of linearly independent rows

The basic Gauss-Jordan algorithm for matrix inversion will be described and illustrated. Consider a matrix W which consists of $N + 1$ columns and N rows. At the start of the procedure, the original matrix A, whose inverse is sought, is placed in the rightmost N columns of W, and the leftmost column is set to the first column of the identity matrix (one followed by $N-1$ zeros). After the algorithm is completed, the inverse matrix will be the leftmost N columns of W. Since the operations are a bit difficult to follow in words, the reader is advised to follow the discussion by referring to Fig. 2.13.1, which shows an example 3 X 3 matrix as well as a APL program. The basic cycle within the program is to use the I-th row of W as a *pivot* in certain row operations with all other rows in order to, in effect, eliminate one variable from all the equations represented by the original matrix A. To do this, I, the index designating the pivot row, is

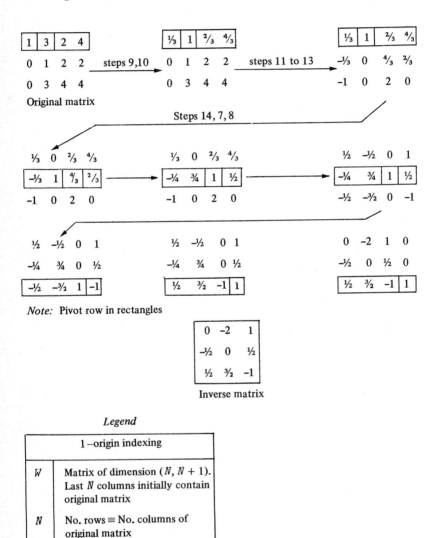

Note: Pivot row in rectangles

Inverse matrix

Legend

1–origin indexing	
W	Matrix of dimension $(N, N + 1)$. Last N columns initially contain original matrix
N	No. rows $\equiv$ No. columns of original matrix

Fig. 2.13.1 Basic algorithm and example of Gauss-Jordan matrix inversion.

```
     ∇ GAUSSJ
[1]     'ENTER MATRIX AS A ROW LIST'
[2]     A←□
[3]     N←(ρA)*0.5
[4]     W←(N,N+1)ρ0
[5]     W[;1+ιN]←(N,N)ρA
[6]     I←1
[7] JSET:J←1
[8]     W[;I]←I=ιN
[9]     P←W[I;I+1]
[10]    W[I;]←W[I;]÷P
[11] IJTST:→(J=I)/JUP
[12]    W[J;]←W[J;]-W[J;I+1]×W[I;]
[13] JUP:→(N≥J←J+1)/IJTST
[14]    →(N≥I←I+1)/JSET
[15]    'INVERSE IS'
[16]    W[;ιN]
     ∇
```

Fig. 2.13.1   Basic algorithm and example of Gauss-Jordan matrix inversion (continued).

initially set to 1, and column I of W to $I=ιN$, which is column I of the identity matrix. The pivot element P is then found from

$$P←W[I;I+1]$$

Row I is then divided by P, thus normalizing the pivot element to 1

$$W[I;]←W[I;]÷P$$

A copy of the $W[I;]$ pivot vector is then multiplied by the element in the pivot column of another row, and the resulting vector is then subtracted from that row. This is repeated for all rows of W except the pivot row itself. In the resultant W matrix, the $I+1$ column is now identical to column I of the identity matrix. The index I is then increased by 1 giving a new pivot row and column, and the entire process of setting column I to $I=ιN$ followed by the row reductions is repeated. This continues until every row has served as a pivot once. As mentioned above, the inverse matrix is then the leftmost N columns of W.

A significant improvement in numerical precision often results if instead of selecting pivots in strict order, the pivot-column index is advanced by 1 successively but the pivot element in column $I+1$ is selected as the largest element in the column (considering only those elements in rows not yet used as a pivot). The index of the selected row, say J, is recorded in the I position of a permutation vector PV, and column I is set to all zeros except for 1 in position J. The row operations then proceed as described above, using row J as the pivot row. After all rows have been used as a pivot row, the inverse of the original matrix A is again in the leftmost N columns of W but the rows and columns are scrambled and must be reordered using the permutation vector PV. To obtain the final inverse, the unscrambling is done by

$$W \leftarrow W[PV;]$$
$$W[;PV] \leftarrow W[;\iota N]$$

Although we have described the Gauss-Jordan matrix-inversion algorithm in words and as an APL program which can be transcribed to other computer languages, in APL there is an operator for matrix inversion. The symbol is a composite formed by typing a quad (shifted L) then a backspace and then overstriking with the divide. Thus

$$Y \leftarrow \boxdot A$$

results in Y being the inverse of matrix A. Also

$$X \leftarrow B \boxdot A$$

is a dyadic form which multiplies (inner product) vector B by the inverse of matrix A, giving X as the solution to the system of linear equations

$Ax \equiv b$

As mentioned earlier in this section, one approach to solving linear equations is called *indirect* since it is based on successive approximations. The *Gauss-Seidel* algorithm, which uses this method, will converge to the solution vector if the matrix of coefficients A satisfies the following condition of dominance of the elements on the main diagonal:

(12) $(|A[I;I]|)>(+/|A[I;]|)-|A[I;I]|$ for all I

Somewhat weaker conditions for convergence also exist that are relevant to many electric-network and heat-transfer problems. In any case, a test like Eq. (12) can be included in the program.

To understand the process (or at least one variation of it) first consider the expression for the *residual* or the typical equation J. This is defined as

(13) $R[J] \equiv B[J]-A[J;]+.\times X$

If X were indeed the solution vector, every $R[J]$ would be zero. Since the process of solution is one of successive approximation, the R will not in general

Lines	Remarks
1–4	Enter elements of matrix A as row list and reshape to matrix
5–6	Enter right-side constants B
7–8	Enter allowable residuals E
9	Initialize solution vector X and current residuals R to all zeros
10	Set J to 1
11	Branch to *ETST* if last residual has been adjusted
12	Increment J by 1
13–14	Compute residual, compute new approximation to X
15	Branch to *JTST* (line 11)
16	Entered from test at line 11: branch to *JSET* (line 10) if all residuals not less than allowable
17–18	Print solution vector X; then exit

```
    ∇ GAUSSDEL
[1]    'ENTER MATRIX A'
[2]    A←□
[3]    N←(ρA)*0.5
[4]    A←(N,N)ρA
[5]    'ENTER VECTOR B'
[6]    B←□
[7]    'ENTER VECTOR OF ALLOWABLE RESIDUALS'
[8]    E←□
[9]    R←X←Nρ0
[10] JSET:J←0
[11] JTST:→(J=N)/ETST
[12]   J←J+1
[13]   R[J]←B[J]-A[J;]+.×X
[14]   X[J]←X[J]+R[J]÷A[J;J]
[15]   →JTST
[16] ETST:→(~∧/E≥|R)/JSET
[17]   'SOLUTION IS X= '
[18]   X
    ∇
```

Fig. 2.13.2 Gauss-Seidel algorithm for solution of linear equations.

be 0. The basic idea is to adjust $X[J]$ so that $R[J]$ is forced to 0. As this is done for each value of J, the X vector changes so that previously calculated residuals are no longer 0. The user specifies a vector of *allowable residuals;* these will be called E. When the magnitude of every element of the residual vector is less than or equal to E, the process terminates.

The key expression is the one for that value of $X[J]$ which we temporarily call $X[J]'$ such that $R[J]$ will be 0. This may be found by setting $R[J]$ to 0 in Eq. (13). The expression is made more suitable for computation if $A[J;J]\times X[J]$ is both added to, and subtracted from, the right side. The term added may be absorbed in the sum so the expression for 0 residual may be written

(14) $0 \equiv (B[J]+A[J;]+.\times X[J])+A[J;J]\times X[J]'-A[J;J]\times X[J]$

Solving for $X[J]'$, remembering from Eq. (13) the definition of $R[J]$, and using $X[J]'$ to replace $X[J]$ as the result gives

(15) $X[J]\leftarrow X[J]+R[J]\div A[J;J]$

A program with line-by-line comment is given in Fig. 2.13.2.

2.14 FUNCTIONS

The notion of a function is fundamental to mathematics and information processing. In conventional notation,

(1) $y \equiv F(x)$

is read "*y* is a function F of x." The variable x is called the *argument,* or *independent variable; y* is called the *function,* or *dependent variable.* A function is a statement of dependence of one list of values on another. The symbol F will be the name of a precise procedure by which a value of y can be obtained for any given value of x.

A general way to think about a function is as a table of number pairs (x,y). If an argument value is specified, the table may be searched in the x column for a value equal to the argument, and the corresponding element in the y column is the function value. A function is sometimes called a *mapping* or *transformation* since it maps or transforms each argument value into a function value.

A graphical interpretation of a function follows from interpreting each (x,y) pair as coordinates of a point in a plane. The function is then represented by a configuration of points which may be connected as a curve.

Another method of specifying a function is by a computation rule or equation such as

(2) $y \equiv x^2$

Substitution of each x value gives a y value, and such a pair can again determine a point in a plane. Equation (2) plots as a parabola.

Thus far two forms of a function have been described:

1. **Tabular Representation**   a list of argument-function correspondence
2. **A Procedure** a method of linking functions together as in an algebraic expression or program

Of these, the first is perhaps more fundamental because it covers a wider class of functions, including, for example, data taken in an experiment. Moreover, if a function is given in algebraic form, it is possible to construct a list of number pairs by evaluating the function at successive points. On the other hand, if the function is given as a table of values, then it is often possible to represent it by any of a number of algebraic expressions.

An algebraic specification of a function has several advantages over the table representation. From a theoretical viewpoint, a most important advantage is that an algebraic expression can be manipulated by the general and powerful rules of algebra, calculus, etc., from which important inferences can often be drawn. From the viewpoint of computation, an algebraic specification of a function often allows computation time to be traded for storage space in the representation of the function.

For n values of a function, the storage required for the table is $2n$ numbers. In the algebraic form, practically no data storage is required: y is calculated for each argument as needed. Since arithmetic computing can be more time-consuming than looking up tables (particularly when the table is ordered on the arguments), computation required for the algebraic representation can be more costly in time but cheaper in (storage) space than the tabular representation.

For practical purposes, the space advantage of the algebraic representation may sometimes be kept even if the function appears first in a tabular form, e.g., as the result of an experiment, survey, or data-gathering operation. The idea is to:

1. Adopt a form of algebraic function which is to be used to "fit," i.e., approximate, the table in some sense. This algebraic function must have *parameters* that can be adjusted as a function of the data to ensure a "good" fit to the data values given.
2. Once the parameters of the approximating algebraic function are determined, they are used to represent the original function at least over the given range of arguments.

Procedure 1 above is likely to be quite time-consuming relative to 2 but is done only once for a given set of data. Procedure 2 is employed whenever the function must be evaluated from a given argument. Often, the value of the argument may not even be a value tabulated in the original function table. In this case, the algebraic expression performs an *interpolation* function.

It is possible to combine the table and algebraic representation in a single scheme. For example, a relatively small table may be stored and other values computed by interpolation. This is done in the familiar function-determination procedure such as using a table of sines and cosines in a handbook. Most people are trained to use linear interpolation to "read between the lines" of a table. There are also more accurate interpolation procedures, which, however, are more time-consuming.

It is important to recognize that it is not always feasible to derive an algebraic representation of a function. For example, consider a business file where the customer number is the argument variable and the customer account balance is the function variable. There is little chance here of approximating the function by an algebraic function. There is no choice but to hold the function in tabular form. This is one reason why commercial data-processing problems are dominated by the need to access large volumes of stored information. In contrast, scientific functions are quite often represented in some algebraic form.

The notation for functions in our programming language begins with the idea that the familiar operations such as $+, -, \times, \div$ are "standard" functions denoted by special symbols whose procedures are supplied implicitly. More generally, a function is defined by writing a program for computing the function value(s) from the argument value(s). That a program is in fact a function is emphasized by the fact that APL's term for "program" is the word "function."

2.15 FUNCTION NAMING: GLOBAL AND LOCAL VARIABLES

Every APL function starts with a header line whose first character is the symbol ∇, called *del*. Every header line must contain the name of the function, but it may also specify one or two argument variables and possibly a result variable, as shown in Fig. 2.15.1. To understand the various possible forms of header, it is first essential to understand certain naming conventions. In APL, a variable, say *JOE*, is said to be *global* if the name *JOE* which appears in more than one function refers to the *same* data. Thus, by using the same name as a global variable, several programs (functions) can communicate with each other through access to the same named data.

Although global variables are very useful for multiple-program manipulation of data, it is sometimes desirable to have named data private to only one program

Header syntax	*Remarks*
[1] ∇FUN	No arguments
[2] $\nabla FUN\ X$	One argument X
[3] $\nabla Y \leftarrow FUN\ X$	One argument X and result Y
[4] $\nabla X\ FUN\ Y$	Two arguments
[5] $\nabla Z \leftarrow X\ FUN\ Y$	Two arguments and result
[6] $\nabla FUN\ X;P;I;J$	Same as line 2 but with additional local variables

Rules:

1. All variables global unless specified as local.
2. All variables appearing in function header are local;
   this is only way variables become local.
3. In forms 3 and 5, if when calling the function, the result variable and arrow
   are omitted, upon exit from the function the result is printed.
4. The syntax of calling the function must agree with the header except
   for rule 3 and additional local variables.

Fig. 2.15.1   Function heading and global/local variables.

rather than the "togetherness" of shared global data. In APL, *a local* variable accomplishes this privacy, i.e., a local variable names a copy of data used uniquely in one function and distinct from all other data that may have the same name in other functions. The rules governing local and global names are summarized in Fig. 2.15.1. Briefly, in APL, all names are global unless specified as local. A local name is one that appears in a function heading.

Figure 2.15.2 shows one function $FUN1$ that calls another function $FUN2$. In analyzing these very simple programs, we may gain insight into the difference between global and local variables. When function $FUN1$ is called by typing $FUN1$, then APL behaves as follows:

1. Statements 1, 2, and 3 of $FUN1$ are executed as usual, in this case X is set to 1, Y to 2 and A to 19.
2. Statement 4 is a call on the function $FUN2$ with arguments X and Y. APL executes this call by first accessing the header of $FUN2$, from which it determines from the positions of the names in the call and in the header that X is to correspond to A and Y to B. It then makes local copies of X and Y data and labels them A and B. Some storage is also labeled C for the result.

```
      ∇FUN1
[1]    X←1
[2]    Y←2
[3]    A←19
[4]    Z←X FUN2 Y
[5]    Z
[6]    Q
[7]    A
       ∇
```

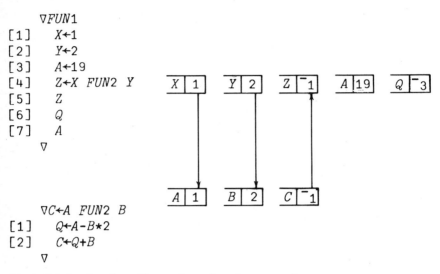

```
      ∇C←A FUN2 B
[1]    Q←A-B*2
[2]    C←Q+B
       ∇
```

Fig. 2.15.2 One function calling another and passing arguments.

3. An internal branch (within APL) is taken to line 1 of the called function *FUN2*. All references to A and B in this function will refer to the *local* copies A and B, *not* to the original X and Y (nor to any other global A and B which may exist in any other function).

4. In executing *FUN2*, the value of global variable Q is computed to be $1-2*2≡ ^-3$. Then at line 2, C is computed to be $^-3+2≡ ^-1$.

5. At exit from *FUN2*, APL copies the result data C into Z and returns to function *FUN1* at the point following the call, i.e., line 5. Lines 5 to 7 print Z, Q, and A, which are

```
 ¯1
 ¯3
 19
```

Note that the A printed is global A, *not* the A local to *FUN2*.

To summarize: in the above program, variables X, Y, Z, Q, A are global, and variables C, A, B are local to the function *FUN2*. The name A is *both* local and global, but different data are named in the two cases. The scheme just described for name and data translation is termed *call by value*, since each time a function is called, a separate copy is made of argument values; at exit from each call, this copy is no longer accessible.

2.16 FORMULA EVALUATION: ONE FUNCTION
OF MANY VARIABLES

Computing the values of a function specified by a formula is a frequent problem. The formula gives the function value in terms of the argument variables. Often there are several argument variables, and we are interested in several values for each variable. Moreover, we seek the value of the function for each argument-value configuration. To be specific, refer to Fig. 2.16.1 which shows the formula for the accumulated amount of money in a savings account that is being credited with compound interest. In this particular problem there are three argument variables, each of which is to take on several values. The variables in the type of problem considered vary linearly, or, in other words, successive values of a variable differ by some fixed value. For *this type* of variation, each variable can be described by three numbers:

1. Starting (first) value
2. Increment value
3. Final (last) value

The current values of the arguments will be called vector X, so ρX is the number of argument variables. We also identify three other vectors, each of the same dimension as X, which give the starting, increment, and final values for each argument. Values for all these vectors are obtained from the problem statement in the manner shown in the example of Fig. 2.16.1. Figure 2.16.2 shows a program that handles all details of advancing the values of the arguments systematically to ensure that all possible combinations of the X values are generated. Note line 2 of the program that "escapes" to the desired function to be evaluated (in general different for every function).

There are two major limitations of Fig. 2.16.2 for general formula evaluation. The first is that it is applicable only where the S, D, and M vectors are independent of each other. In practice this is sometimes not the case.

A somewhat less fundamental, but nonetheless important, limitation of the program is its rather poor control over the display format of the results of the program. In particular, each time a computed value of the function is obtained, not only this value but the values of all parameters are printed. Although this gives complete information, the form of the results is neither elegant nor easy to read. One improvement, at least for three variables, is for one variable to vary across the page and the second down the page so that one complete cycle of the two variables constitutes a two-dimensional table. One such table is produced for each value of the third variable. For four or more variables, things get complicated as far as display is concerned!

Controlling the output format of the results of computation is an important programming problem but is difficult to discuss with any generality.

Problem:

Given the following formula for the amount of money in a savings account accumulating compound interest

$$P \equiv A(1+R/4)^N$$

where

$A \equiv$ initial amount deposited
$R \equiv$ annual interest rate
$N \equiv$ the quarter since A was deposited
$P \equiv$ the accumulated amount on deposit at Nth quarter

Values of P are desired for all combinations of the following:

$A \equiv 1000,2000,3000, \ldots ,10,000$
$R \equiv .04,.045,.05, \ldots , .07$
$N \equiv 1,2,3, \ldots , 20$

Problem Name	Program Name	S	D	M
A	$X[1]$	1000	1000	10,000
R	$X[2]$	.04	.005	.07
N	$X[3]$	1	1	20

An APL form of formula:

$$P \leftarrow X[1] \times (1+X[2] \div 4) \star X[3]$$

Fig. 2.16.1 Preparing a problem using program of Fig. 2.16.2.

```
      ∇  FORMULAS
[1]      X←S
[2]      COM:Y←F X
[3]      X
[4]      Y
[5]      I←1
[6]    XCOM:→(X[I]<M[I])/XUP
[7]      X[I]←S[I]
[8]      →((ρX)≥I←I+1)/XCOM
[9]      →0
[10]   XUP:X[I]←X[I]+D[I]
[11]     →COM
      ∇
```

Fig. 2.16.2 Program for a function of many variables.

2.17 RECURSIVE DEFINITION OF FUNCTIONS*

It is often necessary to compute values of a function for not one but several argument values. Of course a direct approach is simply to repeat the entire function-evaluation calculation for each argument value. In many cases, however, a significant improvement in efficiency is possible by expressing the function value for the current argument in terms of the function values of some previous argument. Some possibilities of this type will now be explored with a familiar concrete example, the factorial function, defined by

(1) $k! \equiv 1 \times 2 \times 3 \times \cdots \times k$

for values of $k \equiv 1, 2, \ldots, n$. A direct method of computing $k!$ for n values of k is to write an inner loop that computes $k!$ and embed this in an outer loop that steps k by 1 until n is reached. To compute $k!$ then requires $k - 1$ multiplications in addition to loop-control operations. The entire problem requires $n(n - 1)/2$ multiplications in all.

A better method follows from writing

(2a) $k! \equiv f(k) \equiv k \times f(k - 1)$

(2b) $f(0) \equiv 1$

Successive substitution into Eq. (2a) (implemented by a program loop) will now require only n multiplications (and loop traversals) to obtain *all* factorials from 1! to n.

Suppose now, for the moment, only $n!$ is to be computed. Substitution of n into Eq. (2a) (say for $n \equiv 4$) gives

(3) $f(4) \equiv 4 \times f(3)$

This expresses $f(4)$ in terms of $f(3)$, but how is $f(3)$ to be obtained? Let us again substitute into Eq. (2a) with $k \equiv 3$, and so on, to obtain the equations (not yet numerical values):

(4) $f(3) \equiv 3 \times f(2)$

(5) $f(2) \equiv 2 \times f(1)$

(6) $f(1) \equiv 1 \times f(0)$

(7) $f(0) \equiv 1$ by Eq. (2b)

Notice that at this point all necessary arguments have been specified to the function *f(k)* but there has yet to be any multiplication. The next step in this procedure is to back-substitute into the above equations, i.e., substitute Eq. (7) into (6), then (6) into (5), etc., until Eq. (3) is reached, which will appear as

(8) $f(4) \equiv 4 \times f(3) \equiv 4 \times 6 \equiv 24$

which is 4!.

The back-substitution process references the list of functions in the reverse order from which they were first encountered. Such a list and list-reference process is called *last-in-first-out* or *LIFO,* for short. It is also called a *push-down* list or *stack.* The LIFO list is found in several distinct procedures in data-processing systems. Later in this chapter it appears in a program translation procedure and also in the execution of the translated program. Details of programs for entry and access to a LIFO list are given in Chap. 9.

A program that includes a call on itself is said to be *recursive.* Whenever a call for a function is executed, it may conceptually be considered to initiate a "fresh" copy or level of the called procedure and to pass the argument to this copy (however, only one copy of the procedure need actually be stored). The program (or copy) in which the call arose remains stalled at the point of the call until the execution of the called copy is completed by an exit, at which point the statement execution proceeds in the normal right-to-left manner. Arguments are passed in succession by successive calls, and results are returned to calling levels in reverse order, which is equivalent to the LIFO referencing scheme described earlier.

To illustrate the above principles, a recursive program for the factorial function specified as

    R←FACT N

is given in Fig. 2.17.1. For example, if $N \equiv 3$, a trace of the program will show that it calls itself three times, the succession of arguments N being 2, 1, 0. At the last level, $R \equiv 1$ is computed at line 2, and exit is made to the previous level at line 3. The value of N at that level was 2, so line 3 computes a value of 2 and

```
    ∇ R←FACT N
[1]    →(N≠0)/COM
[2]    →0,R←1
[3]  COM:R←N×FACT(N-1)
    ∇
```

Fig. 2.17.1 Recursive function for N.

exits to the previous level line 3 where the value 6 is computed. The exit from this level is the final exit.

Recursive function calling can be a powerful technique. However, it can be wasteful of storage, as in the above case, where to compute N! requires a stack depth of N. By programming factorial in the more usual way, only a few storage locations for N and result need be used.

2.18 SELECTION, SEARCH, AND ORDERING OPERATIONS†

The ability to select from, search, and order elements of an array represents powerful data-processing operations. APL's capabilities in this respect are indicated in Fig. 2.18.1 which illustrates these operations on numeric vectors (they are equally applicable to bit vectors). All except grade-up/grade-down are also applicable to character vectors.

The *index-of* operator (as in $X \iota Y$) results in a vector of equal dimension to Y; these are *indices* giving the position numbers pointing to where each element of Y *first* appears in X. If no match is found for a given Y value, an index 1 larger than the dimension of X is posted in the result index vector. The *membership* operator ($X \in Y$) results in the bit vector of dimension equal to that of X, each bit specifying whether or not (1 or 0) the corresponding element of X is found *somewhere* in Y.

The *take* operator ($K \uparrow X$) results in a vector which consists of the leftmost K values of X if K is positive and the rightmost $|K$ elements if K is negative. The *drop* operator ($K \downarrow X$) is complementary to the take operator. Drop results in a vector consisting of the elements of vector X with its leftmost or rightmost K elements deleted as K is positive or negative respectively.

The *rotate* operator ($K \phi X$) moves (shifts) a vector K places in end-around fashion. If K is positive, the rotation is to the left; if negative, to the right. For matrices, K may be a vector; each element specifies the rotation of the corresponding matrix row.

The *compress* and *expand* operators both use one argument (U) as a *bit map* to specify selections on a vector X to form a result. In *compress,* the result consists of only those elements of X for which corresponding elements of U are 1. *Expand* results in a vector of elements of X and 0s with the elements in X filling those positions of the result corresponding to $U=1$. Other positions of the result are 0 (or blank if X is a character vector).

Grade-up and *grade-down* are closely related to sorting operations. Since they are similar except for the direction of the ordering, we describe only grade-up. This operator applied to a vector X produces an *index vector* whose elements are

†See the chart of Fig. 2.18.2 for formal definitions and more examples.

in an order that, if used, will place the elements of X in sorted order. Thus if

$X \equiv 1 \ 3 \ 8 \ 2$

then

$\blacktriangle X \equiv 1 \ 4 \ 2 \ 3$

EXAMPLE VECTORS

$X \leftarrow 3 \ 8 \ 24 \ 29 \ 2 \ 87$

$Y \leftarrow 8 \ 2 \ 12 \ 24$

$U \leftarrow 1 \ 0 \ 1 \ 1 \ 0 \ 1$

EXAMPLES OF OPERATORS

INDEX-OF	$X \iota Y$	2 5 7 3
MEMBERSHIP	$X \epsilon Y$	0 1 1 0 1 0
TAKE	$3 \uparrow X$	3 8 24
	$^{-}3 \uparrow X$	29 2 87
DROP	$2 \downarrow X$	24 29 2 87
	$^{-}2 \downarrow X$	3 8 24 29
ROTATE(LEFT)	$2 \phi X$	24 29 2 87 3 8
(RIGHT)	$^{-}2 \phi X$	2 87 3 8 24 29
COMPRESS	U / X	3 24 29 87
EXPAND	$U \backslash Y$	8 0 2 12 0 24
GRADE-UP	$\blacktriangle X$	5 1 2 3 4 6
GRADE-DOWN	$\blacktriangledown X$	6 4 3 2 1 5

Fig. 2.18.1 Examples of selection, search, and ordering operations (primitive mixed functions).

and using this as an index vector sorts X

   $X[\Delta X]\equiv 1\ \ 2\ \ 3\ \ 8$

The reason APL produces an index list rather than the sorted data directly is that often the reordering is to be done based on X values to *another* vector, say Y.

2.19 SOME STATISTICS APPLICATIONS

Statistics may be considered the art and science of finding a few numbers to represent essential properties of a large set of numbers. Some "measures of central tendency" that are frequently used to characterize a data vector X may be expressed in APL by:

1. Number of data values $\equiv N \equiv \rho X$
2. Range $\equiv R\equiv(\lfloor/X),(\lceil/X)\equiv$ smallest and largest values of X
3. Mean $\equiv M\equiv(+/X)\div N$
4. Median $\equiv X\leftarrow X[\Delta X]$
       $MD\leftarrow(X[\lceil N\div 2]+X[\lceil(N+1)\div 2])\div 2$
5. Standard deviation $\equiv SD\equiv((+/(X-M)\star 2)\div N)\star.5$
6. Coefficient of variation $\equiv SD\div M$
7. A relative-frequency vector $\equiv F$ giving the fraction of the number of data values falling into each of NB "buckets," the buckets dividing the range equally. The user of the program can specify the number of buckets he wants.

An APL program including all the above is shown in Fig. 2.19.1. Most of the statements are straightforward, so we confine attention to those that are not. One of these is the rather neat way the *median* is found. First, the numbers X are placed in ascending order using the grade-up operator. The median is defined as the middle value of this sorted list if there is an odd number of numbers and the average of the two middle X values if there is an even number. Although it might appear that a test for *n* being even or odd must be made, in fact this is *not* necessary as the program shows (try a few cases to see the principle).

The computation of the relative-frequency vector F involves first setting up the bucket vector BUK specifying the lower boundary of each bucket. Each data value is then compared with BUK using the relational statement $X[I]\geq BUK$ and then summing the 1 values in this result. This count is the bucket number J in which $X[I]$ falls. $F[J]$ is then incremented by 1. These computations then loop on I values until all $X[I]$ are counted.

The $STAT$ program output is given in several statements. Line 9 specifies a mixture of character and numeric data to be printed on the same line; these data

Name	Sign†	Definition or example‡
Size	ρA	ρP ↔ 4 ρE ↔ 3 4 ρ5 ↔ ι0
Reshape	VρA	Reshape A to dimension V 3 4ρι12 ↔ E 12ρE ↔ ι12 0ρE ↔ ι0
Ravel	,A	,A ↔ (×/ρA)ρA ,E ↔ι12 ρ,5 ↔ 1
Catenate	V,V	P,ι2 ↔ 2 3 5 7 1 2 'T','HIS' ↔ 'THIS'
Index §¶	V[A] M[A;A] A[A;..] ..;A]	P[2] ↔3 P[4 3 2 1] ↔7 5 3 2 E[1 3;3 2 1] ↔ 3 2 1 11 10 9 E[1;] ↔ 1 2 3 4 ABCD E[;1] ↔ 1 5 9 'ABCDEFGHIJKL'[E] ↔ EFGH IJKL
Index generator §	ιS	First S integers ι4 ↔ 1 2 3 4 ι0 ↔ an empty vector
Index of §	VιA	Least index of A Pι3 ↔2 5 1 2 5 in V, or 1+ρV PιE ↔ 3 5 4 5 4 4ι4 ↔ 1 5 5 5 5
Take	V↑A	Take (drop) |V[I] first 2 3↑X ↔ ABC elements on coordinate EFG
Drop	V↓A	I. (Last if V[I]<0) ‾2↑P ↔ 5 7
Grade-up††	⍋A	The permutation which ⍋3 5 3 2 ↔ 4 1 3 2 would order A (ascend-
Grade-down††	⍒A	ing or descending) ⍒3 5 3 2 ↔ 2 1 3 4
Compress††	V/A	1 3 1 0 1 0/P ↔ 2 5 1 0 1 0/E ↔ 5 7 9 11 1 0 1/[1]E ↔ 1 2 3 4 ↔ 1 0 1⌿E 9 10 11 12
Expand††	V\A	A BCD 1 0 1\ι2 ↔ 1 0 2 1 0 1 1 1\X ↔ E FGH I JKL
Reverse††	φA	DCBA IJKL φX ↔ HGFE φ[1]X ↔ ⊖X ↔ EFGH LKJI φP ↔ 7 5 3 2 ABCD
Rotate††	AφA	BCDA 3φP ↔ 7 2 3 5 ↔ ‾1φP 1 0 ‾1φX ↔ EFGH LIJK
	V⍉A	AEI Coordinate I of A 2 1⍉X ↔ BFJ becomes coordinate CGK
Transpose		V[I] of result 1 1⍉E ↔ 1 6 11 DHL
	⍉A	Transpose last two coordinates ⍉E ↔ 2 1⍉E

Fig. 2.18.2 APL array operators.

Membership	$A\epsilon A$	$\rho W\epsilon Y \leftrightarrow \rho W$ $P\epsilon\iota 4 \leftrightarrow 1\ 1\ 0\ 0$	$E\epsilon P \leftrightarrow \begin{matrix} 0 & 1 & 1 & 0 \\ 1 & 0 & 1 & 0 \\ 0 & 0 & 0 & 0 \end{matrix}$
Decode	$V\perp V$	$10\perp 1\ 7\ 7\ 6 \leftrightarrow 1776$	$24\ 60\ 60\perp 1\ 2\ 3 \leftrightarrow 3723$
Encode	$V\top S$	$24\ 60\ 60\top 3723 \leftrightarrow 1\ 2\ 3$	$60\ 60\top 3723 \leftrightarrow 2\ 3$
Deal§	$S?S$	$W?Y \leftrightarrow$ random deal of W elements from ιY	

Notes:

†Restrictions on argument ranks are indicated by S for scalar, V for vector, M for matrix, A for any. Except as the first argument of $S\iota A$ or $S[A]$, a scalar may be used instead of a vector. A one-element array may replace any scalar.

‡Arrays used in examples:

$$P \leftrightarrow 2\ 3\ 5\ 7 \qquad E \leftrightarrow \begin{matrix} 1 & 2 & 3 & 4 \\ 5 & 6 & 7 & 8 \\ 9 & 10 & 11 & 12 \end{matrix} \qquad X \leftrightarrow \begin{matrix} ABCD \\ EFGH \\ IJKL \end{matrix}$$

§Function depends on index origin.

¶Elision of any index selects all along that coordinate.

††The function is applied along the last coordinate; the symbols $\not{/}$, $\nwarrow$, and $\ominus$ are equivalent to $/$, $\backslash$, and ϕ, respectively, except that the function is applied along the first coordinate. If $[S]$ appears after any of the symbols, the relevant coordinate is determined by the scalar S.

Fig. 2.18.2   APL array operators (continued).

types are separated by semicolons. Line 21 prints the F-vector information. Since three columns are to be printed, we reshape the three vectors into a 3-row matrix and then transpose this matrix to obtain 3 columns. Although APL prints vectors and matrices in easily readable format, there is no user control over spacing. For this reason it is difficult to position headings properly. However, every APL system has APL functions providing quite flexible formatting (we forgo details here).

Another kind of statistical analysis arises from an attempt to represent a trend in relationship between two data vectors say x and y each having p elements. Each x and the corresponding y value may be considered to specify the coordinates of a point in a plane. The plot of these data is then a collection of points called a *scatterplot*.

It is desired to determine the coefficient vector a of a polynomial of degree n which "best" fits these data. The term "best polynomial" will refer to that polynomial (of degree n) among all polynomials which, when evaluated at the values of x, gives values the sum of the squares of whose differences from the data ordinates y are a minimum. This *least-squares criterion* is not the only possible one. It is, however, reasonable since deviations of unlike sign do not

```
      ∇ STAT
[1]   'ENTER DATA VALUES'
[2]   X←,□
[3]   N←ρX
[4]   R←(⌊/X),(⌈/X)
[5]   M←(+/X)÷N
[6]   S←((+/(X-M)*2)÷N)*0.5
[7]   X←X[⍋X]
[8]   MD←(X[⌊N÷2]+X[⌈(N+1)÷2])÷2
[9]   'NO. OF VALUES= ';N;'   RANGE= ';R
[10]  'MEAN= ';M;'   STD. DEV.= ';S;'   COEF. OF VAR.= ';S÷M
[11]  'MEDIAN= ';MD
[12]  'ENTER NO. OF BUCKET INTERVALS'
[13]  NB←,□
[14]  BUK←R[1],R[1]+((R[2]-R[1])÷NB)×⍳NB
[15]  F←(1+NB)ρ0
[16]  I←1
[17]  NXTI:J←+/X[I]≥BUK
[18]  F[J]←F[J]+1
[19]  →(N≥I←I+1)/NXTI
[20]  'BUCKET NO.          RANGE           FREQ.     REL. FREQ.'
[21]  ⍉(4,ρF)ρ(⍳ρF),BUK,F,F÷+/F
      ∇
      STAT
ENTER DATA VALUES
□:
      2 8 3.5 6 9 14 3 5 22 16.3
NO. OF VALUES= 10    RANGE= 2  22
MEAN= 8.88 STD. DEV.= 6.232142489    COEF. OF VAR.= 0.7018178478
MEDIAN= 7
ENTER NO. OF BUCKET INTERVALS
□:
      2
BUCKET NO.          RANGE            FREQ.     REL. FREQ.
    1                 2                7           0.7
    2                12                2           0.2
    3                22                1           0.1
      STAT
ENTER DATA VALUES
□:
      X
NO. OF VALUES= 10    RANGE= 2  22
MEAN= 8.88 STD. DEV.= 6.232142489    COEF. OF VAR.= 0.7018178478
MEDIAN= 7
ENTER NO. OF BUCKET INTERVALS
□:
      4
BUCKET NO.          RANGE            FREQ.     REL. FREQ.
    1                 2                5           0.5
    2                 7                2           0.2
    3                12                2           0.2
    4                17                0           0
    5                22                1           0.1
```

Fig. 2.19.1 A program for range, mean, median, standard deviation, and relative frequency of data X.

cancel. Also, the least-squares criterion simplifies the derivation of the computation rule. The form of the polynomial of approximation is

$$(1) \qquad \text{Poly} \equiv \sum_{j=1}^{n+1} a_j x_i^{n+1-j}$$

Note that the coefficients a_j are at the moment unknown, and finding them is the aim of what follows.

The expression for the sum of squares of ordinate difference between data and poly is

$$(2) \qquad s \equiv \sum_{i=1}^{px} \left(y_i - \sum_{j=1}^{n+1} a_j x_i^{n+1-j} \right)^2$$

To derive an expression for the a for which s is a minimum, set the partial derivatives of s with respect to the a values to 0. A typical term (the one for index k) is

$$(3) \qquad \frac{\partial s}{\partial a_k} \equiv 0 \equiv 2 \sum_{i=1}^{p} \left(y_i - \sum_{j=1}^{n+1} a_j x_i^{n+1-j} \right) x_i^{n+1-k}$$

or

$$(4) \qquad \sum_{j=1}^{n+1} a_j \left(\sum_{i=1}^{p} x_i^{n+1-j} x_i^{n+1-k} \right) \equiv \sum_{i=1}^{p} y_i x_i^{n+1-k}$$

It can be shown that the process of Eq. (3) yields a minimum rather than a maximum of s.

The equations typified by Eq. (4) are $n + 1$ in number (one for each value of k). These equations are linear in the a_j since the known values of x_i^{n+1-j}, x_i^{n+1-k}, and $y_i x_i^{n+1-k}$ are constants.

The problem of solving for the coefficients of the polynomial that best fits data in the least-squares sense is then a problem in solving a system of linear equations.

A case of special interest is where the "fitting polynomial" is a straight line. In this case, $n \equiv 1$ and Eq. (4) applied twice ($k \equiv 1,2$) gives

$$(5) \qquad a_1 \sum_{i}^{p} x_i^2 + a_2 \sum_{i}^{p} x_i \equiv \sum_{i}^{p} y_i x_i$$

$$(6) \qquad a_1 \sum_{i}^{p} x_i + a_2 p \equiv \sum_{i}^{p} y_i$$

The straight line called the *regression line* has the equation

$$(7) \qquad y \equiv a_1 x + a_2$$

a_1 is the slope and a_2 is the y intercept. It may be shown that the regression line passes through the point determined by the mean of x and mean of y.

Equations (5) and (6) can be put in a more convenient form for program solution as

$$(8) \qquad a_1 m + a_2 q \equiv u$$

$$(9) \qquad a_1 q + a_2 r \equiv z$$

where

$$(10) \qquad m \equiv +/x \times x$$

$$(11) \qquad q \equiv +/x$$

$$(12) \qquad r \equiv p$$

$$(13) \qquad u \equiv +/y \times x$$

$$(14) \qquad z \equiv +/y$$

Equations (8) and (9) can be solved by determinants

$$(15) \qquad a_1 \equiv ((u \times r) - (z \times q)) \div \Delta$$

$$(16) \qquad a_2 \equiv ((m \times z) - (u \times q)) \div \Delta$$

$$(17) \qquad \Delta \equiv (m \times r) - q \times q$$

Equations (10) to (17) may be used for the actual computations. For polynomials of higher degree than 1, the corresponding computation will consist of solving a system of linear equations.

The computations for obtaining the two parameters of the regression line may be included in the program *STAT*. Also, the above derivation extends in a straightforward way to the case of fitting a plane to three vectors of data (multiple linear regression)

2.20 SOME NONNUMERICAL APPLICATIONS

Although the computer had its origins in scientific numerical calculation, its value is equally great in handling nonnumeric data such as is found in commercial files and social science applications, to name but a few. We now give some examples of processing data of this kind.

As a simple first example, consider a character string composed of substrings (fields) separated by commas. The program of Fig. 2.20.1 extracts each substring and moves it to a row of a character matrix *NL*. The program handles (say) up to 20 substrings where a substring can be from 0 to (say) 10 characters long. The statements of special interest are:

```
     ∇  SCAN1
[1]     'ENTER CHARACTER VECTOR'
[2]     C←,⎕
[3]     I←1
[4]     NL←(20 10)ρ' '
[5]  NXT:J←Cι','
[6]     NL[I;]←10↑(C[ιJ-1],10ρ' ')
[7]     →((J>ρC),J=1)/LAST,CHOP
[8]  CHOP:I←I+1
[9]     C←J↓C
[10]    →NXT
[11] LAST:NL←NL[ιI;]
[12]    'EXPRESSION LIST IS'
[13]    NL
     ∇

        SCAN1
ENTER CHARACTER VECTOR
JOE,PETE,JOE+7,,JIM,X-56
EXPRESSION LIST IS
JOE
PETE
JOE+7

JIM
X-56
```

Fig. 2.20.1 Program and example run, field extraction.

Line 2   The ⌷ symbol requests input from the user in the form of an unquoted character vector.

Line 5 J is determined as the index of the first appearance of the comma.

Line 6   The first $J-1$ characters are sent to the NL matrix. Note the "padding out" of the string to ensure that 10 characters are moved.

Line 9   Drop the first J characters of C to form new C.

The next program is called a *radix sort*. It takes C, a matrix of characters, each row being one item, and sorts and prints these items. Figure 2.20.2 shows a

```
      ∇ RADSORT KEY
[1]      '***ORIGINAL***'
[2]      C
[3]      ALF←' ABCDEFGHIJKLMNOPQRSTUVWXYZ'
[4]      I←KEY[2]
[5]   REP:J←ALFιC[;I]
[6]      C←C[⍋J;]
[7]      →(KEY[1]≤I←I-1)/REP
[8]      '***SORTED LIST***'
[9]      C
      ∇
```

```
         RADSORT 1 4
***ORIGINAL***
DAN
PETE
WALT
JIM
JOE
WALTER
BILL
***SORTED LIST***
BILL
DAN
JIM
JOE
PETE
WALT
WALTER
```

Fig. 2.20.2   Radix sort.

program *RADSORT* with an argument vector (*KEY*) of two integers specifying the *sort key*, i.e., the first and last character positions over which the sorting decisions are to be made. Sorting of course implies an arithmetic ordering of the items. As stated earlier, the APL language has no built-in ordering of character data. Our program constructs the basis of such an ordering in line 3 by creating vector *ALF* specifying the ordered alphabet of the data expected, in this case blank followed by *A* through *Z*. Line 5 uses the *index-of* operator to find the position in *ALF* of each character to be compared. The result is *J*, an index list which gives the position number and hence an order number to each character of the *I*th column of *C*. Line 6 then permutes the rows of *C* according to this ordering. Starting with the rightmost-character position (column), the orderings proceed column by column to the left until the leftmost position specified by *KEY* [1] is reached. The sort is then complete.

There are many sort algorithms other than the radix sort here illustrated (see Chap. 4 for more on sorting).

Manipulation of text information often involves handling *strings* of characters of *variable length*. Some simple but powerful APL functions for handling strings are shown in Fig. 2.20.3. The strings of interest are catenated together to form one long character vector *STF*. Each element of the *pointer vector ST* gives the position in *STF* of the first character of a string. Manipulating strings then involves using *ST* to locate the string of interest. The length of each string is easily found from *ST* also, since the last position of a string in *STF* is 1 less than the position of the start of the next string. Thus,

> Position in *STF* of start of string $I=ST[I]$
> Position in *STF* of end of string $I=ST[I+1]-1$
> Length of string $I=ST[I+1]-ST[I]$

The functions in Fig. 2.20.3 can initialize the string at start-up, accept insertion, deletion, and replacement of a string, and search for a match between a given string (*X*) and the other string. In brief, these functions may be described as:

∇*CLEAR*	Initializes the string *STF* to null and the pointer vector *ST*. This function is used only to start up string manipulation.
∇*INSX N*	Inserts the string named *BUF* between substrings *N* and *N*+1.
∇*DELTX N*	Deletes the *N*th substring of *STF*.
∇*REPLX N*	Replaces the *N*th substring of *STF* by the string named *BUF*.
∇*X STRMTCH STR*	Searches the string *STR* for a match with a string *X*. The result is the index vector *IXX*, each element

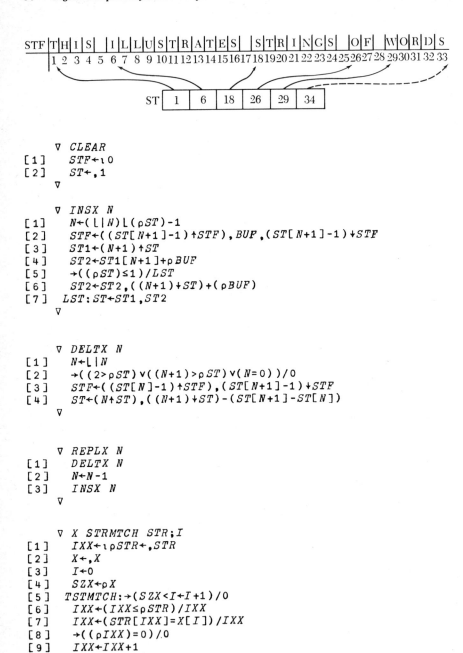

```
      ∇ CLEAR
[1]    STF←ι0
[2]    ST←,1
      ∇

      ∇ INSX N
[1]    N←(⌊|N)⌊(ρST)-1
[2]    STF←((ST[N+1]-1)↑STF),BUF,(ST[N+1]-1)↓STF
[3]    ST1←(N+1)↑ST
[4]    ST2←ST1[N+1]+ρBUF
[5]    →((ρST)≤1)/LST
[6]    ST2←ST2,((N+1)↓ST)+(ρBUF)
[7]  LST:ST←ST1,ST2
      ∇


      ∇ DELTX N
[1]    N←⌊|N
[2]    →((2>ρST)∨((N+1)>ρST)∨(N=0))/0
[3]    STF←((ST[N]-1)↑STF),(ST[N+1]-1)↓STF
[4]    ST←(N↑ST),((N+1)↓ST)-(ST[N+1]-ST[N])
      ∇


      ∇ REPLX N
[1]    DELTX N
[2]    N←N-1
[3]    INSX N
      ∇


      ∇ X STRMTCH STR;I
[1]    IXX←ιρSTR←,STR
[2]    X←,X
[3]    I←0
[4]    SZX←ρX
[5]  TSTMTCH:→(SZX<I←I+1)/0
[6]    IXX←(IXX≤ρSTR)/IXX
[7]    IXX←(STR[IXX]=X[I])/IXX
[8]    →((ρIXX)=0)/0
[9]    IXX←IXX+1
[10]   →TSTMTCH
      ∇
```

Fig. 2.20.3   String processing functions and data structure.

pointing to the position 1 higher than the *last* position of a string in STR that matches all of string X. If no substrings of STR match X, then IXX is a null vector.

One interesting principle that emerges from the string-manipulation functions is that *replacement* of a given string (the function $REPLX$) is done by the simple sequence: deletion ($DELTX$) followed by insertion ($INSX$).

Using the few functions given, it is easy to write other functions to do such tasks as display all strings or some subset (say string N to $N+K$) or to count the number of matches of some given string X in STF.

PROBLEMS

2.1 Which of the following are legal APL names?

a) X
b) $X1$
c) $X1Y$
d) $X12$
e) $1X$
f) $X.1$
g) $X\iota Y$

2.2 Execute the following statements by hand to test your understanding of primitive scalar operators. Use as values:

$$W\equiv3;X\equiv2;\ Y\equiv4,12,\bar{}1,5;IX\equiv12,9,2,3$$

Note: Be careful to use the right-to-left and element-by-element rules.

a) $Z\leftarrow(W\times2)+(X*2)+W\times X$
b) $Z\leftarrow W\times2+X*2+W\times X$
c) $Z\leftarrow X\times W+Y\times IX\div X$
d) $Z\leftarrow X+Y\times2|IX$
e) $Z\leftarrow2|\iota\rho IX$
f) Every other element of IX (start with $IX[1]$)
g) $Z\leftarrow X+Y\times IX\lceil Y$
h) $Z\leftarrow X+Y\times\lceil IX\div W$
i) $Z\leftarrow Y+Y>IX$
j) $Z\leftarrow(Y>W)\wedge(IX\leq W)$
k) Show that the same answer as in part (*j*) is obtained by

$$Z\leftarrow\ \sim(Y\leq W)\vee(IX>W)$$

2.3 Polynomials are often used as approximation functions. As suggested in Sec. 2.4, the method of *nesting* is a simple, elegant, and fast way to evaluate polynomials.

a) Evaluate, by nesting, the following for $X \equiv 4$:

$$P \equiv 5\,X^3 + 4\,X^2 + 2X + 9$$

b) More generally, call the coefficients vector A, that is, $A \equiv 5,4,2,9$ in part (*a*). A single-loop program to evaluate polynomials can then be written around the statement

$P \leftarrow A[I] + P \times X$

where initial values are $I \equiv 1$, $P \equiv 0$. Write such a program.
c) Trace your program of part (*b*) using part (*a*) as example.
d) How many statements are executed for a polynomial of degree N?
e) The method of nesting can often be expressed as a single statement rather than a program loop. Discuss the pros and cons of these two methods.

2.4 Obtain the value represented by interpreting the vector 2,1,3 as a 3-digit radix-4 number.

2.5 The Newton algorithm for R, the approximate square root of X, consists of successive use of

$$R \leftarrow .5 \times (R + X \div R)$$

until the residual (error) condition

$$E \geq |X - R \times R|$$

is satisfied, in which case R approximates the square root of X sufficiently closely. Select an initial R (say $R \equiv 1$) and an E value (say .0001).

a) Write a program.
b) Trace the program for $X \equiv 3$.

2.6 One way to represent the result of division of two positive integers X and Y is by two integers called quotient Q and remainder R. This may be expressed as

$Q \leftarrow \lfloor X \div Y$
$R \leftarrow Y \mid X$

The second representation is as an integer I and fraction (decimal) F

$I \leftarrow \lfloor X \div Y$
$F \leftarrow (Y \mid X) \div Y$

Verify the above formulas for the examples

a) 9÷3
b) 9÷4
c) 9÷45

2.7 *a*) Verify by several trials and by analysis that the following statement replaces X by X rounded to N decimal places

$$X \leftarrow (\lfloor .5 + X \times E) \div E \leftarrow 10 \star N$$

b) Is this expression valid if X is negative or 0?

2.8 The date and time (in hours, minutes, seconds) of an event may be conveniently expressed as the character string typified by MMDDHHMMSS where each two-character sequence denotes month, day, hour, minute, and second as a 2-digit integer value. It is often desired to change this type of representation into a single integer giving the number of seconds since the start of the year (this makes it much easier to compute time intervals). Write a program that produces the transformation (assume no leap year). The program should also be able to compute the number of days, hours, minutes, and seconds between any two given times. Check your program for the following cases:

a) 0101000100   (Jan. 1, one minute A.M.)
b) 0301183045   (March 1, 6:30:45 P.M.)

2.9 The number of combinations of n things taken k at a time (the binomial coefficient) can be expressed as

$$c(n,k) \equiv \frac{n!}{k!(n-k)!} \quad \text{for } n \geqslant k$$

A more efficient recursive formula is

$$C(n,k) \equiv C(n-1,k) + C(n-1,k-1)$$

where

$$C(n,0) \equiv 1 \quad \text{and} \quad C(n,n) \equiv 1$$

a) Verify algebraically that the recursive form is correct.
b) Write a program for $C(n,k)$ for all n,k such that $k < n$.

2.10 The formula for the amount p of each of n *equal* payments to retire a loan (mortgage) a at an interest rate r on the unpaid balance is

$$p = \frac{ra(1 + r)^n}{(1 + r)^n - 1}$$

Write a program to generate a table of p values for all r, a, n values as follows:

$.03 \leqslant r \leqslant .07$	in steps of .005
$1 \leqslant n \leqslant 30$	in steps of 1
$1000 \leqslant a \leqslant 5000$	in steps of 1000

2.11 Define the difference vector D of vector Y as

$$D \leftarrow (1 \downarrow Y) - (\bar{} 1 \downarrow Y)$$

If D is substituted for Y and the statement executed again, the result is called the *second difference* of Y. By repeating this process, higher-order differences are generated. Given the polynomial

$$y = 4x^3 + 2x^2 + x + 9$$

Using $X \leftarrow \iota 7$, compute seven Y values (YV). Compute difference vectors D through the fourth difference. This illustrates the important principle that for a polynomial of degree n, evaluated at values of x equally spaced, all differences of higher order than n are zero.

2.12 As seen in the program of Fig. 2.19.1 the mean m and variance v (square of standard deviation) of n numbers x is

$$m = \frac{1}{n} \sum_{i=1}^{n} x_i$$

and

$$v = \frac{1}{n} \sum_{i=1}^{n} (x_i - m)^2 = \left(\frac{1}{n} \sum x_i^2\right) - m^2$$

a) Derive the rightmost form of v from the left form using algebra.
b) Write a detailed *single-loop* program that computes *both* m and v.

2.13 Rewrite the statistical program of Fig. 2.19.1 as follows:

a) No vector operations may be used. Such a program is similar to those written in FORTRAN or other languages.
b) Include computation and printout of cumulative relative frequencies.

2.14 Write detailed (element-by-element) programs for the following where U,

X, Y are vectors and M is a matrix:

a) $Z \leftarrow X + Y$
b) $Z \leftarrow X + . \times Y$
c) $Z \leftarrow M \wedge . = Y$
d) $Z \leftarrow U / X$

2.15 Explain in words the meaning of parts (*c*) and (*d*) of Prob. 2.14.

2.16 The approximate area under a curve specified by ordinate values y spaced at equal intervals h can be obtained by Simpson's rule:

$$a = h/3 \ (y_1 + 4y_2 + 2y_3 + 4y_4 + \cdots + y_n)$$

The total number of ordinates must be odd; the first and last are weighted by 1, the other ordinate weights alternate as 4 and 2. Write an expression for a.

2.17 A Fibonacci sequence is one in which each term is the sum of the immediately preceding two terms. It is sometimes used to generate random numbers and test data. A concise expression for a new term of the sequence X as appended to X is

$$X \leftarrow X , +/ ^- 2 \uparrow X$$

a) Starting with $X \equiv 0 , 1$ list the first 20 elements.
b) Write a detailed program to compute N elements.

2.18 Write expressions for the following selections from X to form Y. Assume 0-origin indexing and $(\rho X) \equiv 32$.

a) Six consecutive elements starting at element 4
b) Nine consecutive elements starting at the element 12 positions from the rightmost end
c) All nonzero elements
d) Every other element starting with element 0
e) Every fifth element starting with element 0

2.19 Write a *detailed* program for the "multiplication" of two matrices A and B, that is, in the usual notation

$$C[I;J] \equiv \sum_{K \equiv 1}^{(\rho A)[2]} A[I;K] \times B[K;J] \qquad \begin{matrix} 1 \leqslant I \leqslant (\rho A) \ [1] \\ 1 \leqslant J \leqslant (\rho B) \ [2] \end{matrix}$$

2.20 Write a concise expression for that value of a matrix A which is the minimum of the row-by-row maxima.

2.21 The Gauss-Seidel algorithm converges if each main diagonal element of matrix A is larger in absolute value than the sum of the absolute values of all other elements of the row. Write a concise program for this test.

2.22 Execute the following statements by hand (use the same W, X, Y, IX values as Prob. 2.2).

a) $Z \leftarrow IX + +/Y$
b) $Z \leftarrow +/(Y>X) \wedge (IX \leq W)$
c) $Z \leftarrow +/5<9$
d) $Z \leftarrow 1 \downarrow 3 \uparrow Y$
e) $Z \leftarrow \bar{\ }1 \uparrow \bar{\ }2 \downarrow Y$
f) Series approximation to sine x: $z \equiv x - \dfrac{x^3}{3!} + \dfrac{x^5}{5!} - \dfrac{x^7}{7!} \cdots \dfrac{x^{11}}{11!}$
(write a concise program)
g) $Z \leftarrow Y[IX[W]] + IX[W] \uparrow Y$
h) $Z \leftarrow +/Y < X \times IX[\spadesuit Y]$

2.23 Use the Gauss-Jordan algorithm to obtain the inverse of the matrix

$$\begin{array}{rrrr} 2 & -1 & -1 & 0 \\ -1 & 3 & 0 & -1 \\ -1 & 0 & 3 & -1 \\ 0 & -1 & -1 & 3 \end{array}$$

Check your answer by multiplying $(+.\times)$ the answer by the original matrix and comparing the result to the identity matrix.

2.24 Carefully analyze the programs for string processing given in Fig. 2.20.3. Using them, write programs to:

a) Find and print the Ith substring.
b) Print all substrings on successive lines.
c) Find I, the first substring number whose characters include a match on any given substring T. The result should be I and a pointer to the matching substring in substring I.

2.25 Given a text as a character string containing words, where no word is longer than (say) 10 characters. Words are defined here as any continuous string of nonblank alphabetic or digit characters between blank characters. Write a program that:

a) Produces a list of all distinct words in the text and the frequency of occurrence of each

b) Sorts the list of part (*a*)

2.26 Given a line of text (a character vector C). Write a program to spread the words in C by inserting blanks between words so that the text fills N characters ($N \geqslant C$). When this program is used on multiline texts, all lines can be printed so that the lines lineup on the right as well as left margins. *Note:* Your program must of course insert blanks between words. This can be done in several ways; an elegant method is to use the APL random-number generator (operator $?$); since there is then, no uniform pattern to the number of inserted blanks, this makes the output more pleasing to the eye.

REFERENCES

1. Abramowitz, H., and I. A. Stegun: "Handbook of Mathematical Functions," *U.S. Dept. Comm. Appl. Math. Ser.* 55, June 1964.

2. Barron, D. W.: "Recursive Techniques in Programming," American Elsevier, Inc., New York, 1968.

3. Bellman, R. E.: "Introduction to Matrix Analysis," McGraw-Hill Book Company, New York, 1960.

4. Birkhoff, G., and S. MacClane: "A Survey of Modern Algebra," The Macmillan Company, New York, 1951.

5. Branin, F. H.: DC and Transient Analysis of Networks Using a Digital Computer, *IRE Int. Conv. Rec.,* 1962.

6. Dijkstra, E. W.: Translator for the XI, annual review in R. Goodman (ed.), "Automatic Programming," vol. 3, Pergamon Press, Oxford, 1963.

7. Dorn, W. S., and D. D. McCracken: "Numerical Methods and Fortran Programming," John Wiley & Sons, Inc., New York, 1964.

8. Falkoff, A. D., and K. E. Iverson: "APL/360 User's Manual (GH20-0683)," IBM Corp., White Plains, N.Y.,

9. Gilman, R. E., and A. Rose: "APL Programming: An Interactive Approach," Prentice-Hall, Inc., Englewood Cliffs, N.J., 1971.

10. Hastings, C.: "Approximations for Digital Computers," Princeton University Press, Princeton, N.J. 1955.

11. IBM Corporation: "APL/360-OS and APL/360 DOS System Manual (LY20-0678)," White Plains, N.Y.,

12. Iverson, K. E.: "A Programming Language," John Wiley & Sons, Inc., New York, 1962.

13. Kemeny, J. G., H. Mirkil, J. L. Snell, and G. L. Thompson: "Finite Mathematical Structures," Prentice-Hall, Inc., Englewood Cliffs, N.J., 1959.

14. Knuth, D. E.: "The Art of Computer Programming," vol. I, Addison-Wesley Publishing Corporation, Reading, Mass., 1968.

15. Leeds, H. D., and G. M. Weinberg: "Computer Programming Fundamentals," 2d ed., McGraw-Hill Book Company, New York, 1966.

16. McCracken, D. D.: "A Guide to COBOL Programming," John Wiley & Sons, Inc., New York, 1963.

17. Newell, A., and C. J. Shaw: Programming the Logic Theory Machine, *Proc. 1957 West. Jt. Comput. Conf.,* February 1957.

18. Orden, A.: in A. Ralston and H. Wilf (eds.), "Mathematical Methods for Digital Computers," John Wiley & Sons., Inc., New York, 1960.

19. Richtmyer, R. D.: "Finite Difference Methods for Partial Differential Equations," Interscience Publishers, Inc., New York, 1960.

20. Scarborough, J. B.: "Numerical Mathematical Analysis," The Johns Hopkins Press, Baltimore, 1958.

21. Spiegel, M. R.: "Statistics," McGraw-Hill Book Company, New York, 1961.

22. Steifel, E. L.: "An Introduction to Numerical Mathematics," Academic Press Inc., New York, 1963.

23. Weinberg, G. M.: "PL/I Programming Primer," McGraw-Hill Book Company, New York, 1966.

3

Program Translation

Any program is a transformation of certain input operands into output operands by means of a well-defined sequential process. Although this is a very general property, it is useful to define classes of programs according to the intended purpose of the inputs and outputs.

Perhaps the most obvious class of programs is that (already discussed) in which the inputs are problem data such as the constants of a system of equations or records of a payroll file. In these cases, the outputs might be the solution values of the variables or the updated payroll file.

Another class of program, called a *translator program,* accepts a program as input and delivers another form of program as output. Of course, although the input is a program from the user viewpoint, it is treated as data by the translator program to produce the translated program. One basic objective of this process is to give the user convenience in stating his problem for machine execution. The program written by the user is called the *source* program. The rules, symbols, and conventions which he must follow in writing a source program and the meaning given to them are called the *source language.* The result of translation is a program called the *object program.* The object language is usually a machine language and hence can be executed by the machine directly.

An *assembler language* is a source language which is logically very similar to a machine language. Languages that are more convenient and usually more distant from machine languages are often called *high-level* languages. Most modern programming is done in a high-level source language, which must be translated.

In many computer installations, the translation process accounts for up to 30 percent of machine time.

The basic advantages of assembler or high-level languages over machine language directly are:

1. Convenience and flexibility in program statement.
2. Portability: the same source program can be taken from one machine to another.
3. Ease of detecting and correcting errors and making changes in the program.

The second advantage follows from the fact that it is quite feasible to define source languages independent of any machine. Of course, a translator program must be available for each language for each machine type. A machine-independent language permits the statement of problems as source programs, with the assurance that they can be executed on any of several computers which may differ greatly in hardware properties. In principle, examples of machine-independent languages include FORTRAN, ALGOL, COBOL, PL/I, and others. Unfortunately, in practice many source languages actually available for machine execution are almost, but not entirely, machine-independent.

A valuable way to view a translator is that it disguises the actual physical machine as a pseudomachine whose instructions are specified by the source language. In other words, the source language is in effect the "machine" to the programmer.

Every source language requires adherence to definite rules of syntax, i.e., conventions for combining symbols into operands, names, expressions, statements, and programs. It is quite possible to make errors in syntax in writing programs. Fortunately, it is relatively easy to design translators that include many tests for proper syntax and notify the programmer by diagnostic messages where those errors occur in the program. Syntax-error detection is normally included in the syntax-analysis portion of the translator. Syntax errors should be distinguished from errors in program logic. The translator is much less effective in detecting the latter type.

There are two extreme kinds of organization to language-translator programs which are called *interpreter* and *compiler.* These differ in time/storage efficiency and also have subtle effects on user convenience. Understanding the distinctive characteristics of these translation methods is fundamental to computer science and will be discussed in the next few sections. In practice, any given translator is predominantly either a compiler or interpreter although each type may use certain techniques found in the other.

3.1 INTERPRETERS

An *interpreter* is a type of translator program that first translates and then executes each source statement in turn; translation and execution alternate in close time proximity. Figure 3.1.1 shows the principle of interpreter logic. A pointer p points to the location in storage of the next source statement to be executed. The statement is accessed from storage to some work area, where it is scanned to determine what data and operations are to be worked on; then this

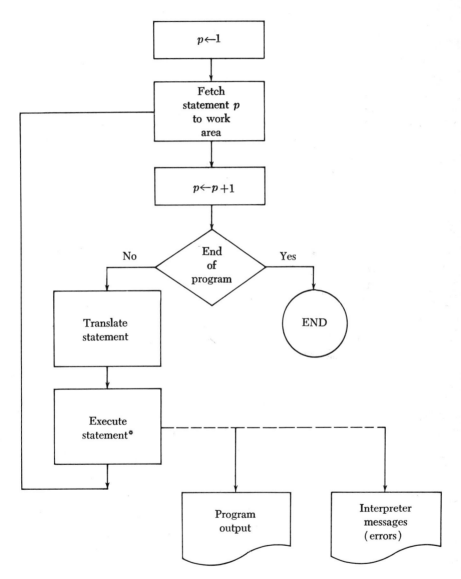

Note: A branch statement may replace p by a new value.

Fig. 3.1.1 Basic interpreter logic.

work is actually done (the statement is executed), and the cycle repeats for the next statement.

Because of the intimate alternation in the times of translation and execution, the interpreter program usually shares high-speed main storage with the source program and data, thereby reducing the storage available for these latter two kinds of information. The interpreter is a time-consuming translation method because each statement must be translated every time it is executed, instead of only each time it appears in the written source program. This time penalty is, however, smaller the more powerful the source language. For example, in an array-oriented language like APL, which states operations on entire arrays in a single statement, a good deal of productive execution can result from translation of a single statement.

The interpreter has an advantage over the compiler (see Sec. 3.2) if fast response to *changes* in the source program is required, as in many timesharing systems. This is because in conventional compilers a change in even one statement requires retranslation of the entire program. However, some compilers are now available that can process changes with acceptable speed.

The principle of the interpreter includes the sequence of switching operations performed by every computing machine while executing each of its instructions. These particular sequences are called *microprograms* and *to them* the object program produced by a language-translator program is the source program! In a real sense, the design of the control logic of a computer is a problem in the design of an interpreter-translator (see Chaps. 8 and 9 for details).

3.2 COMPILERS

A compiler is a type of translator program that translates each source statement to one or more object statements once for each *appearance* of the statement in the source program. The compiler should be contrasted to the interpreter, which must translate each statement each time it is *executed.* Thus, the compiler yields savings in time for any statement executed repetitively, such as entire programs run several times on different data or, more importantly, statements in a program loop.

A compiler (Fig. 3.2.1) translates an entire source program in one distinct phase of the programming-translation-execution process. Once the compilation has been completed and the object program produced, this program is executed without any further translation. The separation in time of compilation and execution results in simple and efficient use of high-speed processor storage. For example, during compilation, problem data need not be present in the high-speed processor storage. Although the entire source program must be available, compilation is typically divided into two phases so that even further

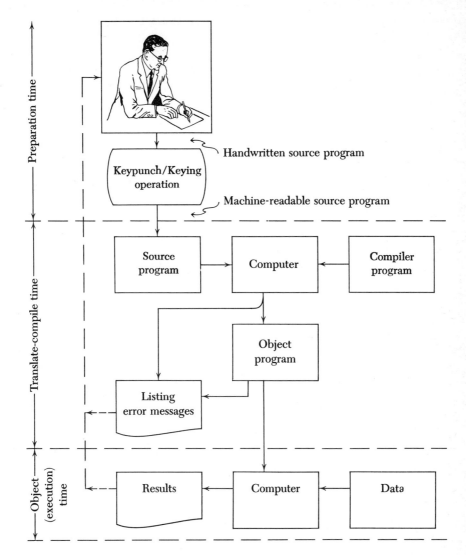

Fig. 3.2.1 Information flow in a compiler system.

space economy is possible. In the first phase the definitions of variables are extracted from the source program and machine addresses are assigned to them. This procedure produces a *symbol-address table*. No object program is produced in this phase, and only a fraction of the compiler program itself need occupy processor storage. In the second phase of compilation, the symbol table must be accessible, but in many cases processor storage is only required for one source statement and the object code resulting from it. This is because as each source statement is translated (compiled), it may be replaced by the next source statement, say, drawn from cheap, low-speed storage such as a deck of cards or a magnetic tape. As each statement is processed, the object code may likewise be sent to auxiliary storage so that its space in processor storage may be used again for the next statement.

The object-program output of the compiler and the problem data are then sent back into the machine for execution. Notice that at execution time neither the source program nor the compiler program need share processor storage with the object program and data.

Since "compiler" has been here defined in terms of the properties of the translator program, it is independent of any particular source language. Thus a given source language may be translated by a compiler or an interpreter-translator. Compilers exist for translating FORTRAN, ALGOL, COBOL, PL/I, and several other source languages to a variety of machine object languages.

Although the time-space efficiency advantages of the compiler over the interpreter might seem (and often are) quite substantial, the interpreter source program (or a condensed version of it) is usually very compact compared to the object program. Since the interpreter does its work from the source program and never produces an object program, program storage would favor the interpreter. This partially offsets the space disadvantage that results from the necessity of keeping the interpreter in main storage. Another factor that often softens the space inefficiency is in a timesharing or multiprogramming system, where the same copy of the interpreter can service several users. However, compilers (WATFOR and PLC) have appeared that can also remain main-storage-resident to serve several users.

As we have seen, there are several advantages and disadvantages of the interpreter compared to the compiler. At this time, the balance seems to favor the compiler, which is the type of translator most frequently used in practice.

3.3 ASSEMBLER PROGRAMS

An assembler language is a symbolic form of a machine language which may also include other powerful features (like *macros*). The purpose of the assembler language is to give the programmer *convenient* access to *all* machine features by permitting him to use symbolic names for program variables and the machine's operation codes and also to simplify specification of constants and reservation of storage space.

Figure 3.3.1 shows an example of machine-instruction format. For simplicity, it uses decimal rather than binary (or hexadecimal) representations. The instruction is seen to be a 9-digit number composed of four fields as follows:

OP   Specifies a machine-operation code like ADD or COMPARE.

R   Specifies one of 10 registers that can hold a number.

X   Specifies one of the same set of registers as R except that if X=0, no register is used. The register specified by X is used as an *index*; i.e., its content is added to the ADDRESS field to determine the location in storage of an operand or instruction.

ADDRESS Specifies a storage location holding an operand or instruction.

Figure 3.3.1 shows two examples of machine instructions and the way they might be specified in the assembler language. Figure 3.3.2 is an OP code-correspondence table relating each symbolic code to a machine code. It is *not* essential for the present discussion to understand the meanings of the machine instructions. What *is* important is the assembler-language representation of the machine instructions since we shall now show how the assembler program

Machine instruction: *Assembler instruction:*

 OP R X ADDRESS   OP R,NAME,X

              Note:
              If last ,X is omitted, a 0 is assigned
              for X.

Example 1:
Add content of cell named JOE (address 00109) to register 4:

   ADD 4, JOE 214000109

Example 2:
Add content of cell located at: JOE + (content of register 1) to register 4:

   ADD 4, JOE, 1 214100109

Fig. 3.3.1 Machine and assembler instructions.

Symbolic	*Machine*
LOD	01
ADD	21
COM	24
BNH	25
HLT	12

Fig. 3.3.2 Some assembler and machine OP codes.

Line		Source statement	Meaning
1		DORG 100	Start address assignments at 00100
2		LOD 1, ZER	Load reg 1 from cell ZER
		LOD 0, ZER	Load reg 0 from cell ZER
4	REP	ADD 0, NUM, 1	Add content of cell (located at) NUM+reg 1 to reg 0
5		ADD 1, ONE	Add content of cell ONE to reg 1
6		COM 1,LIM	Compare reg 1 to LIM,set condition code (CC)
7		BNH 0,REP	Branch to REP if CC is not high
8		HLT	Halt (stop sequencing)
9	ZER	DC 0	ZER is constant 0
10	ONE	DC 1	ONE is constant 1
11	LIM	DC 10	LIM is constant 10
12	NUM	DS 10	NUM is an area of 10 words
		END	End-of-program

(*a*) A simple source program to sum 10 numbers (already in storage).

REP	00102
ZER	00107
ONE	00108
LIM	00109
NUM	00110

(*b*) Symbol table resulting from pass 1 of assembler.

Source statements		Location	Object instructions
			OPRXADDRESS
	DORG 100		
	LOD 1,ZER	00100	011000107
	LOD 0,ZER	00101	011000107
REP	ADD 0,NUM,1	00102	210100110
	ADD 1,ONE	00103	211000108
	COM 1,LIM	00104	241000109
	BNH 0,REP	00105	250000102
	HLT	00106	120000000
ZER	DC 0	00107	000000000
ONE	DC 1	00108	000000001
LIM	DC 10	00109	000000010
NUM	DS 10		
	END		

(*c*) Source and assembled (object) program.

Fig. 3.3.3 Assembler language program to sum 10 numbers.

translates assembler-language instructions into machine-language instructions. Assembler programs are almost always compiler-translators and will be assumed to be here.

Figure 3.3.3*a* shows a simple assembler-language program to add 10 numbers presumed to be already in storage. Since a line-by-line explanation is given, we here only note some general properties. There are two kinds of assembler-language statements:

1. Machine instructions
2. Assembler instructions

Each machine instruction corresponds to, and will be translated into, a machine-language instruction. An assembler instruction (DC,DS,DORG) signals the assembler program, i.e., the translator, with certain information; these do *not* result in machine-language instructions. The DC statement specifies a constant; the DS statement reserves N words of storage for an array. The DORG statement specifies the beginning of a new area of storage for the statements that follow.

Let us now sketch how an assembler program might translate the source program of Fig. 3.3.3*a*. As shown in Fig. 3.3.3*b*, pass 1 of the translation results in a *symbol*-address *table*. This is constructed using a programmed storage-allocation counter (SAC) which is initially set (to 00100) by the DORG statement and incremented by 1 for every machine or DC statement. Just after a DS statement is encountered, SAC is incremented by the value of the DS parameter. Using these rules, it is easily seen that the statement named REP is assigned to location 00102 and similarly for all of the other named words in the program. During pass 2 of the assembler program, the symbol table constructed in pass 1 is used to translate all names and supply the ADDRESS part of each instruction. The OP codes are translated using the OP code table of Fig. 3.3.2. The R and X parts of the instruction are found directly from their references in the assembler-language statements. The result of the translations is the machine-language object program listed in Fig. 3.3.3.

3.4 PRINCIPLES OF SUBROUTINES

In the specification of sequential processes, it is very convenient to be permitted to give a name to a sequence of statements and to refer to such a subsequence in much the same manner as a single statement. A sequence of statements which can be handled in this way will be called a *subroutine*. The adjectives "closed" and "open," which will be explained shortly, are useful in classifying implementations of subroutines.

Use of subroutines removes the necessity of repeating in detail commonly used subsequences. This simplifies the expression of a program and has the following important advantages:

1. *Storage Economy*   A good subroutine structuring system will permit a single copy of a subroutine to be *called* by any number of program segments. A subroutine which can be used in this way is called a *closed* subroutine.
2. *Logical Separability*   A subroutine can be written with a high degree of logical independence from the rest of the program or other subroutines. This permits great flexibility and ease of introducing changes in the overall program, since it is relatively easy to keep track of such changes and their effects. The program check-out or debugging process also is made simpler by this property.

The storage economy is especially important for subroutines of appreciable length. On the other hand, since a small amount of storage is necessary for each call, or *linkage,* for very short subroutines, the size of the linkage may be comparable to the size of the subroutine itself. In such a case, it is often economical to insert a copy of the subroutine into the program wherever it is needed. This is called an *open* subroutine.

The property of logical separability has an important consequence to the organization of people to produce a large program. Different people or groups of people can be given parts of a large programming job; the mechanism of linking to subroutines imposes a precise technical discipline on how these groups communicate with each other.

Most machines include at least one instruction to facilitate subroutine control. Most programming languages include statements for subroutine linking either implicitly through the ability to define functions or even extended functions (i.e., functions of functions) and/or by explicit subroutine call.

Some programming systems permit subroutines written in two or more different source languages to be linked together in the same program. This is especially important where one of these languages is the machine assembly language and the other a high-level language. In this case, the latter gives good user convenience; yet where ultimate performance or full machine logic is required, the programmer can use the machine instruction also. As usual with data-processing features, different systems differ in implementation details and generality. The following discussion focuses on principles common to many systems. One general rule of good language design is that any program should be eligible to become a subroutine with minimal preplanning by the programmer.

Designing and using closed subroutines involve the following concepts:

1. *Subroutine Definition*   This refers to the subroutine as a written program beginning with a *header line*(s) that includes:

Language	Typical headers	Typical calls	Exit	Remarks
ALGOL	*PROCEDURE* FUN (X,Y,Z); *PROCEDURE* FUN (X,Y,M,N); *VALUE* M,N;	FUN (A,B,C); FUN(A,B,MN,NN);	*END*	Call by name except for parameters declared call by value by a *VALUE* declaration in header
APL	∇FUN;U;W ∇FUN X ∇Y←FUN X;P;Q;R ∇Z←Y FUN X	FUN FUN A B←FUN A C←B FUN A	→0	All passed parameters are call by value; all variables global except those in header, which are local
FORTRAN IV	*SUBROUTINE* FUN (X,/Y/,Z) *SUBROUTINE* FUN (X,Y)	CALL FUN (A,B(1),C) CALL FUN (5*A,B)	*RETURN*	1. Call by value for nonarray or nonsubprogram variables or expressions 2. Call by name for array variables or for other variables by enclosing in slashes in header
PL/I	FUN:*PROCEDURE* (X,Y,Z);	CALL FUN (A,(B),C);	*RETURN;* or *END FUN;*	1. Call by value for constants, expressions, and parenthesized names 2. Other arguments are passed call by name

Notes:
1. Language key-words shown in italics.
2. Only some example cases shown; see language manuals for full details and restrictions.

Fig. 3.4.1   Examples of subroutine headers and calls.

a. A symbol or keyword identifying the line as a header
b. The name of the subroutine
c. A list of parameters

See Fig. 3.4.1 for examples from several languages. In high-level languages, the body of the subroutine directly follows the header. The subroutine definition is ended by a symbol (∇ in APL) or a key-word (RETURN in FORTRAN).

In machine and assembler languages, the part of the subroutine immediately following the header is usually responsible for storing machine registers that the subroutine requires and often accesses parameter values from the calling program (see Sec. 3.6). The last part of the subroutine restores the original register contents and branches back to the calling program.

2. **Subroutine Linkage** (calling sequence) This refers to a type of statement which *calls* for the execution of a subroutine. Aside from the special symbol or key-word used to identify the calling type of statement, the syntax of the call usually closely follows the syntax of the subroutine header. In particular, both include the name of the subroutine and a list of parameters in corresponding order.

In most high-level languages, exit from a subroutine results in implicit return to the statement following the linkage. At the assembly-language level, more detail is usually involved. Return of program control from the subroutine to the calling routine is the most obvious part of the exit procedure. This cannot be done with an ordinary branch statement in the subroutine, since the place where the control must return depends on the calling sequence. The return point can be handled like another parameter, or else there must be common agreement between subroutine and calling routine about where the return location is placed and can be accessed. Where machine registers or common storage are used by both calling program and subroutine, the subroutine is usually responsible in its exit procedure for restoring these from the places where they were saved in the linkage or subroutine initialization.

3.5 MACROS

The term *macro* refers to a kind of subroutine structuring system which is most frequently (but not exclusively) found in assembler languages and which features copying of subroutines, with substitutions, into specified places in a program. Macros are therefore usually implemented as *open* subroutines.

Figure 3.5.1 shows some principles of macros using the IBM System/360 assembler macro language as the source of some simple idealized examples. Part

	Remarks
MACRO	MACRO is a key-word starting all definitions
FUN1 &X, &Y, &Z	FUN1 is name of the macro; parameter list follows (parameters start with & symbol)
Body	Body is any sequence of assembler statements
·	
·	
·	
MEND	MEND is a key-word ending all definitions

(*a*) Typical macro definition format.

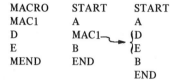

MACRO	START	START
MAC1	A	A
D	MAC1	{D
E	B	{E
MEND	END	B
		END

(*b*) Macro definition, a program and expansion.

MACRO	START	START
FUN &X, &Y, &Z	A	A
&X	FUN U, V, W	{U
&Z+&Y	B	{W+V
MEND	END	B
		END

(*c*)   Similar to (*b*) but macro includes parameters.

Fig. 3.5.1   Macro expansion principle in IBM System/360 assembler syntax.

(*a*) of the figure shows the format of a macro definition: it must start with the key-word statement MACRO; the immediately following statement begins with the name of the macro followed by an optional-parameter list. The variables in this list must start with the ampersand (&) character. These parameters will be replaced during compilation by corresponding parameters from the statement calling the macro. The body of the macro can contain any assembler statements as well as calls on other macros. Every macro definition signals its end with the key-word statement MEND.

Parts (*b*) and (*c*) of Fig. 3.5.1 show the effects of processing a simple program containing a call on a macro. In the first simplest case, it is seen that the body of the macro (statements D and E) are simply compiled into the place in the program where the call appeared. In the second case (*c*), the call on macro FUN with parameters U, V, W again results in the compilation of the macro body replacing the call, but now, wherever the first parameter (&X) appeared in the macro definition the first parameter in the call (U) appears in the expansion, and similarly for all other parameters.

The macro is a powerful technique that permits a programmer to exert considerable control over the compilation process. Thus far in our discussion this is due entirely to the operations of copying subroutines and making symbol substitutions. Many macro systems extend this concept to include conditional *compilation (or assembly)*. This means that statements such as a special type of conditional branch are designated to signal the *compiler* either to compile or not to compile a statement (including a macro call) depending on some parameter value. Conditional compilation permits arithmetic operations and decision making to be based on information available or computable at compile time. This can significantly improve space-time efficiency of the resulting object program. For example, suppose we have a generalized macro for finding the value of an N-degree polynomial from an X value and several coefficients. Suppose we know that in a certain case, only even powers of X appear. The use of the general macro would be wasteful of time and space since it must pad out the missing coefficients with zeros and also do the multiplications for these. A conditional compilation technique can include compilation of statements to first square X and then halve N before entering the main body of the macro. Note that this technique is applicable only if the knowledge about options is available at compile time. More generally, conditional compilation gives the macro user a very significant increase in language power and machine efficiency which he can use to better control the compilation process.

3.6 SUBROUTINE COMMUNICATION: PARAMETER TRANSLATION

The fundamental principle by which several programs or even several computers can communicate is for them to share some common storage. All subroutine-communication methods use this idea, but there are several significant differences; often a single language will use several methods. The differences occur in how the common space is named, how such names are translated, and how and when information is moved into and out of such storage.

One very simple scheme, used in the FORTRAN language, is to have a special named area of storage called COMMON, in which several programs can store and access data. Special FORTRAN language statements permit the programmer to declare that any variables he desires are to be assigned to COMMON, and since COMMON space is always allocated by the FORTRAN compiler starting at the same storage cell for every program and subroutine, corresponding COMMON variables in different programs can occupy the same storage cells.

A more elegant scheme allows certain variables and subroutines to communicate selectively with each other without requiring the programmer to keep track of the ordering of thc variables in COMMON. We have already encountered the principle called *positional parameters* in our discussion of APL function linking and also in the section on macros earlier in this chapter. Briefly, the subroutine is written in terms of some variables that are expected to be passed as parameters. Thus, in APL

(1) $\nabla P \leftarrow X \ POLY \ A$

denotes the start of a subroutine (function) definition whose name is $POLY$ and whose parameter names are P, X, and A. To *invoke* (or *call* or *link*) to this subroutine, we write a statement like

(2) $Y \leftarrow U \ POLY \ C$

The symbols in the call, namely Y, U, and C, name (or give) actual data values which will be associated with the names in the subroutine definition header (in this example P, X, and A) in corresponding order so that in sketch form

$$Y \Rightarrow P \quad U \Rightarrow X \quad C \Rightarrow A$$

The header names are sometimes called *dummy* variables. Note that the user of the subroutine needs only minimal knowledge about the subroutine, namely:

1. The name of the subroutine
2. The order in which the parameters must be listed but *not* their particular names

   There are at least two schemes of variable translation. The first, already described in some detail for APL in Chap. 2, is named *call by value* because upon call, a copy is made of the *values* specified in the linkage, and then during subroutine execution, the corresponding names appearing in the header are used to name these data copies. Upon exit from the subroutine, the result is copied into the result variable (Y in the above example). Any modifications to linkage-named data by the subroutine are made only to the copies (not the originals).
   A second method of variable translation is *call by name*. Here, the *names* of the linkage parameters are passed to the subroutine (but not data copies of the named data). Since only a name correspondence is established, any modification of a value by the subroutine changes the single copy of data. The call-by-name scheme can save storage space especially when the variables name large arrays, since separate copies of the data are not made. However, call by name is not suitable for multiple calling of the same subroutine before completion, as required in recursive-function calling, when the data for each call must be kept distinct.

Several modern languages (see Fig. 3.4.1) permit arthmetic or other expressions in the place of variables in a call on a subroutine. Two possible meanings that can be given this substitution will now be considered using a very simple example. In both cases, single-variable parameters are handled in the usual ways described above.

1. Call by Value

CALL FUN(A,A+C+1,C)   for   *PROCEDURE:* FUN(X,Y,Z)

In this case the expression A+C+1 is evaluated once at call time, and the result is named as local Y for the duration of the procedure FUN.

2. *Call by Name* For the above CALL and PROCEDURE, a program fragment to compute A+C+1 is inserted every place Y appears in the procedure FUN. Hence any changes in A or C during execution of FUN will result in new values computed wherever Y originally appeared in FUN.

An issue quite distinct from handling the variables to be passed is how the other variables are to be translated. In Chap. 2 we saw that in APL, all variables not passed through a linkage or specified in the header (by semicolon separators) are *global,* i.e., reference the same data for all programs. Although this convention applies in APL, other languages have other rules for what makes a variable local or global; the reader must discover this for himself in each language of interest.

As illustrated many times above, the most widely used syntax for linking to subroutines is the *positioned-parameter* list. This is a satisfactory method where only a few parameters are involved. Even in this case it is often convenient (but not permitted in many languages) to be able to omit one or more parameters. Thus for example, instead of

(3)   CALL FUN(X,Y,U)

we might wish to write

(4)   CALL FUN(X,,U)

Note that although a parameter is omitted, its comma cannot be deleted since it tells us (and the compiler) that U is the third and not the second parameter. Assuming that the second form is permitted, we must now face the problem of what value should be used by the subroutine FUN for the omitted parameter. This is usually handled by the *default* value, i.e., a value supplied automatically by the subroutine (usually the most expected value). The convenience of omitting parameters can be considerably enhanced if the parameters most likely to be defaulted are assigned rightmost positions in the parameter list. It is then quite easy to arrange that the final cluster of commas simply be omitted.

In a system requiring many parameters, it is tedious for the user to remember the order in which they must be listed especially if, as is often the case, only a few of the large number of possible parameters are to have nondefault values in any one call of the subroutine. It is then desirable to permit each parameter to carry its own identifier as a *key-word* rather than depend on its position in the parameter list. It often makes sense to combine both positional designations and key-word designations in the same language. In the IBM Operating System OS/360, the job-control language uses mixed position and key-word parameters. For example, one of the statements in this language is called a JOB statement since it specifies several parameters that apply to an entire job. An example job statement is

$$//ACGO \quad JOB \quad 9990,SMITH,MSGLEVEL=1$$

This statement is interpreted as follows: the leftmost // symbols are mandatory for all job-control statements of this class, ACGO is the name of the job, the word JOB is a key-word identifying this as a JOB statement (there are several other statement types in the language). The next two parameters (9990,SMITH) are positional parameters which denote account number and name respectively. The JOB statement also permits five other key-word parameters of which only one (MSGLEVEL=) is specified in this instance.

3.7   REENTRANT SUBROUTINES

In many cases it may be assumed that although several routines may call the same subroutine, each call will complete its use of the subroutine before the next call takes place. This is often a good assumption in single processor systems, where program interruption may not take place or, if a subroutine is permitted to be interrupted, resumption of the subroutine will always be at the point of interruption for the call that was in process. These conventions are quite restrictive but also quite common. As systems developed in the direction of greater emphasis on multiprogramming and multiprocessing (multiple processor units), pressure increases for a more general scheme whereby a subroutine may be interrupted and subsequently a new call may be made on it before the old call is completed. Such a subroutine is said to be *reentrant*. It is written in such a way that it never modifies its own instructions. Yet many subroutines require data and index-address parameters particular to each call. Reentrant subroutines manage these areas in one of two basic ways (Fig. 3.7.1). In the first method, all write-type storage required by the subroutine (including space for storing registers if interrupted) is provided by the *calling* routine. Since this is named and allocated by each calling sequence, each call is kept distinct, so there is no confusion between calls on the common routine. This method also has the advantage that an indefinite number of distinct calls can be made without a

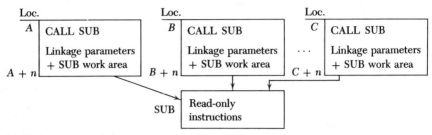

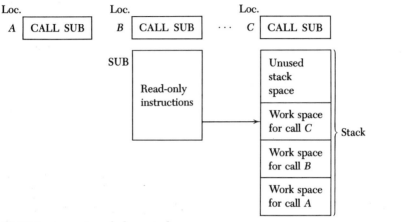

(a) Write-storage in linkage.

(b) Write-storage in push-down stack.

Fig. 3.7.1 Two methods of control of reentrant subroutines: (a) write-storage in linkage; (b) write-storage in push-down stack.

storage-allocation burden on the subroutine. The method has the disadvantage that each calling sequence requires knowledge of the storage needs of the subroutine. Another method of controlling multiple calls on a single subroutine is to have the subroutine obtain distinct space for its data manipulations for each call made on it. Since after each call is completed, space can be released for a subsequent call, a storage-allocation function is required. One simple scheme is called a *push-down list* or *stack*. The subroutine assigns a block of space from a pool of storage for use by each call. It releases space from the top of the stack of used space as a call is completed. With this rule, it is necessary that the calls be completed in the reverse order in which they were made. For this reason a push-down list is sometimes called a last in, first out (LIFO) list (see Sec. 9.6). The stack has the dual advantages and disadvantages of the scheme mentioned earlier. One of the main problems is the amount of space to be reserved for the stack—this requires knowledge of the maximum number of uncompleted calls that can exist at one time. Since calls arise dynamically, such information is not always available. On the other hand, the stack requires minimum knowledge by the calling routine of the needs of the subroutine. This is consistent with good subroutine structuring practice.

3.8 TRANSLATION OF ALGEBRAIC EXPRESSIONS

An algebraic expression is a symbol string which, when constructed according to certain rules of syntax, specifies a procedure for obtaining a function value from several argument values and primitive operations. An example of an algebraic expression written in the usual manner is

$$(1) \qquad ((ax + b)^2 + 2(y - a))p$$

This example is intended to suggest that an expression may be of essentially indefinite extent, although in computer work there is usually some large upper limit. As a practical matter, any number of variables, operators, and subexpressions denoted by parentheses may appear in an expression.

Most computer languages do not permit expressions to be entered exactly in the form of Eq. (1) for several reasons: (1) Often only uppercase (capital) letters are available. (2) Most typewriters and keypunches cannot type or otherwise designate above-line or below-line positions such as are commonly used for exponents and subscripts or superscripts. (3) Most computer-oriented languages require all operator symbols to be shown explicitly; the usual practice of omitting the multiplication symbol is not permitted. This is done to allow variables to be designated by multiple-letter names.

Typical of the way these conventions are implemented is the set of rules followed in the FORTRAN language. The variables are always uppercase, the exponentiation operation is denoted by a double asterisk before the exponent variable, and multiplication is designated by a single asterisk. A FORTRAN expression for Eq. (1) is

$$(2) \qquad ((A * X + B) ** 2 + 2 * (Y - A)) * P$$

Equation (2) is a symbol string such as a user of the system may set down to specify a computation.

Now there are several schemes of syntax possible for algebraic expressions. Three of these are shown in the example of Fig. 3.8.1; they all specify the same transformation on the literals and argument variables A,B,C,D,E,F.

The first representation is that of ordinary algebra except that all operator symbols are shown explicitly. The second representation is called *completely parenthesized* because the range of each operator symbol is shown explicitly by a pair of parentheses. Completely parenthesized expressions are easier to translate than conventional algebraic form, but they impose a bothersome

Algebraic form:

$$A+B\times C\times D\times (E+F\times (A-B))$$

Completely parenthesized form:

$$(A+(((B\times C)\times D)\times (E+(F\times (A-B))))) $$
$$\begin{array}{ccccccccc} 1 & & 234 & & 4 & 3\,5 & 6 & 7 & 76521 \end{array}$$

Note: Parentheses with same number identify a matching pair. Method of assigning numbers is: assign integers in order (left-to-right) to left parenthesis; for right parenthesis, assign last number assigned to left parenthesis and unused for right parenthesis.

Polish (parenthesis-free) form:

$$ABC\times D\times EFAB-\times+\times+$$

Precedence tree representation:

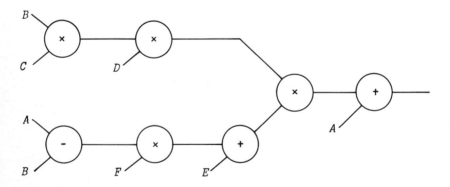

Fig. 3.8.1   Three forms of algebraic expression.

burden on the writer of the expression. The third form of expression is called *parentheses-free, Polish,* or *Lukasiewicz* notation. It has the property that parentheses never appear and that a simple procedure exists for translating a Polish symbol string into a machine program. Before discussing this, however, it is necessary to specify the interpretation given to the operators of a Polish string.

The Polish string, in the form discussed here, is read from left to right. In interpreting an operator symbol, the operator is understood to operate on the number of operands appropriate for the operator; these are obtained from the symbols immediately to the left of the operator. The result of each operation is then considered to be an operand for subsequent operators. Thus the Polish string

$$AB + C*D +$$

means, in fully parenthesized and ordinary algebraic notation,

$$((A + B) * C) + D \quad \text{or} \quad (A + B) * C + D$$

If we accept for the moment that translation of a symbol string from Polish form into machine instructions is relatively easy, then the problem of translation has as its central task the translation of algebraic symbol strings into Polish symbol strings. It should be stressed at this point that translation into Polish form is not essential—it is simply one technique of translation.

Later in this chapter a quite different method will be sketched for translating arithmetic expressions whereby the relative precedence of the operators is embedded in the syntax equations that describe the entire language. For the moment, however, we are interested in the technique of conversion of a parenthesized expression into Polish form.

A trace of the APL program for the conversion algorithm is shown in Fig. 3.8.2 as an aid in understanding how it works. The program itself is given in Fig. 3.8.3. The program begins by requesting a parenthesized expression as the source string (vector) S. The program then prints a position number under each character of S to help the reader follow the trace (in actual practice where the trace is not used, this step and several trace printout statements in Fig. 3.8.3 would of course be omitted). Every character of S is then assigned its rank value, which for this operator set follows the usual algebraic precedence convention:

$$+ - \times \div * ( ) \Delta$$
$$1\ 1\ 2\ \ 2\ 3\ 4\ 5\ 5$$

Every variable symbol is given a rank of 0. The vector of ranks in S is C. The program maintains a stack of operator symbols D, and their corresponding ranks constitute vector E. We are now ready to state the basic idea of the algorithm, which is to examine each character of S and compare its rank with the rank of

```
        POLISH
ENTER A SOURCE EXPRESSION, USE OPERATOR SYMBOLS +-×÷*()
A+B×C×D×(E+F×(A-B))
00000000011111111112 ←CHAR. POSITION
12345678901234567890
1A
   2 +
3AB
   4 +×
5ABC
6ABC×
   6 +
   6 +×
7ABC×D
8ABC×D×
   8 +
   8 +×
   9 +×(
10ABC×D×E
  11 +×(+
12ABC×D×EF
  13 +×(+×
  14 +×(+×(
15ABC×D×EFA
  16 +×(+×(-
17ABC×D×EFAB
18ABC×D×EFAB-
  18 +×(+×(
18 +×(+×
19ABC×D×EFAB-×
  19 +×(+
19ABC×D×EFAB-×+
  19 +×(
19 +×
20ABC×D×EFAB-×+×
  20 +
20ABC×D×EFAB-×+×+
  20
THE ORIGINAL EXPRESSION IS:
A+B×C×D×(E+F×(A-B))
THE POLISH EXPRESSION IS:
ABC×D×EFAB-×+×+
```

Fig. 3.8.2   Illustrating algebraic to Polish conversion (see Fig. 3.8.3 for program).

the symbol at the top of the operator stack D. Depending upon the outcome of this comparison, the symbol from S may be sent directly to the Polish string P or else the S symbol may be entered into D (and its rank taken from C to E) or else symbols may be removed from D and sent to the Polish string P. In the trace, the integer at the far left of each line gives the position number of the character in S currently being processed; lines starting at the extreme left show the Polish string every time a new entry is made, and indented lines show the operator stack D every time symbols are entered or taken out. Examination of Fig. 3.8.2 or analysis of Fig. 3.8.3 reveals the essence of the algorithm, which may be simply stated as:

1. Variable symbols go directly to P.
2. If the rank of the current S symbol is higher than that at the top of the D

stack, the S symbol is entered at the top of the D stack.

3. If the rank of the current S symbol is equal or lower than that of the symbol at the top of D, then symbols are removed from D and copied into P until a symbol is reached with lower rank. The S symbol is then entered into D.

4. A right parenthesis is treated specially: it empties the D stack into P until its left mate is found, which is then deleted from D.

```
      ∇ POLISH
[1]      A←'+-×÷*()∆'
[2]      R← 1 1 2 2 3 4 5 5
[3]      'ENTER A SOURCE EXPRESSION, USE OPERATOR SYMBOLS +-×÷*() '
[4]      S←⎕,'∆'
[5]      ((9ρ'0'),(10ρ'1'),(10ρ'2'),(10ρ'3'),(10ρ'4'))[ιρS];' ←CHAR. POSITION'
[6]      (50ρ'1234567890')[ιρS]
[7]      C←(ρS)ρ0
[8]      D←P←(ρS)ρ' '
[9]      I←1
[10] CSET:C[(S=A[I])/ιρC]←R[I]
[11]     →((ρA)≥I←I+1)/CSET
[12]     I←J←K←1
[13]     E←(ρS)ρ0
[14] ETST:→(S[I]='∆')/JCOMP
[15]     →(C[I]≠0)/STST
[16]     P[K]←S[I]
[17]     I;P
[18]     I←I+1
[19]     K←K+1
[20]     →ETST
[21] STST:→(S[I]=')')/JCOMP
[22] STTST:→((C[I]>E[J])∨(D[J]='('))/CESTAK
[23]     XSTAK
[24]     →STTST
[25] CESTAK:ESTAK
[26]     →ETST
[27] JCOMP:→(J=1)/PRINT
[28]     →(D[J]≠'(')/CXSTAK
[29]     J←J-1
[30]     I;D[ιJ]
[31]     I←I+1
[32]     →ETST
[33] CXSTAK:XSTAK
[34]     →JCOMP
[35] PRINT:'THE ORIGINAL EXPRESSION IS:'
[36]     S[ι¯1+ρS]
[37]     'THE POLISH EXPRESSION IS:'
[38]     P
      ∇


      ∇ XSTAK
[1]      P[K]←D[J]
[2]      I;P
[3]      J←J-1
[4]      '  ';I;D[ιJ]
[5]      K←K+1
      ∇


      ∇ ESTAK
[1]      J←J+1
[2]      D[J]←S[I]
[3]      '  ';I;D[ιJ]
[4]      E[J]←C[I]
[5]      I←I+1
      ∇
```

Fig. 3.8.3 Program to convert algebraic to Polish notation.

3.9 SYNTAX DESCRIPTION: BNF EQUATIONS

The syntax of a computer language can usually be described in a precise way by a set of *syntax equations* which give the rules for recognizing and classifying legal symbol strings. We must realize, however, that these equations are themselves symbol strings, which to be meaningful must follow some set of syntax rules. In other words, the description of the syntax of a language itself requires a language! A language that describes another language is called a metalanguage. Clearly, this process of layers of precise description can go on indefinitely. We avoid this by resorting to an informal natural-language description of the metalanguage and also choose the metalanguage to be exceedingly simple so that there can be little (if any) doubt about its properties. The particular metalanguage that we shall use is called BNF (short for *Backus-Nauer Form*, after two pioneers in the practical description of computer languages).

The symbols and conventions of BNF may be summarized as follows (see below for examples):

1. Certain symbols have special meanings in the metalanguage:
    a. → means "is *defined* as."
    b. <> is used to *delimit* a string that is the *name* of another string.
    c. | means "or else," i.e., separates *alternatives*.
2. All symbols except those above denote themselves.
3. Symbols or strings or names in any combination that follow in succession implicitly specify the operation of *concatenation*.
4. The order of application of the operations in the metalanguage is first concatenations, then alternatives, then the definition arrow.
5. Unless otherwise stated, the syntax equations shall be applied to strings in left-to-right order.

EXAMPLE 1:

(1) $<DIG> \rightarrow 0|1|2|3|4|5|6|7|8|9$

May be read "the object named DIG is defined as the string 0 or else 1 or else 2 . . . or else 9."

EXAMPLE 2: Consider Eq. (1) along with the following equations for the syntax of integers, fractions, and numbers:

(2) $<INT> \rightarrow <DIG>|<DIG><DIG>$

(3) $<FR> \rightarrow .<INT>$

(4) $<NUM> \rightarrow <INT>|<FR>|<INT><FR>$

Using the five rules of the metalanguage, we can interpret these four BNF equations as a *grammar* for recognizing 1- or 2-digit integers as INT or up to 2 digits following a period as FR, or any instance of INT or of FR or of INT followed by FR as (numbers) NUM.

Each alternative term of a syntax equation is called a *production*. The problem of recognition can then be described as a sequence of searches of the productions for matches to the string to be translated, both directly and by means of intermediate named classifications that are matched to productions and then used to form later matches. We shall see examples of this presently.

It often happens that strings of indefinite length are of interest. For this purpose, the metalanguage permits *recursive* statements as illustrated by

(5) $<INT> \rightarrow <DIG> \mid <INT><DIG>$

This equation is recursive because it defines INT and INT also appears on the right side of the arrow. To see the power of this kind of equation consider the string

    23473658

The first symbol, 2, is found to match an alternative in Eq. (1) so 2 is classified as DIG. Using DIG as an argument in Eq. (5), it is found to be an INT. Consider now the second symbol, 3, which is also first found to be a DIG. The string 23 is at this point then classified as <INT><DIG>. This matches the second alternative of Eq. (5), making the string an INT. This process of using Eqs. (1) and (5) continues and clearly may be used to recognize a string of any number of digits. Also, Eqs. (1), (5), (3), and (4) are then able to recognize numbers of any length.

With the specification of the property of recursion, we have completed the informal definition and illustration of the BNF metalanguage. It is worth noting that although strings of arbitrary length can be handled, there is no provision for simple specification of strings of a definite or of maximum length like "names can be up to eight characters long." There are versions of BNF that can conveniently specify properties such as these (see Ref. 10).

Figure 3.9.1*a* shows a set of syntax equations that define a grammar typical of arithmetic expressions. The expressions may be of any length and include parenthesized subexpressions to any depth. Although names are here restricted to the single letters A, B, or C, it is easy to modify the syntax to permit multiple-letter names. One important property of this particular syntax is not obvious; the usual precedence rule that multiplication (*) is done before addition (+) is built into the syntax. This occurs in the following way: consider the string A+B*C. In the left-to-right scan, the substring A+B will initially be classified, but this classification (as an EX) used with the following string *C will

	Syntax equation	Meaning
1	<AOP> → + | –	Add-operator symbol is + *or* –
2	<MOP> → * | /	Multiply-operator symbol is * *or* /
3	<V> → A | B | C	A variable symbol is A *or* B *or* C
4	<F> → <V> | (<EX>)	A factor is <V> *or* left paren *then* <EX> *then* right paren
5	<T> → <F> | <T> <MOP> <F>	A term is <F> *or* term *then* <MOP> *then* <F>
6	<EX> → <T> | <EX > <AOP> <T>	An expression is <T> *or* <EX> *then* <AOP> <T>

(*a*) An arithmetic-expression grammar.

	Successive classifications*		Equations used	Compiled subexpression
1	A + B *(C + A *C) + B		*Original expression*	
2	V + V * (V + V * V) + V		3	
3	V + V * (V + T * F) + V		4,5	
4	V + V * (V + T) + V		5	T1 = A*C
5	V + V * (EX + T) + V		4,5,6	
6	V + V * (EX)+V		6	T2 = C + T1
7	V + V * F	+ V	4	
8	V + T *F	+ V	4,5	
9	V + T	+ V	5	T3 = B*T2
10	EX + T	+ V	4,5,6	
11	EX	+ V	6	T4 = A+ T3
12	EX	+ T	4,5	
13	EX		6	T5 = T4 + B

Notes:
1. In this example, AOP is + and MOP is *.
2. Equation (3) of (*a*) is used to replace all variable symbols by V. For clarity on this chart, angle brackets are omitted.

(*b*) Example of use of syntax equations.

Fig. 3.9.1 A set of syntax equations and example.

be found *not* to match any production. The scan must then abandon the tentative classification of A+B as an EX and seek another sequence of classifications which can be found as A is an EX, B*C a T, and finally, the entire expression is an EX followed by + followed by T which is found to match the last alternative of Eq. (6) of the figure. Thus in this expression, B*C is recognized as a legal operation while A+B is not. The chart of part (*b*) of the figure shows some key steps in the analysis of an example statement.

Using the technique described above, it is possible to determine whether any given string representing a program or a statement is a legal one of a given syntax. Since the string is recognized by a sequence of matches of its substrings with the syntax productions, this process can *parse* the string, i.e., identify the "parts of speech" such as operators, variables, product and sum terms, indexes, etc. Parsing is a major task of a language-translator program such as a compiler.

BNF is a valuable way to start the orderly design of a compiler. However, this first step must be followed by a host of other difficult judgments such as:

1. Does a given set of BNF equations consistently and unambiguously define a grammar?
2. If the grammar is unambiguous, precisely how are the equations to be scanned with the string to be translated? This depends on how the equations are represented.
3. The *semantics* of the language must somehow be specified so that the compiler can compile object instructions when it recognizes the productions. Fortunately, most semantic rules are rather simple, but the fact remains that there is no instrument as powerful and as widely accepted as BNF to specify semantics. There is also the issue whether the semantics, which usually take the form of a list of object instructions for each kind of production, should be applied just after each recognition or whether pointers to the substrings should be kept until the scan is complete and the object instructions assigned at the end.
4. Syntax errors are naturally detected during the syntax scan. However, in order to keep enough information about errors to best communicate the place where they occur, careful attention is required in the design of the compiler.
5. The many efficiency questions are of two classes: the efficiency of the compilation process itself and the efficiency of the object code produced by the compiler. By efficiency we mean storage space and time.

The above should give the reader some feel for the kinds of considerations that must be weighed in compiler design.

3.10 SYNTAX-DIRECTED COMPILING: COMPILER OF COMPILERS

A process of compilation that is based on formal syntax equations is called *syntax-directed* compiling. Usually the information in the syntax equations is represented by a table. A program in the compiler scans this table using the source string (and intermediate results) as arguments. The techniques for converting syntax equations into table form and the scan program for searching this table for matches with the productions will not be detailed here. It suffices to assure the reader that these techniques are well known in the compiler art and are based on a considerable body of theory (see Refs. 3, 6, and 7).

Thus far, we have sketched a way to do much of a compiler's job of translating a program written in a source language whose syntax is specified in BNF into some object language which is represented as a collection of rather simple sequences of instructions, each sequence corresponding to some syntax production. From a very gross view, the input to a compiler is then a source string which is a source program, and the compiler output is an object program. Consider now another layer of translation called a *compiler of compilers*. We shall now sketch the nature of such a program. Its name implies that its output should be a *compiler* and its input must specify the source language that this compiler accepts. BNF syntax equations are a suitable input to a compiler of compilers. The compiler of compilers program is capable of scanning BNF equations and transforming them into a table representation. The syntax-analysis part of the resulting compiler program consists of this table plus a program to scan this table for parsing; much of this scan program can be the same no matter what the source language. One quite practical simplification results if the object language is fixed, as it would be for a compiler of compilers designed for a particular computer. The object language is then known once and for all; however, object code sequences for each production, which may well differ from language to language, must be constructed for each compiler.

3.11 TRANSLATING INDEXES INTO ADDRESSES

Most modern programming languages permit the user to manipulate elements of vectors, matrices, and even higher-order rectangular arrays. References to such source-language data structures must be translated into *addresses,* i.e., location numbers in the simple linear machine-memory structure. We now consider how this index-to-address translation can be accomplished.

The case of vector indexing is the simplest since a vector, like the machine memory, is a linear structure (we here assume that the elements of the vector are the addressable units of the machine). Thus, if B is the address of the first word of vector X, then

| X[1] | is at address | $A \equiv B$ |
| X[I] | is at address | $A \equiv B + I - 1$ |

For a *matrix* X having R rows and C columns, the matrix elements are usually stored in row or column order; i.e., the successive matrix elements of a row or of a column follow each other in memory. Either scheme is feasible and used in practice. In the following discussion we assume column order as in FORTRAN. With this convention, a little thought will show that if B is the address of the 1;1 element of the matrix, then the address of an element can be computed as typified by

X[1;1]	is at address	$A \equiv B$
X [I;1]	is at address	$A \equiv B + I - 1 \equiv (B - 1) + I$
X [I;2]	is at address	$A \equiv B + (1 \times R) + I - 1 \equiv (B + R) - 1) + I$
X [I;J]	is at address	$A \equiv B + ((J - 1) \times R) + I - 1$
		$\equiv (B - (R + 1)) + I + J \times R$

The rightmost form of the computations emphasize that part of the computation like $(B - (R + 1))$ in the matrix case, can be done at compile time, while only the parts involving I,J need be compiled into object code (since only I,J change values). This reduces the number of *executed* instructions (from four adds/subtracts and one multiplication to two add/subtracts and one multiplication in the last example). Of these, the multiplication is the most time-consuming. A clever compiler can often avoid most of these multiplications by recognizing when the user will be marching down a matrix, i.e., referencing its elements successively in the same row or column. In this case, only one multiplication may be required to locate the first element of a column; successive references are then obtained by simple addition (by 1 down a column or by R if across a row). This kind of time savings of course requires that the compiler recognize array marching. This is easiest to do in an array-oriented language like APL, where the user is likely to indicate this point by specifying a row or column vector or even an entire matrix as a variable. In FORTRAN, array marching must be deduced from the structure of a sequence of statements and hence is harder to detect (but still feasible).

3.12 EFFICIENCY CONSIDERATIONS IN PROGRAMMING SYSTEMS

A precise measure of the efficiency of a program is a most difficult and thus far elusive entity. However, it is relatively easy to list some of the important parameters which influence the efficiency. As usual, the two main factors are space (storage) and time.

Contributions to these may be considered separately as follows:

1. Problem-to-program translation time including debugging time
2. Translator efficiency
   a. Translator running time
   b. Storage used by translator
3. Object-code efficiency
   a. Storage required for object program and data
   b. Running time of object program

Because trade-offs can often be made whereby some of these efficiencies may improve at the expense of others, careful attention must be paid to the objectives of the system before sound judgments can be made as to how to weight the above factors.

For example, consider a program which is to have very high volume use once it is operational. Here the efficiency of the compiler itself as well as the problem preparation time is of relatively low importance, while the efficiency of the object program is of prime importance.

As another example, consider the evaluation of a formula by a scientist. Here, the problem-preparation and compile time may well be of greatest concern; object running time may be sacrificed in order to obtain short overall response to "one-shot" running of the program.

3.13   CONCLUDING REMARKS

Programming is the science and art of precise description of sequential processes. A rather vague but valuable distinction is sometimes made between programming and *coding;* the former refers to the general planning and strategy aspects, whereas the latter refers to stylizing a procedure in a particular machine-readable form.

To an increasing extent, the facilities available to a programmer are not merely a machine and a program translator, but a whole set of facilities called a *programming system.* These systems typically include several translator programs for different source languages and for the same source language with different biases in efficiency. A "library" of programs is made available under program control, and its contents may be used as simple programs or incorporated in other programs under program control. Programs may be added to the library as they are developed by system or problem programmers.

Programming languages play key roles in the use of computer systems. Even the computer machine itself may be considered as an interpreter program of a single language, the machine language, that is implemented in the machine's components and their physical interconnections. Languages much more convenient for direct human use greatly enhance the ease with which people can use a computer productively. The same computer can easily process source programs of several different languages provided a translator program is provided for each language. The art of specification of a language, writing translators (compilers and interpreters), and even producing programs that can produce compiler programs is now fairly well understood although many judgments of course must be made in each individual system according to the user-convenience and efficiency objectives desired.

The allocation of equipment resources such as processor storage, auxiliary storage, and input/output devices is usually vested in an important special program called variously a *control,* a *monitor,* a *supervisor,* or an *operating-system* program. It is usually written and maintained by the system manufacturer, and it coordinates both the programming and equipment facilities in response to problem program requests. In multiprogrammed systems it also resolves all conflicts among problem programs for calls on common facilities and ensures privacy among the several users that may be sharing these facilities.

The broad objectives of programming systems are (1) increased user convenience and (2) efficient use of the system's equipment and programs. The result is not only lower direct costs but also economical opportunities for direct human interaction with a computer system. The implications for expanding human abilities in problem solving and learning are just beginning to be explored.

PROBLEMS

3.1 Use the following symbols for operators:

Addition	Subtraction	Multiplication	Division	Exponentiation
+	-	×	/	↑

Assume a left-to-right scan with precedence: exponentiation (highest), then multiplication and division (equal), and then addition and subtraction (equal). Using a parenthesis pair for each operator, show the evaluation of the following expressions for $A \equiv 3$, $B \equiv 2$, $C \equiv 4$, $X \equiv 7$, $D \equiv 2$:

a) $A*B+B*C \uparrow 2-4$
b) $A*B/C*D$
c) $A/C*B/D$
d) $A+B*C*(4-A*B)$
e) $A+X*(B*X*(C+X))$

3.2 Give the Polish strings for each expression in Prob. 3.1.

3.3 Show a stack implementation of the execution of each expression in Prob. 3.1 and give the maximum depth of the stack in each case.

3.4 Use the grammar of Fig. 3.9.1*a* to show compiled subexpressions (each with a single operator) for evaluating each of the expressions of Prob. 3.3.

3.5 Suppose we have a character set consisting of the 26 English letters; 10 digit symbols; blank; period; and comma. A <NAME> is defined as any string starting with a letter and followed by any number of digit or alphabetic symbols. Write a BNF expression for a <NAME>.

3.6 Given a matrix declared to be 40 rows and 30 columns in a system that stores a matrix as a *row* list. Assume 1-origin indexing and the first element at location 1000.

a) Give the locations of the first five elements of row 3.
b) Give the locations of the first five elements of column 3.
c) Give the locations of the first five elements along the main diagonal.
d) For each of the above cases, give the number of addition and multiplication operations required to compute the locations.

3.7 Given the following calls and definitions of subroutines. Assume (as in ALGOL) that all parameters are passed call by name unless declared otherwise with a *VALUE* declaration in the header. For each case, give the values of A, B, C after the return from the CALL.

a) A=5   *PROCEDURE:* FUN(X,Y,Z)
     B=3   X=X+Y
     CALL FUN(A,B,C)   X = X + Y
                                Z=X+Y
                                RETURN

b) A=5   *PROCEDURE:* FUN(X,Y,Z) *VALUE*(X)
     B=3   X=X+Y
     CALL FUN(A,B,C)   X=X+Y
                                Z=X+Y
                                RETURN

c) A=5   *PROCEDURE:* FUN(X,Y,Z)
     B=3   X=X+Y
     CALL FUN(A,A+1,C)   X=X+Y
                                  Z=X+Y
                                RETURN

d) Same as part (*c*) except that all passing is call by value.

Answers: (*a*) 11,3,14 (*b*) 5,3,14 (*c*) 23,3,47 (*d*) 5,3,23.

3.8 Compare the call-by-value and call-by-name methods with respect to storage requirements, execution time, and convenience.

REFERENCES

1. Bobrow, D. G., and B. Raphael: A Comparison of List Processing Languages, *Commun. ACM,* vol. 7, pp. 231–240 (April 1964).

2. Chatham, T. E., and K. Sattley: Syntax Directed Compiling, *Proc. AFIPS Spring Jt. Comput. Conf.,* 1964, vol. 25, pp. 31–57.

3. Cohen, D. J., and C. C. Gotlieb: A List Structure Form of Grammars for Syntactic Analysis, *ACM Comput. Surv.,* vol. 2, no. 1 (March 1970).

4. Feldman, J., and D. Gries: Translator Writing Systems, *Commun. ACM,* vol. 11 pp. 77-113 (February 1968).

5. Floyd, R. W.: Syntactic Analysis and Operator Precedence, *J. ACM,* vol. 10, no. 3, pp. 316-333 (October 1963).

6. Floyd, R. W., The Syntax of Programming Language: A Survey, *IEEE Trans. EC-13,* pp. 346–353 (August 1964).

7. Foster, J. M.: "Automatic Syntactic Analysis," American Elsevier Inc., New York, 1970.

8. Hellerman, H.: Addressing Multidimensional Arrays, *Commun. ACM,* April 1962.

9. Johnson, L. R.: "System Structure in Data, Programs and Computers," Prentice-Hall, Inc., Englewood Cliffs, N.J., 1970.

10. Lee, J. A. N.: "The Anatomy of a Compiler," Reinhold Publishing Corporation, New York, 1967.

11. McIlroy, M. D.: Macro Instruction Extensions of Compiler Languages, *Commun. ACM,* vol. 3, pp. 214–220 (April 1960).

12. McKeeman, W. M., J. J. Horning, and D. B. Wortman: "A Compiler Generator," Prentice-Hall, Inc., Englewood Cliffs, N.J., 1970.

13. Nauer, P. (ed.): Revised Report on the Algorithmic Language Algol 60, *Commun. ACM,* vol. 6, pp. 1–17 (January 1963).

14. Rosen, S. (ed.): "Programming Systems and Languages," McGraw-Hill Book Company, New York, 1967.

15. Samelson, K., and F. L. Bauer: Sequential Formula Translation, *Commun. ACM,* vol. 3, no. 2, pp. 76–83 (February 1960).

16. Sammet, J.: "Programming Languages: History and Fundamentals," Prentice-Hall, Inc., Englewood Cliffs, N.J., 1969.

4

Storage Organization and Searching

Technology makes available a variety of storage devices that differ in cost per unit of information stored and performance as measured in access speed. In general, devices with lower unit cost are also slower, so that large volumes of program and data are typically held most of the time in slow, cheap storage such as magnetic tape, disk, or drum and moved in segments to faster, more expensive, but smaller processor storage prior to processing. All systems thus contain a *storage hierarchy*. It extends to the still better access but smaller capacity of the few high-speed registers directly accessible to the high-speed processing circuitry. Because the speed of transfer of information between two members of the hierarchy is limited to the speed of the slower member, during transmission there would appear to be an enforced idleness on the faster member. This can be avoided, especially in the important case where this faster member is processor storage, by a technique called *overlapping,* whereby information already in the processor storage is processed during the relatively long intervals of slow (input or output) transmissions with slower devices.

The choice of the members of the storage hierarchy and design of equipment features to achieve good overlap are important responsibilities of the system designer. The design of strategies for moving information within a given hierarchy is an important problem in programming. In some recent systems, this is made *transparent* (invisible) to most programmers by a combination of equipment and system program. Users of such systems are given the great convenience of uniform reference to a large *virtual* storage independent of its true hierarchal nature. However, in most other types of systems, scheduling of transmission within the storage hierarchy is the job of the programmer.

Although the physical properties of storage devices can be quite complex, most fall into one of a few classes, and each class can be characterized by a few parameters for purposes of logical description and performance analysis. This will be done in the early sections of this chapter.

Quite independent of the physical hierarchy is the logical structure of stored information, typically divided into substructures for convenience in referencing and making changes. Thus, for example, a book is divided into chapters, these into sections, these into paragraphs, etc. Search of information is often facilitated by a table of contents and an index.

Any volume of stored information will be called a *file* or *data set.* Techniques of ordering and otherwise arranging subdivisions of a file are of great importance because the speed at which information can be accessed and hence processed depends not only on the physical properties of the storage device but also most critically on where information is stored relative to other information or with respect to the criterion for searching. A simple familiar example will introduce some terminology and principles to be expanded later. Consider the telephone directory of a large city. Its information, considered as a file, is organized into entries called *records;* each record contains a number of *fields:* subscriber's surname, address, and telephone number. One of the fields, the subscriber's surname, is the usual criterion for search; this is then called the key-field or *key.* The telephone directory is ordered alphabetically on this field. As a consequence of this ordering, finding the telephone number or the address of a subscriber whose surname is known is easy (fast). On the other hand, to obtain the telephone number of a single residence whose address is known but whose occupant's name is not available is much harder (slower). This illustrates two important principles of the logical organization of storage: (1) the organization of information in a file should reflect how the file is to be used, and good performance can be expected only for that use; (2) files ordered on a given key will generally be far easier to search on that key than on any other key. Of these two principles, the first is more general, but both are applicable to many if not most file organization problems. Several sections of this chapter classify and describe logical properties of files, methods of obtaining these, and ways to search such files efficiently.

4.1 BASIC STORAGE OPERATIONS; DIRECT, SEQUENTIAL, AND ASSOCIATIVE ACCESS

This section introduces a somewhat simplified abstract model of storage devices for the purpose of focusing attention on fundamental properties and terminology.

A storage will be characterized by the following parts:

1. A *storage array* contains a space distribution of some physical representation of the information stored. Often this takes the form of magnetized spots on a recording surface or the state of magnetization of tiny donut-shaped magnetic cores. The entire array is subdivided into subarrays for reference and access purposes. In one scheme of such partitioning, all subarrays must be of equal length. Another method allows variable-length subarrays called *records*. Records often specify their extent by a special terminating character called a *record* or *group mark*. Whatever method is used, each identifiable subarray will henceforth be called a *record*.
2. An *access mechanism* is the means by which some record of storage can be located for the purpose of copying or replacement. At any instant the access mechanism is in some definite state or position relative to the storage array. A position operation consists of changing the state of the access mechanism from its present state to a new state.
3. A *data buffer* is a device with very limited storage capacity which serves as the immediate source or destination of information en route between the storage array and other devices.

Basic operations on storage are:

1. *Access*   The access mechanism is positioned to the beginning of a record in the storage array.
2. *Flow*   Flow may start only after access. There are two types of flow:
    a. *Read* (copy) whereby information (starting at the access position) is copied from the storage array to the data buffer. From a logical viewpoint, the read operation is always nondestructive; i.e., information in the storage array is not modified by reading it.
    b. *Write* (replace) whereby information in the data buffer replaces information in the storage array (starting at the access position).

A *direct-access* storage device is one whose access mechanism requires the same number of position-operations to arrive at any record. Another term for direct access is *random access*. An example of a direct-access storage device is magnetic-core storage.

A *sequential-access* storage device is one whose access mechanism can only advance from the position of the present record to the position of the next record. Magnetic or paper tape devices are examples. They often depend on a program to test identifier information embedded in the data to determine whether the desired data unit is in access position. In general, then, search for a particular record requires moving all records past the access station from the currently accessible one to the desired one.

Many storage devices such as magnetic disks or drums, while not strictly direct access, are often classified as such because their access mechanisms can usually arrive at any record from any position in less time than it takes to access all intervening records sequentially.

Data may be referenced in three basic ways: by addressing, i.e., giving the position number in the storage array; by sequential advance to only the next record; and by search-key, i.e., specifying a part of the data as identifier. Of these methods, addressing has greatest potential for high-speed access because all identifiers or names have been *mapped* into equipment-significant position numbers, the addresses.

An *associative* storage is one in which stored data can be identified for access by some portion of the data itself. This is contrasted to access by addressing (position number) or by next position (sequential access). Associative storage has an interesting history of potential application, and a considerable number of experimental units have been reported.

Related to the associative retrieval principle are *scan* features available on some disk, tape, and drum units. A scan feature permits the program to specify a search argument (data identifier) to the control unit of the storage device; the control unit then performs a search for a match between the argument and some specified portion of each record in storage. This search, which may be quite time-consuming, can often be done concurrently with computer processing. When the search is complete, the information necessary to directly access the record is made available to the processor program. Such a scan feature displays some of the logical properties of an associative memory with storage units which are physically direct access or sequential access. This may be done with only a small addition to the amount of equipment over conventional storage devices. However, even the modest expenditure for equipment to implement the scan feature may often be challenged on the basis that without scan hardware the scan may still be performed by program means. If it can be shown that this requires only a small fraction of processor time, a program solution may well be best.

Direct equipment implementation of associative storage, especially high-speed direct-access associative storage, is apparently awaiting demonstration that it can significantly improve processing on real problems over the best use of conventional storage structures.

4.2   A BRIEF DESCRIPTION OF SOME STORAGE DEVICES

Details of magnetic-core storage organization are given in Chap. 6. Access time is defined as the delay between when the storage unit receives an address (position number) and when the data become available. Because of the nature of the magnetic-core device, information read-out is physically destroyed in the array by the reading process. It is, however, automatically regenerated; but this requires an additional delay. The sum of access and regeneration time is called *cycle time*. Cycle time is the minimum time between which successive accesses can be made. Cycle time is usually about twice access time. Another important parameter of core storage is the width, i.e., the number of bits (or bytes or words) which are retrieved with each access. The *bandwidth* of a core storage unit is defined as the width divided by the cycle time. It represents the maximum rate at which the device can deliver or accept information. Bandwidth is the most significant single parameter of performance of a core storage device.

A magnetic drum is physically composed of a plated recording surface on a cylindrical frame. The recording surface rotates at a uniform speed and is not started or stopped during access operations. Read/write heads are placed at fixed positions along the axis of the cylinder. Each head can access a band or *track* on the drum. Data are stored as magnetized spots on the surface. The change in magnetic field produced by a spot moving past the read head is converted by the head circuits into an electric signal. Access then consists of waiting for the desired position of the drum to reach the read/write head and then routing the signal between the head and the storage data register. After the rotation delay (which is typically in the 10-msec range), data flow from the read head(s) at a rapid rate, which may approach the rate obtainable from magnetic-core storage. Several techniques exist for reducing access time at the expense of capacity, e.g., the "revolver" method of positioning heads. Also, for a given rotational delay, it is possible to improve the flow rate by having several heads read several bits at the same time. This latter technique improves the flow rate but not the access time.

Access times for rotational-access devices are often specified by minimum, maximum, and average; i.e., the shortest, longest, and average delay from the time access is initiated to the time the desired information reaches the position of the head.

Magnetic-disk storage is available in a variety of arrangements (Fig. 4.2.1). In one common scheme the recording surfaces are on rotating disks; all disks rotate together at a fixed speed—they are not stopped or started for access purposes. Read/write heads are mounted in a "comb" arrangement; each comb (there may be only one) has one head for each recording surface. Data are typically stored serially by bit along each of several concentric circles (tracks) of each disk. Since all heads are positioned together, a single comb position makes a set of tracks (one track per disk) available. Such a set of tracks is called a *cylinder*. Since head-positioning (seek) time requires the longest delay for random access, the capacity of a cylinder is important. In addition to seek time, random access also requires a rotational delay (of the same order as for drum storage). Flow rates in the 800 kilobytes/sec range are presently available.

Some disk units allow the disks to be removed easily. This permits replacement of one set of data by another for the access mechanism.

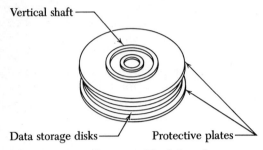

Vertical shaft

Data storage disks —   Protective plates —

(*a*) Appearance of a removable disk pack.

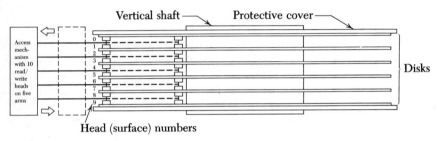

Vertical shaft —   Protective cover —

Disks

Head (surface) numbers

(*b*) Disks, access mechanism, and read/write heads.

Number bytes per track	13,030
Number tracks per cylinder = number recording surfaces	19
Number cylinders per pack = number tracks per surface	404
Number bytes per pack	100,000,000
Number of drives	8
Total on-line capacity per disk storage unit	800,000,000

Avg. access (head move)	30 msec
Avg. latency (rotation delay)	8.4 msec
Data rate	806 kilobytes/sec
Number bytes accessible with no arm motion = number bytes/cylinder	248 kilobytes

(*c*) IBM 3330 disk storage characteristics.

Fig. 4.2.1 Typical desk-file characteristics.

Magnetic-tape devices are of the sequential-access variety. Data are recorded as magnetic spots on typically nine positions across the *width* of the tape (Fig. 4.2.2). Such a set of nine positions may for example represent 8 information bits and 1 bit for parity checking (see Chap. 8). Corresponding to each bit position is a read/write head used for recording or sensing information on the tape. Thus data are retrieved or sent 1 byte at a time (9 bits in parallel) to the recording heads.

Assuming the tape is at rest, recording or reading can start only when the tape is accelerated to (or near) maximum speed. This delay is called the *start time;* it is on the order of 5 msec. Once the *start* period is over, tape devices deliver information at byte flow rates which are typically in the 20 to 500 kilobytes/sec range.

Tape units are usually designed to recognize and generate bit patterns, called *interrecord gaps,* which separate byte clusters that constitute the tape records. Generally, tape units are controlled by specifying that the next tape record is to be read or written. Tape records may be of any length—different length records

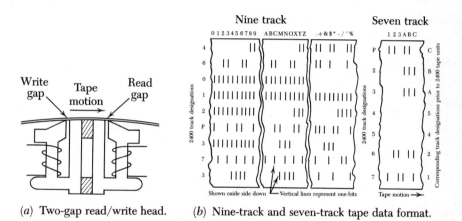

(*a*) Two-gap read/write head.   (*b*) Nine-track and seven-track tape data format.

(*c*) Blocked and unblocked records.

Fig. 4.2.2 IBM 2400 series magnetic tape.

Device	Typical values
Magnetic-core storage:	
Capacity, megabits	0.065-8
Access time, μsec	0.25-4
Cycle time, μsec	0.5-8
Bandwidth (flow rate), megabits/sec	8-64
Magnetic drum:	
Capacity, megabits	6-32
Access time (average), msec	8
Bandwidth (flow rate), megabits/sec	1-8
Magnetic disk:	
Capacity, megabits	20-2000
Access to a cylinder (SEEK), msec	80 (avg)
Rotation delay, msec	10 (avg)
Capacity of one cylinder, megabits	0.2-1
Bandwidth (flow rate), megabits/sec	2.4
Magnetic tape:	
Capacity (one reel), megabits	100-500
Start-stop (access) time, msec	3-10
Flow rate, megabits/sec	0.15-2.5

Fig. 4.2.3   Parameters of storage devices with typical values in year 1965.

may exist on the same tape. The programmer also usually considers this information on tape as organized into records. For example, a subroutine or one employee's payroll record are typical problem records. It is not necessary for each problem record to correspond directly with a tape record. In fact, it is quite feasible and advantageous to *block* records; i.e., group several problem records into a block, each block of problem records constitutes a single tape record. Blocking improves the speed at which records can be read or written and saves gap space since most gaps between individual records are eliminated. The choice of size of a block is an important programming problem—this depends on many factors, particularly the amount of processor storage that can be allocated for *buffering* the records, i.e., for accumulating the flow from (or to) tape.

4.3 METHODS OF CONTROLLING TRANSMISSION

Auxiliary storage devices usually have rather long access delays but good flow rates once the access delay is over. This suggests that flow from such devices should be in the form of long strings of data.† Maintenance of continuous flow is a problem that can be visualized with the aid of a fluid analogy. Picture a pipe supplied at one end with fluid at a steady rate while at the same time a pumping action removes fluid from the other end. It is required that inflow be maintained although outflow is occasionally stopped. In the computer case, this stoppage may be due to competition of other devices for processor storage cycles or other timing reasons. In any case, a storage device called a *buffer* is required to accumulate inflow during the intervals when outflow is blocked. Simple flow-conservation principles dictate that over long-enough time intervals, the average outflow rate must equal or exceed the average inflow rate. With this understood, the buffer can free the system from many detailed timing constraints and tolerances.

The buffer principle appears in many equipment and programming problems. For example, a two-register buffer is frequently used in flow control from a tape device to processor storage. As one buffer register is filled from tape, it is emptied into the other and a signal is sent requesting a processor storage cycle. While this register is awaiting service, the other continues to accept the flow from tape.

There are several methods of specifying control of flow. All require the following facilities:

1. Selection of the desired device.
2. Description of the record in storage. Typically, this consists of a starting location (address) of the record in processor storage and a count of the number of words or bytes to be transmitted.
3. Update of location of data in processor storage.
4. Indication of end-of-transmission.

Perhaps the simplest implementation is to add a very few instructions to the machine's repertoire. One of these is a SELECT instruction that typically selects the device and initiates access and flow into the buffer. A READ instruction transmits one word (say) from buffer to processor storage. Since successive words are usually entered into successive storage locations, the address of the destination is updated by a fixed value after each word transmitted. The address update and test-for-completion may be done by the usual program means by including instructions for them (as well as the READ instruction) in a program loop called a *copy loop*. The copy-loop method is economical since it relies on already present program-control facilities. For the same reason, the copy-loop method gives full program logical power for address updating and counting.

---

†Transmission is assumed to be from external device *to* processor storage (READ). Similar considerations apply to flow in the opposite direction (WRITE).

Disadvantages of the copy-loop method are that it may not be able to control high data rates, and it requires the programmer to time the execution of the copy loop so that the interval between execution of successive READ instructions is no longer than buffer-fill time. This can be a difficult restriction on the programmer, especially if he attempts other program execution aside from copy-loop instructions between READ executions.

Another approach to control is typified by a logical device called a *channel,* which may be viewed as a special-purpose computer whose command-set is specialized for control of transmission between main storage and other devices. A channel command (or control word) typically specifies all of the parameters necessary for transmission of a block of information between a device and processor storage. Commands may be "chained" to form a channel program; i.e., after each block transmission is complete, the channel may automatically access the description for the control of the next block. Since the channel controls functions that are logically independent from the processor, channel operations may be overlapped with computing.

Although the channel program runs independently of the processor, the latter controls initiation of a channel program. The processor can also sense the state of a channel for decision making on starting the channel on a new program. When a channel has completed executing a chain of commands, it typically sends an "interrupt" signal to the processor. For more details on this see Chaps. 9 and 10.

4.4   CYCLE STEALING AND I/O-COMPUTE OVERLAP

A system that permits logically independent control of transmission between processor storage and an input/output (I/O) device can be organized to overlap I/O transmission and computation. To understand the basic principle, the following ideas should be understood: (1) I/O transmission control and the processor each require storage cycles. (2) Because of relatively slow speed, I/O requests for cycles are usually (especially in the larger machines) far less frequent than for the processor. (3) The I/O flow must generally be maintained or there will be a long delay for reaccess. Access by the processor may, however, be delayed with no severe access penalty. One method of storage access control is to make storage switchable to the processor and each I/O controller. The switch is controlled by demand from these units; in the event of competition among them on any given cycle, priority is given to the controllers since they are penalized most if their request to unload their buffers are not satisfied. In the usual case, especially for fast processors, most cycles will be taken by the processor; occasionally an I/O channel will require and "steal" a memory cycle to empty its buffer register into storage on READ, or refill its buffer from storage on **WRITE**. The storage cycle to satisfy the I/O may delay execution of the processor instruction, but only if the processor requires storage access at the same time.

Aside from "stealing" storage cycles for transmission of data, the logical I/O controllers may make other demands on storage or even the processor. For example, each I/O controller must update an address to storage for the next byte and count to completion the block of bytes being transferred. Such updating of control information may be done by separate independent circuits in the controller. An alternative is to hold this information for each controller in processor storage and move these as required to one set of registers for updating. These may even be processor registers! In these latter cases the economies of timesharing common logic registers for control operations are at the expense of delays in processing due to more storage cycles for the access and return of control information held in storage. These cycles are in addition to cycles taken for transmission.

The general phenomenon of delay in processing due to all I/O demands is called *interference*. It may be expressed as the percent of the total number of storage cycles taken for I/O activity.

Interference is a function of the way the I/O controllers are implemented as well as the problem being run. Although its effect is to lengthen the run time of

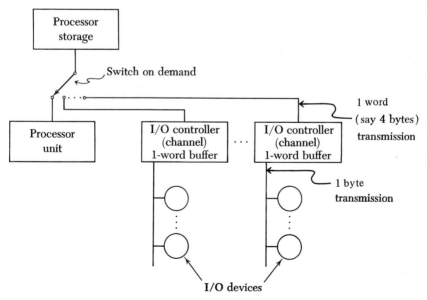

Fig. 4.4.1   Schematic of cycle stealing.

a problem, especially where there is heavy I/O activity, it need not have any effect on the logic of the program. Interference is generally most important in smaller systems where the economy incentives are the greatest and the processor is slower relative to I/O rates than in the larger systems.

The cycle-stealing principle not only permits concurrency between I/O and processor activity, it also permits sharing of the large processor storage for I/O buffering, i.e., for accumulating flow from an external device so that continuous flow may proceed without loss of information. Because of the low cycle time of processor storage and the facility to break in at these small intervals, the I/O controller need only have a small (and hence cheap) buffer to accumulate one storage word (or less) of information.

4.5   A SIMPLE MODEL FOR I/O-COMPUTE OVERLAP

To illustrate some of the relationships between computation time, I/O flow and access times, and the size of blocks (and buffer areas), a simple model of a system processing uniform-size records will be described. Assume equal computing time for all records. Of the several possibilities shown in Fig. 4.5.1, the discussion corresponds to (b), i.e., input overlapped with compute. Finally, assume that the flow of records (and computation) has reached a steady-state condition; i.e., we neglect considerations at the very start or end of the entire job.

The model assumes that uniform-size physical records flow between the storage device and processor storage in blocks of r problem records. The time to transfer r records is given by

(1) $t_b \equiv t_a + rk_f$

where $t_a \equiv$ one-time interval per block of r records, e.g., start time for tape
   $r \equiv$ number of problem records in the block
   $k_f \equiv$ time to flow one problem record
The time for the processor to process the block of r records is

(2) $t_p \equiv t_s + rk_p$

(3) $k_p \equiv k_p' + k_i$

where $t_s \equiv$ one-time interval per block of records required for processing, e.g., time to execute the Input/Output Control system (IOCS) routine to initiate block transmission
   $k_p \equiv$ elapsed processor time per record (not counting t_s)

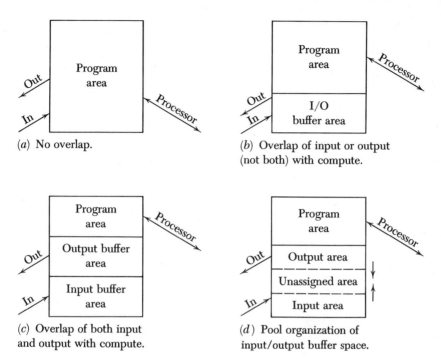

(a) No overlap.

(b) Overlap of input or output (not both) with compute.

(c) Overlap of both input and output with compute.

(d) Pool organization of input/output buffer space.

Fig. 4.5.1 Simple models of overlap.

Equation (3) is simply a reminder that k_p is the sum of two parts; one is processing time per record k_p' and the other is the CPU interference time per record k_i.

Now in a strictly sequential system, i.e., one with no overlap, the time to completely process the block of r records is the sum of t_p and t_b, Eqs. (1) and (2). In an overlapped system, however, computation, access, and flow may take place, at least to some extent, at the same time. In fact, *if the smaller of t_p, t_b can be overlapped with the larger, the elapsed time will be the larger of the two.* As a measure of the degree of overlap, the ratio of t_p to t_b is defined

(4)　　$u \equiv \dfrac{t_p}{t_b}$

If $t_p > t_b$, the time to process r records is larger than the time for them to enter the buffer area of storage; the system is then said to be processor-bound. This and the other two cases may be stated as

(5)　　$u > 1$　　or　　$t_p > t_b$　　processor-bound

(6) $u \equiv 1$ or $t_p \equiv t_b$ balanced

(7) $u < 1$ or $t_p < t_b$ I/O-bound

Dividing Eq. (2) by Eq. (1),

(8) $$\frac{t_p}{t_b} \equiv u \equiv \frac{t_s + r k_p}{t_a + r k_f}$$

One important decision in such a system is the value of r, since r multiplied by the number of bytes per record is the needed area in core storage to receive the flow (on READ). Not only must there be space in processor storage for *buffering* (accumulating) the r records, but space for the r records currently being processed must also be provided (in addition to space for the program). To understand how the value of r can be determined, solve Eq. (8) for r and use the nearest integer equal or higher than the value obtained.

(9) $$r \equiv \left\lceil \frac{u t_a - t_s}{k_p - u k_f} \right.$$

For all parameters fixed except u, Eq. (9) indicates that as u rises from a small value, i.e., to the case of processor-bound operation, the required block size increases. A particular case of interest is balanced overlap, that is, $u \equiv 1$ in Eq. (9)

(10) $$r_0 \equiv \left\lceil \frac{t_a - t_s}{k_p - k_f} \right.$$

Equation (10) shows that if the time to flow one record (k_f) is equal to the time to process one record (k_p), then the buffer size required is infinite; i.e., it is impossible to obtain full overlap. This is because access time is then an excess interval over which the processor can have no work available. If k_p, the processor time per record, is larger than flow time per record, the required buffer size increases directly as the difference between access and overhead time $t_a - t_s$.

The elapsed time to process each of r records is the larger of the total elapsed time due to processing or I/O alone.

(11) $$\frac{t_p}{r} \equiv k_p + \frac{t_s}{r}$$

(12) $$\frac{t_b}{r} \equiv k_f + \frac{t_a}{r}$$

A typical schematic plot of Eqs. (11) and (12) with r as the independent variable is shown in Fig. 4.5.2. The time for any value of r is the larger of the two ordinate values. For a small buffer, the system is I/O-limited; for a larger buffer it is processor-limited.

Notice that the curves indicate that little is gained in improved performance as the buffer size increases beyond a certain point. If t_s is 0, this value of r is the value at $u \equiv 1$, Eq. (10). For t_s nonzero there is some speed improvement with larger and larger block sizes.

The identical form of the equations for t_b and t_p suggests that each plot of these functions represents two sets of curves; the second can be obtained from the first by systematic interchange of variables.

The equations also indicate that if

$$t_a > t_s$$

and

$$k_f > k_p$$

complete overlap is not possible (since the curves do not intersect). It is also not possible if both inequalities are reversed.

Thus far, the problem of buffer size and its relationship to timing parameters to achieve a high degree of overlap has been considered. We now turn to the

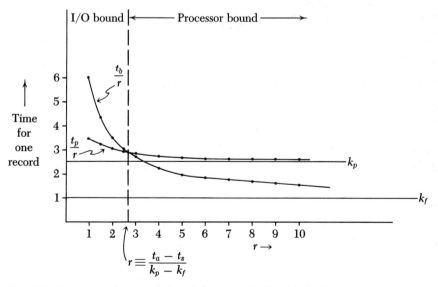

Fig. 4.5.2 Representative plot of elapsed time versus buffer (block) size.

design of a program to control input, output, and compute phases of a task which must obtain blocks of data from auxiliary storage, process it, and return the result to auxiliary storage. Assume the system to include two I/O channels so that input of the soon-to-be processed data and output of completed data can be transmitted concurrently with computation on the current data (see Fig. 4.5.1c).

Processor storage is partitioned into three areas called input buffer, compute or work area, and output buffer. The logic of the program demands that the data flows of a block of problem data be in the order:

Input device → input buffer → work area → output buffer → output device

Although a given batch of data must follow this sequence, the system may have several of these phases in progress at one time on different batches of data. Each phase may require a different amount of time for its completion than the other phases; in fact, completion time may be data-dependent. The problem is to so organize the control of flow of information to achieve the greatest degree of concurrent operation while ensuring that the program logic (the sequence specified above) is preserved for each batch of data.

One approach to the design of a program of this type using the two channels (and hence read-while-write-while-compute) will now be described.

To begin, it is recognized that each of the three areas can be in one and only one of three possible states at any one time:

Idle   Available for the next batch of data.
Busy   In the midst of handling a batch of data.
Ready   Completed handling a batch of data and ready to transmit it to the successor area (or modify a pointer designating the subject area as now being the successor).

The transitions between states for each of the three areas are in the order:

Input buffer   Idle → busy → ready
Compute area   Idle → busy → ready
Output area   Idle → busy

(The output area does not have a ready state since it has no successor area.) The first step is to construct a state-transition table listing each possible state of the three areas and its successor state. Such a listing of state transitions using the abbreviations B for busy, R for ready, and I for idle is shown in Fig. 4.5.3. Also listed with each state transition is the source of the signal which initiates the transition. The following signals are presumed available to initiate state transitions:

Initiation signal	Current state			Next state		
	Input area	Compute area	Output area	Input area	Compute area	Output area
i	B	I	I	R	I	I
i	B	I	B	R	I	B
i	B	B	I	R	B	I
i	B	B	B	R	B	B
i	B	R	I	R	R	I
i	B	R	B	R	R	B
c	I	B	I	I	R	I
c	I	B	B	I	R	B
c	B	B	I	B	R	I
c	B	B	B	B	R	B
c	R	B	I	R	R	I
c	R	B	B	R	R	B
o	I	I	B	I	I	I
o	I	B	B	I	B	I
o	I	R	B	I	R	I
o	B	I	B	B	I	I
o	B	B	B	B	B	I
o	B	R	B	B	R	I
o	R	I	B	R	I	I
o	R	B	B	R	B	I
o	R	R	B	R	R	I
START	I	I	I	B	I	I
cp/LAST	I	I	B	B/I	I	B
cp/LAST	I	B	I	B/I	B	I
cp/LAST	I	B	B	B/I	B	B
cp/LAST	I	R	I	B/I	I	B
cp/LAST	I	R	B	B/I	R	B
cp	B	I	I	B	I	I
cp	B	I	B	B	I	B
cp	B	B	I	B	B	I
cp	B	B	B	B	B	B
cp	B	R	I	B	I	B
cp	B	R	B	B	R	B
cp/LAST	R	I	I	B/I	B	I
cp/LAST	R	I	B	B/I	B	B
cp/LAST	R	B	I	R	B	I
cp/LAST	R	B	B	R	B	B
cp/LAST	R	R	I	B/I	B	B
cp	R	R	B	R	R	B

Fig. 4.5.3 State transitions for a two-channel I/O system.

i   Input operation complete
o   Output operation complete
c   Compute operation complete

For the moment, consider state transitions due to these signals only. Although all possible combinations of signals and states can be listed, it is easy to see that some will never occur and need not be shown. For example, since an i signal denotes completion of an input operation, it must accompany an input-area state of B, and hence rows whose arguments are of the form iIXX or iRXX need not be listed. Similar reasoning excludes rows whose arguments are of the form cXRX, cXIX, or oXXI. Each row of the function side of the table gives the next state corresponding to the argument side of the corresponding row. This is obtained by changing only the state of the area signaling completion to R (ready). In constructing the table, all rows are considered independently of all other rows, and rows can be listed in any order although a systematic enumeration is indicated.

The next task in table construction is the cp (control-program) section of the table. The major purpose of the cp is to start new operations wherever possible. Using this principle, the next-state entries are determined and listed.

In addition to the i, o, and c signals, the control program is also assumed to receive two less-frequent signals: START and LAST, denoting the start of the program and a notification that the last record has entered the input area. Although these could be shown in separate rows, compaction of space in the table is gained by showing each with a slash separating a LAST entry from one due to some other signal.

After constructing the large table, it is partitioned into four smaller tables, each for a signal initiating signal (see Fig. 4.5.4). Also, any row whose current state cannot be found somewhere as a next state (except for START) may be deleted. The cp table is accompanied by an explanation of the action taken to accompany each state transition (in practice, each of these would be a branch to a subroutine to execute the action).

The tables constitute the heart of the program logic. They are referenced by a simple scan program whose function will now be described. Consider that the system is in one of its states with an ongoing execution. Eventually, an i, o, or c signal will be generated. As indicated previously, this causes a machine interrupt that includes identification of the signal. The scan program then:

1. Uses the signal to be searched.
2. Searches this table using the current state as an argument. When a match is found, the next state becomes the new current state.
3. The current state is used as an argument to the cp table. If a match is found, the next state replaces the current state, the action is taken, and execution

returns to the preinterrupt activity or continues with a new activity. If no match is found, this indicates an error in constructing the tables.

EXAMPLE: Consider that the current state is BBB when a c (interrupt) signal is received denoting completion of processing in the compute area. The c table is search with BBB and the new state is found to be BRB. Using this in the cp

i table		*c table*		*o table*		
States		*States*		*States*		
Current	*Next*	*Current*	*Next*	*Current*	*Next*	
BII	RII	IBI	IRI	IIB	III	→ PROGRAM
BIB	RIB	IBB	IRB	IBB	IBI	ENDS
BBI	RBI	BBI	BRI	IRB	IRI	
BBB	RBB	BBB	BRB	BIB	BII	
BRI	RRI	RBI	RRI	BBB	BBI	
BRB	RRB	RBB	RRB	BRB	BRI	
				RIB	RII	
				RBB	RBI	
				RRB	RRI	

cp and cp/LAST table

Signal	States		Action taken followed by return to prior activity
	Current	*Next*	
cp/START	III	BII	Start input (and start program)
cp/LAST	IIB	–/I,IB	cp–not enterable; LAST (no action)
cp/LAST	IBI	B/I,BI	cp–start input; LAST (no action)
cp/LAST	IBB	B/I,BB	cp–start input; LAST (no action)
cp/LAST	IRI	B/I,IB	Move c to o, start output; cp–start input
cp/LAST	IRB	B/I,RB	cp–start input; LAST (no action)
cp	BII	BII	
cp	BIB	BIB	
cp	BBI	BBI	
cp	BBB	BBB	
cp	BRI	BIB	Move c to o, start output
cp	BRB	BRB	
cp/LAST	RII	B/I,BI	Move i to c, start compute; cp–start input
cp/LAST	RIB	B/I,BB	Move i to c, start compute; cp–start input
cp	RBI	RBI	
cp	RBB	RBB	
cp/LAST	RRI	B/I,BB	Move c to o, i to c, start compute, output; cp –start input
cp	RRB	RRB	

Fig. 4.5.4   Partitions of state-transition table by initiating signal.

table, it is seen that no new activity is started and control returns to the ongoing i and o activities, the state remaining at BRB. Eventually, say an o interrupt is next received. Using the state BRB to the o table, the new state is BRI. Using this state to the cp table, the action is to move the c area to o and start the output activity. (Instead of moving the data, pointers to the areas may be changed.) The state is now BIB. The above process now continues with new interrupts processed in a similar manner.

The table method of program organization is especially valuable for some nonnumerical problems, such as the one illustrated above, and for syntax-analysis procedures used in many compilers. It is also closely related to the technique used to design sequential circuits (see Chap. 7). A major advantage of this organization of a program over a pure procedure (without tables) is systematic consideration of *all* cases in a routine manner. In some problems, the table would be too large, and a procedure approach or a combination of procedure and the table method may be advantageous.

4.6 STATEMENT OF A SEARCH PROBLEM

A basic requirement appearing in many data-processing problems is the need to search a mass of information for certain information associated with specific information on hand. The latter is called the *search argument.*

We begin with some terminology and symbol definitions for an abstract statement of a search problem.

F	Denotes a *file,* here considered as a matrix of characters.
$F[I;]$	Denotes record I of the file (also called item I).
$F[;J]$	Denotes character position J of *all* records of the file. $F[;J]$ is a column vector of F.
X	Denotes an argument to be used as the basis of search. X will usually correspond to a part of a record and is here considered a vector of characters.
M	Denotes a *mask* or *format* bit vector which specifies by its "1" elements which columns of F are to participate in the search.
$K \equiv M/\iota(\rho F)[2]$	Denotes the position (columns) of F which participate in the search. The vector K is called the *key.* Note the simple correspondence between the key and the mask M and that $\rho X \equiv +/M$.

With the above terminology, a simple but common search problem may be stated in words as: Given a file F, a format vector M, and argument X. Find G, a submatrix of F containing all those records of F whose contents in the key positions match the argument.

An expression for G is

(1) $G \equiv ((M/F) \wedge . = X)/[1]F$

This may be understood by decomposing the expression into its parts:

(2) M/F

selects from F only those columns of F which correspond to the key specified by M.

(3) $(M/F) \wedge . = X$

is a bit vector, each element corresponding to a row of F. The Ith bit of this vector is 1 if the corresponding row of F (item in F) contains a match to the argument X.

i	Employee number				Last name						Dept.			ED code		Other fields
	0	1	2	3	4	5	6	7	8	9	10	11	12	13	14	
0	0	3	0	0	A	B	L	E	–	–	2	7	5	0	3	. . . .
1	0	4	0	1	J	O	N	E	S	–	4	8	2	0	1	. . . .
2	0	5	0	2	B	R	O	W	N	–	0	3	5	0	5	. . . .
3	0	2	0	3	S	M	I	T	H	–	2	6	1	0	4	. . . .
4																
5																
6																
7																
8																
9																

File search for equality

Argument $X \equiv 2,7,5,0,4$

Key $K \equiv 10,11,12,13,14 \equiv$ department and education code

Key mask $M \equiv 0,0,0,0,0,0,0,0,0,0,1,1,1,1,1,0, \ldots ,0$

Fig. 4.6.1   Example of file and search terminology.

Using (3) to select rows (compression on columns) of F gives Eq. (1), which is capable of two distinct interpretations:

1. A precise definition of the search problem stated in words above.
2. By using the definitions of the operators in sequence, Eq. (1) describes a procedure for finding all the records whose key-fields match the argument by a linear (successive) search through each record of F.

4.7 BIT MAPS VERSUS INDEX VECTORS

In considering the ways to represent the results of a search, three approaches may be contrasted. The first, which may be called direct, is simply an accumulation of all items which satisfied the search. The second method is an indirect representation whereby a bit map U gives the result of the search by $U[I]$ being 1 if item I satisfied the search; otherwise, $U[I]$ is set to 0. The search map U may be used to compress the matrix of items to extract those which satisfied the search. If the compression is done with $\sim U$ instead of U, then all items not satisfying the search will be extracted. Another important use of U is to take its sum reduction; this results in the count of the number of items which satisfied the search. In still another application of the map representation several map vectors are available where each was derived from a different search criterion. In this case, the set of U vectors may be combined to satisfy complex search criteria by using logical operators to derive a final map used for selection. This may well have an advantage in speed of processing because only access to the maps, not to the much more voluminous file is required.

A third method of representing the results of a search is a vector of index values "pointing" to those items which satisfied the search. This approach can be much more economical in storage than the bit map if the density of search "hits" is small. For example, consider a file with 1000 items of which no more than 10 can possibly satisfy a certain search criterion. The map approach requires 1000 bits (one for each item). The index vector requires 10 index values, each of which must be capable of pointing to 1 of 1000 items and hence requires 10 bits. It therefore requires 100 bits in all as contrasted to 1000 bits for the map.

The discussion above may be summarized in parametric form by noting that for n items, the map requires n bits, the index list requires $\lceil \log_2 n$ bits per hit, or a total of $h \times \lceil \log_2 n$ bits in all. Figure 4.7.1 gives k, the largest value of h for which the number of bits required by the index list is at least as economical as the map. The table indicates that as larger search problems are handled, smaller hit densities are required before the index-list approach is more economical.

n	k	$k \div n$
2	2	1
4	2	0.5
8	2	0.25
16	4	0.25
32	6	0.19
64	10	0.156
128	18	0.141
256	32	0.125
512	56	0.109
1024	102	0.099
2048	186	0.091
4096	341	0.083
8192	630	0.077
16,384	1170	0.072

$$k \equiv \lfloor \frac{n}{\lceil \log_2 n \rceil}$$

Fig. 4.7.1 Table giving k, the largest number of ON conditions of n conditions for which an index vector is cheaper than a bit map.

The above discussion was concerned with storage economy. As usual, processing speed should also be considered as the other primary factor in choosing a search representation. Most existing computers with random-access storage can make almost direct use of an entry in an index list by using it as an address in the item-storage matrix. The bit map on the other hand must be "decoded" by counting 0s until a 1 is encountered. This count could then be used as an index. Thus, the bit map would appear to require somewhat more processing than the index vector to yield usable access information.

4.8 LIST MAINTENANCE USING A SINGLE STORAGE POOL

A frequent problem in storage organization is the allocation of a pool of storage (say about N cells) to N items, where each item requires one cell and each item is identified with one of M categories, or *lists*. The number of items belonging to each list is *not* known in advance. Furthermore, it is desired that all items of any given list be accessible without the need to search items of any other list. An example of this kind of structure is shown in Fig. 4.8.1 where the file is represented as a vector of single-integer items F and a chaining or pointer vector C for each item in F. There is also a *category directory* vector D. The elements of these vectors have the following meanings:

	C	F			C	F			C	F	Remarks
1	2	0		1	0	222		1	0	222	Last on list 2
2	3	0		2	0	333		2	0	333	Last on list 3
3	4	0		3	0	444		3	0	444	Last on list 4
4	5	0		4	1	222		4	1	222	
5	6	0		5	3	444		5	3	444	
6	7	0		6	2	333		6	2	333	
7	8	0		7	4	222		7	4	222	
8	9	0		8	7	222		8	7	222	First on list 2
9	10	0		9	8	222		9	12	222	First on free list
10	11	0		10	5	444		10	5	444	First on list 4
11	12	0		11	6	333		11	6	333	First on list 3
12	13	0		12	13	0		12	13	0	
13	14	0		13	14	0		13	14	0	
14	15	0		14	15	0		14	15	0	
15	0	0		15	0	0		15	0	0	

D | 1 0 0 0 0 | D | 12 9 11 10 0 | D | 9 8 11 10 0

List no. 1 2 3 4 5   1 2 3 4 5   1 2 3 4 5

(a) Initial after *STLIST*   (b) After a sequence of *ENTER*s.   (c) Lists of (b) after 222 *DELETE* 2.

Note: List 1 is the free list.

Fig. 4.8.1 Snapshots of list structure at 3 times.

$F[I]$ Contents of cell I holding one item (file entry).

$C[I]$ Pointer to the index of the next file entry which is on the same list as $F[I]$. $C[I]=0$ indicates end-of-list.

$D[J]$ Pointer to the *first* cell of a chain of cells linking the items of list J. $D[J]=0$ indicates that the J list is empty.

Part (a) of the figure shows the storage and pointers before any entries are made. List 1 is, by convention here, the free list, i.e., the list of unused cells. Thus at start-up, $D[1]\equiv1$, $C[1]=2$, $C[2]=3$, etc., placing all cells of F on the free list. Although F values of 0 are shown initially in the empty cells, this is *not* essential. Part (*b*) shows the state of the storage after several entries have been made into cells belonging to two lists. Part (*c*) shows the state of the storage after a *DELETE* operation on the storage state of part (*b*).

It is very helpful to notice that since the location (index) in F of the first item on list J is easily found as $D[J]$, it is fastest to insert new items in front of the first item on a list. It follows that the latest items entered are the first encountered in each list. For this reason, the type of list shown is called last in, first out.

Before proceeding to the programs for entering, deleting, and searching the lists, the reader is advised to study Fig. 4.8.1 and follow the pointers to identify the lists and how they change with entry and deletion.

The functions shown in Fig. 4.8.2 are typical of those used to maintain a list structure but also include list printouts for tutorial reasons. They may be briefly described as follows:

$\nabla STLIST$	Initializes list structure using parameters supplied by the user specifying the total number of items SS and number of lists NC
$\nabla X\ ENTER\ J$	Enters item value X into list J
$\nabla X\ DELETE\ J$	Deletes the first item having value X from list J. Note that this fucntion calls the function $FIND$
$\nabla X\ FIND\ J$	Determines I, the index of the first occurrence of X in list J
$\nabla P\ PFIND\ J$	Determines I, the index of the Pth item in list J
$\nabla II{\leftarrow}CHAIN\ I$	Moves down a specified chain by one item; checks for end of chain
$\nabla TEST\ J$	Tests for whether requested list J is illegal or empty

The list scheme shown is an important example of a *data structure,* i.e., a way to organize information through the relationships existing in the data, in this case a scheme of pointers. The flexibility of use of storage is its main advantage in the example illustrated; the items belonging to each list are "in one place" logically, and this is so even though we do not know in advance how many items are to be on each list and these may be changing from one moment to the next. The price of this flexibility is twofold:

1. Space for the pointers and for the list programs
2. The time to execute the list programs

The first is relatively smaller the larger the item compared to the size of the pointer value. Often the items are records of several (say 80) bytes while the pointers are typically 4 or 5 bytes each. The execution time of the programs to deal with the list structure can be appreciable, but it is minimized by certain techniques discussed in the next section.

We should emphasize that we have illustrated only a most elementary kind of list structure. A more powerful type permits items to be of different lengths and also allows an indefinite number of lists; i.e., each item may start a new list. In

```
      ∇ STLIST
[1]    'ENTER NO. CELLS FOR ITEM STORAGE'
[2]    SS←□
[3]    'ENTER NUMBER OF CATEGORIES TO BE KEPT BY LISTS'
[4]    NC←□
[5]    D←NCρ0
[6]    D[1]←1
[7]    F←(SS)ρ0
[8]    C←(1+ι(⁻1+SS)),0
[9]    C[ρC]←0
[10]   (3,SS)ρ(ιSS),C,F
[11]   D
      ∇
      ∇ENTER[□]∇
      ∇ X ENTER J
[1]    →(J>ρD)/EM1
[2]    →(D[1]=0)/EM2
[3]    I←D[1]
[4]    D[1]←C[I]
[5]    C[I]←0
[6]    F[I]←X
[7]    →(D[J]=0)/FINIENT
[8]    C[I]←D[J]
[9]    FINIENT:D[J]←I
[10]   (3,SS)ρ(ιSS),C,F
[11]   D
[12]   →0
[13]   EM1:'UNDEFINED LIST'
[14]   →0
[15]   EM2:'NO SPACE AVAILABLE IN STORAGE'
[16]   →0
      ∇
      ∇DELETE[□]∇
      ∇ X DELETE J
[1]    X FIND J
[2]    →(K≠0)/CREP
[3]    D[J]←C[I]
[4]    →SKPDEL
[5]    CREP:C[K]←C[I]
[6]    SKPDEL:C[I]←D[1]
[7]    D[1]←I
[8]    (3,SS)ρ(ιSS),C,F
[9]    D
      ∇
```

Fig. 4.8.2 List processing functions.

```
      ∇TEST[□]∇
    ∇ TEST J
[1]   →(J>ρD)/ER1
[2]   →(D[J]=0)/ER2
[3]   I←D[J]
[4]   K←0
[5]   →0
[6]  ER1:'LIST IS ILLEGAL'
[7]   →
[8]  ER2:'LIST IS EMPTY'
[9]   →
    ∇

      ∇CHAIN[□]∇
    ∇ II←CHAIN I
[1]   →(C[I]=0)/ER1CH
[2]   K←I
[3]   II←C[I]
[4]   →0
[5]  ER1CH:'END OF LIST REACHED, NO MATCH'
[6]   M←II←0
[7]   →
    ∇

      ∇FIND[□]∇
    ∇ X FIND J
[1]   TEST J
[2]  TSTTST:→(X=F[I])/FNFINI
[3]   I←II←CHAIN I
[4]   →(I=0)/FNFINI
[5]   →TSTTST
[6]  FNFINI:→0
[7]   →0
    ∇

      ∇PFIND[□]∇
    ∇ P PFIND J
[1]   TEST J
[2]   II←I
[3]   M←P-1
[4]  MTST:→(M≤0)/PFNDFIN
[5]   I←II←CHAIN I
[6]   M←M-1
[7]   →MTST
[8]  PFNDFIN:→0
    ∇
```

Fig. 4.8.2   List processing functions (continued).

many such structures, the unused space is not kept on a chained free list. Instead, all unused space begins as a contiguous string of cells available for allocation to new items. Deleted items are marked as "garbage" to be retrieved later. When the structure exhausts its contiguous unused space, it then calls a "garbage collection" program that reorganizes the storage so that all used items are in one contiguous part of the storage and the unused space is in the remaining contiguous area. This kind of scheme can be faster for entry and deletion of items since no manipulation of the free list is required. This is especially true if the items are of variable size. The equivalent of free-list operations are of course done during garbage collection, but this occurs only when necessary.

4.9 SOME FACTORS IN FILE ORGANIZATION

Files exist only because of the information they contain. Extraction of file information will be called *file searching.* The purposes of search are of course many and diverse—updating records, report generation, etc. In this chapter we are interested less in the motivation than in the technique for search.

A basic factor in the organization of any file is the knowledge *at file load time* of certain parameters of the file search. In general, the more known at file load time about how the information in the file is to be accessed, the better the file-search algorithm which can be devised. Conversely, if knowledge is lacking at load time of the type of information desired from the file, an efficient search procedure will not be possible. In a sense, then, file search may be considered to start at file load time rather than just when the search argument is presented to the search procedure. This is true because search can be made faster by proper placement of data and control information.

In some cases, it will be necessary to accumulate large volumes of information and only subsequently specify the nature of the search arguments. Such a situation, which arises in real-time telemetering and other applications, represents a difficult challenge to system innovation. These are examples of unavoidable ignorance (or uncertainty) of the nature of the search at file load time. On the other hand, every effort should be made to identify at least the high-activity file-search properties and use them as inputs to design the file organization.

The identification of high-activity items, i.e., those that are referenced very frequently, can be a major factor in achieving high performance. An old rule of thumb, called the *80-20 rule,* asserts that in many systems 80 percent of the accesses are to 20 percent of the records. Although there is nothing sacred about these particular numbers, many actual files exhibit similar activity. In some cases it is possible to predict in advance which records are the high-activity ones. It is more reliable, however, and quite feasible for the file-processing program to keep a frequency-of-access counter with each record (or block of records). This of course assumes that the records referenced most frequently in the past will be most active in the future. Once the high-activity records are identified, the

A. Application description
  1. File size
  2. Single or multiple keys
     a. Dominance (frequencies of access) of keys
  3. Allowable number of arguments in a batch
  4. Activity
     a. Access activity
     b. Change activity
     c. Knowledge of high-activity items
  5. Ratio of argument size to item size
  6. Homogeneity of item size
  7. Homogeneity of argument size

B. Description of storage medium
  1. Tape
     a. Start/stop time
     b. Character flow time
     c. Read forward/backward
     d. Rewind time
     e. Record gap time
     f. Capacity
  2. Disk
     a. Seek time(s)
     b. Rotation time
     c. Character flow time
     d. Maximum number of characters available in 1 seek time
     e. Capacity
     f. Number of concurrent seeks possible
  3. Core storage
     a. Cycle time
     b. Memory bandwidth
     c. Capacity

C. System organization
     a. Number of logical channels
     b. Core storage interference factor per channel
     c. In nonchannel systems, number of instruction executions to control I/O byte entry or exit
     d. Types and extent of overlap
     e. Special autonomous search mechanism
     f. Number of storage units per channel

Fig. 4.9.1 Check list of file processing parameters.

strategy is to move them into the places in the storage structure where access is fastest. For example, if the system storage consists of a hierarchy of small fast devices and large slower ones, the highest-activity items should be moved to the fastest store. Even if only one type of device is used, organization of the records to reflect frequency of use can be very beneficial. For example, consider the list structure discussed in Sec. 4.8. Since all records in a given category are chained in sequence, to find an item, the list must be searched sequentially. The number of probes into the list will be fewer and hence the speed faster if the more frequently accessed records are kept closest to the start of the list. This ordering is quite different from ordering the records according to when they arrived to the structure. Of course, reordering a list itself requires processing. This processing is justified in those cases where there will be a sufficiently high frequency of accesses for each execution of the reordering procedure.

Figure 4.9.1 lists some of the factors to be considered in designing a file system. The above discussion relates particularly to the application description, although all the factors have an important bearing on a system design. The listing is probably incomplete and very qualitative. It is centered on modeling the system for algorithm design and evaluation. Other important practical system factors, such as those that effect reliability and security against unauthorized access, are not included.

4.10 SEARCHING AND ORDERING FILES: GENERAL DISCUSSION

The interest in ordering (sorting) records on some field arises because of the ease with which an ordered file can be searched, especially where only serial-access devices (such as tapes) are available for storage. With serial-access devices, there is little advantage to ordering the file if it is only required to search for a single argument, since it is necessary in any case to pass all of the file past the argument (and compare each record with the argument) in order to be certain that the matching entry is found. The situation is, however, quite different if n arguments (called the *activity file*) are to be used to search another file (called the *master file*) of N records. Now, if both files are unordered, it will take at most about n passes through the master file to be sure of finding all matching entries, or approximately p operations where

(1) $p \equiv nN$ assume $N \gg n$

If, however, the files are ordered, then the maximum number of operations is approximately

(2) $p \equiv N + n$ if duplicates may be present

(3) $p \equiv N$ if no duplicates

The search is done by passing the master file past the first entry of the activity file until a match is found. If it known that there are no duplicates, the search of the master would then be continued using the next argument of the activity file, etc. The fact that the files are ordered ensures that all matches will be found in a single pass.

These two simple alternate ways of searching illustrate the effect of batching (collecting) search arguments before starting the search; in particular, the larger the "batch" of search arguments (activity file) the more it pays to order the files before searching. "Traditional" commercial file processing almost always is done by batching activity items, sorting them to form an activity file and searching (or updating) by passing it against the ordered master file. The updated master file produced is ordered by this process.

The above discussion was concerned with serial-access devices for storing the files. These assume that no (or little) saving in access time can be obtained from knowledge of the position of the desired record.

It would seem that the situation would be different if the files are stored in random-access devices such as magnetic-core storage or disk files. In this case, there are indeed other techniques which may be used. However, some of these, e.g., binary search (see below), still require the file to be ordered.

The problems of searching or file updating thus naturally divide into the following broad categories:

1. Search methods: ordered files
    a. Search procedures on sorted files
    b. Methods of ordering (sorting)
2. Search methods: unordered files

4.11 UPDATING ORDERED FILES

Figure 4.11.1 shows a program for a very common type of file-update problem often encountered in commercial data processing. To simplify the exposition, file items are here considered to be single numbers rather than the character (byte) records that would be found in practice. Despite this simplification, the basic logic of the program is quite typical. Two files, *both ordered low to high,* are to be combined to produce a single result file. One of the files M, called the *master,* represents the current records, say of customer accounts. The second file A, called the *activity,* contains new information (such as purchases) to update records of M and also possibly new records for M. In the particular program illustrated, update of an existing record is indicated by the call of some update program $UPDATE$ (line 13) which depends on the particular problem being considered and is not detailed here. A new record, i.e., one in the activity file

```
      ∇ FILEMAINT
[1]   'ENTER ORDERED MASTER FILE'
[2]   M←□
[3]   M←M,99999
[4]   'ENTER ORDERED ACTIVITY FILE'
[5]   A←□
[6]   A←A,99999
[7]   R←⍳0
[8]   I←1
[9]   J←1
[10]  MENDTST:→(M[J]=99999)/FMTST2
[11]  →(A[I]=99999)/FMTST1
[12]  →(A[I]≠M[J])/NINSERT
[13]  B←A[I] UPDATE M[J]
[14]  →FUPDATE
[15]  NINSERT:B←(M[J],A[I])[1+M[J]>A[I]]
[16]  FUPDATE:T←I+M[J]≥A[I]
[17]  J←J+M[J]≤A[I]
[18]  I←T
[19]  R←R,B
[20]  →MENDTST
[21]  FMTST1:J FMAINTST M
[22]  →FMAINTEND
[23]  FMTST2:I FMAINTST A
[24]  FMAINTEND:R←R,99999
[25]  'THE UPDATED MASTER FILE IS:'
[26]  R
[27]  →0
      ∇

      ∇FMAINTST[□]∇
      ∇ P FMAINTST X
[1]   FSTTST:→(X[P]=99999)/0
[2]   R←R,X[P]
[3]   P←P+1
[4]   →FSTTST
      ∇

      ∇UPDATE[□]∇
      ∇ Q←A UPDATE M
[1]   Q←M
      ∇

      FILEMAINT
ENTER ORDERED MASTER FILE
□:
      3 19 27 30 35 68 96 103 125 243 554 665 777
ENTER ORDERED ACTIVITY FILE
□:
      21 38 39 105 245
THE UPDATED MASTER FILE IS:
3  19  21  27  30  35  38  39  68  96  103  105  125  243  245  554  665  777  99999
```

	Legend
	1-origin indexing
M	Master file
A	Activity file
R	Result file
99999	Record mark
UPDATE	Record-update program (not detailed here)

Fig. 4.11.1   Update of ordered master file with ordered activity file.

Line	Description
1–6	Entry of ordered master and activity files each terminating with an end-of-file mark here denoted by the integer 99999.
7	Initialize result file to null.
8, 9	Initialize pointers to activity and master files (I, J).
10	If end of master file is reached, branch to line 23.
11	If end of activity file is reached, branch to line 21.
12	If activity record does not match master record, branch to line 15.
13, 14	Since master record and activity record match, call the file-update routine (not detailed here). After return, branch to 16.
15	Specify B, the next result record, as either the old master or else the activity record.
16	Specify T as the pointer to A by increasing I by 1 (or not) as the master is (or is not) larger than the activity record.
17	Update the pointer to the master file.
18	Specify I as T.
19, 20	Append the record B to the result file R; branch to line 10.
21, 22	Calls the function *FMAINTST* to append remaining master records to result file; branch to line 24.
23	Calls the function *FMAINTST* to append remaining activity records to result file.
24–27	An end-of-file mark is placed on the end of the result file, and the result file is then printed.

Fig. 4.11.1 Update of ordered master file with ordered activity file (Continued).

not matching one in the master file, is inserted into the result file. The logic of the program proceeds from the fact that both the master and activity files are assumed to be ordered beforehand so the program can then be described as passing an ordered activity file against an ordered master to produce an ordered result file R. The result file can become the new master for the next round of updating.

For a full understanding of the logic of the program, it is suggested that the reader follow the step-by-step description with a simple example of say 10 master and 5 activity values (both vectors ordered).

The function *FMAINTST* is used to run out either the master or activity records that remain when the end-of-file mark is reached on the other file.

The fact that the files are processed on serial-access devices is indicated by the index increments of only 0 or 1.

Although, for simplicity, single-field file items were assumed, in practice there generally are several fields per item, and the files are ordered on one field but the updating of the entries is on some other field. The result file is then automatically ordered and hence is eligible for use as a master file in a later updating operation. Another important property is that *every* master-file item is accessed whether its argument field is matched by an activity argument or not. This is not necessary in methods for direct-access devices and is one reason why the latter can be faster, especially if the activity file is much smaller than the master.

4.12 PRINCIPLES OF ORDERING (SORTING)

Since the literature on sorting is vast, only a few of the many procedures (algorithms) that have been used will be described here.

A simplifying assumption made throughout the rest of this section is that only a file of arguments is to be sorted; in most practical problems each argument is part of a record. This means that either the record itself or a pointer to the record is implicitly assumed to accompany each argument.

An abstract statement of a sorting problem is as follows. Given a vector of arguments X, find P an index vector (also called a permutation vector) for X such that

(1) $X[P[I]] \geq X[P[I-1]]$ for all I

To illustrate the definition, Fig. 4.12.1 shows an example vector X together with its position numbers, followed by the required permutation vector P, followed by the sorted list $X[P]$. In many practical situations, P is not explicitly developed.

The representative sorting methods given below illustrate the fact that there is no one "best" sorting method; several algorithms exist which have important efficiency and inefficiency properties relative to each other. A short word description is given for each of three sort procedures, and the states of the partially sorted files are given as an aid in understanding each method.

The *bubble sort* is very efficient in use of storage but requires a rather large

	X	P	$X[P]$
1	382	5	004
2	004	1	042
3	249	4	101
4	101	3	249
5	042	2	382
6	777	7	706
7	706	6	777
8	999	8	999
	(*a*) Original vector	(*b*) Permutation vector	(*c*) Sorted vector

Fig. 4.12.1   Role of permutation (index) vector in sorting.

number of operations. A program is given in Fig. 4.12.2. The principle is to start at the bottom of the argument file and compare pairs of arguments in turn. The smaller argument of a pair is placed in the lower index position of the pair; the larger argument value is placed in the higher index position. The comparisons continue until element $X[1]$ has been processed. The result is that the smallest argument in the file has "bubbled" to the top position, $X[1]$. The bubbling procedure is then repeated on the result file reduced by the top member, which need not be processed any longer. The second pass bubbles the second smallest value to its proper position on the file. After $n - 1$ passes, a file of n items will be sorted. A count of the number of operations (compare and index-advance)

```
         ∇ BUBBLE P
[1]      'ENTER VECTOR'
[2]      N←ρX←,□
[3]      J←0
[4]   JUP:→(N<J←J+1)/PRINT
[5]      I←1+N
[6]   IUP:→(J≥I←I-1)/JUP
[7]      →(SWAP,IUP)[1+P≠X[I]≥X[I-1]]
[8]   SWAP:T←X[I]
[9]      X[I]←X[I-1]
[10]     X[I-1]←T
[11]     →IUP
[12] PRINT:'SORTED VECTOR:'
[13]  X
         ∇
         BUBBLE 0
ENTER VECTOR
□:
         382 4 249 101 42 777 706 999
SORTED VECTOR:
4    42   101   249   382   706   777   999
         BUBBLE 1
ENTER VECTOR
□:
         382 4 249 101 42 777 706 999
SORTED VECTOR:
999   777   706   382   249   101   42   4
```

Fig. 4.12.2 Bubble sort with option parameter.

may be made as follows: in the first pass, $n - 1$ operations are performed; in the next pass, $n - 2$ operations, etc. The total number of operations is then

$$(2) \qquad n - 1 + n - 2 + n - 3 + \cdots + 1 \equiv n \times (n - 1) \div 2$$

For large n this is approximately half the square of n. Note that very little intermediate storage space is required.

The bubble-sort algorithm discussed thus far can be improved in a number of ways. For example, it may easily be modified as shown in the program to accept a specification of whether the result file is to be in high-to-low or low-to-high order. A further improvement can be made by recognizing that for certain files of data the file may be sorted after fewer passes than the worst case of n passes. An indicator variable may be introduced and set ON at the start of each pass and set OFF after each bubble interchange. After each pass is complete, a test of the value of this indicator will determine if a subsequent pass is necessary.

Radix-sorting methods require d successive passes through the arguments, where d is the (common) number of digits (or characters) in each argument. In

Original

382	004	004	004	004	004	004	004
004	382	042	042	042	042	042	042
249	042	382	101	101	101	101	101
101	249	101	382	249	249	249	249
042	101	249	249	382	382	382	382
777	706	706	706	706	706	706	706
706	777	777	777	777	777	777	777
999	999	999	999	999	999	999	999

(*a*) Bubble sort.

Original	Pass 1	Pass 2	Pass 3
382	101	101	004
004	382	004	042
249	042	706	101
101	004	042	249
042	706	249	382
777	777	777	706
706	249	382	777
999	999	999	999

(*b*) Radix sort.

Note: For merge sort see Fig. 4.12.4.

Fig. 4.12.3   Three sort procedures on the same data vector.

the first pass, the entire file of arguments is ordered only on the rightmost (low-order) digit position of the arguments. Since the range of values of a digit position is small (0 to 9 for decimal numeric digits), the ordering may be done by pigeonholing; e.g., 10 storage areas are set up and each *complete* argument entered into the area corresponding to the *value* of its rightmost digit. In the next pass, the procedure is repeated using the second digit position (from the right) for pigeonholing and starting with the 0 pigeonhole as the source of arguments and progressing to higher-numbered ones, as each is emptied. This procedure is repeated for successive passes until all d passes have been made.

Radix sorting is very popular on punched-card equipment, largely because card storage for the pigeonhole is very cheap; each area is simply a bin on the sorter. The principal difficulty with radix sorting is that the required capacity of each pigeonhole is unpredictable and hence there is no simple way to share a pool of space among the pigeonholes. This storage-allocation problem is especially severe when sorting in core storage. There is an exception for binary radix (radix 2), since then the single core storage can be filled from each end—in effect one pigeonhole starts from the high end of storage and works downward (to lower addresses), whereas the other pigeonhole starts at the lowest end and works upward. Despite the lack of a storage-allocation problem, binary-radix sorting is still not too attractive, since it does not make use of the parallel-by-bit processing ability of most machines.

The *merge sort* in its many variations is a very efficient method from a speed viewpoint and is the most popular method used in magnetic-tape systems. To begin, it is important to understand the idea of a string; an ascending string of arguments of length n is a succession of n arguments whose successive values do not decrease. An ordered file of n arguments is simply a single string of length n. The simple binary merge assumes there is no inherent ordering in the original file, so at the start of processing, this file of n arguments is considered as being constituted of n strings each of length 1. The objective of each pass is to take *pairs* of strings and merge each pair into a single string. Thus, after each such pass, the length of each string is twice as long as the length of each string in the previous pass and there are half as many strings. Successive merge passes of this type finally result in a sorted file (a single string).

The number of passes required for an n-argument file is

$$(3) \qquad p \equiv \lceil \log_2 n$$

In each pass, there are at most n move operations. Hence the total number of operations is about

$$(4) \qquad M \equiv np \equiv n \lceil \log_2 n$$

```
     ∇ MERGE
[1]     'ENTER VECTOR'
[2]     N←ρX←,□
[3]     INC←PASS←1
[4]     Y←Nρ0
[5]   IPSET:'MERGES FOR PASS ';PASS
[6]     IP←1
[7]   UPD:II←IP+INC-1
[8]     JJ←N⌊II+INC
[9]     →(II≥JJ)/NXTPASS
[10]    MERGE2
[11]    →(KK=N)/PRINT
[12]    IP←JJ+1
[13]    →UPD
[14]  NXTPASS:→(IP=1)/PRINT
[15]    INC←INC+INC
[16]    PASS←PASS+1
[17]    →IPSET
[18]  PRINT:' SORTED VECTOR:'
[19]    X
     ∇


     ∇ MERGE2
[1]     I←IP
[2]     J←II+1
[3]     K←1
[4]   TST:→(I>II)/RUN1
[5]     →(J>JJ)/RUN2
[6]     U←X[I]≤X[J]
[7]     Y[K]←X[(J,I)[1+U]]
[8]     I←I+U
[9]     J←J+~U
[10]    K←K+1
[11]    →TST
[12]  RUN1:Y[(K-1)+ιKK]←X[(J-1)+ιKK←JJ+1-J]
[13]    →MOVE
[14]  RUN2:Y[(K-1)+ιKK]←X[(I-1)+ιKK←II+1-I]
[15]  MOVE:□←X[⁻1+IP+ιKK]←Y[ιKK←JJ+1-IP]
     ∇
```

Fig. 4.12.4 Merge sort with trace statements.

```
        MERGE
ENTER VECTOR
□:
        382  4  249  101  42  777  706  999
MERGES FOR PASS 1
4    382
101    249
42    777
706    999
MERGES FOR PASS 2
4    101    249    382
42    706    777    999
MERGES FOR PASS 3
4    42    101    249    382    706    777    999
 SORTED VECTOR:
4    42    101    249    382    706    777    999
```

	Legend	
	1-origin indexing	
X	Argument and result vector	
P	Option parameter: 0 = sort low to high 1 = sort high to low	

Fig. 4.12.4   Merge sort with trace statements (continued).

More generally, an r-way merge can be done in each pass. With this scheme, m sets of strings are merged in each pass; after k passes, each string is (at least) m^k long. The total number of passes is at most

(5) $p \equiv \lceil \log_m n$

The number of move operations is

(6) $N \equiv n \lceil \log_m n$

Characteristics of the three sort algorithms are shown in Fig. 4.12.5.

	Maximum number of passes	Maximum number of moves	Approximate number of data storage words
Bubble	$n - 1$	$n \times (n - 1) \div 2$	n
Radix (q digits, radix r)	q	$n \times q$	$n \times (r + 1)$†
Merge (m-way)	$\lceil \log_m n$	$n \times \lceil \log_m n$	$2 \times n$

†Can be reduced to $2 \times n$ by list structure for storage organization (not counting pointers).

Fig. 4.12.5   Performance comparison of three sort algorithms.

4.13 BINARY SEARCH (ORDERED FILES, DIRECT-ACCESS DEVICES)

The binary search is useful only on *ordered* files and is especially useful for random-access files. The basic idea is to probe the file successively with *midpoint* indices; each such index value is calculated from a pair of end-point values. Each index is used to extract a record and compare its key fields with the search argument. If these match, the desired record has been found and the search is complete. Otherwise, depending on the result of the comparison, one of the limits for the next index calculation is reset with the present index. The procedure is shown in Fig. 4.13.1 in example and program form.

The *maximum* number of probes in the binary search of a vector X is

$$1 + \lceil \log_2 \rho X$$

The *average* number of probes is only slightly less than the maximum:

$$(\lceil \log_2 \rho X) - 1$$

The binary search of Fig. 4.13.1 requires division by 2 and rounding operations. In a machine having binary arithmetic this is easily done by a right shift by one position. However, in a decimal machine or in binary machines without shift capability in address arithmetic, the division and shift of an address or index will be more awkward.

The division by 2 and subsequent rounding operations may be eliminated and replaced by addition/subtraction operations at search time. This is done by constructing a vector D of index increments at file load time. Although this list requires division or multiplication, this is done only once at file set-up time instead of at every search.

One of the disadvantages of the binary search follows from the property that it depends on the file being in strict order; new entries cannot be made unless the new item is inserted in its proper position which maintains the ordering. This can be a very time-consuming operation.

```
       ∇ J←A BINSEARCH X
[1]      N←⌈2⍟1+ρX
[2]      L←1
[3]      I←0
[4]      H←1+ρX
[5]    ITST:→(N<I←I+1)/NMTCH
[6]      J←⌊(L+H)÷2
[7]      →((A=X[J]),(A>X[J]))/0,UPL
[8]      H←J
[9]      →ITST
[10]   UPL:L←J
[11]     →ITST
[12]   NMTCH:'NO MATCH'
[13]     J←0
[14]     →0
       ∇
```

```
INDEX   FILE(X)   PROBE

    1      4
    2     50
    3     56
    4     64        ←2
    5     89        ←3
    6    120        ←4  →
    7    146        ←1
    8    356
    9    390
   10    760
   11    777
   12    789
   13    842
```

Fig. 4.13.1 **Binary search (for** $A \equiv 120$**).**

4.14 SEARCH OF AN UNORDERED FILE

An unsorted file can always be searched *linearly,* i.e., by comparing the argument to the first entry in the file; if there is no match, the search advances to the next entry in the file, etc., until a match is found. For a file of n items this requires at most n operations or $(n + 1) \div 2$ operations on the average. Linear searching is simple and hence requires little program space.

The advantages of sorting both the activity and master file for the case of files stored on strictly serial devices (e.g., tapes) were discussed in the previous section.

In some cases, it may be possible to contain the activity file if not the master file in a small random-access store (e.g., core storage). It may then well pay to sort the activity file, place it in the random-access storage and pass the *serial, unordered* master file past the activity file. During this process each item of the master file is used to search the activity file with the binary-search algorithm. With this procedure, the search is completed in one pass of the master file.

4.15 SEARCH OF UNORDERED FILES STORED ON DIRECT-ACCESS (RANDOM- ACCESS) DEVICES

The following classification is useful for systematic examination of some important strategies in file organization. Let

$n \equiv$ number of items in the file vector X

$d \equiv$ number of digits required to represent an item in some radix system r

For simplicity, each item is considered to be a single number (argument).

Case 1 $n \equiv r^d$, and all arguments are unique (no duplicates). Each argument can then be used as an index (address) for locating it in the file in a single access.

Case 2 $n > r^d$, which implies duplicate entries. This case may be handled efficiently as a multiple-category problem using a list organization (see Sec. 4.8).

Case 3 $n < r^d$, which is illustrated by a file of say 1 million names each 10 letters long, the letters chosen from the English alphabet of 26 letters. The number of possible names is 26^{10}, clearly greater than 10^6.

A strategy for case 3 is to find some transformation for mapping the arguments into integers in the range of addresses. However, since the set of arguments is larger than the set of addresses, the mapping is many to one; i.e., in general, several arguments may transform to the same address. These are called *transformation synonyms* and will be discussed more fully in the next sections.

Thus far nothing has been said about a specific means of performing the transformation of argument to address. One scheme applicable to the binary radix, for example, is to square the bit representation of the argument Y and select the middle k bits of the product, where k is the extent of the address. Such a process is called *randomizing* or *hashing*. Another hashing technique uses the nearest prime number P smaller than n. The transformation is the residue of Y modulo P, that is, divide Y by P and keep only the remainder

$$A \leftarrow P \mid Y$$

By the definition of the residue operation (Chap. 2), A will be in the range of indices of the file. This method will preserve some of the ordering in the arguments.

4.16   TRANSFORMATION-SYNONYM PROBLEM

The many-one nature of the argument-address transformation requires the system to handle the many arguments which may transform to the same address. Most random-access devices such as disks have the property that, following a long access delay (head movement), a rather large block of storage is available at a high transmission rate. Capacity permitting, it is then feasible to consider each such block of storage as a *bucket* capable of holding several items of the file. Since each bucket can hold several items, some synonyms can be handled without requiring additional head access. (After access to the beginning of a bucket the bucket is searched linearly.)

With completely random-access devices, e.g., core storage, there is no advantage to bucket size larger than 1.

Even in those cases where buckets larger than a single item are used, the system must still cope with bucket overflow. At load time, a synonym appears when it is found that a transformed address is already occupied. One approach, termed the *open method,* starts at the transformed address and searches linearly for the first available unfilled bucket. At file-search time, after argument-address transformation, the argument is compared with the key-fields of the item found at the addressed location; if no match is found, the search proceeds in the same direction as used at file load time.

The performance (number of file probes to find an item) of the open method of file organization depends on several factors, the most important of which are:

1. Bucket size
2. File loading factor, i.e., the fraction of the file which is actually occupied
3. Success of the hash transformation in randomizing the arguments

Analysis based on idealized models shows that for a bucket capacity of 1 and the file half loaded, an average of 1.5 probes is required to find an item. As the loading factor increases, the average number of probes increases.

Another procedure for organizing a file stored in a random-access medium is called *chaining.* It differs from the open method described above in the manner of handling the transformation synonyms. One way to describe a common chain organization is to consider the entries to be made to the file in two stages (Fig.

4.16.1). First, all nonsynonym entries are made at the transformed addresses; synonym items are set aside for entry in the second stage. After the first stage is completed, the synonyms are then entered into the empty file positions; all items that transform to the same address carry a pointer to the cell number of the next entry in the chain. After the second stage of loading, all items have been entered and all chains established.† At file-search time, the search argument is transformed, the item at the addressed cell retrieved, and the search argument compared with the key-field. If these match, the search is complete; otherwise the chain part of the cell is used as an address to probe the file once more. The process continues until the argument matches the key-field, in which case the search is completed successfully, or until the end of chain is reached, in which case there is no matching argument in the file.

A formula for the performance of a chain-organized file can be derived with

---

† Loading can also be done in one stage instead of two by proper maintenance of chains already established when it becomes necessary to start a new chain at an address already used by a chained item. A chained file is an example of a list structure.

Argument	Transformed address
JONES	4
SMITH	2
BLACK	1
BROWN	4
JOHNSON	9
TAYLOR	4
BARONE	1
CHASE	4

(*a*) Listing of arguments and transformed addresses.

Address	Item	Chain		Address	Item	Chain
1	BLACK	–		1	BLACK	6
2	SMITH	–		2	SMITH	–
3	–	–		3	BROWN	5
4	JONES	–		4	JONES	3
5	–	–		5	TAYLOR	7
6	–	–		6	BARONE	–
7	–	–		7	CHASE	–
8	–	–		8	–	–
9	JOHNSON	–		9	JOHNSON	–

(*b*) File after first stage.   (*c*) After second stage.

Fig. 4.16.1 Chain organized file.

the help of some combinatorial analysis and probability theory. Assume a file containing a addresses, each of a cell that can hold a single item (bucket size of 1). Consider the file after loading, with n of the a cells filled. The list of transformed arguments which determined the cell addresses is a string of n integers each in the range from 1 to a. There are a^n such *possible* strings. Imagine these recorded so that the properties of all such strings can be examined. A chain of length k is represented by the appearance of an address k times in one of the strings. Suppose we now focus attention on any single address. What is the probability of finding a chain k long starting at the address? This probability can be found by considering a series of n drawings from a set of a objects with the appearance of our address called a success and the nonappearance called a failure. In any given drawing, the probability of success is

(1) $$p \equiv \frac{1}{a}$$

The probability of k successes in n such trials is given by the binomial distribution†

(2) $$b(k,n,p) \equiv p^k(1 - p)^{n-k}\frac{n!}{k!(n-k)!}$$

In terms of our list of all possible strings of addresses, $b(k,n,p)$ is the fraction of the a^n possible strings that contain k appearances of any given address.

Now for a chain of length $k,$ one probe is required to obtain the first item on the chain, two probes for the second, etc. To obtain all items on a chain k items long therefore requires a total number of probes equal to the sum of the first k integers:

$$\frac{k(k + 1)}{2}$$

If this is multiplied by the probability of Eq. (2) and the product summed, the result is the number of probes required to retrieve all items on all chains for a given address divided by the number of possible address strings. Now this may be divided by the total number of items on these chains divided by the total number of address strings to obtain the average number of probes to retrieve an item from the file. Performing the substitutions described gives

---

†See W. Feller, "An Introduction to Probability Theory and Its Applications," 2d ed., vol. 1, John Wiley & Sons, Inc., New York, 1957. See also Appendix B.

(3)   Average number of probes $\equiv \dfrac{\displaystyle\sum_{k=1}^{n} \dfrac{k(k+1)}{2} b(k,n,p)}{\displaystyle\sum_{k=1}^{n} kb(k,n,p)}$

(4) $\equiv \dfrac{\dfrac{1}{2}\displaystyle\sum_{k=1}^{n} k^2 b(k,n,p)}{\displaystyle\sum_{k=1}^{n} kb(k,n,p)} + \dfrac{1}{2}$

Use is now made of two results in the theory of probability for the binomial distribution of Eq. (2):

(5) $\displaystyle\sum_{k=1}^{n} kb(k,n,p) \equiv np$

(6) $\displaystyle\sum_{k=1}^{n} k^2 b(k,n,p) \equiv np + (np)^2 - np^2$

Substituting into Eq. (4) and simplifying

(7)   Average number of probes $\equiv 1 + \dfrac{np}{2} - p$

For a large file $a \gg 1$, and hence

$$p \equiv \frac{1}{a} \ll 1$$

Equation (7) therefore simplifies to

Average number of probes $\equiv 1 + \dfrac{n}{2a}$

This rather remarkable result states that the average number of probes required to retrieve an item is 1 plus half the fraction of the file that is loaded. Even for a fully loaded file, this is only 1.5. Note that this average value is relatively independent of the size of the file, and the chain organization is therefore particularly good for large files. However, Eq. (7) is only the average number of probes; it is not impossible for a particular retrieval to require a large number of probes. A further disadvantage of the method is its unsuitability for a file with nonuniform record lengths.

4.17 CHAINING ON SECONDARY KEYS

The performance of the hashing methods, especially the chaining method, is quite high; fewer probes are required on the average than with the binary search. Moreover, the average number of probes is independent of the size of the file.

Although many problems require rapid search on a single key only, in other cases, search on several keys is desirable. For example, it might be required to find all people in a given department (department constitutes one key) with a certain education code (education code is another key). Of course, one possibility is to duplicate the file and order one file on one key, the other on the other key. However, the file may also be organized for search on two keys using the hash transformation method, provided the keys are known at file load time. One method of doing this is shown in Fig. 4.17.1.

The procedure may be described briefly as follows:

1. Part (*a*) of the chart simply shows the file with its two sets of key-fields $Y[;1], Y[;2]$ and the transformed addresses corresponding to these, $T\ Y[;1]\ T\ Y[;2]$. None of the items are yet assigned addresses.
2. Part (*b*) shows the file after entry of those items which do not correspond to synonyms on the primary key $Y[;1]$. Although there are no primary-key chains at the end of this first stage, chains have been established for the secondary keys of all the items entered. Two chain pointers are kept with each item for possible chaining on the secondary key. $X[I;1]$ is a pointer to the address of the first item in the chain on the secondary key which transforms to address $I. X[;2]$ serves as pointers to other items in the chains for the secondary key.
3. Part (*c*) of the chart shows the file after the final step of entering synonyms on the primary key (and establishing their chains).

File		Transformed arguments	
Y[;1]	Y[;2]	T Y[;1]	T Y[;2]
Jones	105	5	2
Black	309	3	3
Smith	608	1	6
White	004	6	7
Brown	367	3	2
Davis	852	2	7
Kelly	057	5	8
Doe	924	8	2
Lewis	777	3	9
Johnson	665	4	0

(a) File and transformed arguments.

Address	X[;1]	X[;2]	X[;3]	File		Sequence in loading
0		4				
1				Smith	608	3
2		5		Davis	852	5
3		3		Black	309	2
4				Johnson	665	7
5			8	Jones	105	1
6		1	2	White	004	4
7		6		—	—	—
8				Doe	924	6
9				—	—	—

(b) After first-stage loading (nonsynonyms on primary key).

Address	X[;1]	X[;2]	X[;3]	File		Sequence in loading
0	9	4√		Brown	367	1
1				Smith	608	
2		5√		Davis	852	
3	0	3√		Black	309	
4				Johnson	665	
5	7		8√	Jones	105	
6		1√	2√	White	004	
7		6√		Kelly	057	2
8		7	0	Doe	924	
9		9		Lewis	774	3

(c) After second-stage loading (loading complete; √ denotes entered in stage 1).

Chain vectors

X[;1] – Pointers in chains on primary key Y[;1]

X[I;2] – Pointer to first item in chain for secondary key which transforms to address I

X[;3] – Pointers in chains on secondary key

Fig. 4.17.1 Chained file on two keys.

4.18 SEARCHING DIRECT-ACCESS DEVICES: INDEX LISTS AND DIRECTORIES

A philosophy of file organization quite different from the key-address transformation suitable for direct-access devices is the index-list, or directory, method. As usual there are many variations, only a few of which will be discussed here.

The main idea is to construct at file load time a directory of argument-address correspondences. Such a directory can require space much smaller than the file partly because argument fields are typically much smaller than the records and also because if the records are sorted on the argument field as the key, the directory need only have entries for blocks of records such as one entry per track. As a specific example consider a disk file with a comb-access-head arrangement so that one position of the comb makes a cylinder of tracks available without further comb motion. Assume several tracks per cylinder and several records per track. Records need not be of the same length. One track of each cylinder is set aside as a directory of argument-address pairs for the first record of each track of the cylinder. If the data and directory are assumed sorted high to low, search of a record in the cylinder will be narrowed to a single track by searching only the directory track.

The principle of the directory may be extended to larger data units than the cylinder. Thus it is feasible and may well be efficient to create a directory to cylinders (as well as tracks) or even larger data units.

4.19 BRIEF SUMMARY OF FILE-MAINTENANCE PROCESSES

For files that must be updated or searched with activity rate and response time that permit accumulating a large batch of arguments, the serial file-maintenance scheme can be very efficient. Here the activity records are sorted on the key-field and then passed (once) against the sorted master file. This produces a new sorted master file that can be used later in another updating operation. Note that the old master file is still available and may be saved for history reasons or as a *backup* file if for some reason the new file is found to be erroneous. Magnetic tape is well suited to serial files.

Certain jobs require such fast response that they do not permit accumulation of a sizable batch of activity items or search arguments. Airline reservations and some command and control systems are classical illustrations. For this type of problem the direct-access file is required. Fastest retrieval of *individual items* may be obtained with a computed argument-address transformation process.

Direct-access devices may be used as serial-access devices, but the reverse is not true at least as a practical matter in most cases. Many applications can batch items for most processing but require fast response to high-priority requests that occur only infrequently. Direct-access files organized according to the directory method are directly applicable here.

PROBLEMS

4.1 Is the cycle-stealing principle of I/O transmission applicable to the copy-loop method of I/O control? Why or why not?

4.2 In a certain computer the following parameters apply to reading or writing a tape record of 80 *characters:*

Tape start time	5 msec
Tape flow rate	60,000 bytes/sec
Time to execute IOCS routine	1 msec
Time to process a record	2 msec

a) What buffer size (in bytes) is required to achieve balanced overlap?
b) Estimate the time to run a 5000-record problem.

4.3 Repeat part (*b*) of Prob. 4.2, assuming that 10 problem records are blocked into one tape record.

4.4 Explain the meaning and advantage of blocking when referring to records on magnetic tape.

4.5 Assume core-storage cycle time of 1 μsec with 4 bytes/word. Attached to the channels are:

Channel 1: Disk device:	
Head-move time	100 msec
Rotation delay	15 msec (avg)
Flow rate	90 kilobytes/sec
Channel 2: Tape device:	
Start/stop time	5 msec
Flow rate	90 kilobytes/sec

Assume two words of register buffer per channel.
a) With both channels running concurrently, what percent of storage cycles is used to service the channels?
b) Repeat part (*a*) if four storage cycles are required for control-word update per word serviced.

4.6 It is desired to interchange (swap) the contents of two areas of storage, one extending from cells numbered *a* through $a + n-1$, the other numbered *b* through $b + n - 1$. Write a detailed single-loop program for the swap that uses no more than one intermediate cell for data.

4.7 Given: a one-channel I/O system which is to use two storage areas, one for compute and output, the other for input. Output is expected to be relatively infrequent. Give design tables for control of the system. Include a program for receiving and processing completion signals i and c and any others deemed necessary.

4.8 A search is to be made of 10,000 items, and the maximum number of items satisfying the search is known to be 200.

a) Does the index list or bit map give better storage economy?
b) If the maximum number that can satisfy the search is 1500, which is more economical of space?
c) What other factors besides economy of space (storage) should be considered?

4.9 Given: a file of variable-length records stored as a vector of characters C. A directory vector D specifies in $D[I]$ the position of the start of record I in C.

a) Write an expression for record I in terms of I,D,C.
b) Write a program to search the file for a match on the first three characters of each record (assume all records are at least three characters long).
c) Comment on the ease of searching for a record I.
d) Comment on the ease of changing record contents.
e) Comment on the ease of deleting records and utilizing the space released.

4.10 In a certain program the programmer knows that 10,000 available storage cells M are to be used for T tables (T is known in advance), but he does not know how many entries will be necessary for each table. Suggest as simple a scheme as possible to utilize the 10,000 cells in each of the following cases. Include the cost (in cells) of control information such as pointers.

a) $T \equiv 2$
b) $T \equiv 3$
c) $T \equiv 50$

4.11 Given: a file with each record formatted as follows:

Field	Character positions	Meaning
0	0–5	Man number
1	6–26	Name
2	27–29	Age
3	30–35	Job code
4	36–39	Dept. no.

The file is held in storage according to a list structure. There are three lists, one for each of the last three fields. Consider the file entries as a matrix of characters. In writing programs, subroutines given in the text may be used.

a) Write a program to obtain all records which contain a specified age.

b) Write a program to obtain all records which contain a specified age *and* job code.

c) Write a program for entering a new record into the file showing the updating of the three lists.

4.12 *a)* Modify the file-maintenance program of Fig. 4.11.1 so that each record of the activity or master file contains two number values (fields), a key-field and an update field. Use as an example:

Activity file:

Record	1	2	3
Key-field	2	19	24
Update field	75	20	14

Master file:

Record	1	2	3	4	5	6	7
Key-field	1	7	11	14	19	25	27
Update field	19	12	14	37	140	90	77

Write an UPDATE function that adds the activity update field to the master update field for matching key-fields.

b) Give the program output for the above example.

4.13 Generate a vector X of 27 random numbers by the Fibonacci process; i.e., the first two elements should be 0, 1, the next the sum of the immediately preceding pair, etc. Then take

$$X \leftarrow 100 \,|\, X$$

Sort X and show the results for each pass using:

a) The two-way merge

b) The three-way merge

c) Bubble sort (first three passes only)

4.14 *a)* Write a program for a radix sort using binary radix. Original numbers are called X, sorted numbers Y.
b) What are the disadvantages of the radix-sort method?

4.15 Use the sorted vector X of Prob. 4.13 to perform the binary search for the following arguments:

a) 5
b) 0
c) 75

List the sequence of indices to X generated by the binary search in each case.

4.16 A binary-search program that does not require division (or shifting) for each probe uses a precomputed index increment/decrement vector V. This vector contains only powers of 2 as follows: $V \equiv 1,2,4,8 \ldots (\rho X) \div 2$. Write a binary-search program that uses V. Include generation of V at the start of the program.

4.17 An unordered file of 10,000 records each 100 characters long is to be searched for equality using a 10-character key corresponding to the first 10 characters of the record. The search is to be made against one hundred 10-character arguments, the file records satisfying any argument are to be extracted.

a) Write a program to define the problem.
b) Assuming the file is on magnetic tape, describe and justify a good system procedure to perform the required search.

4.18 A file of 10,000 records is contained in a direct-access device capable of holding 15,000 records.

a) How many accesses on the average are required to retrieve any desired record if the file is chain-organized using the hashing method?
b) If the file were ordered on the search argument, how many accesses would be required and what method could be used?
c) Discuss briefly the pros and cons of the methods in (*a*) and (*b*).

4.19 Given a value A to be used to search vector X in a table-look-up process to an X,Y table. Since X is in ascending order, when A is found to lie between two X values, say $X[I]$ and $X[I+1]$, the value YE corresponding to A can be estimated by *linear interpolation* given by the formula

$$YE \leftarrow Y[I]+(A-X[I]) \times (Y[I+1]-Y[I]) \div (X[I+1]-X[I])$$

a) Draw an X versus Y curve sketch and verify the above relationship geometrically (using similar triangles).

b) Write a program for table look-up including linear interpolation.

4.20 Some matrices, like those representing distances (see Sec. 2.12) have all-zero main-diagonal values and are symmetric about the main diagonal. In this case, considerable storage can be saved by storing (say) *only* the below-diagonal elements as a dense row list. If the original matrix is $n \times n$ and b denotes the location of the first stored element:

a) Show that the number of values that needs to be stored is $n(n-1) \div 2$ (rather than n^2).

b) Show a 4×4 matrix and label each element with its location.

c) Show that the location (address) of the i,j element of the original matrix can be found by the formula

$$a \equiv b + (j-1) + \sum_{k \equiv 2}^{i} (k-2) \equiv (b-1+j) + (i-2)(i-1) \div 2$$

for $i > j$, and for $j > i$, first interchange j and i and then use the above formula for a.

d) Calling S the vector of stored values, write a program whose inputs are the row and column values I,J of an element in the original matrix and whose output is the desired element value. It must handle all cases of $I=J$, $I>J$, and $I<J$.

REFERENCES

1. Buchholz, W.: File Organization and Addressing, *IBM Syst. J.,* June 1963. (This contains a good bibliography on random-access file-search techniques.)

2. Clark, W. A.: The Functional Structure of OS/360, II: Data Management, *IBM Syst. J.,* vol. 5, no. 1 (1966).

3. *Commun. ACM,* vol. 6, no. 5 (May 1963). (Contains several papers on sorting.)

4. Falkoff, A. D.: Algorithms for Parallel Search Memories, *J. ACM,* vol. 9, p. 488 (1962).

5. Friend, E. H.: Sorting on Electronic Computer Systems, *J. ACM,* vol. 3, pp. 134–168 (1956).

6. Heistand, R. E.: An Executive System Implemented as a Finite State Automaton, *Commun. ACM,* vol. 7, no. 11 (November 1964).

7. Hellerman, H., and H. J. Smith: Thruput Analysis of Some Input/Output and Compute Overlay Configurations, *ACM Comput. Surv.,* vol. 2, no. 2 (1970).

8. Hoagland, A. S.: "Digital Magnetic Recording," John Wiley & Sons, Inc., New York, 1963.

9. IBM Corporation: "Sorting Techniques," no. C20-1639, White Plains, N.Y.

10. Iverson, K. E.: "A Programming Language," John Wiley & Sons, Inc., New York, 1962.

11. Johnson, L. R.: An Indirect Chaining Method for Addressing on Secondary Keys, *Commun. ACM,* May 1961, pp. 218–222.

12. Kiseda, J. R., H. E. Petersen, W. C. Seelbach, and M. Teig: A Magnetic Associative Memory, *IBM J. Res. Dev.,* vol. 6, no. 2 (April 1962).

13. Knuth, D. E.: "The Art of Computer Programming," vol. I, "Fundamental Algorithms," Addison-Wesley Publishing Company, Inc., Reading, Mass., 1968.

14. Martin, W. A.: Sorting, *ACM Comput. Surv.,* vol. 3, no. 4 (December 1971).

5

Logic and Logic Circuits

The subject called *logic* originated as a branch of philosophy, with the purpose of studying reasoning and improving its validity. In the Western world, logic is generally recognized to have begun with the great Greek philosopher Aristotle, who lived in the fourth century B.C. An independent development of logic also took place in India beginning in ancient times. Although much use of Aristotle's logic was made in philosophy and religion, logic itself developed only slowly until about the seventeenth century. Beginning then, contributions were made by several men of renown including Leibniz, Euler, Kant, Hegel, and Bolzano. An important step was taken in 1847 by George Boole and Augustus De Morgan, who independently proposed algebras for symbolically representing and manipulating logical expressions. Boole's extended work was published in 1854 under the (abbreviated) title "An Investigation of the Laws of Thought." By the end of the nineteenth century, the foundations of mathematics were recognized to contain certain difficulties. These were to some extent solved by A. N. Whitehead and B. Russell in 1910 to 1913 in their monumental treatise "Principia Mathematica." This work nearly established logic as the basis of mathematics.

Logic is a subject applicable to a very broad spectrum of problems, especially those concerned with classifications of symbols and symbol strings. Principles of logic are particularly valuable in problem analysis, programming, and logic design. This chapter presents an introduction to logic in the context of the design of logic circuits. Such circuits are found not only in computers but also in telephone, relay switching, and other systems. Their chief characteristic is that they are composed of large collections of similar devices, each of which is relatively simple. Complex functions are obtained by the interconnections of the devices and the timing of signals which excite them. In keeping with the simplicity of device operation, each circuit excitation and output usually operates (at least nominally) with only two values of signal. Depending on the physical nature of the signal, these are often called by different names, e.g., relay contact open or closed, transistor cut off or saturated, etc. This type of device operation leads to great reliability and relative ease of manufacture. It is convenient to give standard designations to the two possible signal values no matter what their physical origin. The techniques of mathematical logic can then be applied to the analysis and design of switching circuits.

A logical variable, sometimes called a Boolean variable, is one that can take on only two distinct values or classes of values. The value assigned to a variable thus represents a choice between two classes or alternatives.

The two possible values that can be specified by a logical variable will be denoted by the symbols 0 and 1. These are by no means the only common designations; in philosophy they are often denoted by F and T (for false and true). In our notation, although the symbols 0 and 1 will have no numerical significance when used in a strictly logical context, we shall, however, permit values of logical variables to have their usual numerical significance when used with numerical operators such as addition and multiplication. In other words, the meaning assigned to a value depends upon the particular operation applied to it. This makes it essential that all operators contain in their definition a specification of the range or domain of the operands upon which they operate. This principle also forbids use of the same symbols for both arithmetic and logical operators as is done in some systems of notation.

Because of the finite choice of distinct values (namely two) that can be assumed by each variable, a *function* of one or more variables may be *completely* specified by a table listing all possible argument values and the corresponding function value for each. Such a finite-length table, called a *truth table,* will be discussed in detail later. Although a finite table can define a logical function, it is not possible to represent the common mathematical functions such as polynomials by finite tables because the number of possible argument values is usually infinite, e.g., when the argument variable can assume values over a continuum.

Although tables of argument-function correspondence completely define logical functions, it is valuable to develop algebraic methods for manipulating variables and their functions. An algebra is essential for proving and demonstrating general relations among variables. Boolean and other logical algebras are important tools in the design of logic circuits.

A necessary step in the development of a logical algebra is the choice of a set of functions as *primitive.* Such a set, an example of which is AND, OR, NOT, should be *complete;* i.e., all other functions should be expressable in terms of only the primitives.

From a circuit viewpoint, each primitive can be thought of as a logic-block type, i.e., a fairly small circuit capable of implementing the primitive function. Thus, we have, for example, AND, OR, and NOT (inverter) logic blocks. Since any logical function can be expressed in terms of only the members of a complete set of primitives, any logic circuit can be implemented as an interconnection of logic blocks.

A further insight into the nature of logic circuits is that since a logical function can be expressed as a truth table and each primitive function is also defined as a truth table, complex functions, specified by large tables, are implemented as a succession of small tables, the logic blocks.

Logic circuits are broadly classed as *combinational* or *sequential.* A combinational circuit is one whose output(s) at any instant is a function only of its inputs at that same instant; a combinational circuit does not contain any storage. In fact, even simple time delay between input and output would be excluded by strict application of the definition. As a practical matter, models of combinational circuits are often permitted to include simple time delay of input to output. A sequential circuit (see Chap. 7) is one whose outputs at any instant depend not only on its present inputs but also on its past history; i.e., a sequential circuit includes the property of storage or memory. The usual ingredients of sequential circuits are combinational circuits and time delays in a feedback arrangement. In fact, any sequential circuit including an entire computer may, in theory, be represented by combinational circuits and time delays.

From a computer viewpoint, logic circuits may be classified as follows:

1. *Routing or Bus Circuits* These implement the *data-flow* structure of the system and serve to conduct information from point to point within the machine, i.e., between the other circuit types.
2. *Transformation Circuits* These typically perform addition, complementation, parity checking, and selection operations.
3. *Sequencing* These generate the time sequence of pulses and other waveforms for control of the routing circuits.
4. *Storage* This class includes fast-access storage such as machine registers, flip-flops for holding control information, as well as storage elements in large-capacity storage arrays such as magnetic-core or thin-film storage.

Routing and transformation circuits are usually combinational circuits; the other types are sequential circuits. Finally, it must be mentioned that every computer contains other circuits besides logic types, power-supply circuits and memory-sense amplifiers among others.

In this chapter only combinational circuits are discussed; these are viewed as circuit implementations of logical functions. The main emphasis is on the theory of such circuits and some important simple examples. Other more extensive combinational circuits as well as sequential circuits are discussed in later chapters.

5.1   THE TRUTH TABLE AS A LOGIC-CIRCUIT SPECIFICATION

A truth table is a very general method of stating the exact function which a logic circuit is to perform. Since each input can take on only one of two values, a circuit with n inputs has 2^n possible argument (input) configurations of its values. A truth table lists all these input combinations and the desired output corresponding to each. For convenience and standardization, the 2^n rows will be listed in a standard manner using 1 and 0 for each position and in such order as if they represented consecutive binary numbers (see Fig. 5.1.1). The array of possible inputs (arguments) in this form of a truth table can easily be constructed by noting that in the rightmost column the pattern 01 repeats, in the next column to the left the pattern 0011 repeats, in the next column the pattern 00001111 repeats, etc. The matrix of arguments having 2^n rows and n columns will be denoted by A.

The listing of all possible inputs as rows of the table is routine by the above procedure. On the right of each row the designer enters one of the three symbols 0, 1, or X, depending on the desired assignment of output value for the combination of inputs represented by the row. The 0 or 1 entries are made if

Row No.	a b c	y		a b c	y
0	0 0 0	0		0 0 0	0
1	0 0 1	0		0 0 1	0
2	0 1 0	0		0 1 0	0
3	0 1 1	1		0 1 1	1
4	1 0 0	0		1 0 0	0
5	1 0 1	1		1 0 1	1
6	1 1 0	1		1 1 0	X
7	1 1 1	1		1 1 1	X

(a) Truth table for a simple majority function.

(b) Truth table for a majority function with a and b never 1 at the same time.

(c) Minterm list for Problem (a) ...... $P \equiv 3,5,6,7$
Maxterm list for Problem (a) ...... $S \equiv 0,1,2,4$

Fig. 5.1.1   Logical functions as truth tables.

there is a definite specification of the output value. In some problems, certain input combinations may never actually appear in the circuit. They must, however, appear in the truth table. In such cases an X denoting a "don't care" assignment is entered as the function value. As will be seen later, knowledge that certain input combinations will never occur permits a measure of design freedom which can yield important circuit economies. An X in the function column of a truth table reminds the designer that he is free to later assign a function value of 0 or 1 to the corresponding entry in the truth table.

To illustrate, the truth table for a three-input *majority* function is given in Fig. 5.1.1. The function takes on a 1 value only when at least two of its three inputs are 1 values.

Since the listing of all possible input combinations is now a routine matter, the essential information in a truth table is the number of variables and the function column. The function column is a bit vector which will be denoted by F. If the inputs are called X, then the manner of listing the inputs implies that the output Y may be obtained for any given X by treating X as a binary-encoded integer and using this integer as an index (position-number) in F. In other words:

(1) $Y \leftarrow F[2 \perp X]$

In this statement and throughout this and the following chapters, 0-*origin indexing will be assumed unless stated otherwise.* Thus, if X is all zeros, $Y \equiv F[0]$. Since the argument side of a truth table contains *all* possible input combinations, the table is somewhat redundant. For example, it may be reconstructed only from knowledge of *all* rows for which the function value is 1. This is true since all other rows correspond to a function value of 0. One representation of a logic function is as a list of row numbers for which the function value is 1. Such a list is called a *minterm* or P list. An equally valid specification is the list of row numbers for which the function value is 0. Such a list will be called a *maxterm* or S list. Expressions for P and S lists in terms of the truth vector F and argument matrix A are

(2) $P \leftarrow 2 \perp F / [1] A$

(3) $S \leftarrow 2 \perp (\sim F) / [1] A$

5.2 CANONICAL FORMS AND BOOLEAN ALGEBRA

Although any function can be expressed as a truth table, it is important to seek an algebra which specifies rules of manipulating functions to produce new functions. Such an algebra is the mechanism by which new properties of functions and relations can be inferred. Another important use of algebraic manipulation of functions is to derive expressions which are functionally equivalent to the original functions but simpler or cheaper to build.

To derive an algebra of logical functions, we begin by choosing a small number of functions as *primitive*. These are analogous to addition and multiplication in arithmetic. It is convenient to choose as three primitive logical functions NOT, AND, OR defined by the truth tables shown in Fig. 5.2.1. These are not the only primitive functions which can be chosen. They do have a certain intuitive appeal, however.

Although the AND and OR functions are given in the truth table for two variables, the AND function is easily extended to n variables by the P-list expression:

(1) $P \equiv 2^n - 1$ AND

Similarly, the OR function is defined in general by

(2) $S \equiv 0$ OR

By Eq. (1), the AND of n variables yields a 1 result only when *all* inputs are 1. By Eq. (2), the OR of n variables yields a 0 only when *all* inputs are 0. Since we are about to study the properties of logic functions using a logic algebra, it is important to explain our notation clearly. We could of course use APL notation exclusively, but this extreme and purist approach has the price of often cumbersome expressions and also a significant departure from other commonly used notations. For these reasons, in writing logical equations, we shall use the following conventions which are illustrated along with their APL equivalents:

1. An overbar will signify complement

$$\bar{a} \equiv {\sim}A$$

2. Single-letter names will always be used, which permits omission of the AND symbol; it is implicit in the catenation of names (this is like the similar rule

a	b	$a{\wedge}b$	a	b	$a{\vee}b$	a	$\bar{a}$
0	0	0	0	0	0	0	1
0	1	0	0	1	1	1	0
1	0	0	1	0	1	NOT $(-)$	
1	1	1	1	1	1		

AND $(\wedge)$ OR $(\vee)$

Fig. 5.2.1   Definitions of AND, OR, NOT by truth tables.

for multiplication in ordinary algebra)

$$abc \equiv a \wedge b \wedge c \equiv A \wedge B \wedge C$$

3. Operators will be assigned the following precedence: first complement, next AND, next OR. Expressions will be scanned from left to right to break precedence ties:

$$\overline{abc} \vee \overline{a} bc \vee ac \equiv (A \wedge B \wedge {\sim}C) \vee ((\sim\!A) \wedge B \wedge C) \vee A \wedge C$$

The last example indicates the simplicity gained by the changed notation. The above conventions will be used in logic equations and with lowercase letters; it will never be used in programs or in specification statements (those containing ←), where APL will always apply.

The AND and OR operators obey the associative law; i.e., variables may be grouped in the following alternative ways without changing the value of the result:

(3) $a \wedge b \wedge c \equiv (a \wedge b) \wedge c \equiv a \wedge (b \wedge c)$

(4) $a \vee b \vee c \equiv (a \vee b) \vee c \equiv a \vee (b \vee c)$

The equivalences shown can be established by truth tables. For example, consider Eq. (3) (Fig. 5.2.2). First the arguments are listed, then the function columns, numbered from 4 to 9 obtained by using the AND truth table for two variables. The fact that columns 6 and 9 agree in all positions establishes Eq. (3) as true.

The AND and OR functions also obey two other important laws, the *commutative law:*

(5) $a \wedge b \equiv b \wedge a$

(6) $a \vee b \equiv b \vee a$

and the *distributive law:*

(7) $a \wedge (b \vee c) \equiv (a \wedge b) \vee (a \wedge c)$

(8) $a \vee (b \wedge c) \equiv (a \vee b) \wedge (a \vee c)$

Having established these properties of the functions chosen as primitive, we can show that the following identities hold by using the appropriate truth tables:

1	2	3	4	5	6	7	8	9
a	b	c	$a{\wedge}b$	c	$(a{\wedge}b){\wedge}c$	a	$b{\wedge}c$	$a{\wedge}(b{\wedge}c)$
0	0	0	0	0	0	0	0	0
0	0	1	0	1	0	0	0	0
0	1	0	0	0	0	0	0	0
0	1	1	0	1	0	0	1	0
1	0	0	0	0	0	1	0	0
1	0	1	0	1	0	1	0	0
1	1	0	1	0	0	1	0	0
1	1	1	1	1	1	1	1	1

Fig. 5.2.2   Proof by truth table of $(a \wedge b) \wedge c \equiv a \wedge (b \wedge c)$.

(9a) $a \wedge 0 \equiv 0$

(9b) $a \wedge 1 \equiv a$

(9c) $a \vee 0 \equiv a$

(9d) $a \vee 1 \equiv 1$

(9e) $a \wedge a \equiv a$

(9f) $a \vee a \equiv a$

(9g) $a \vee \bar{a} \equiv 1$

(9h) $a \wedge \bar{a} \equiv 0$

(9i) $a \equiv \bar{\bar{a}}$

(9j) $a \vee (a \wedge b) \equiv a$

(9k) $a \vee (\bar{a} \wedge b) \equiv a \vee b$

(9l) $a \wedge (a \vee b) \equiv a$

(9m) $\overline{a \wedge b} \equiv \bar{a} \vee \bar{b}$ or $a \wedge b \equiv \overline{\bar{a} \vee \bar{b}}$

(9n) $\overline{a \vee b} \equiv \bar{a} \wedge \bar{b}$ or $a \vee b \equiv \overline{\bar{a} \wedge \bar{b}}$

Equations (9m) and (9n) are called *DeMorgan's laws*. They show essential relationships between AND and OR expressions. For example, Eq. (9m) states that an AND may be expressed as an OR if all variables (including the result) are complemented and the AND is replaced by an OR.

Another important identity valuable in circuit simplification is

(10) $(a \wedge b) \vee (a \wedge \bar{b}) \equiv a$

This can be established by recognizing that the left side is equivalent to

(11) $a \wedge (b \vee \bar{b})$

by the distributive law and that application of Eq. (9*g*) and then Eq. (9*b*) to Eq. (11) will produce the right side of Eq. (10).

It is well to pause at this point to understand where we stand in the development of a logical algebra. First the logical function was introduced and expressed as a truth table. It was shown how all the information in the truth table could be expressed as one of two lists of row numbers P or S. Of all possible functions, three, AND, OR, NOT, were selected as primitives for a logical algebra. Certain general relations satisfied by expressions were stated and derived.

The next task at hand is to show how *any* truth table can be expressed as an algebraic expression. To start, consider the P list and a given input combination x. If x matches (bit for bit) any row of the truth table whose number is in the P list, then the output (function) value for this x is 1; otherwise it is 0. Each element of the P list may be represented by an AND expression of the x elements which produces a 1 only for the particular combination of x values corresponding to the row. For example,

(12) $\bar{x}_0 x_1 \bar{x}_2 x_3 x_4$

is 1 only for x values as follows:

$$x_0 \equiv 0 \quad x_1 \equiv 1 \quad x_2 \equiv 0 \quad x_3 \equiv 1 \quad x_4 \equiv 1$$

that is, for the row in the truth table

0,1,0,1,1

Any other assignment of 0, 1 values to x corresponds to another row, and by the same token will yield a 0 when substituted into (12). Since the function value is 1 if a given argument combination corresponds to *any* row listed in P, a logical function may be written as an OR of terms like (12). This is shown in Fig. 5.2.3 for the majority function. The first form of the equation is called the *minterm, disjunctive,* or *P canonical* form. It consists of an OR of AND terms; each variable appears in each AND term.

By analogous reasoning, an S or *maxterm* or *conjunctive* canonical form can be derived from the rows given in the S list. Since if a given input combination corresponds to any such row, the function is to be 0, the S canonical form is an AND of terms each of which is an OR containing all input variables (see Fig. 5.2.3).

To summarize the procedure for obtaining the P canonical form from a truth table:

Row	a	b	c	y
0	0	0	0	0
1	0	0	1	0
2	0	1	0	0
3	0	1	1	1
4	1	0	0	0
5	1	0	1	1
6	1	1	0	1
7	1	1	1	1

$P \equiv 3,5,6,7$

$y \equiv \bar{a}bc \vee a\bar{b}c \vee ab\bar{c} \vee abc$

$S \equiv 0,1,2,4$

$y \equiv (a \vee b \vee c)(a \vee b \vee \bar{c})(a \vee \bar{b} \vee c)(\bar{a} \vee b \vee c)$

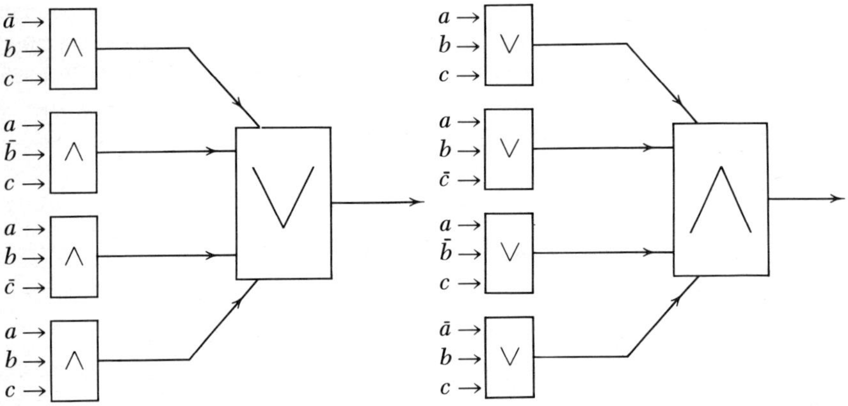

P form

S form

Fig. 5.2.3 Canonical forms and circuits for the majority function.

1. Select a row of the truth table whose *function* entry is 1.
2. Form an AND of *all* input variables; then place an overbar (complement) over each variable whose corresponding entry in the selected row is a 0. (Any variable whose corresponding entry in the row is 1 is not given an overbar in the AND expression.)
3. Repeat steps 1 and 2 for *all* rows in the truth table whose function value is 1.
4. Form an OR of all AND terms obtained in previous steps; this is equal to the function (output).

The procedure for obtaining the S canonical form from the truth table is identical to the above procedure if each time a 0 appears in the description of the procedure a 1 is substituted and vice versa; and each time the word AND appears, the word OR is substituted and vice versa.

Once a logical expression has been obtained, a circuit can be set down in terms of AND, OR, NOT logic circuit blocks. It is usual practice to assume that the complements of all input variables are available (without explicit NOT functions). This is justified by the fact that input lines to most circuits often come from registers which make available both true and complement outputs.

To summarize, it has been shown that a truth table is a means of specifying a logical function and that two forms of algebraic expressions called *P* (minterm) and *S* (maxterm) forms may be derived from any truth table. All such expressions use only three primitive operators: AND, OR, NOT. If circuit blocks which can perform the three primitive operations are assumed available, any logical function can be synthesized as an interconnection of blocks.

5.3 LOGIC-BLOCK CIRCUITS

Logic circuits are usually designed in two distinct stages called logic-block-circuit design and logical design. The design of logic-block circuits is concerned with the synthesis of physical parts such as diodes, resistors, transistors, and capacitors into circuits which have primitive logical properties such as the AND or OR function and can operate under prespecified loading and delay conditions. Logical design generally assumes the availability of specified logic blocks and is concerned with their interconnection to synthesize complex logical functions. In practice there is, of course, some interaction between these two phases of circuit design; nevertheless, it is important that they also maintain distinct identities because different skills are required to do each of them well and because separation of circuit and logical design by clear specification interfaces encourages good design and manufacturing practices. Circuits are usually designed very conservatively because of the high reliability required in a system that may include millions of parts. One common circuit-design philosophy is called *worst case* because the circuit is built so that it will work properly even when all parts have values at the extreme unfavorable ends of their tolerance ranges.

A few of the many logic-block circuits which have been used in computers are shown below. The circuits are constructed with such parts as relays, resistors, diodes, transistors, and capacitors. The details of the physical operation of the circuits require knowledge of the electrical properties of the components, which will be described very briefly later. Of more immediate interest is the block representation of the circuit which relates the electrical properties of the circuit to its logical properties. One block representation consists of three sections (Fig. 5.3.1 illustrates an OR circuit). The leftmost section informs us that a + 6-volt level is considered a logical 1 and a 0-volt level is considered as a logical 0. The rightmost section gives the corresponding convention for the output line. The

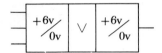

Fig. 5.3.1   Symbol for logic-physical correspondence.

center section denotes the logic function (OR) performed by the circuit with the electrical-logic correspondence shown.

A few representative circuits with relay, diode, and transistor components are illustrated in Fig. 5.3.2.

The relay circuits are controlled by coils which activate the contacts. The logic inputs correspond to electrical inputs on the coils. The output is a connection path which is either closed (a logical 1) or open (a logical 0).

A diode is represented by an arrowlike symbol and has the (idealized) electrical property that when the polarity at its arrowhead terminal is + relative to its other terminal, the diode acts as a conductor; the opposite polarity causes the diode to block conduction. Notice that in all diode circuits a resistor (wavy line) appears; a resistor limits the current in the circuit to safe values and also permits voltage signals to be developed across it. The symbols +, – at the ends of certain resistors indicate that these are connected to power supplies of fixed magnitude and designated polarity.

The diode OR and AND circuits perform these functions for the polarity logic correspondences shown (+ for 1, – or zero for 0). The top circuit is an OR circuit because a + signal applied to any diode causes that diode to conduct; the + signal then appears at the output. If all diodes are excited by 0 inputs, the diodes still conduct but a 0 voltage (and hence a logical 0 also) appears at the output.

The diode AND circuit is similar in structure to the OR circuit except both the diodes and power-supply polarities are reversed. The circuit gives an AND function since if a 0 signal is applied to any of its inputs, the corresponding diode conducts and the output is 0. However, if all inputs are + signals, the output will also be + (and hence a logical 1).

In the type of logic circuits illustrated here, diodes cannot supply the NOT (complement) function; a transistor can be used for this function. Also, the transistor can supply signal *power gain;* i.e., the output signal can be of higher power than the input because the transistor is capable of using the input power to convert power-supply energy to output signal power. The transistor is a three-terminal device. In most (but not all) circuits the input is to the terminal called the *base;* the output is at the terminal called the *collector.* There are two types of transistors, *n-p-n* and *p-n-p;* these have similar electrical functions except for reversal of polarities. The simple *n-p-n* transistor inverter circuit works as follows. A positive input signal at point *a* causes the transistor to conduct heavily, thus drawing a large current *I* from the collector supply. This

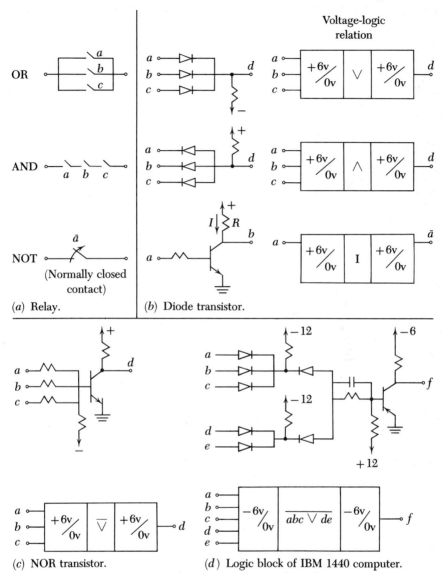

Fig. 5.3.2   Some representative building-block circuits.

current is limited by the collector resistor. Because of the high *IR* drop across the resistor, the voltage at *b* is very low, i.e., a logical 0. A 0 input at point *a*, on the other hand, causes the transistor to conduct very little; the collector current *I* is therefore small, the *IR* drop is small, and almost all the supply voltage appears at point *b,* a logical 1. It is seen that the simple transistor circuit functions as an *inverter* (or NOT circuit).

If the input to the transistor is a resistor network with proper power-supply value and polarity, the circuit can yield a NOT-OR, or NOR, function; if any input is positive, the transistor conducts, and the output level at *d* is 0. If all inputs are 0, the transistor is cut off and the output level is positive (logical 1).

For efficient packaging, and to reduce external wiring, many actual computer block circuits are combinations of AND, OR, NOT functions. One of these circuits from an actual computer is shown. Note that the transistor is *p-n-p* and in this circuit a "−" signal is considered as a logical 1.

Most of this book is concerned with logical rather than logic-block design. The logical designer must however characterize each logic block for timing and loading properties. A single number is usually specified for each of the following parameters even though they are all really complex functions of loadings and other factors.

1. *Time Delay*   This is due partly to unavoidable energy storage in electronic devices or distributed capacitance and partly to the finite time for electric signals to travel from one point to another. In air, propagation time is about 1 nanosecond (10^{-9} sec, or 1 nsec) per foot of wire length. Propagation delay is a fundamental limitation on circuit speed. It can be reduced only by miniaturization and careful placement of parts.
2. *Fan-in*   The number of inputs allowed per block.
3. *Fan-out*   The number of blocks permitted to load the given block.

Thus far, the problem of characterizing only a single logic block has been considered. Logical functions generally require several circuit blocks—but only of a very few types. Manufacturing uniformity, as well as reliability, indicates a small number of block types. In the simplest case, properties required of all blocks will be determined by the most stringent requirement on any one block in the circuit. If this rather conservative policy is adopted, the definitions of the three parameters given above may be extended to entire circuits as follows:

1. *Time Delay*   Total delay—the sum of block delays through the longest path from any input to any output. This may also be specified as the number of *levels* in the circuit, i.e., the number of blocks in tandem when tracing the longest path through the circuit.
2. *Fan-in*   The maximum number of inputs required of any single block.
3. *Fan-out*   The maximum number of blocks loading any single line. The input lines to the circuit must be included in the fan-out specification because several input lines with the same label are usually supplied by a single line.

4. Cost Although the cost of a logical expression may be defined in a number of ways, one common method, which we shall adopt, reckons the cost as a count of the number of input lines to all blocks of a circuit. This is especially meaningful for diode circuits, where the input to each block is in series with one diode.

To illustrate these definitions, consider the circuit obtained by the *P*-form *canonical* expression. If

(1) $n \equiv \rho X$ = number of input variables (inputs to each AND circuit)

(2) $k \equiv +/F$ = number of 1s in truth vector F (inputs to the OR circuit)

then

Number of levels $\equiv 2$
Fan-in $\equiv n \lceil k$ (larger of n or k)
Fan-out $\equiv k$ (maximum value for circuit inputs)
Cost $\equiv k(n + 1)$

The logic-circuit designer is typically presented with a specification of a logical function and a maximum time delay for the circuit which is to implement this function. He is also usually restricted to using specified logic blocks with their fan-in, fan-out, and time-delay constraints. His job is to design an interconnection of the blocks to perform the desired logical function within the specified delay time at minimum cost. Often these requirements are in conflict; for example, the lowest-cost circuit may require a relatively large number of circuit blocks in tandem, thus yielding a long circuit delay. On the other hand, any logical function can be implemented with only two logical levels in tandem if cost and fan-in and fan-out considerations are relaxed. In the following sections it is important to learn of the possibilities of trading time, cost, fan-in, and fan-out in the various classes of circuits and design methods described.

It must be emphasized that rational logic-circuit design includes the problem of optimizing a cost function subject to certain constraints. For historical reasons and ease of analysis, as well as to illustrate ideas, the classical cost function has been defined above. With new technologies, however, the nature of the cost function may be quite different. For example, with some modern integrated circuit fabrication techniques, devices can be so cheap that it is more important to minimize the number of interconnections or pins leading to external circuits than to minimize the number of diodes or transistors.

5.4 CIRCUIT MINIMIZATION OR SIMPLIFICATION

The problem of simply obtaining a valid circuit for a given specification was seen earlier to be purely routine and hence rather trivial. A central problem in logic-circuit design is obtaining an economical or *low-cost* circuit. One form of this problem assumes:

1. Cost will be defined as the total number of inputs to all blocks in the circuit. This way of reckoning cost is simple and particularly applicable to diode circuits.
2. The circuit building blocks will be of the types AND, OR, NOT.
3. Each input variable and its complement is available on a separate line.
4. Fan-in and fan-out restrictions are ignored.
5. Circuits produced by most of the procedures described below are two-level circuits.

It should be understood that the above assumptions are restrictive, and modern logic simplification algorithms are attempting to meet this criticism. Nevertheless, techniques subject to the above assumptions are fundamental to most simplification algorithms.

A *cube* of order 1 is defined as two minterms which have identical variables except for one variable which appears complemented in one of the minterms and uncomplemented in the other. Each one of such a pair of minterms is said to be distance 1 from the other since they differ in only one position.

EXAMPLE:

$$\left\{ \begin{array}{l} \bar{a}b\bar{c}d \\ \bar{a}\bar{b}\bar{c}d \end{array} \right\}$$

is a cube of order 1 since all variables agree in the two minterms except for b. Now if a minterm expression contains a cube of order 1, an OR of these minterms has the form

$$u\bar{v} \lor uv$$

where u represents the part of the minterm common to the pair. By applying Eq. (10) of Sec. 5.2, v can be eliminated. For example, b can be eliminated in the expression for y, yielding the reduced expression

$$y \equiv \bar{a}b\bar{c}d \lor \bar{a}\bar{b}\bar{c}d \equiv \bar{a}\bar{c}d(b \lor \bar{b}) \equiv \bar{a}\bar{c}d$$

Note that the reduced expression has a cost of 3 compared to 10 for the original.

The idea of minterm grouping can be extended to a cube of order 2. A cube of order 2 consists of a group of four minterms such that they can be divided into two groups where each group is a cube of order 1; and after reduction of each of these, the resulting two terms constitute a cube of order 1. Thus for a group of minterms constituting a cube of order 2, the final reduced expression, logically equivalent to the OR of minterms, is a single AND term with two variables absent.

EXAMPLE:

$$y \equiv \bar{a}b\bar{c}\bar{d} \vee \bar{a}bc\bar{d} \vee \bar{a}b\bar{c}d \vee \bar{a}bcd$$

The four minterms in this expression constitute a cube of order 2 as may be seen as follows:

$$
\left.
\begin{array}{c}
\left. \begin{array}{c} \bar{a}b\bar{c}\bar{d} \\ \bar{a}bc\bar{d} \end{array} \right\} \rightarrow \bar{a}b\bar{d} \\
\left. \begin{array}{c} \bar{a}b\bar{c}d \\ \bar{a}bcd \end{array} \right\} \rightarrow \bar{a}bd
\end{array}
\right\} \; \bar{a}b
$$

Hence the original expression is equivalent to the reduced expression

$$y \equiv \bar{a}b$$

The cost of the original expression (an OR of four minterms of four variables) is 20. The cost of the reduced expression is 2.

The importance of recognizing high-order cubes should now be clear; they permit reduction in the cost of circuits to realize a given function.

In general, a group of minterms containing p variables constitutes a cube of order n if there are 2^n minterms in the group and if the OR of these minterms are equivalent to a single term which is an AND of $p - n$ variables.

This definition unfortunately does not tell us how to identify cubes other than by testing a group of minterms exhaustively. Since cube identification generally leads to logically equivalent but lower cost expressions, techniques to identify high-order cubes in expressions are very important in simplification procedures. A few such methods are given below.

Although the above discussion has been entirely in terms of minterms and hence are directly applicable only to P-form expressions, analogous processes apply to S-form expressions. For conciseness, the discussion will continue to refer to P-form expressions.

5.5 KARNAUGH MAP TECHNIQUE OF SIMPLIFICATION

A graphical or map technique for identifying cubes is useful for expressions involving a small number of variables (say no more than four or five). The map method is also valuable to help visualize the process of simplification.

Consider first a minterm expression of three variables in canonical form. Such an expression may be visualized as plotted on corners of a three-dimensional cube where each variable is represented as a 0 or 1 distance along one direction of the cube edges. Each minterm appears as a vertex of the cube. Now it is possible to map the cube on to a plane by arranging a chart containing eight squares, one for each possible minterm of three variables. By proper assignment of labels to the squares, adjacent vertices or corners on the cube plot will also be adjacent on the chart. Since two adjacent corners constitute a 1-cube, two adjacent squares will then also identify a 1-cube. If this principle is extended to higher-order cubes, it will be possible to identify high-order cubes by certain types of clusters of 1s on the map. With some practice, the eye can be used to identify the clusters and hence the cubes.

The manner of labeling the squares of the map is most vital. The labeling scheme is shown for three- and four-variable maps (Fig. 5.5.1). For example, in the three-variable map, the top line is labeled to represent terms for variables *a* and *b*. The left side is labeled for the variable *c*. Note that the labels are assigned so that adjacent labels differ in only one position. The labeling scheme can be standard for all maps of a given number of variables. Groups of squares indicated by braces represent minterm groups which reduce to a single variable.

Any minterm function in canonical form can be plotted on the map. Each minterm is plotted as a 1 in the appropriate square. A "don't care" is plotted as an ×. After plotting, the task of grouping the squares to identify cubes may begin. Any set of groups which contain all the 1s on a map is called a *cover* (since all terms in the original function are covered). The problem of simplification is to obtain a minimum-cost cover.

The process of obtaining a minimum-cost cover may be summarized as follows:

1. Plot the function on the map. If the function is given in equation form, this may be done by inspection or by expanding any missing variables to obtain the expression in canonical form. For example, for a four-variable problem, the following term of three variables can be plotted in two squares by

$$ab\bar{d} \equiv ab(c \vee \bar{c})\bar{d} \equiv abc\bar{d} \vee ab\bar{c}\bar{d}$$

2. Search the map for high-order cubes, i.e., for adjacency groups of 1s. A group constitutes a cube only if its elements obey the *adjacency rules* as illustrated below for the four-variable map. The grouping should start with 1-squares

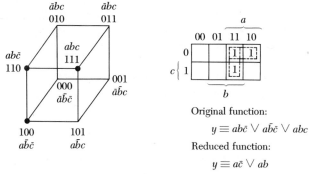

Original function:

$$y \equiv ab\bar{c} \vee a\bar{b}\bar{c} \vee abc$$

Reduced function:

$$y \equiv a\bar{c} \vee ab$$

(a) Three-variable—cube plot and map.

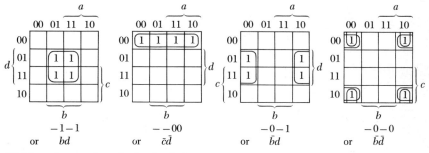

(b) Maps of some cubes of order-2 with their expressions
(four-variable maps shown).

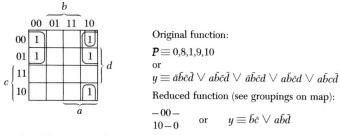

Original function:

$$P \equiv 0,8,1,9,10$$

or

$$y \equiv \bar{a}\bar{b}\bar{c}\bar{d} \vee a\bar{b}\bar{c}\bar{d} \vee \bar{a}\bar{b}\bar{c}d \vee a\bar{b}\bar{c}d \vee a\bar{b}c\bar{d}$$

Reduced function (see groupings on map):

$$\begin{array}{l} -00- \\ 10-0 \end{array} \quad \text{or} \quad y \equiv \bar{b}\bar{c} \vee a\bar{b}\bar{d}$$

(c) Simplification of a four-variable function in *P* form.

Fig. 5.5.1 Karnaugh maps of functions of three and four variables.

which can be included in a cube in one way only. Any square may be
included in as many cubes as desired (provided it satisfies adjacency
conditions). Any × entries are now assigned 1 or not for best clustering.

3. When the best cover has been obtained, i.e., all 1-squares have been included

in at least one group (cube) and all squares have been included in as high order a cube as possible, it is quite likely that a true minimum-cost cover has been found. This minimum-cost cover may not, however, be unique. Also, in some cases grouping in lower cubes may reduce the number of cubes leading to a lower-cost expression.

4. Finally, the entire process should be repeated with the S form of expression. The resulting expression should be compared in cost with the P form and the lower-cost expression retained.

The circuit obtained by the map method is always a two-level circuit.

The circuit cost can be computed from the reduced expression. It is also given by the formula

$$\text{Cost} \equiv \sum_{j=0}^{n-2} q_j \times (n-j) + \sum_{j=0}^{n-1} q_j$$

where $q_j \equiv$ number of cubes of order j in reduced function
$n \equiv$ number of variables

5.6   QUINE-McCLUSKEY SIMPLIFICATION ALGORITHM

The map technique of simplification is primarily useful for simplification of functions of three or four variables. For more variables, the ability of the eye to recognize high-order cubes drops rapidly. Aside from this, however, it is desirable that the graphical map method be replaced by a symbol-manipulation method if the simplification process is to be mechanized as a computer program. Such programs do in fact exist; many of them are based on the Quine-McCluskey technique. The method is directly applicable to combinational circuits with any number of input variables and a single output variable (extensions also exist for multiple-output circuits). It applies directly to circuits using AND-OR type logic blocks, it neglects fan-in and fan-out restrictions, and it produces a minimum-cost two-level circuit.

As an aid in understanding the general description of the Quine-McCluskey simplification technique, it is recommended that the reader follow the specific example in Fig. 5.6.1.

At the start of the process, the function to be simplified is assumed to be available as a list of rows of the truth table defining the function—the rows listed are those for which the function value is 1. To facilitate row-matching operations, to be described shortly, the rows are placed in the order of the number of appearances of 1s. Thus, all rows having the same number of 1s

Table I		Table II		Table III		Table IV
0	0000√	0,4	0−00√	0,4,8,12	−−00	No entries
4	0100√	0,2	00−0√	0,2,8,10	−0−0	
2	0010√	0,8	−000√	2,3,10,11	−01−	
8	1000√	4,12	−100√			
3	0011√	2,3	001−√			
10	1010√	2,10	−010√			
12	1100√	8,10	10−0√			
13	1101√	8,12	1−00√			
11	1011√	3,11	−011√			
		10,11	101−√			
		12,13	110−			

Prime implicants are unchecked rows:

12,13	110−
0,4,8,12	−−00
0,2,8,10	−0−0
2,3,10,11	−01−

(a) Tables to obtain prime implicants.

		110−	−−00	−0−0	−01−
0	0000		√	√	
4	0100		√ *		
2	0010			√	√
8	1000		√	√	
3	0011				√ *
10	1010			√	√
12	1100	√	√		
13	1101	√ *			
11	1011				√ *

(b) Choice of prime implicants for minimum-cost cover.

Selected prime implicants:

$$\begin{pmatrix} 110- \\ --00 \\ -01- \end{pmatrix}$$

Simplified equation:

$$f \equiv ab\bar{c} \vee \bar{c}\bar{d} \vee \bar{b}c$$

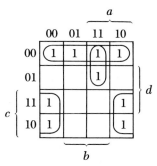

(c) Map of function (shown for comparison purposes).

Fig. 5.6.1 Steps in Quine–McCluskey simplification technique.

appear in a group—the rows and their tags (original row numbers) with lines delineating the groups constitute Table 1 in Fig. 5.6.1a. Thus Table 1 is simply a particular arrangement of the information in the truth table defining the function to be simplified.

The algorithm has as its first objective the construction of Table 2; each entry is obtained by combining a pair of rows from Table 1. Two rows constitute a pair if they differ in only one position, i.e., if they are a *1-cube* (are distance 1 apart). Such a pair yields a reduction in cost since it represents application of the theorem

$$\bar{a}b \vee ab \equiv a$$

where a represents the AND of all variables common to both minterms. To facilitate making table entries, the following notation will be adopted for a reduced row pair:

$$\begin{matrix} 01011 \\ 01111 \end{matrix} \to 01 - 11$$

The reduction yields one AND term shown in 0, 1 form with a $-$ as a placeholder for the variable that is eliminated. Thus, each row of Table 1 is compared with every other row for a distance-1 pair; the process may systematically start with the top row and work downward. Whenever a pair has been identified, the following is done:

1. An indicator (check mark) is placed next to both rows that contribute to the reduction.
2. The reduced term and both sets of tags are entered into the subsequent table.

The search for the row pairs is simplified by the method of ordering entries in Table 1. This is true because it is not necessary to search for a distance-1 match *within* a group, since two distinct bit vectors that have the same number of 1s must differ in more than a single position. Also, notice that the two tags of terms for a reduced pair differ by a power of 2.

The process of identifying row pairs of Table 1 to form Table 2 continues until all rows of Table 1 have been tested. The process is then repeated on Table 2 to produce Table 3. Since now the rows being matched contain either 0, 1, or $-$ elements, the matching rule demands agreement in all positions containing a $-$ and agreement in all other positions except for a single position. Using this extended match rule, Table 3 is constructed from Table 2.

The process of building successive tables continues until there are no entries possible in the successor table. At this point, the first phase of the process is complete. The result of this phase is the set of *unchecked* rows in *all* the tables.

These are called *prime implicants.* Since each time a pair-reduction took place, the reduced term encompassed (or covered) the two contributory terms, a cover of all original rows and hence the original function is included in the set of prime implicants. However, the complete set of prime implicants may not be essential; in this case the choice of a subset that still covers the function can give a lower-cost expression. Thus, the next step is to select only necessary prime implicants for a cover. To do this, a table is prepared with the prime implicants as column headings and original terms (Table 1) as row headings. A check mark is placed wherever a prime implicant covers an original term; this information is readily available from the tags associated with each prime implicant. Since the complete set of prime implicants constitute a cover, each row of this table will contain at least one check mark. Consider now a row (if one exists) containing only one check mark. Such a check mark is shown with an *. The prime implicant that supplies this check mark is *essential* for the cover since no other one will cover the same term. All such essential prime implicants should be identified first. Once this is done, the next step is to choose other prime implicants so that each original term is covered; i.e., so that the check marks under the set of all selected prime implicants include at least one check in each row and the total cost of these is as low as possible. This last procedure requires good judgment or exhaustive trial. At the end of the process a final test for a cover should be made by making sure that the set of selected prime implicants (columns) includes at least one check mark in every row.

5.7 DESIGN OF A 1-BIT FULL ADDER

The addition of two binary numbers can be mechanized in much the same way as by the pencil-and-paper method. Addition is done bit by bit starting at the rightmost bit position. Each bit addition produces a sum bit and also a carry to the next position to the left; the carry may have either a 1 or 0 value depending on the inputs to the bit adder and carry from the previous position. A 1-bit adder must therefore be capable of accepting three inputs. Two are the original bits (called a, b in this discussion) and the third input c is the carry out from the previous bit position. There are two outputs of the adder: the sum bit (s) and the carry out (c') (Fig. 5.7.1). We mention in passing that the linking of the successive 1-bit adders to perform addition of entire binary numbers can be done in several ways (see Chap. 8). In this section, we are interested in an adder for a single-bit position only as an example of a logic circuit.

The first step in the design of the adder is to set down the functions for sum and carry. Since both these functions have the same input variables, a single truth table with two function columns is used. Logical equations may be set down for the functions in a number of ways. The canonical minterm form for s is

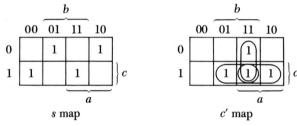

a	b	c	s	c'
0	0	0	0	0
0	0	1	1	0
0	1	0	1	0
0	1	1	0	1
1	0	0	1	0
1	0	1	0	1
1	1	0	0	1
1	1	1	1	1

(*a*) Truth table for sum bit (*s*) and carry out (*c'*) for a full 1-bit adder.

(*b*) Maps for *s* and *c'*.

$s \equiv \bar{a}\bar{b}c \lor \bar{a}b\bar{c} \lor a\bar{b}\bar{c} \lor abc$
$c' \equiv ab \lor ac \lor bc$

(*c*) Equations derived from maps.

Fig. 5.7.1 Design of minimum two-level full adder.

(1*a*) $s \equiv \bar{a}\bar{b}c \lor \bar{a}b\bar{c} \lor a\bar{b}\bar{c} \lor abc$

Another type of expression using the EXCLUSIVE OR operation is:

(1*b*) $s \equiv a \neq b \neq c$

The canonical *P* form for the carry function is found from the truth table:

(2) $c' \equiv \bar{a}bc \lor a\bar{b}c \lor ab\bar{c} \lor abc$

The cost of Eqs. (1*a*) and (2) is 32. Maps of these functions show that only *c'* can be reduced:

(3) $c' \equiv bc \lor ac \lor ab$

This has a cost of 9. At this point the adder cost has been brought down to 25 from 32.

Further reduction is not possible with the map method. However, a lower-cost circuit for the full adder is still possible, although the number of levels for the sum (s) function will be higher than two. This may be done by recognizing a pattern or relation between the two function columns of the truth table. Inspection shows that c' is the complement of s in all positions but the top and bottom entries. These two exceptions can be handled with separate correction terms. We use Eq. (3) for c' both because this is already a somewhat reduced expression and also because it is a two-level expression and it is desirable to keep the carry circuit fast to reduce overall carry propagation. The s function in terms of the c' function may be written

(4) $s \equiv \bar{c}'(a \lor b \lor c) \lor abc$

Equations (3) and (4) are the equations of a low-cost adder. The cost of this circuit is 19 plus one inverter to generate $\bar{c}'$. The $\bar{c}'$ circuit is two level; the s circuit is five level.

A slightly lower cost full adder is represented by the system of equations

(5) $h \equiv a\bar{b} \lor \bar{a}b$ }
                                          half-adders
(6) $s \equiv c\bar{h} \lor \bar{c}h$ }

(7) $c' \equiv ab \lor ch$

The cost is 18 plus one inverter (for h). However, this circuit requires five levels for s and four levels for c'.

The 1-bit full adder is only the beginning of the design of practical adder circuits. For more details see Chap. 8.

5.8   FUNCTIONS OF n VARIABLES

The question may well be raised whether the AND, OR, NOT set of primitive functions is the only possible set for representing general logical functions or for primitives of a logical algebra. To understand this problem, consider the possible functions of two variables. Since for two variables, any *single* function (truth vector) is a configuration of 4 bits, there are 2^4 possible functions. These are enumerated in Fig. 5.8.1. The functions (or connectives as they are sometimes called) numbered 1, 7, 10, or 12 are the familiar AND, OR, NOT functions.

Notice that for n variables, the number of possible functions is

(1) $\quad 2^{2^n}$

The most common case of interest is $n \equiv 2$; that is, the 16 functions of two variables. Several important functions of more than two variables can be expressed as functions of two variables by use of the commutative, distributive, and associative laws. The functions of two variables are of great interest not only in circuit design but also in programming because the application of logical operators is a powerful problem-solving tool. For this reason, most computers include instructions in their repertoire for logical operators such as AND, OR, NOT, EXCLUSIVE OR ($\neq$).

Suppose it is desired to include the ability to perform *all* of the 16 Boolean connectives as machine instructions.

The scheme presented below is the same as is used in the IBM 7030 (STRETCH) computer. The basic principles are as follows:

If we interpret 0 as false and 1 as true, it is possible to array all 16 possible results of operating on two variables X and Y as follows:

X	0	0	1	1	*Boolean name*	*Example*	*Mathematical name*	*Logic symbol*	*Class*
Y	0	1	0	1					
0	0	0	0	0	0	0	False	F	I
1	0	0	0	1	AND	XY	And	$\wedge$ or	III
2	0	0	1	0	X AND NOT Y	$X\overline{Y}$	~ Conditional	⊅	I,III
3	0	0	1	1	X	X	Identity	X	
4	0	1	0	0	(NOT X) AND Y	$\overline{X}Y$	~ Conditional	⊄	I,III
5	0	1	0	1	Y	Y	Identity	Y	
6	0	1	1	0	EXCLUSIVE OR	$X \neq Y$	Exclusive or	$\neq$	I
7	0	1	1	1	OR	$X \vee Y$	Or	$\vee$	III
8	1	0	0	0	NOR	$X \downarrow Y$	Peirce	$\downarrow$	I,II,III
9	1	0	0	1	EQUAL	$X = Y$	Biconditional	$\equiv$	II
10	1	0	1	0	NOT Y	$\overline{Y}$	Negation	~ Y or $\overline{Y}$	I,II
11	1	0	1	1	X OR NOT Y	$X \vee \overline{Y}$	Conditional	⊂	II,III
12	1	1	0	0	NOT X	$\overline{X}$	Negation	~ X or $\overline{X}$	I,II
13	1	1	0	1	(NOT X) OR Y	$\overline{X} \vee Y$	Conditional	⊃	II,III
14	1	1	1	0	NAND (NOT BOTH)	$X \uparrow Y$	Sheffer stroke			I,II,III
15	1	1	1	1	1	1	True	T	II

The categorization into classes allows us to state without proof the following theorem:

If a subset of all the connectives should be chosen such that all three classes are represented and, in addition, such that if T is the only connective of class II, then F is not the only connective of class I, or such that if F is the only connective of class I, then T is not the only connective of class II, all possible connectives can be generated from this subset and the subset is complete.

Fig. 5.8.1 The 16 logical connectives of two variables.

1. Consider the operand bits to be held in two registers X and Y. The same Boolean connective will be applied to each bit pair $X[I]$ and $Y[I]$; the result will be placed in the result register $Z[I]$.

2. A 4-bit code is necessary to specify the particular connective desired since there are 2^4 possible connectives. Let the 4 bits which supply the designation of the connective be denoted by C. Physically C is a 4-bit register which may be part of the machine's operation-code register.

3. The heart of the circuit follows from the idea of encoding the contents of C so that it contains the 4-bit column which is the function of the truth table for the desired connective. For example, consider the connective EXCLU-SIVE OR (see next page)

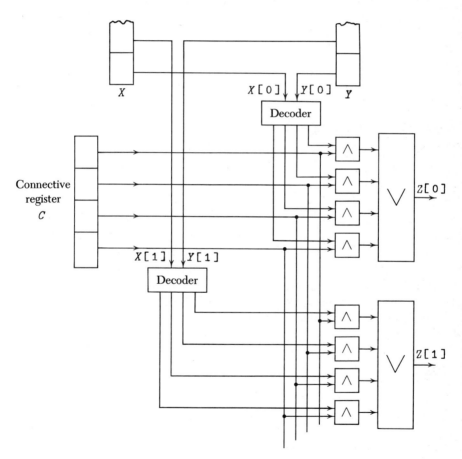

Fig. 5.8.2   Circuit implementing all functions of two variables on bit pairs from X and Y registers.

$X[I]$	$Y[I]$	C
0	0	0
0	1	1
1	0	1
1	1	0

4. With the connective specified as described above, the circuit uses each bit pair $X[I]$, $Y[I]$ to select one line from C for routing to Z (see Fig. 5.8.2). This selection is done by a decoder circuit. One and only one of the four output lines of a decoder is 1 at any one time; the line which is a 1 corresponds to the state of the input lines.

5. Properties of the circuit are

Cost (number of inputs) $\equiv 20N$
Number of levels $\equiv 3$
Fan-in $\equiv 4$
Fan-out $\equiv N$ (from connect-code register C)

5.9   NOT-AND (NAND OR SHEFFER STROKE) LOGIC

The NAND function is defined by

(1) $f \equiv \sim \wedge/x \equiv \curlywedge(x_0, x_1, \ldots)$

The logical function NOT-AND, or NAND, like the NOR function, is complete; i.e., it is sufficient by itself to realize an expression for any truth function. This may be illustrated by constructing the operations NOT, AND, OR using only NAND elements (Fig. 5.9.1). A single logic-block type is desirable since there is economy in manufacturing as few different parts as possible.

Any logical function expressed in a minterm-type expression can easily be converted to an expression using NAND only by the following reasoning. The minterm form is

(2) $f \equiv j \vee k \vee l \vee m$

where j, k, l, m are an AND expression of the input variables. Using DeMorgan's law on Eq. (2),

(3) $f \equiv \overline{\overline{j}\,\overline{k}\,\overline{l}\,\overline{m}} \equiv \curlywedge(\overline{j}, \overline{k}, \overline{l}, \overline{m})$

Here we introduce the symbol $\curlywedge$ to denote NAND; this is followed by a list of the input variables to which the NAND is applied. Now since j, k, l, m are each AND expressions of the input variables, Eq. (3) is seen to be a NAND function of variables which are NAND functions of the original variables. Equation (3) therefore illustrates the following principle:

To translate a minterm-type expression to a NAND expression, change all AND terms and all OR terms to NAND.

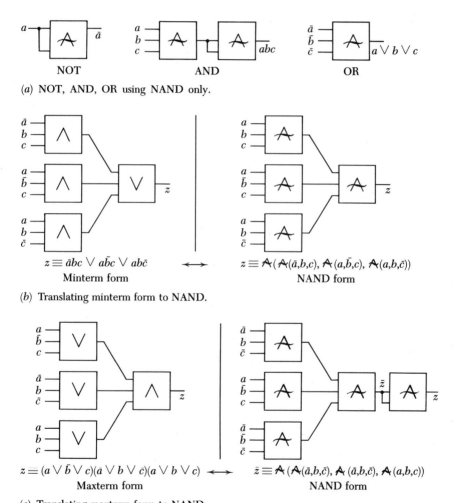

(*a*) NOT, AND, OR using NAND only.

$z \equiv \bar{a}bc \lor a\bar{b}c \lor ab\bar{c}$

Minterm form

$z \equiv \text{A}(\text{A}(\bar{a},b,c), \text{A}(a,\bar{b},c), \text{A}(a,b,\bar{c}))$

NAND form

(*b*) Translating minterm form to NAND.

$z = (a \lor \bar{b} \lor c)(\bar{a} \lor b \lor \bar{c})(a \lor b \lor c)$

Maxterm form

$\bar{z} \equiv \text{A}(\text{A}(\bar{a},b,\bar{c}), \text{A}(\bar{a},b,\bar{c}), \text{A}(a,b,c))$

NAND form

(*c*) Translating maxterm form to NAND.

Fig. 5.9.1 NAND functions and conversion from AND, OR, NOT logic.

A somewhat more involved rule exists for conversion of maxterm-type expressions to NAND form:

First negate (complement) all input variables. Then replace each OR term and the AND expression with a NAND term. The result thus far is the complement of the original function. A NAND of this, either with itself or with a 1 value, will therefore finally give the original function in terms only of NAND functions.

The NOR function defined as

$$f \equiv \sim \lor / x \equiv \forall(x_0, x_1, \ldots)$$

has properties analogous to NAND. To convert AND-OR logic to NOR, it is most convenient to start with the maxterm form, and equations like Eqs. (2) and (3). The above description then applies except that the words minterm, NAND, AND, OR are replaced by maxterm, NOR, OR, AND respectively.

5.10 DECOMPOSITION USING TWO-INPUT BLOCKS

Consider now the problem of designing logic circuits with logic blocks having a fan-in of 2. A straightforward approach is to first obtain a reduced minterm form and then partition each AND into as many two-input ANDs as necessary (and similarly for the OR). The explicit groupings and hence the logic-block designations can be indicated by explicit parenthesis pairs:

$$\overline{abcd} \equiv ((\overline{ab})\,(cd))$$

which represents three AND circuits, each with two inputs. It often pays to factor an expression before such grouping. Thus

(1) $y \equiv a\overline{bc} \lor \overline{a}bc \lor a\overline{bc} \equiv \overline{a}(\overline{bc} \lor \overline{b}c) \lor a\overline{bc}$

or

(2) $y \equiv ((\overline{a}((b\overline{c}) \lor (\overline{b}c))) \lor ((a\overline{b})\overline{c}))$
$\qquad\quad$ 12 34 4$\quad$ 5 532$\quad$ 67 7 61

where the numbers help identify the parenthesis pairs. Equation (2) has a cost of 14 compared to a cost of 16 by decomposing the AND and then OR terms directly without first factoring.

The above example, although a particular case, is suggestive of a general property: if y is a function of several variables denoted by the vector x, then y can be expressed as follows in terms of any x_i selected for attention:

(3) $y \equiv f(x) \equiv \overline{x}_i g_i \lor x_i h_i$

Original function:

$$y \equiv \overline{abcd} \vee \overline{ab}c \vee \overline{a}cd$$

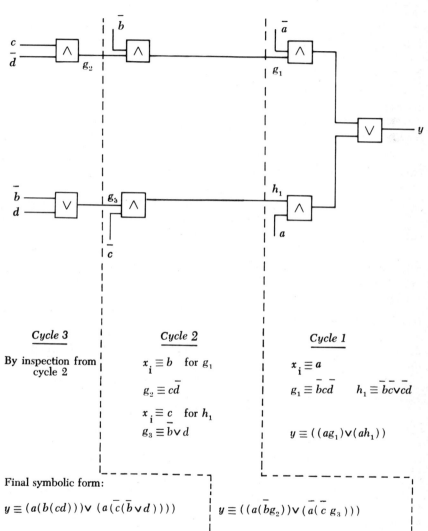

Fig. 5.10.1 **Example of decomposition design method.**

where the two functions g_i and h_i are easily verified by substitution into Eq. (3) to satisfy

(4) $g_i \equiv y$ for $x_i \equiv 0$

(5) $h_i \equiv y$ for $x_i \equiv 1$

An elegant design procedure consists of *decomposing* the given function by using Eqs. (3) to (5) in successive cycles, eliminating one variable per cycle (see Fig. 5.10.1).

NAND circuits can be decomposed by using the same idea, specifically the NAND form of Eq. (3):

(6) $y \equiv \curlywedge(\curlywedge(\overline{x_i},g_i),\curlywedge(x_i,h_i))$

Care must be taken to apply the method consistently until *all* variables are decomposed. For example, the simple AND function (which might well appear at the end of a cycle) must be handled as follows:

(7) $z \equiv ab \equiv \overline{a}0 \vee ab \equiv \curlywedge(\curlywedge(\overline{a},0),\curlywedge(a,b)) \equiv \curlywedge(1,\curlywedge(a,b))$

5.11 BINARY DECODERS

A binary decoder is a circuit with n input lines and 2^n output lines arranged so that for each of the possible 2^n *states* of the input lines, one and only one output line is a 1 and the rest are 0. Such a circuit is sometimes called a 1-out-of-N circuit. In equation form, the circuit properties are

(1) $\rho Y \equiv 2 * \rho X$

(2) $Y \equiv (2 \bot X) = \iota 2 * \rho X$

To help visualize a decoder function, a specific example is shown in Fig. 5.11.1; the 3-bit input 1,1,0 is seen to produce an output of all 0s except for line 6, which is a 1.

The decoder function is very important because it translates the representation of a number from the conventional highly compact positional-notation to a 1-out-of-N form that is required for physical selection of a single desired object from among several objects. Decoder circuits are often used in the storage-selection (addressing) circuits of core storage and the operation decoder which controls instruction execution. The principle of the decoder circuit is also

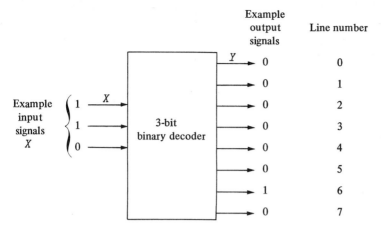

Fig. 5.11.1   3-bit decoder with inputs (1,1,0).

fundamental to many communication circuits such as telephone dialing. Here, the act of dialing specifies a desired telephone as a number; equipment must translate this number to a selection of a single telephone from all phones connected to the system.

From a circuit viewpoint, a decoder is a circuit with many inputs and many outputs. A design may be made by truth table and using one of the simplification techniques described earlier. This is not too practical for several reasons: (1) Because the number of outputs (as well as inputs) is often very large, the truth table would be unwieldy. (2) A little thought (or a simple example) shows that for a decoder, the (output) columns of the truth table contain all 0s except for a single 1 entry; with this simple property, it is wasteful to list the full truth table. (3) The previous minimization processes are not useful for decoder structures because those methods were designed primarily for single-output circuits. Other methods will be used.

We assume that the inputs to the decoder are $2n$ lines; n of these are the bits, the other n the complements of the bits. These are usually available from a register in the system. The output of the decoder is a set of 2^n lines. As noted previously, each input bit configuration results in a 1 for one and only one of these lines.

A one-level design (Fig. 5.11.2) can be obtained by recalling that each output has a truth vector containing a single 1. It follows that each output is a logical AND function of the inputs. If N_A is the number of AND circuits, $N_{D/A}$ the number of diodes per AND circuit, and N_D the total number of diodes, we see that the one-level approach for an n-bit decoder requires

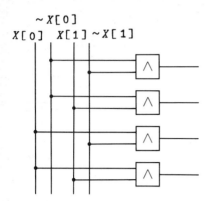

Fig. 5.11.2 A one-level 2-bit decoder.

(3) $N_A \equiv 2^n$

(4) $N_{D/A} \equiv n$

(5) $N_D \equiv n2^n$ (cost)

The diode count N_D becomes very large for even moderate n; for example, there are 2048 diodes for $n \equiv 8$. Moreover, each AND circuit must be capable of eight inputs. One advantage of the one-level circuit is its speed: all signals propagate through only one stage.

A less costly approach, called the *simple tree* decoder, is shown in Fig. 5.11.3 in both relay and logic-block implementation. To help follow the operation of the circuit, a particular input configuration (1,0,1,1) is illustrated; in the relay circuit, each contact closed for these inputs is shown accompanied by an arc. The circuit supplies a closed path only to line 11.

The *dual-tree* decoder is a different circuit and less costly than the simple tree, although its internal fan-out requirements are higher. The basic idea is to decode the input variables in pairs in one level of circuit then combine each output of these with every other output to produce the next level of outputs. This process continues until all outputs are derived. A circuit for four input variables is shown in Fig. 5.11.4; again to help follow the circuit operation, the particular input (1,0,1,1) is shown.

The dual tree may be designed by a symbolic procedure which will now be described and illustrated (Fig. 5.11.5). Let n equal the number of input variables. A diagram containing boxes with a number in each box is constructed according to the following rules (these follow the pair-combination principle described above):

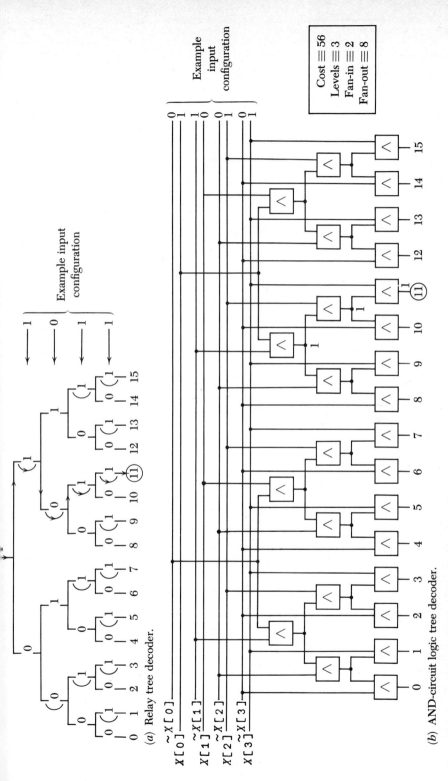

Fig. 5.11.3 Two implementations of simple tree decoders ($n \equiv 4$).

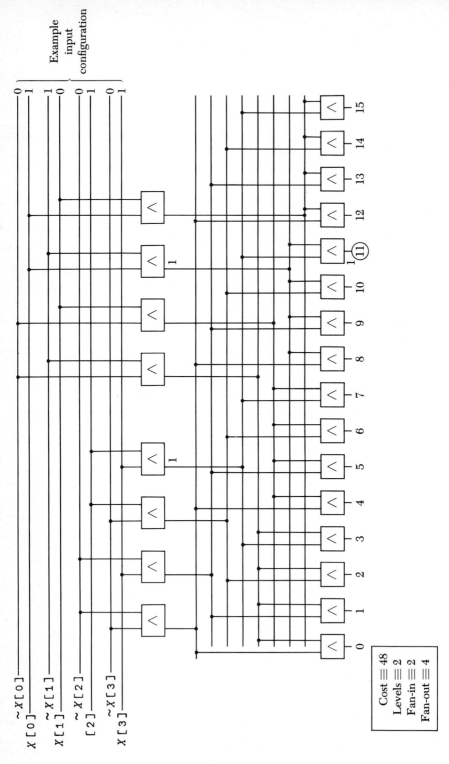

Fig. 5.11.4 Dual-tree decoder showing 1 signals for inputs (1, 0, 1, 1).

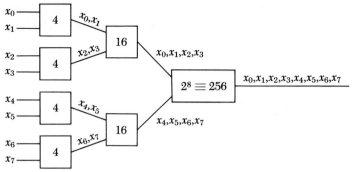

Number of AND circuits $= 256 + 16 + 16 + 4 + 4 + 4 + 4 = 304$
Number of inputs/AND circuits $= 2$
Cost $\equiv 608$
Number of levels $\equiv \lceil \log_2 8 = 3$
Fan-out $\equiv 16$ (feeding last level)

(*a*) 8 bit.

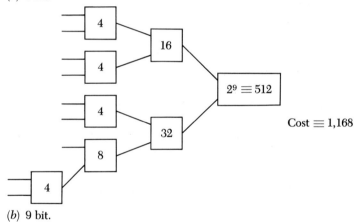

(*b*) 9 bit.

Fig. 5.11.5 Symbolic design of dual-tree decoder.
Note: $x_i \equiv X[I]$.

1. The box on the far right is labeled 2^n.
2. Each box (except the last) feeds one and only one box.
3. Work back to successive boxes, each box requiring two inputs. The numbers in the two boxes feeding any given box must be such that:
   a. Their product is the label on the given box.
   b. Each number is a power of 2 and as nearly equal as possible.

There are no boxes labeled 2 since these correspond to inputs.

Each box in the symbolic diagram represents a *set* of two-input AND circuits. The number of AND circuits in a set is the number placed in the box. Note that this is the product of the numbers in the boxes feeding the box in question.

Inputs	Outputs	One level				Simple tree				Dual tree			
n		c	L	FI	FO	c	L	FI	FO	c	L	Fi	FO
2	4	8		2	2	8	1	2	2	8	1	2	2
3	8	24		3	4	24	2		4	24	2		
4	16	64		4	8	56	3		8	48	2		4
5	32	160		5	16	120	4		16	96	3		
6	64	384		6	32	248	5		32	176	3		
7	128	896		7	64	504	6		64	328	3		
8	256	2,048		8	128	1,016	7		128	608	3		16
9	512	4,604		9	256	2,040	8		256	1,168	4		
10	1,024	10,240		10	512	4,088	9		512	2,240	4		
11	2,048	22,528		11	1,024	8,184	10		1,024	4,368	4		
12	4,096	49,152		12	2,048	16,376	11		2,048	8,544	4		

One-level circuit:

c — Count $\equiv n2^n$
L — Levels $\equiv 1$
FI — Fan-in $\equiv n$
FO — Fan-out $\equiv 2^{n-1}$ (input drivers)

Simple tree:

c — Count $\equiv 8(2^{n-1} - 1)$
L — Levels $\equiv n - 1$
FI — Fan-in $\equiv 2$
FO — Fan-out $\equiv 2$ (internal); 2^{n-1} for input drivers

Dual tree:

c — Count $\equiv 2n \displaystyle\sum_{j \equiv 1}^{\lceil \log_2 n \rceil} \frac{2^{2^j}}{2^j}$ for n a power of 2

$$c_{2m} \equiv 2c_m + 2^{2m+1} \qquad \left.\begin{array}{l}\\ \end{array}\right\} \text{for } n \text{ not a power of 2;}$$
$$c_{2m+1} \equiv c_m + c_{m+1} + 2^{2m+2}; c_1 \equiv 0 \left.\begin{array}{l}\\ \end{array}\right\} \text{substitute } 1 \leqslant m \leqslant n$$

L — Levels $\equiv \lceil \log_2 n \rceil$
FI — Fan-in $\equiv 2$
FO — Fan-out $\equiv 2\lceil n \div 2 \rceil$ (internal); 2 for input drivers

Fig. 5.11.6 Properties of decoder circuits.

Each symbolic line represents a set of physical lines, each line in the set being a 1 only for one of the combinations of the variables involved. The number of AND blocks is the sum of the numbers in all the boxes; the circuit cost is twice this.

A formula for the diode count may be obtained for the case where n is a power of 2.

$$(6) \qquad N_D \equiv 2n \sum_{j \equiv 1}^{\lceil \log_2 n \rceil} \frac{2^{2j}}{2^j}$$

$$(7) \qquad N_{D/A} \equiv 2$$

If n is *not* a power of 2, no such simple formula exists. However, the diode count may easily be determined using the symbolic-synthesis approach as shown in Fig. 5.11.5 for a 9-bit decoder ($n \equiv 9$).

Several properties of interest for the three methods of decoder implementation are summarized in chart form in Fig. 5.11.6.

5.12 DESIGN OF A DECIMAL (BCD) DECODER

A binary-coded-decimal (BCD) decoder for a single decimal digit is a circuit having four input variables and 10 output variables. For each input combination, one and only one output is a 1 (the rest are 0). Since the four input lines represent a decimal digit, only 10 combinations (of the possible 16) can actually appear.

One approach to the design is to use the principles developed earlier for a binary decoder—say, the dual-tree type of circuit. If the input bits are called a, b, c, d, first decode the pairs (a,b) and (c,d) by AND circuits as follows:

$$\bar{a}\bar{b}, \bar{a}b, a\bar{b}$$
$$\bar{c}\bar{d}, \bar{c}d, c\bar{d}, cd$$

notice that the ab combination never occurs if the inputs represent BCD encoding. The cost of the seven AND circuits is 14. Their outputs are then combined in pairs; there are 10 of these AND circuits. Total cost of this BCD decoder is then 34.

A somewhat lower-cost circuit is possible based on further properties of the 10 valid combinations of inputs. Thus, since a *must* be 0 if b is 1, the term $\bar{a}b$ need not be implemented (only b need be supplied). Also, the term $a\bar{b}$ is not required since wherever a is 1, b must be 0 for any valid input combination. The decoder design may then be expressed as follows:

$$p \equiv \bar{a}\bar{b} \qquad y_0 \equiv pq \qquad y_5 \equiv br$$
$$q \equiv \bar{c}\bar{d} \qquad y_1 \equiv pr \qquad y_6 \equiv bs$$
$$r \equiv \bar{c}d \qquad y_2 \equiv ps \qquad y_7 \equiv bt$$
$$s \equiv c\bar{d} \qquad y_3 \equiv pt \qquad y_8 \equiv aq$$
$$t \equiv cd \qquad y_4 \equiv bq \qquad y_9 \equiv ar$$

The cost of this circuit is 30.

Another approach to BCD decoder design is to set down the truth tables for all 10 outputs. Since 6 of the 16 combinations never occur, these are "don't care" conditions (entries of X are made for them in the function columns). Each function may be separately reduced–i.e., by the map method. However, with judicious "don't care" assignments good clustering and reduction will be possible.

5.13 BINARY ENCODERS

A binary encoder circuit performs the inverse function to the binary decoder; it produces on n output lines a configuration of 0,1 values which when interpreted

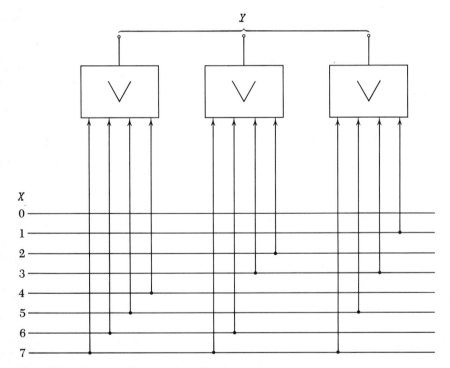

Fig. 5.13.1 Binary encoder (eight-input liner).

as a binary number is the position number of which (single one) of its input lines is a 1. If X denotes the input lines and Y the output lines, the function may be expressed as

(1) $Y \leftarrow ((\lceil 2 \circledast \rho X) \rho 2) \top X / \iota \rho X$

A circuit is shown for $\rho X \equiv 8$ (Fig. 5.13.1). The circuit has the following properties:

> Number of levels $\equiv 1$
> Cost $\equiv \lceil ((\rho X) \div 2) \lceil 2 \circledast \rho X \equiv 12$
> Fan-in $\equiv \rho X \div 2 \equiv 4$
> Fan-out $\equiv \lceil 2 \circledast X \equiv 3$ from X

PROBLEMS

5.1 Give the truth table for each of the following:

a) $f \equiv ab\bar{c} \vee abc \vee \bar{a}\bar{b}c \vee \bar{a}\bar{b}\bar{c}$
b) $f \equiv (a \vee b \vee \bar{c})(\bar{a} \vee \bar{b} \vee c)(\bar{a} \vee \bar{b} \vee c)$
c) $f \equiv ab \vee c\bar{d} \vee a\bar{b}c$

5.2 Express $f \equiv abc \vee a\bar{b}c \vee ab\bar{c}$:

a) As a P list
b) As an S list
c) In canonical P form
d) In canonical S form

5.3 Repeat Prob. 5.2 for the function $f \equiv abc \vee \bar{a}bc \vee \bar{b}\bar{c}$.

5.4 Use DeMorgan's law to obtain an expression for f in Prob. 5.2 using only AND and NOT primitives.

5.5 Given

$$f \equiv \bar{a}b\bar{c}d \vee ab\bar{c}d \vee \bar{a}bcd \vee ab\bar{c}\bar{d} \vee ab\bar{c}d$$

a) Draw the circuit.
b) Give cost, fan-in, number of levels, fan-out.
c) Simplify the expression for f using Boolean algebra.
d) Repeat (*b*) for the simplified expression.

5.6 A 1-bit *full subtracter* has three inputs—minuend m, subtrahend h, and borrow in b— and two outputs—difference d and borrow out b'.

   a) Give the truth table.
   b) Design a circuit.

5.7 Simplify in AND-OR-NOT logic using Boolean algebra

   a) $f \equiv \bar{a}\bar{b}cd \vee ab\bar{c}d \vee \bar{a}bc\bar{d} \vee abc\bar{d}$
   b) $f \equiv a\bar{d} \vee ab\bar{c}d$

5.8 *a)* Simplify the function of Prob. 5.7 using the Karnaugh map. Give cost, fan-in, fan-out, number of levels.
   b) Simplify $f \equiv a\bar{d} \vee ab\bar{c}d$ using the Karnaugh map.
   c) Simplify the function represented by $P \equiv 9,10,11,12,13,14,15$ in S and P form.

5.9 Repeat Prob. 5.8 using the Quine-McCluskey method.

5.10 *a)* Design a 1-bit full adder using NAND blocks only. Your circuit should be as low cost as possible.
   b) Repeat (*a*) using NOR blocks only.
   c) Design the circuit using AND/OR blocks with fan-in of 2.

5.11 Using NOR blocks only show circuits for:

   a) EXCLUSIVE OR (half-adder)
   b) NAND
   c) $a \wedge \bar{b}$

5.12 A four-input NAND function is desired but only two-input NAND blocks are available; show a circuit for $\bar{\wedge}(a,b,c,d)$ using only two-input NAND blocks.

5.13 Given n lines X. Design a circuit for obtaining a parity signal; the output of the parity circuit p should be

$$P \equiv 2 \mid +/X \quad \text{or} \quad P \equiv \neq /X \quad \text{for} \quad \rho X \equiv 4$$

5.14 Show the symbolic design of a 7-bit dual-tree decoder. What is the cost, fan-in, fan-out, and number of levels for this circuit?

5.15 Design a 4-bit BCD *one-upper* circuit; i.e., a circuit for the function of X given by

$$Y \equiv (4\rho 2) \top 10 \mid 1 + 2 \bot X$$

5.16 Given a set of four lines X. Design an economical circuit whose outputs are Y such that Y is the encoding of the *number* of lines in X which are 1, that is,

$$Y \equiv (4\rho 2)\top + /X$$

5.17 In a ternary (three-valued) logic system, how many functions are there of two variables?

5.18 This is a research problem. Write an APL program for the Quine-McCluskey method. The problem may be divided into two parts:

a) Obtaining the prime implicants
b) Choosing the lowest cost cover from the prime implicants

5.19 This is a project. Write a logic-simulator program that accepts from the user a description of any combinational logic circuit, the inputs to this circuit, and computes/prints:

a) Output of every line in the circuit
b) Fan-in and fan-out of every logic block
c) Circuit cost

The user would prepare to use the program by first drawing the circuit and numbering every line. Each logic block is considered to have the same number as its output line. From the diagram, the user enters the following data for each logic block:

1. The number of the block
2. The numbers of the lines feeding the block
3. The logic-block type (indicating AND, OR, NOR, NAND, NOT, etc.)

For each logic-block type, the user must define the logic function by giving its truth vector. *Note:* A three-input AND is therefore a distinct block type from a two-input AND.

REFERENCES

1. Boole, G.: "An Investigation of the Laws of Thought on Which Are Founded the Mathematical Theories of Logic and Probabilities," Dover Publications, Inc., New York, 1951.
2. Burks, A., et al.: Complete Decoding Nets: General Theory and Minimality, *J. Soc. Ind. Apl. Math*, vol. 2, pp. 201–243 (1954).
3. Chu, Y.: "Digital Computer Design Fundamentals," McGraw-Hill Book Company, New York, 1962.

4. Culbertson, J. T.: "Mathematics and Logic for Digital Devices," D. Van Nostrand Company, Inc., Princeton, N.J., 1958.

5. Huntington, E. V.: New Sets of Independent Postulates for the Algebra of Logic with Special Reference to Whitehead and Russell's Principia Mathematica, *Trans. Am. Math. Soc.,* vol. 35, pp. 274–304 (1933).

6. Karnaugh, M.: The Map Method for Synthesis of Combinational Logic Circuits, *AIEE Commun. Electron.,* November 1953, pp. 593–599.

7. McCluskey, E. J.: Minimization of Boolean Functions, *Bell Sys. Tech. J.* November 1956, pp. 1417–1444.

8. Maley, G. A., and J. Earle: "Logic Design of Transistor Digital Computers," Prentice-Hall, Inc., Englewood Cliffs, N.J., 1963.

9. Miller, R. E.: "Switching Theory," vol. I, "Combinational Circuits," John Wiley & Sons, Inc., New York, 1965.

10. Phister, M.: "Logical Design of Digital Computers," John Wiley & Sons, Inc., New York, 1958.

11. Pressman, A. I.: "Design of Transistorized Circuits for Digital Computers," John F. Rider, Publisher, Inc., New York, 1959.

12. Quine, W. V.: "Methods of Logic," Holt, Rinehart and Winston, Inc., New York, 1950.

13. Richards, R. K.: "Arithmetic Operations in Digital Computers," D. Van Nostrand Company, Inc., Princeton, N.J., 1955.

14. Staff of Computation Laboratory: "Synthesis of Electronic Computing and Control Circuits," Harvard University Press, Cambridge, Mass., 1951.

15. Whitehead, A. N., and B. Russell: "Principia Mathematica," 2d ed., Cambridge University Press, London, 1962.

6

Data-flow Circuits and Magnetic-core Storage

The economies inherent in the centralization of fast expensive processing circuitry imply the ability to store information not currently processed and to move stored information between the central processing points and the storage locations. This basic idea applies not only among the large units of the system but also within each unit. Thus the processing unit itself contains registers for storing operands, a few fast transformation circuits such as an adder, shifter, etc., and paths for moving information between the registers and the transformation circuits. Circuits that provide paths for movement of information are called *data-flow* or *bus circuits*. The organization of the data-flow structure is a fundamental property of a data-processing system.

The study of data-flow organization may well begin with the question: What are the ways of interconnecting, say, *s* sources and *d* destinations? Some answers to this are summarized in this chapter with special emphasis to the trade-offs possible between economy and speed. Illustrations of these rather abstract considerations are then discussed for some concrete cases.

A proper focus for understanding magnetic-core storage is the scheme for routing the contents of any storage cell to the data register. Some methods for doing this and their implications for computer organization are considered.

Aside from the paths themselves, another important consideration is the orderly control of the information sent along these paths. Of special interest is the case of several sources (or destinations) that provide continuous flow that must be maintained; i.e., routing to the paths must be done within strict time constraints, yet time is available for interleaving flow of many sources along common paths if the switching is carefully controlled. Some idealized models will be proposed and analyzed.

6.1 INTERCONNECTION CONFIGURATIONS

In this section we consider several ways to connect s sources and d destinations. Figure 6.1.1 shows an abbreviated circuit notation which will be used on

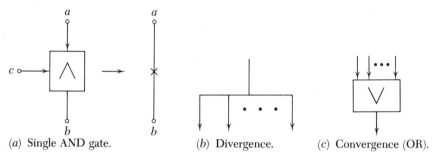

(a) Single AND gate.   (b) Divergence.   (c) Convergence (OR).

Fig. 6.1.1 Notation and elementary operations.

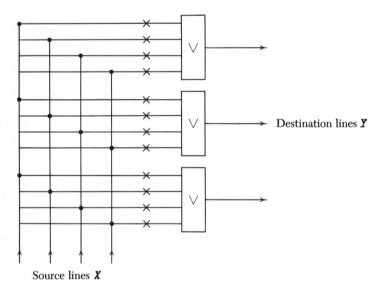

Destination lines **Y**

Source lines **X**

Fig. 6.1.2 Grid-type circuit ($s \equiv 4; d \equiv 3$).

subsequent diagrams in this chapter. In particular, a cross symbol will denote an AND circuit; the line supplying the control will not be shown explicitly since the main objective is to display the data flow not the control.

Figures 6.1.2 to 6.1.5 show several ways of interconnecting s sources and d destinations. The methods differ in the amount of logic circuitry required and in the degree of concurrency, i.e., the maximum number of source-destination transmissions possible at the same time. In reckoning concurrency, we omit *broadcast*-type transmission (where a single source transmits to several destinations at once). Note that at most, only one line at a time should be 1 into an OR circuit or else there will be confusion at the output of the OR.

Figure 6.1.2 permits the maximum possible concurrency, which is the smaller of the number of sources or destinations. Figure 6.1.3 is a low-cost circuit called

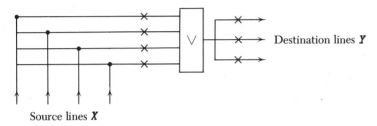

Source lines X

Fig. 6.1.3   Single bus ($s \equiv 4; d \equiv 3$).

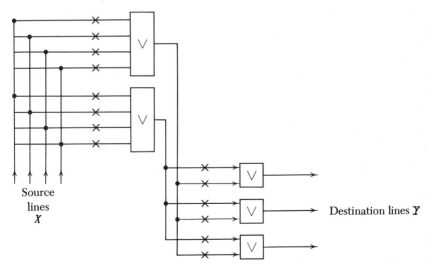

Source
lines
X

Destination lines Y

Fig. 6.1.4 k-bus type A ($s \equiv 4; d \equiv 3; k \equiv 2$).

a *single bus.* The idea of the single bus is analogous to the central train terminal used by railroads to bring commuters to their offices. Instead of directly routing each commuter to his office from his suburban station line, all such lines are brought to a central point, and the commuters use facilities from there to connect to their destinations. Although the single bus is economical in circuitry, only one transmission at a time, a concurrency of 1, is possible.

If the direct connection and single bus are limits of economy and concurrency, some intermediate circuits are also possible. For example Fig. 6.1.4 uses k intermediate switching points. Figure 6.1.5 is valuable when it is possible to group the sources so that only one source in any one group is active at one time.

The circuits given by no means exhaust the possible types of interconnection logic.

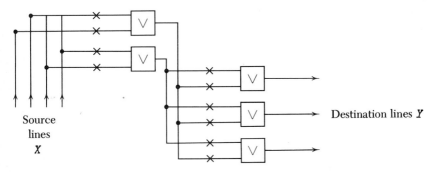

Fig. 6.1.5 k-bus type B ($s = 4; d = 3; k = 2$).

Table 6.1.6 Cost concurrency for interconnection methods

Type	Cost	Concurrency
Direct	$3sd$	$s \sqsubset d$
Single bus	$3s + 2d$	1
Bus type A	$3k(s + d)$	k
Bus type B	$3s + 3kd$	k with group constraint

6.2 BUS PRIORITY CONTROL FOR NONCRITICAL SOURCES

By a noncritical source (or destination) we mean a source with no strict time constraint on the interval between its request for service and the granting of the request.

Consider a set of N noncritical sources which is to be connected to a single noncritical destination. The sources may be ranked with regard to their priority. At any given bus time available to noncritical sources, the highest-priority source requesting service is to be selected for switching to the bus. One way of determining the highest-priority source which is "on" is by performing a sequential scan starting with the highest-priority source and proceeding to the lower-priority ones until an "on" request line is found. The successive lines selected for testing can be specified as the outputs of a clock or a decoder fed by a counter. When a 1 request line is encountered, counter-stepping ceases and the decoder output indicates the line found in 1-out-of-N code directly suitable for bus-switch selection.

In place of sequential scanning of the source "request" signals, combinational circuits may be used for selecting the highest-priority source to be switched. Two circuits of this type are shown in Figs. 6.2.1 and 6.2.2. In Fig. 6.2.1 each request line contributes to the conditioning of all lower-priority lines. The

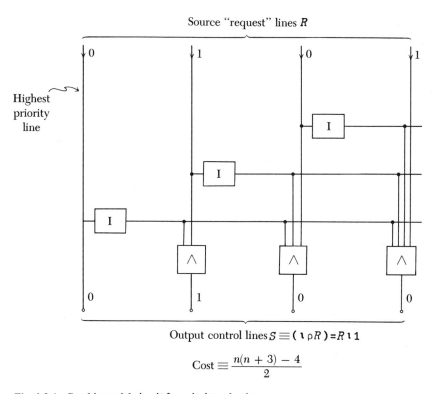

$$\text{Cost} \equiv \frac{n(n+3)-4}{2}$$

Fig. 6.2.1 Combinatorial circuit for priority selection.

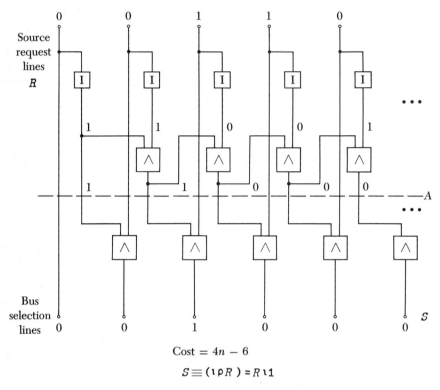

$$\text{Cost} = 4n - 6$$

$$S \equiv (\imath \rho R\,) = R \imath 1$$

Fig. 6.2.2 Low-cost circuit for priority selection.

circuit cost is proportional to the square of the number of request lines.

Figure 6.2.2 shows a circuit which is cheaper but slower than the circuit of Fig. 6.2.1 because in Fig. 6.2.2 the outputs cannot be sensed until at worst all signals pass the successive AND circuits above the line A. The source request lines are shown at the top, 0 indicating "no request," 1 indicating "request." Priority decreases from the left. The circuitry from the input lines to dashed line A transforms the input-line pattern to one wherein there are all 1s from the left until the position where the first 1 is found in the input configuration and all lines to the right of this position are 0. To obtain the desired output configuration, it remains to operate on the lines at level A to detect the transition between 1 and 0 at this level. Hence, below level A there are pairwise AND circuits for this detection. Cost of the combinational priority circuit is linear in the number of input lines.

6.3 DATA FLOW OF A SIMPLE PROCESSOR

A data-flow diagram shows the explicit paths provided between various parts of the system. It normally does not show control lines or the manner of generating control signals. Each line may represent a multiplicity of similar lines, e.g., all the bits of a word, or byte. Where the bit width may be different in different portions of the diagram, the common width may be implicit; other widths are shown by numbers in parentheses. The narrow rectangles denote registers, i.e., circuits for storing bits.

To make the discussion specific, consider the data-flow diagram of the simple hypothetical processor Fig. 6.3.1. The path widths are 32 bits unless otherwise specified. The instruction is also 32 bits long; the current instruction is held in the instruction register I, which is shown in some detail to display the meaning assigned to its various fields. The processor is fed from the storage data register; this line is routed to either the instruction register (for instruction fetching) or to the processor storage register (for data fetching). The processor storage register also has a path back to the storage data register for storing the results of processing. As for the paths within the processor, most registers are bussed to one of the inputs of the ADDER; the processor storage register is routed to the other input of the ADDER. Zeros may also be applied to each ADDER input; this allows the ADDER to be used as a central routing point as well as for arithmetic. Accordingly, the ADDER output is distributed to most registers. The address part of the instruction specifies one of three types of information. The most frequent type is the *address* of data, i.e., its location in storage. The address must be routed to the storage address register. In branch-type instructions, if the branch is successful, the *address* part of the instruction replaces the contents of the program counter P. The third case is typified by the shift instructions in which case the address part of the instruction specifies the number of positions to be shifted. This information can be routed to the shift counter N.

During normal sequencing, where a program branch is not involved, the program counter is normally advanced by 1 to *point* to the next instruction in sequence. This incrementation may be done by the ADDER by routing P to the ADDER and supplying a 1 to the other ADDER input. The result is routed back to P.

In our example machine, the programmer may specify indirect addressing by bit 14 of the instruction being 1. In this case, the address is first used to fetch a data word, but the rightmost 17 bits of this word are routed to replace the corresponding bits of I, the address part of the instruction. From this point, the instruction is executed as if it had just been fetched. (See Chap. 9 for a discussion of the purposes of indirect addressing.)

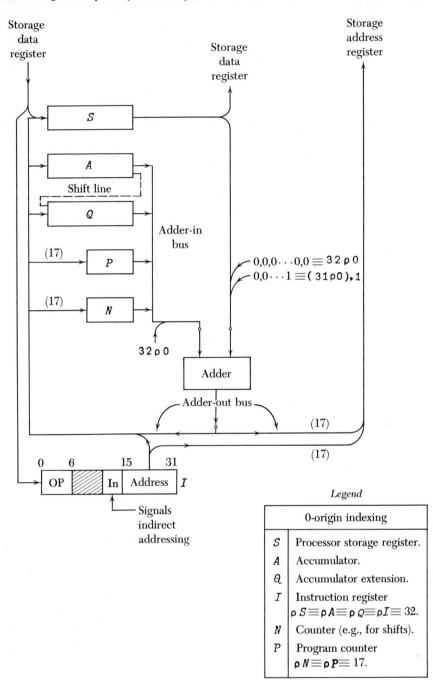

Fig. 6.3.1   Data flow of a simple hypothetical 32-bit processor.

6.4 EXAMPLES OF BUS CIRCUITS IN THE IBM 7090 COMPUTER

Bus circuits appear at many levels of circuit interconnection in a computer system. As an example, consider the IBM 7090, a large binary computer. The most obvious bus configuration is in the unit called the 7606 Multiplexor (Fig. 6.4.1) which is a set of busses for connecting the central processing unit and data channels with the machine's core storage. Basically, the multiplexor contains three busses: (1) data out, (2) data in, (3) address in.† These busses are independent except for a path provided from core storage data out to the channel address switches for channel indirect addressing.

A less obvious but no less important example of bus principles is illustrated by the data-flow organization of the IBM 7090 Central Processing Unit (CPU). Even a superficial glance at the data-flow diagram (Fig. 6.4.2) shows that the storage register and ADDER serve as highly centralized switching points. They are therefore outputs from busses with the numerous input paths as shown.

†The terms "in" and "out" are from the viewpoint of the storage terminals.

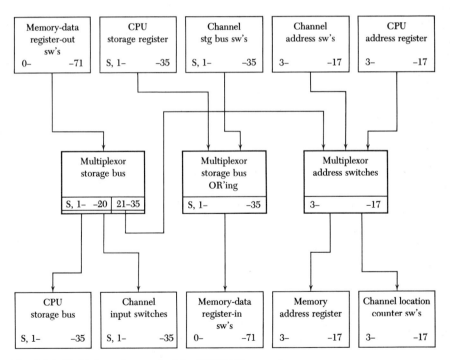

Fig. 6.4.1 Multiplexor (storage bus) for IBM 7090 computer.

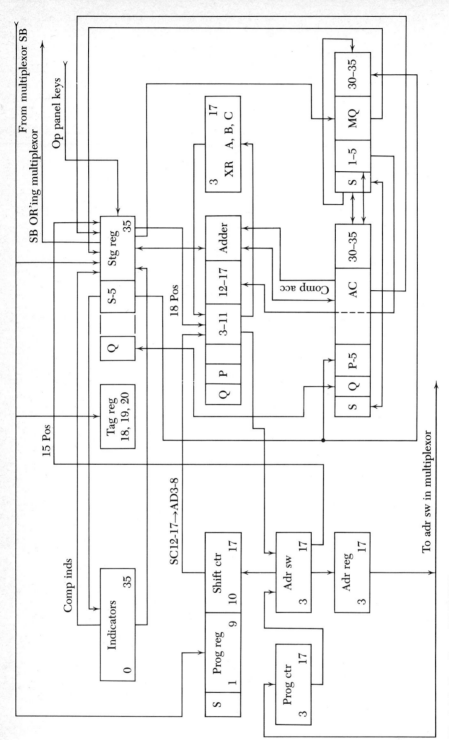

Fig. 6.4.2 Data flow of IBM 7090 processor.

A high proportion of 7090 instructions involves gate openings to and from various bus switches. However, for economy, not all paths are direct since only a limited concurrency of signals along paths is necessary. Thus there is a good deal of routing, sometimes circuitous, in order to move information from source to destination along the few paths provided. As a dramatic example, consider the instruction TRANSFER AND SET INDEX (TSX) used for subroutine linking. It requires that the 2s complement of the contents of the program counter (Progr Ctr) be sent to a specified index register and the program then branch to a location specified in the instruction; this address is held in the processor address register (Adr Reg). Since there is no direct path from program counter to index registers, this instruction is accomplished as follows:

1. Prog Ctr is sent to address switches (Adr Sw).
2. Adr Sw is sent to the storage register (Stg Reg).
3. Stg Reg is sent to the adder.
4. Adder output is sent to the specified index register.
5. The index-register contents are routed back through the adder for complementation and hence back to the index register.
6. The address register (Adr Reg) is routed to the program counter to effect the program branch.

6.5 EFFECT OF DATA FLOW ON INTERNAL SPEED

The data-flow organization of a computer is a basic factor determining its performance. Once the data-flow paths (including path widths and circuit speed) are specified, a good deal of the performance of the system is circumscribed. On the other hand, the *logical* properties of the system, from the user viewpoint, can remain the same as data-flow design, and hence performance is varied over a considerable range. For example, it is possible to design two systems which appear to the programmer as a 10-digit-per-word fixed-word computer with identical instruction sets; yet they will differ in performance by a factor of 10 because in one system the storage and flow paths are 1 digit wide, whereas in the other they are 10 digits wide.

Aside from path widths, another important parameter in data-flow design is the number of *direct* paths provided as distinct from necessary routes which may involve sequences of direct paths. An economical design will contain as few direct paths as necessary for the required routings. However, a minimum path design limits speed in two ways: (1) routing by a sequence of paths increases the number of circuit levels and hence delays to realize the routings; (2) minimum paths limit the number of concurrent routings necessary to achieve speed by overlapping many internal operations.

6.6 MAGNETIC-CORE STORAGE

Magnetic-core storage is widely used for the high-speed main storage directly accessible to the processing unit. Some of the techniques of storage organization used with core storage are also applicable to other technologies especially magnetic films. As a rough indication of speed and capacity commercially available:

	Range among machines
READ/WRITE cycle, μsec	0.5–10
Capacity, bits	40,000–8,000,000

As with most storage systems, information is stored in a space array of elements; in this case each element can store a single bit and physically consists of a tiny donut-shaped object, the magnetic core. Access to information stored may be considered as involving two operations:

1. Selection of the desired bits
2. Routing of the information between the desired bits and a single data register

The storage unit communicates with the outside world by means of an *address register,* into which the *location* of the selected bits is specified, and a *data register,* which on a READ operation will receive the selected bits from storage and on WRITE will serve as the source of bit values for the selected bits. An address almost always specifies a *group* of bits called the *storage byte* or *word.* All the bits of the storage byte are generally routed at the same time between storage and the data register. For the moment, consider each byte to consist of a single bit, and consider the problem of selection of the desired bit as specified by the address. As a concrete example, consider a storage device containing $2^{16} \equiv 65,536$ bytes. The selection scheme must be able to select one out of these many objects. The size of the array indicates that careful thought must be given to economy. For example, the selection could be done by a single decoder for 16 bits. Even the most economical design of a 16-bit diode decoder (see Chap. 5) required 132,288 diodes. A different approach than straightforward decoding is clearly indicated.

If the storage elements are organized into a two-dimensional array, the identification of an element requires two numbers which in our example are each specified by half of the address bits. Thus two wires, one in the x and one in the y direction, thread each core; half of the address is decoded to select an x line and the other half to select a y line. Two decoders each of 8 bits are required instead of one 16-bit decoder. A glance at the symbolic design of a 16-bit decoder indicates that the final stage is fed by two 8-bit decoders. In other words, the two-dimensional selection scheme is equivalent to eliminating the final (and most costly) stage of decoding.

The x, y selection implies that only the core at the intersection of the selected x and y lines be selected. Notice that *half-selection* currents will be received by cores along one row and one column of the array. The physical behavior of the core as well as the strengths of the currents in the selection wires must be such that only the coincidence of currents results in a selection. This property is available from a magnetic core.

A magnetic core with three wires threading it is shown in Fig. 6.6.1*a*. The physical behavior of the core is given by the *BH* curve shown in somewhat idealized form in Fig. 6.6.1*b*. The *H* variable is proportional to the algebraic sum of the currents threading the core. The *B* variable is the amount of magnetic flux density resulting from the *H*. The two stable states of the core corresponding to storage of a 1- or 0-bit value are indicated. Writing a 1 into the core may be done by supplying a sufficiently large positive current to correspond to, say, point *P* on the curve. Similarly a sufficiently large negative current will result in a 0 being stored (point *Q*). Although supplying these currents initiates the 1 and 0 states as indicated, it is important to see what happens when these currents are removed, i.e., are then reduced to 0. For example, suppose a strong positive current is supplied, and the core state is indicated by point *P*. Now suppose the drive current (and hence *H*) is removed, i.e., made 0. The *H* value then follows the upper line of the *BH* curve and finally arrives at point *R*. Notice that the vertical distance of point *R* is the same as point *P;* this vertical distance represents the 1 state of the core. In other words, if the last driving current set the core to the 1 state, it remains in this state even after the drive current is removed; i.e., the core "remembers" its last excitation. This is the reason the magnetic core can store a bit of information. Another property of the *BH* curve

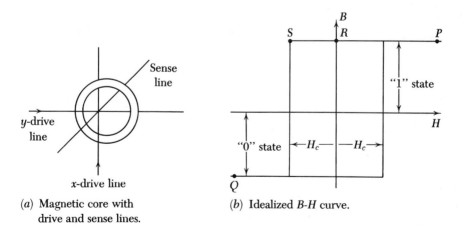

(*a*) Magnetic core with drive and sense lines.

(*b*) Idealized B-H curve.

Fig. 6.6.1 A single magnetic core and its properties.

is that if the core is, say, at point *R,* the application of a negative current less than sufficient to produce the change *RS* in *H* will not switch the core to the 0 state. This fact is important to the success of the coincident-selection principle shown in Fig. 6.6.2, where a *plane* of 1-bit position of 16 words is shown. Thus to drive a given core to the 0 state, its drive currents must sum to produce an *H* corresponding to at least *RS.* Each *x* and *y* drive current is chosen to correspond to less than *RS.* Thus when writing, say, a 1 into a core, a core on the selected *x* line that has a state of 0 will receive a *half-select* drive current; but this is not sufficient to switch the core state. Similarly all cores threaded by the *y*-select line will also be half-selected. Only the core at the intersection of the *x* and *y* drive lines will receive full WRITE excitation and therefore be set to the desired state no matter what its previous state.

Thus far the process of writing into any selected core has been described. The state of the core was said to correspond to the magnetic flux density *B.* To read the information (1 bit) represented by the state of the core it is necessary to sense the state of *B.* Now there is no simple way of directly converting magnetic flux density into an electric signal. The law of electromagnetic induction or *generator* principle states that a *time rate of change* of magnetic flux produces an electric signal. In other words, to generate a signal that senses the state of a core, the state must be changed. From the *BH* curve it is clear that a change of *B* requires a change in the vertical direction, which means that if the core is in the 1 state, it must be switched to the 0 state. Each core is threaded by the common *sense* wire for picking up the sense signal. To sense a given core, i.e., to *read* it, the address of the core is decoded into *x* and *y* selections; these control one *x* and one *y* drive line. These lines are excited to *write* a 0 into the core. If the core was in the 0 state, this produces no change in *B,* and hence a 0 signal appears on the sense winding. If the core state was 1, the drive currents produce a change in *B* and a signal is induced on the sense wire. In either case, the core is sent to the 0 state. The electric signal on the sense wire is amplified, shaped, and sent to the data register. The READ operation is therefore destructive of the information read from storage. It is a universal rule that to the user reading means *copying* and hence must be nondestructive. The storage system must therefore restore the information destroyed. Now this is essentially a writing operation. The address is of course available in the address register, and the data are available from the data register. Hence the restoration or regeneration of the information destroyed by the READ process is done by writing it back into the cores.

From the above discussion it should be clear that a complete READ cycle consists of two parts, an ACCESS and a REGENERATION subcycle. The desired information is available after the ACCESS subcycle, which is typically about half of the total cycle. As will be seen later, this fact can be of considerable importance in the organization of a computer.

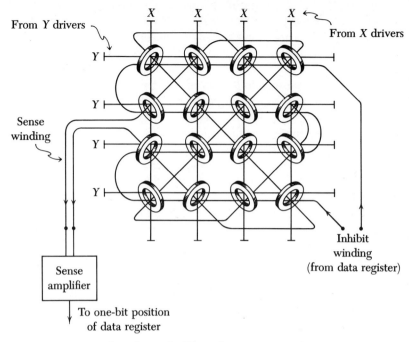

From Y drivers

From X drivers

Sense winding

Sense amplifier

To one-bit position of data register

Inhibit winding (from data register)

One plane of a 16-word-core storage unit

Number of words $\equiv w$
Number of bits per word $\equiv b$
Number of cores per bit position $\equiv w$ (one plane)
Number of planes $\equiv b$
Number of drivers $\equiv 2\sqrt{w}$
Number of sense amplifiers $\equiv$ Number of inhibit windings $\equiv b$

Cycles of Operation:

1. READ cycle
   (a) Write "0" into selected bits (all bits of selected word). This gives a "1" sense output for each bit position which contained a "1." After amplification and shaping, these signals are sent to the data register.
   (b) Regenerate-drive all selected bits to "1"; concurrently, use data register to send an inhibit (cancel) signal through those inhibit windings for which the bits are "0." This process thus restores all selected bits (one word) to the values they had before (a).

2. WRITE cycle—Data to be written initially in data register
   (a) Same as READ (a) except do not sense output.
   (b) Same as READ (b).

Fig. 6.6.2 Operation of 3D organized core storage.

Notice that the sense wire is threaded diagonally through the cores; this is done to obtain cancellation of sense signals due to half-select currents which may arise because the *BH* curve is not actually rectangular.

Thus far the discussion has assumed that a word contains only a single bit. For a storage array of w words each of b bits, b core planes are provided each with w cores (Fig. 6.6.3). A plane therefore contains 1 bit of all words. Each x or y drive line is continued into the next plane; thus a given driver drives one line of cores in all the planes. A separate sense winding is supplied for each plane; the signal from a sense winding eventually sets one bit position of the storage data register. As described thus far, the storage unit can select a word and write either a 1 or a 0 into *all* positions of the word. It can also sense the state of a word by writing 0 into all positions and sending the sense signals to the data register. What is still lacking is the ability to write selectively into the bits of a word, i.e., to set some bits of a single word to 0 and others to 1. In principle, this essential facility could be supplied by logical circuitry on drivers for each plane. However, this is not only expensive in logic circuitry but it also requires independent drivers for each plane. It is recalled that each x driver served all planes since corresponding x (or y) lines are really part of the same wire. To obtain selective bit writing with such a scheme, another winding is introduced for each *plane;* i.e., each such winding threads all cores of one plane. This is called the *inhibit* winding. It is used only on writing operations; when active, it is controlled by a bit of the data register. To write a word into storage, the address of the word is decoded and the selected x and y lines are driven to write 0 into all bits of the selected word. This may be viewed as a clearing operation. The selected lines are then driven to write a 1 into all bits of the selected word, but at the same time, all bits that are to have 0 values are sent an inhibit current, or cancellation current, via the inhibit winding. The proper bits are inhibited since the inhibit windings are excited only by the positions of the data register having 0 values. The inhibit winding simplifies the circuitry for writing. The winding itself is similar in its threading pattern to the sense winding; in some systems the same physical winding is used for both purposes.

A somewhat different method of organizing high-speed storage is called *2D*. Here the storage elements (cores) are arranged, at least conceptually, in a strictly two-dimensional pattern rather than the three-dimensional bit-plane stack of the 3D scheme discussed above. In our picture of a 2D system, a line of vertical cores represents a single word; the vertical lines are therefore called *word lines.* Each horizontal line threads the same bit position of all words; the horizontal lines are called *bit lines.* One apparent disadvantage of 2D organization appears at once: the need to drive each word with a separate driver or w drivers for w words (as compared with only about $2\sqrt{w}$ in the 3D scheme). The success of the 2D organization depends in large measure on obtaining economical word drivers. It is important to note in this connection that a word driver need drive only b cores ($b \equiv$ number bits per word). One approach used often with the

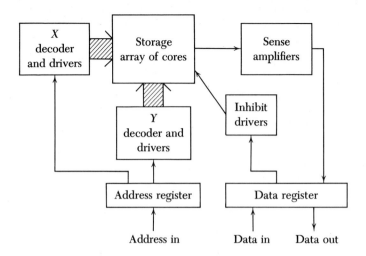

(*a*) Simplified data flow of a core storage unit.

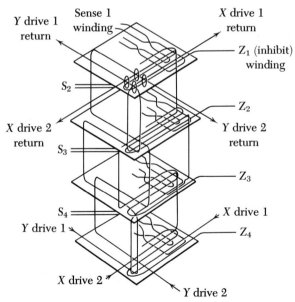

(*b*) Schematic showing 4-bit planes.

Fig. 6.6.3   Detail of drive logic − 3D organized core storage.

core technology is a separate plane of cores used as word drivers. This plane typically has one driver core per word; each such core drives a word line. The driver cores are selected by a coincident-current arrangement of drive lines selected by two decoders each fed from half of the memory address register. This method of selecting the driver cores requires $2\sqrt{w}$ drivers for these cores.

The operation of a typical 2D storage unit is summarized in Fig. 6.6.4 together with a simple example to illustrate the configuration. Notice that the 2D method requires only two wires per core as opposed to at least three and sometimes four

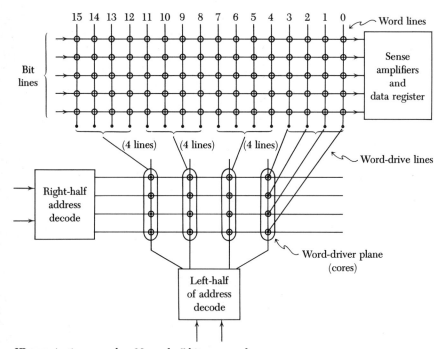

2D-organization example—16 words, 5 bits per word

Read Cycle:

1. Drive selected word to "0"
2. Sense bit lines
3. Regenerate—drive selected word to "1"
   inhibit bit lines for positions requiring "0"
   (from data register)

Write Cycle:

1. Same as Read Cycle 1
2. Same as Read Cycle 3

Fig. 6.6.4   2D organization of core storage.

wires threading each core in the 3D organization (three rather than four wires may be used if both the sense and inhibit functions share the same wire, as they sometimes do). The small number of wires that need thread the core is a definite advantage of the 2D organization; this is especially important as speeds increase, since this requires smaller cores and it becomes increasingly difficult to thread wires through them.

As described thus far, the loading and wire length of the bit lines in the 2D scheme can be quite large. It is the usual practice to improve the "aspect ratio" of the memory by increasing b and decreasing w by the same factor k (thus maintaining the same total number of bits). If the cost of a bit-line circuit and a word-line circuit were the same, the best value of k would be $\sqrt{w \div b}$ and the array would be square. Since bit-line circuitry including the sense amplifier is more costly, k is usually smaller than this value. (The choice of k, and its corresponding circuit arrangements, is independent of the appearance of the memory to the user, who sees w b-bit words.)

A variation of the 2D organization is called $2\frac{1}{2}$D. It is similar in geometry to 2D with a rather large k, but unlike 2D the method of driving is coincident-current. There are kb lines in the bit direction and $w \div k$ lines in the word direction; to select a word, one word line and b bit lines are half-selected. On READ, the sensed signals are found on the same b bit lines that were half-selected and are sent to b sense amplifiers. The sharing of b bit drivers and b sense amplifiers by kb bit lines is done by a switching circuit containing b decoder circuits each capable of 1-out-of-k selection. The meaning of the $2\frac{1}{2}$D designation should now be clear: the organization has properties intermediate between 2D and 3D.

6.7 OVERLAP AND CYCLE SPLITTING

The total cycle time of a core storage unit is the sum of two essentially equal subcycle times; these will be called *access* and *regeneration* subcycles. Full READ and WRITE cycles each consist of both subcycles, as was seen in the description of the operation of magnetic-core storage.

In executing a program, the number of READ cycles exceeds the number of WRITE cycles, in part because all accesses to storage for instructions are READ-type accesses. This fact has some potential in the development of storage devices, since a technology that could yield faster READ than WRITE could improve processing speed considerably.

It is important in the design of a system to fully utilize the potential speed of the processor storage because of its large share of the cost of the system. Methods of improving the effective speed of core storage devices over using the devices in strict cycle fashion will now be described.

Consider a single-address machine whose typical instruction is represented by

$$r \leftarrow r + x$$

Here r specifies a very fast access machine register which contains an operand from a previous instruction, and x specifies a location in storage. To execute this instruction the following microoperations are performed:

I Cycle of the Processor

1. The address of the instruction (IA) is sent from the machine's program counter to the storage address register. The READ-access subcycle of storage is then started to fetch the instruction.
2. Await completion of the READ-access subcycle; when complete, the instruction appears in the storage data register.
3. Storage performs the READ-regeneration subcycle.
4. The instruction is routed from the storage data register to the processor's instruction register, which is connected to circuits that can analyze the instruction.
5. The program counter is incremented by 1 in anticipation of fetching the next instruction.
6. The instruction is *decoded* at least to the extent of determining the *effective* address of data. This may involve extraction of address bits from the instruction and reference to index registers as specified in the instruction.

E Cycle of the Processor

7. The effective address of the operand (DA) (which is denoted by x in the statement given earlier) is sent to the storage address register. The READ-access subcycle of storage is then started to fetch the data.
8. Await completion of the READ-access subcycle; when complete, the data appear in the storage-data register.
9. Storage performs the READ-regeneration cycle.
10. The data are routed to a machine register.
11. The operation is performed on the data fetched and on the data in the register r from a previous operation.

Instead of performing the above sequence in single-step fashion it is quite feasible to perform some parts of it concurrently, i.e., to overlap them in time (Fig. 6.7.1). For example, since the instruction is available to the processor at the end of step 2, steps 4, 5, 6 in that order can be performed at the same time as step 3; steps 10 and 11 can be overlapped with step 9.

Another important case is where the operation on data (steps 10 and 11) requires a longer time than the data-regeneration subcycle (step 9). Then the storage READ cycle for fetching the next instruction can be started while the processor is completing execution of the current instruction.

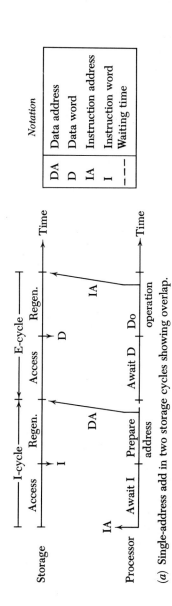

(a) Single-address add in two storage cycles showing overlap.

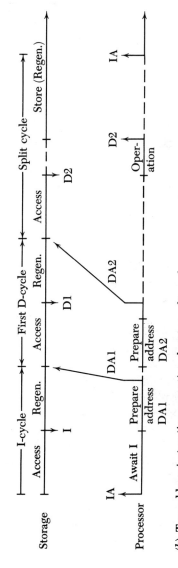

(b) Two-address instruction execution showing split cycle.

Fig. 6.7.1 Overlapped access and split-cycle methods.

Notation	
DA	Data address
D	Data word
IA	Instruction address
I	Instruction word
- - -	Waiting time

By overlapping microsequences, it is quite feasible to often "hide" the time for address indexing and even some of the fast fixed-point arithmetic operations behind portions of the storage cycles.

Another scheme to improve performance follows from the recognition that it is not essential for storage to perform both subcycles in immediate succession; in fact, machine speed may be improved by interleaving processing with storage subcycles rather than cycles. As an important illustration, consider the two-address type of instruction typified by

$$x \leftarrow x + y$$

Here the operand specified by x is added to the operand specified by y and the result replaces x. Note that x appears on both sides of the arrow. If this instruction were executed with full storage cycling, four storage cycles would be required (one for instruction fetch, one each for x and y datum, and one to restore the result in x). The four cycles can be reduced to three by taking full cycles for the instruction and data fetch of y and then taking the READ-access subcycle to fetch x (see Fig. 6.7.1b). The operation is then performed, and only when the result is available is the second subcycle taken—but now the result is written into x. Such a scheme of delaying the second subcycle of storage to wait for an updated result in the last location referenced is called the *split cycle*. It requires an instruction type wherein the result is returned to storage at the same location as one of the operands in the same instruction.

6.8 MULTIPLE-MODULE CORE STORAGE

A module of core storage will be defined as a storage array plus a single address and data register. To achieve a given storage capacity, two distinct approaches to the design may be contrasted: (1) supply all storage in a single module, or else (2) use several modules. The first method tends to be economical since the full capacity shares a single address- and data-register structure. However, the single-module approach faces an important speed limitation particularly in very-high-speed systems because a single module is internally a single-bus scheme; i.e., only one access can take place at one time.

A multiple-module system has two promising characteristics for high-speed operation. First, for a given capacity, a smaller module can usually be designed with faster cycle time because propagation and other delays can be smaller. Second, and most important, a multiple-module system permits several modules to be accessed at one time.

The requests for storage access of course originate ultimately in the program; its instructions in turn are executed only in response to instruction accesses. In other words, we have a feedback system. Under fairly "typical" problem and machine conditions it has been found that with a fairly high degree of probability, successive accesses are often to successively numbered addresses. For this reason, in multiple-module systems, successive addresses are assigned to successive modules (in cyclical fashion). This type of structure is called *interleaved*.

The number of modules that operate concurrently is a measure of the speed improvement over a single-module system. This depends both on the sequence in which addresses are requested and on the ability of the storage control system to queue requests on busy modules. Such queuing, if provided, must ensure that the sequential logic of the program is preserved even if the accesses are made out of turn due to module traffic. The limiting cases of module concurrency for an *n*-module system are clearly 1 when all successive calls are to the same module and a maximum concurrency of *n* when certain fortuitous sequences occur. Most practical cases will fall between the extremes; a fairly simple analysis is possible to gain insight into the case of random calls on the modules. Consider a multiple-module system with the modules numbered $1, 2, \ldots, n$. Assume an input *stream* of calls on the modules; each element of the stream is an integer in the range 1 through *n*. Assume the elements are at random, all equally likely. Also assume that there is an abundance of elements in the input stream so that the system never holds up for lack of work. The time to inspect the input stream is reckoned as 0 or can be overlapped with access to the modules. This means that all modules will be started together and complete their cycles together. Finally, we assume no queuing of requests on busy modules is permitted. With these assumptions, the problem of how many modules on the average are accessed per cycle is equivalent to the average length of sequence of the input integers until a repetition is encountered. The probability of a sequence of exactly two distinct integers is the probability that the second differs from the first, $(n - 1)/n$, times the probability that the third is a repetition of one of the others $2/n$. The probability of encountering a string of exactly k distinct integers with the $(k + 1)$st a repetition of one of the k others is

$$(1) \quad \frac{(n-1)(n-2) \cdots (n-k+1)}{n \quad n \quad \cdots \quad n} \; \frac{k}{n} \equiv \frac{(n-1)!k}{(n-k)!n^k}$$

The average length of sequences is the sum of products of the probabilities and k

$$(2) \quad N_{av} \equiv \sum_{k \equiv 1}^{n} \frac{k^2 (n-1)!}{n^k (n-k)!}$$

This formula has been evaluated for values of n in the range 1 through 45. The results show that in this range, a fairly good approximation is

$$(3) \quad N_{av} \equiv n^{0.56} \qquad 1 \leqslant n \leqslant 45$$

to within about 4 percent.

6.9 CONTROL-SYSTEM MODEL FOR CRITICALLY TIMED SOURCES

This section is concerned with the design of the circuits to generate the gate signals to control a bus where the sequence of signals must satisfy certain time constraints. The model of the system under consideration is as follows:

1. Multiple sources and multiple destinations are to be connected by a bus system of the simple single-bus type shown in Fig. 6.1.3.
2. The destination service time (also equal to the time the connection to the bus must be maintained) plus the time to make the decision on a particular bus switching will be assumed constant (independent of the sources and destinations). This time will usually be taken as the unit time for the system.†
3. Certain sources will be termed critical. Each critical source is characterized by a period p_i (in general, different for each source). The p_i (which may be grouped into a vector p) are integers and are time periods which are multiples of the unit time discussed in 2. Time for the ith critical source may be considered as a succession of p_i intervals. The time constraints require the ith critical source to be connected to the bus once per each p_i interval.
4. In addition to critical sources, other sources having no critical time constraints are presumed present. Bus and destination capacity not utilized in a given time unit by critical sources will be made available for use by noncritical sources.

6.10 ELEMENTARY GUARANTEED SERVICE PROCEDURE

Given: a set of n critical sources, the ith having a period p_i. One strategy to ensure service within the time constraints is to service all sources in each of successive intervals equal to the smallest period. Such a system can be designed provided

$$(1) \qquad \min_i p_i \geqslant n$$

where the system is designed with the equality condition; the total system time must be available for bus switching of critical sources. However, if the system is designed with some margin, only a fraction of each p_i interval need be used for critical-source switching; the remaining time is free for servicing noncritical sources. The design of a bus control using the above principles may be done with the relations set down below. This is followed by an example.

---

†A system consisting of multiple critically timed destinations and a fixed source service interval clearly has properties identical to the system under consideration.

Interval (seconds) between successive scan bursts:

(2) $b \equiv \min \tau_i$

Interval (seconds) between successive switch signals within a scan burst:

(3) $r \equiv c$

Bus-destination time (seconds) available in each b-interval for noncritical sources:

(4) $t_a \equiv b - nc$

where $c \equiv$ bus-connection time, sec
   $\tau_i \equiv$ service interval for source i, sec
   $p_i \equiv \dfrac{\tau_i}{c} \equiv$ normalized interval for source i
   $r \equiv$ sample interval within a burst
   $b \equiv$ intervals between start of successive bursts
   $t_a \equiv$ available bus-destination time between bursts
   $n \equiv$ number of critical sources

EXAMPLE: A 50-terminal system with each terminal having a 500 characters/ sec rate is to be multiplexed to a memory having a 10-μsec (per character) cycle. Find the memory time available for nonterminal access and specify the scan system.

   SOLUTION: From the problem statement and Eqs. (2) to (4), we obtain

$$n \equiv 50$$
$$\tau_i \equiv \frac{1}{500} \equiv 0.002 \text{ sec} \qquad \text{for all } i$$
$$b \equiv 0.002 \text{ sec}$$
$$r \equiv c \equiv 10^{-5} \text{ sec}$$
$$t_a \equiv 0.002 - (50)(10^{-5}) \equiv 0.0015$$

Thus the control initiates a scan burst of source-ready signals each interval spaced 2 msec apart. During a scan burst, each of the 50 sources is considered in turn for bus switching at intervals of 10 μsec. A scan burst of the 50 sources thus leaves a 1.5-msec interval in each 2 msec available for noncritical-source access to the bus and destination.

   A general limitation on the design of any system with n critically timed sources is

(5) $\displaystyle \sum_{i \equiv 1}^{n} \frac{1}{p_i} \leqslant 1$

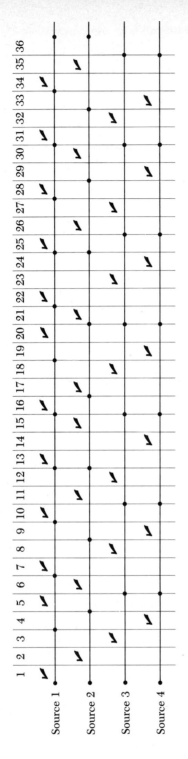

i	$\dfrac{1}{p_i}$
1	0.33
2	0.25
3	0.20
4	0.20
Sum	0.98

Fig. 6.10.1 Timing chart for four mixed-speed sources (idealized).

The physical reason for this relation is that by our normalization of flow rates, the destination rate is unity, and hence Eq. (5) states that the sum of the source flow rates must be less than or equal to the destination rate.

What type of general scheme for switching sources can guarantee no loss of information as long as Eq. (5) is satisfied? Although there is no known rigorous answer to this question, the following is offered as a conjecture. If, while the system is running, the control always selects as the source for switching the one not yet serviced in its current period and having the *least* time remaining in that period, all sources will be serviced properly (see Fig. 6.10.1 for an example). To apply this principle, assume a counter is maintained for each source and all counters are decremented by 1 each unit time. Counter c_i counts down modulo p_i; that is, after the count of 0 is reached, the counter resets to p_i. Associated with source i is a *participation indicator* g_i. If 1, the source i has been serviced in its current p_i interval; if 0, it has not been serviced in that interval. g_i is set to 1 whenever source i is selected for service and is set to 0 when the counter for source i is set to p_i. At any point where the choice of a source to be serviced is made, the control obtains the source number as follows:

(6) $\quad J \leftarrow ((\sim G) \wedge C = \lfloor / (\sim G)/C) \iota 1$

i.e., the source is chosen as the one not yet serviced in its current period and having the least time to wait before the period elapses. In Eq. (6), if more than one counter has the same minimum value, the one with the lowest index is selected. The assignment of indices to sources should be in the order of increasing periods; i.e., the source with the smallest p_i should correspond to $i \equiv 0$, etc.

At first glance it may appear that a multiple-bus scheme can allow more sources to be handled in the system than is possible with a single-bus circuit. This is, however, not the case as may be seen from the limiting situation, where several sources concurrently require service to the *same* destination. Here only one bus can be utilized, and yet all the timing constraints must be met.

Although a multiple-bus system cannot, in general, increase the number of critical sources which can be serviced, it will, on the average, service the critical sources in less time than is possible with a single-bus system. This results in more bus capacity (and destination time) available to service noncritical sources.

PROBLEMS

6.1 Give the cost of a circuit to connect three sources with two destinations. Paths in both directions are to be provided. Assume each path is 1 bit wide and a maximum concurrency of 1.

6.2 Repeat Prob. 6.1 for paths 8 bits wide.

6.3 Repeat the preceding two problems, only now provide a maximum concurrency of 2.

6.4 Estimate the cost of the multiplexor circuit of the IBM 1790 (Fig. 6.4.1).

6.5 A certain 3D core storage unit is to have 4096 thirty-two-bit words, each word directly addressable.

    a) How many cores are needed?
    b) How many sense amplifiers?
    c) How many selection drivers?
    d) What is the cost of the decoder?

6.6 Repeat Prob. 6.5 for a 2D organization using $k \equiv 4$.

6.7 Repeat Prob. 6.5 for a $2\frac{1}{2}$D organization using $k \equiv 32$.

6.8 In the design of a 32,768-byte (8 bits/byte) 3D storage unit, each byte is to be addressable by the programmer. The storage unit may be designed for direct byte addressability or else, say, for selection of 16,384 sixteen-bit bytes and selection from the data register of one-half of its contents for an 8-bit byte. Prepare a table to compare these two designs using the parameters discussed in the text.

6.9 Estimate the effective bandwidth of an eight-module core storage system where the cycle time of one module is 2 μsec.

REFERENCES

1. Allen, C. A., G. D. Bruce, and E. D. Councill: A 2.18 Microsecond Megabit Core Storage Unit, *IRE Trans. Electron. Comput.*, vol. EC-10, pp. 233–237 (June 1961).
2. Forrester, J. W.: Digital Information Storage in 3 Dimensions Using Magnetic Cores, *J. Appl. Phys.*, vol. 22, pp. 44–48 (January 1951).
3. Gilligan, T. J.: $2\frac{1}{2}$D High Speed Memory System: Past, Present, and Future, *IEEE Trans. Electron. Comput.*, vol. EC-15, no. 4 (August 1966).
4. Gluck, S. E.: Impact of Scratchpads in Design: Multifunction Scratchpad Memories in the Burroughs B8500, *Proc. Fall Jt. Comput. Conf.*, 1965.
5. Keister, W., R. W. Ketchledge, and H. E. Vaughn: A New Electronic Switching System, *IEEE Spectrum*, vol. 2, no. 2 (February 1965).
6. Keister, W., A. E. Ritchie, and S. H. Washburn: "The Design of Switching Circuits," D. Van Nostrand Company, Inc., Princeton, N.J., 1951.

7. Minnick, R. C., and R. L. Ashenhurst: Multiple Coincidence Magnetic Storage Systems, *J. Appl. Phys.*, vol. 26 (May 1955).

8. Pohm, A. V.: Magnetic Film Scratch Pad Memories, *IEEE Trans. Electron. Comput.*, vol. EC-15, no. 4 (August 1966).

9. Rajchman J. A.: Memories in Present and Future Generations of Computers, *IEEE Spectrum*, vol. 2, no. 11 (November 1965).

10. "Reference Manual, 7090 Data Processing System No. A22-6528," IBM Corporation, White Plains, N.Y.,

7

Turing, Finite-state, and Sequential-circuit Models

A *model* is an abstract, idealized representation of a system that can reproduce specified aspects of its behavior. The same physical system may be described by several models, depending on the type of behavior of interest. For example, some of a computer's reliability characteristics are included in a model discussed in Chap. 11, while its logical properties can be represented by the Turing and finite-state machine models discussed in the present chapter.

The Turing machine is a model first suggested by the British mathematician A. M. Turing in 1935 as a representation of computational processes. Although it was of exceedingly simple structure, he was able to use it to prove the then existing theorems of computable functions. He further suggested (Turing's thesis) that any function reasonably classed as computable is computable by this machine model. There have been no counterexamples to this conjecture. Hence, a Turing machine is a very simple, easily understood structure that accounts for all the logical properties of the general-purpose computer. It is fitting that we begin this chapter with a description of a Turing machine. An example problem is then discussed, after which we summarize some of the results of Turing machine theory.

The finite-state-machine model (FSM) is somewhat less general than the Turing machine since, unlike the latter, the FSM inputs are completely independent of the machine's operations (the Turing machine can generate symbols to supply its own input later; the FSM cannot). The term *finite-state machine* is synonymous with *sequential circuit* and *finite-state automaton*, also found in the literature.

As is true of many models of physical systems, a major objective is to account for *future* behavior. This depends on three types of factors:

1. The past
2. The system structure
3. The future inputs

The fact that the FSM model depends on its past behavior implies that it has *memory*; i.e., its inputs leave a residue that influences the future. At first glance, this may seem to require recording all past behavior and manipulating this voluminous information in order to predict the future. This is not necessary in FSM models because they use the idea of the state of a system, or more precisely the *state variable,* defined as follows: *the state variable q of a system is the variable whose value at any instant contains all the information about the past history of the system necessary to account for the future.* Although the state variable may be represented by a scalar, it is sometimes convenient to represent it as a vector, say of bits stored in flip-flop circuits.

The idea of the state variable is not unique to FSM models. For example, it appears in physical systems like electric circuits and mechanics, whose model structure is governed by differential equations. These equations can be so written that certain *state* variables, like all capacitor voltages and inductor currents or all particle positions and momenta, if known at any one time, supply the initial-value "constants" needed for the solution of the differential equations.

In FSM models, the system structure is usually described by tables, similar in some respects to truth tables (see Chap. 5) but with a richer symbol alphabet. Inputs are strings of symbols chosen from a specified alphabet. The FSM model is valuable in both programming and equipment design. Programming examples include the buffer-control design given in Chap. 4, table-driven syntax-analyzer algorithms used in compilers, and even some major portions of operating systems (see the Bibliography). In hardware design, most formal design procedures of circuits containing memory are based on the FSM model. Some illustrations are given later in this chapter to the design of counter circuits.

Certain types of sequential devices like ring counters, shift registers, and analog-digital converters are better understood and described from an intuitive viewpoint than a formal one like the FSM. This is done throughout this chapter as appropriate.

7.1 TURING MACHINE MODEL

A description of the Turing machine is given pictorially in Fig. 7.1.1. The description of the function of the various parts will be followed by an example of how the machine is "programmed" to solve a problem.

The facilities are:

1. A *tape* of potentially indefinite extent ruled into discrete squares, each square holding one and only one symbol at any one time.
2. A *read/write head,* in one position (over one tape symbol) at any one time. The head can read the tape symbol (see below) or can replace the current

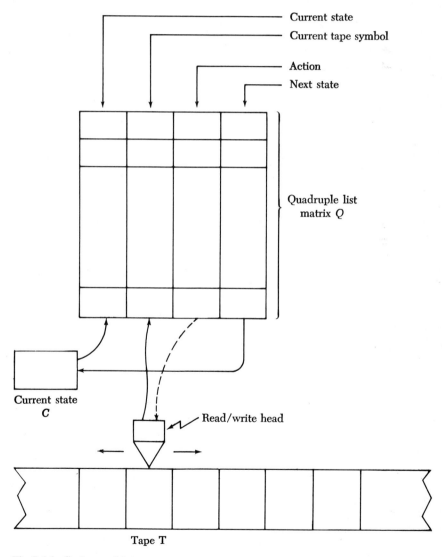

Fig. 7.1.1 Turing machine.

tape symbol by another symbol. The head can be moved past the tape in either direction but only one symbol at a time.

3. A *current-state* "register" C holding the current *state* symbol.

4. A *list of quadruples* used to control the machine's operations; quadruples do not change during any single problem run. The quadruple list, which is the program for the machine, is here represented as the matrix Q, row I holding one quadruple of four symbols whose meanings are described below.

5. A mechanism for using the above facilities according to the following rules:

  a. Initially, the quadruple list Q is supplied, an initial string of symbols is placed on the tape. Unless otherwise stated, the head is first positioned at the left end of the tape and the initial state C is set to the leftmost symbol of the first quadruple, that is, $C \leftarrow Q[1;1]$.

  b. The current state C and the current-state symbol $T[I]$ are used as search arguments to the leftmost two columns of Q. If no match is found, the machine stops and the result of the computation is the contents of the tape. If a match is found, say at row J of Q, then the current state is replaced by the *fourth* quadruple symbol found in row J

  $$C \leftarrow Q[J;4]$$

  and an *action* is taken according to the *third* quadruple symbol;

  $$Q[J;3] = {}'L' \text{ move head one tape symbol to the left}$$
  $$= {}'R' \text{ move head one tape symbol to the right}$$
  $$\text{otherwise replace current tape symbol by } Q[J;3]$$

  c. The process continues as described in *b.*

To illustrate the operation of a Turing machine on numbers, it is first necessary to adopt a representation for numbers. One simple representation for a positive integer n will be in *stone-age binary*—a string of $n + 1$ ones followed by at least one zero. A single 1 therefore represents $n \equiv 0$.

Consider the subtraction of two numbers. The starting configuration on the tape for the example 6 minus 4 is

111111101111100000000000000000000000000 $\cdots$

The problem at hand is to derive a list of quadruples which will specify the computation of the function which is the difference between two numbers in the assumed representation described above. Creating the list of quadruples is analogous to "programming" the Turing machine.

For the problem of subtracting positive integers where the minuend is larger than the subtrahend, the strategy may be described as follows: alternately replace one 1 by a 0 in the minuend and subtrahend representations. When all 1s have been replaced by 0s in the subtrahend, the string remaining in the minuend is the representation of the difference of the original numbers. Figure 7.1.2 shows a possible quadruple list for this procedure. The first quadruple in the list is the first to be executed; after this, each quadruple (and the tape symbol) specifies the next quadruple. In the problem at hand, the current tape symbol starts at the left-most position of the tape shown. The first quadruple is seen to result in a replacement of a 1 on the tape by a 0 and advancement to state 2. The combination of state 2 and a current symbol of 0 results in the second quadruple on the list being the next active one. This quadruple results in a move right one position on the tape and entry into state 3. The third quadruple is then executed repeatedly as the mechanism passes over the first string of 1s. As soon as the first 0 is encountered, the machine enters state 4, whose quadruples specify a search to the right for a 1. When this is found, it is replaced by a 0. The next step (state 5 with symbol 0) is to move right once again and enter state 6. State 6 permits only one tape symbol, a 1. If a 1 is not encountered, since a 60 is illegal, the machine stops. Otherwise, it moves left until it comes to the leftmost 1 of the minuend (state 8) where the above procedure is repeated (execution of quadruple 80R1 returns the machine to state 1).

As described thus far, each problem to be solved must be specified as a quadruple list and hence a Turing machine. Turing proposed a *universal machine* whose quadruple list is in effect capable of accepting any quadruple list from a tape. A universal Turing machine is therefore a general-purpose computer and

```
1102
20R3        Start  11111110111110000 ...
31R3               01111110111110000 ...
30R4               01111110011110000 ...
40R4               00111110011110000 ...
4105               00111110001110000 ...
50R6               00011110001110000 ...
61L7               00011110000110000 ...
70L7               00001110000110000 ...
71L8               00001110000010000 ...
80R1               00000110000010000 ...
81L8        End    00000110000000000 ...
```

(*a*) Quadruple list   (*b*) Tape configurations after each
for computation of: replacement for the example.
$m - n; n \geqslant 0; m \geqslant n.$

Number representations for this problem:

Input n is represented by a string of $n + 1$ ones.
Output n is represented as a string of n ones.

Fig. 7.1.2 Turing machine quadruples and trace of tape.

```
      ∇ TURING
[1]     'ENTER INITIAL TAPE'
[2]     T←▯
[3]     '   TAPE AFTER EACH CHANGE'
[4]     NQ←0
[5]     I←1
[6]     C←Q[1;1]
[7]     NR←(ρQ)[1]
[8]   NXT:J←(Q[; 1 2]∧.=C,T[I])/ιNR
[9]     NQ←NQ+1
[10]    →(0=ρJ)/END
[11]    C←Q[J;4]
[12]    →(Q[J;3]='LR')/LEFT,RIGHT
[13]    T[I]←Q[J;3]
[14]    T
[15]    →NXT
[16]  LEFT:→(0≠I←I-1)/NXT
[17]    T←' ',T
[18]    I←1
[19]    →NXT
[20] RIGHT:→((ρT)≥I←I+1)/NXT
[21]    T←T,' '
[22]    →NXT
[23]  END:'NO. OF EXECUTED QUADRUPLES= ';NQ
      ∇

        Q
1102
20R3
31R3
30R4
40R4
4105
50R6
61L7
70L7
71L8
80R1
81L8
        TURING
ENTER INITIAL TAPE
11111110111110
   TAPE AFTER EACH CHANGE
01111110111110
01111110011110
00111110011110
00111110001110
00011110001110
00011110000110
00001110000110
00001110000010
00000110000010
00000110000000
NO. OF EXECUTED QUADRUPLES= 96
```

Legend

	1-origin indexing
Q	Quadruple list
C	Current state symbol
I	Position on tape
NQ	No. of executed quadruples
NR	No. of written quadruples
T	Tape

Fig. 7.1.3 Turing machine simulator.

because of its formal simplicity can serve as a definition of the property "general purpose."

It is instructive to consider a program capable of simulating the operations of a Turing machine (Fig. 7.1.3). Such a program is not only a precise way of stating what has thus far been said in words, but it may also be used for demonstration or educational purposes. The simulator is capable of executing any list of quadruples. It also keeps a count of the number of quadruples executed and prints the entire tape after each replacement of a symbol on the tape.

As already indicated, the Turing machine exhibits all the necessary properties of a general-purpose computer. A test for any real computer to be classed as general purpose is to demonstrate that it can simulate a Turing machine. Similarly, any general-purpose computer can simulate any other one (with the same alphabet or character set). Some variations of the Turing machine have been suggested; e.g., several tapes instead of one; in Turing's original paper the tape had a definite left end but was of indefinite length to the right. These variants do not alter the fundamental nature of the Turing machine. In all cases, it must be able to reaccess data generated by the machine and must be capable of accessing a tape whose length need not be known in advance.

A *computable function* is one that can be computed by a Turing machine in a finite number of steps (executed quadruples). Certain functions are clearly not computable; they always involve an infinity of some sort. Calculation of the decimal expansion of pi is an example. Advance determination of whether a function is computable or not amounts to determining whether its Turing machine will stop or not. This is the famous halting problem. Note that this very problem can be posed as a function for a Turing machine! Thus, the answer is Y or N (halts or does not), and the input is any quadruple list and starting tape (both symbol strings). It has been shown that this function is *not* computable. In practical terms, this means that it is impossible to write a program that can analyze *all* other programs to determine whether they will come to an end or not. Another result is that it is impossible to write a program that will predict how much storage (tape) all other programs will require.

7.2 FINITE-STATE-MACHINE MODEL

A finite-state machine (FSM) is an abstract model containing an input variable x, output variable y, and state variable q. The model requires specification of:

1. An alphabet of all permitted *input* symbols

$$x \in \left\{ x_1, x_2, \ldots, x_{N_X} \right\}$$

This is read "x is a member of the set (alphabet) $x_1, x_2 \ldots, x_{N_X}$."

2. An alphabet of all permitted *output* symbols

$$y \in \left\{ y_1, y_2, \ldots, y_{N_Y} \right\}$$

3. An alphabet of all permitted *state* symbols

$$q \in \left\{ q_1, q_2 \ldots, q_{N_Q} \right\}$$

4. An *output function g* mapping input and state variables into the output variable

(1) $y \leftarrow g(x, q)$

5. A *state transition function f* mapping input and state variables into the next-state variable

(2) $q \leftarrow f(x, q)$

The *f* and *g* functions are similar to the Turing machine quadruple list and are supplied by tables, as will be discussed shortly. Note the appearance of *q* as both an argument and function variable in Eq. (2). This becomes meaningful in conjunction with a timing convention.

6. *Timing convention:* Successive input symbols are applied one at a time to the FSM at definite times called *event times*. Input and [through Eq. (1)] output variables are observable only at event times. The state transition through Eq. (2) is considered to apply just after each event time. Thus the states used in Eqs. (1) and (2) are the same. If event times are equally spaced in time, they are called *clock times*. The model is displayed pictorially in Fig. 7.2.1

Both input and output variables are intuitively essential for any interesting system model. The need for the state variable arises from the fact that the output of the FSM at any instant depends not only on the input at that same

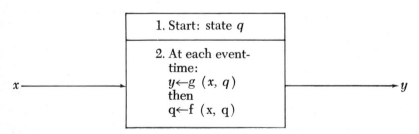

Fig. 7.2.1   Schematic of FSM.

instant but also on the past history of inputs. This of course is due to the fact that the FSM contains *storage* (memory). The purpose of the state variable is to represent all information about the past history of the FSM necessary to predict and determine its future behavior

Consider now three of several possible schemes of representing the two functions f and g. The first method, shown in Fig. 7.2.2a, will be called a *function table.* It lists in its leftmost two (argument) columns *all* possible input and state-symbol pairs. To the right of each such pair are entered the corresponding next-state and output symbols. Each row thus gives a *possible* transition at an event time. However, there is no sequencing of event times implied by the listing of the rows. Hence, rows may be interchanged without changing the FSM. The FSMs of interest in the following discussion can respond to any input symbol when they are in any state. In other words, all possible input state-symbol pairs appear in the table. There is a theory of *input-restricted* machines which cannot accept every input symbol at every state, but such machines will not be considered here.

Figure 7.2.2b shows a second table format, called a *transition table,* which displays the same information as the function table but with a considerable saving in recorded symbols. Here the row headings are the members of the state alphabet and the column-pair headings are the members of the input alphabet. The f and g function values, i.e., the next-state and output symbols, are the table entries.

Figure 7.2.2c and d shows a third way of specifying the f and g functions as a *state diagram* or directed graph; the nodes are the state alphabet, and directed-line segments between them show transitions. These lines are labeled with the input symbol (above the slash) and the output symbol (below the slash) associated with each possible transition. In the case where more than one I/O pair is associated with one state transition, a single line is drawn and the label pairs are separated by the symbol $\vee$. Thus, $0/1 \vee 1/0$ on a line between states A and B would mean that input symbol 0 or else 1 can cause a transition from state A to B but in the first case the output is 1 and in the second it is 0.

To determine the output sequence resulting from any given starting state and input sequence, any of the three representations may be used. However, the state diagram is perhaps easiest to follow so we use it for the following example (the reader should repeat the example with the transition table).

EXAMPLE: Given the FSM of Fig. 7.2.2 with starting state P, find the output sequence if the input sequence 0001011 is applied.

SOLUTION: To solve this simple problem, first locate the starting state (P) on the state diagram and then, since the first input symbol is 0, find the exit line from state P having a 0 above the slash. In this case the line has a 1 below the slash; this then is the output symbol. The transition line leads to state B which is then the next state. The process is repeated, only now the

Input	Present State	Next State	Output
0	P	B	1
0	B	M	1
0	M	B	1
0	R	E	0
0	E	R	0
1	P	M	0
1	B	R	0
1	M	R	0
1	R	M	1
1	E	P	1

(*a*) Function table

Input

Present State	Next State	Output	Next State	Output
P	B	1	M	0
B	M	1	R	0
M	B	1	R	0
R	E	0	M	1
E	R	0	P	1

(*b*) Transition table

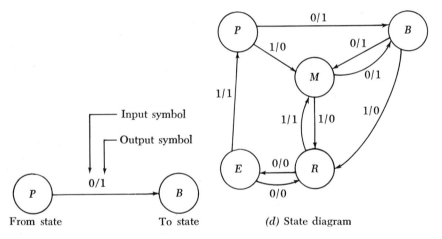

(*c*) Fragment of state diagram showing notation.

For all above representations: $x \in \{0, 1\}$ $y \in \{0, 1\}$ $q \in \{P, B, M, R, E\}$

(*d*) State diagram

Fig. 7.2.2 Three representations of FSMI.

second input symbol (which happens to be a 0) is used. Successive applications of the procedure result in symbols as indicated in the trace table shown in Fig. 7.2.3.

For most purposes, the state transition table will be the preferred representation because of its symbol economy compared with the function table and its

Event times	1	2	3	4	5	6	7	
Input sequence	0	0	0	1	0	1	1	
State sequence	P	B	M	B	R	E	P	M
Output sequence	1	1	1	0	0	1	0	

Fig. 7.2.3   Trace table for example input sequence to FSM1.

suitability to representation as a program data structure. As a further convention, we shall assume unless otherwise stated that the state label of the first row of the transition table is the *initial state* of the FSM.

It is useful for many purposes to standardize the labeling of the states and I/O alphabets. Accordingly, assume that the state alphabet is the English alphabet and the I/O alphabets are the integers (often only 0 and 1). With these conventions, it is possible to define a unique *standard form* for an FSM transition table as follows:

1. The column headings (input alphabet) appear left to right in numerical order, and row headings (state alphabet) appear in alphabetic order.
2. When the rows of the standard-form table (including row headings) are read left to right across each row and then top row to bottom row, the *first* appearance of each state symbol occurs in alphabetical order.

If a table is not initially in standard form, it can be translated by a series of one-for-one symbol translations and possible row interchanges, as illustrated in the example of Fig. 7.2.4. It can be shown that the standard form for a given FSM is unique (see Hennie, 1968).

Two machines having the same transition table except for one-for-one exchange of symbols (and possible row interchanges) exhibit essentially the same

	0		1	
P	B	1	M	0
B	M	1	R	0
M	B	1	R	0
R	E	0	M	1
E	R	0	P	1

		0		1	
P =	A	B	1	C	0
B =	B	C	1	D	0
M =	C	B	1	D	0
R =	D	E	0	C	1
E =	E	D	0	A	1

(*a*) Original table   (*b*) Standard-form table
(with new alphabet)

Fig. 7.2.4   Translation of table to standard form (FSM2).

behavior and are said to be *isomorphic.* If two machines have the same alphabets and are isomorphic, their standard-form tables will be identical. Thus, the standard form is a useful technique for determining isomorphism.

7.3 CONNECTIVITY AND REACHABILITY

A fundamental kind of question about an FSM is whether its states are *reachable* from each other. The following definitions help sharpen this idea:

D1:   A *persistent* state is one that can be reached from at least one other state but cannot reach any other state.

D2:   A *transient* state is one that can reach at least one other state but cannot be reached from any other state.

D3:   A *strongly connected machine* is one for which it is possible by some sequence of input symbols to reach any state from any other state.

In most practical cases, machines contain transient or persistent states because of design errors rather than by intent.

Every state of a strongly connected machine must clearly be able to serve as a start or end state in a reachability test. Since from the above definitions, a transient state cannot serve as a last state and a persistent state cannot serve as a start state, we have the following theorem.

T1:   A strongly connected machine cannot have any transient or persistent states.

The converse of this theorem, however, is not true, as can be seen from the example of Fig. 7.3.1, which shows a machine which has no transient or persistent states and yet is not strongly connected.

Many connectivity and reachability questions can be answered by simple manipulations of a *connectivity matrix* A, as shown in Fig. 7.3.2a. This square

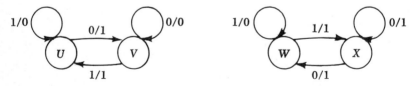

Fig. 7.3.1 Simple example of machine with no transient or persistent states but *not* strongly connected. (State *U* cannot be reached from state *W*.)

	A	B	C	D	E
A	0	1	1	0	0
B	0	0	1	1	0
C	0	1	0	1	0
D	0	0	1	0	1
E	1	0	0	1	0

	A	B	C	D	E
A	0	1	1	1	0
B	0	1	1	1	1
C	0	0	1	1	1
D	1	1	0	1	0
E	0	1	1	0	1

(*a*) Matrix A (=B^1) (states reachable in one transition).

(*b*) Matrix $B^2 = B^1 \vee . \wedge A$ (states reachable in exactly two transitions).

Fig. 7.3.2 Transition matrix and "product" for FSM2 of Fig. 7.2.4b.

matrix has row and column labels which are the states (but row and column numbers will be used to reference the matrix also). The entry in row I and column J is defined as follows:

$$A[I;J]=1 \quad \text{if there is } any \text{ single input symbol that can produce a transition from state } J$$

$$=0 \quad \text{otherwise}$$

The A matrix is clearly an alternative method of showing the line connections of the state diagram.

Tests for persistent and transient states follow almost immediately from the definition of the matrix:

1. If $A[I;J]=0 \quad$ for $I \neq J$

$$=1 \quad \text{for } I=J$$

then state I is persistent (since it is impossible to leave it).

2. If $\wedge/A[;I]=0$, that is, all entries in column I are 0, state I is transient (since it is impossible to reach state I). The number of 1s in any row (state) of the matrix is the number of states reachable by *one* input symbol from the state represented by the row. This number is at most equal to the size of the input alphabet.

If $A[I;J]=0$, there is of course no single input symbol that can cause a transition from state I to state J. However, there may well be a *sequence* of inputs that can produce such a transition. In fact, for a strongly connected machine we are sure there is at least one such sequence for every I, J pair. The following simple process will determine the length of input sequence to cause a transition from each state to every other state. The basic operations consist of AND/OR on successive matrices, starting with the A matrix, to obtain B^1, $B^2, \ldots, B^k$ matrices. The meaning of the matrix B^k is that $B^k[I;J]=1$ (or 0) as state J is (is not) reachable from state I by *some* input sequence of length exactly k symbols. The B matrices are obtainable with the recursion scheme

(1*a*) $B^1 = A$

(1*b*) $B^k = B^{k-1} \vee . \wedge A$ $k \geqslant 2$

Equation (1*b*) is a compact way of stating that for all *I,J* combinations

(1*c*) $B^k[I;J] = \vee / B^{k-1}[I;] \wedge A[;J]$

See Fig. 7.3.2*b* for an example of the computation of B^2. The recursion need be carried only as far as *k=m*, where *m* is the smallest integer for which $B^{m+1} = B^m$.

The length of the *shortest* input sequence required to reach state *J* from state *I* is the smallest value of *k* for which $B^k[I;J] = 1$. If all B^k are ORed,

(2) $R^k = B^1 \vee B^2 \vee \cdots \vee B^k$

the result is a matrix R^k whose *I,J* element specifies whether state *J* is reachable from state *I* by *any* input sequence of *length k or less*. Also, the positions of row *I* of R^k which contain 1 values are the states reachable from state *I* by sequences of at most *k* input symbols.

In many cases of interest we desire information on only those states reachable from a particular starting state, say state *I*. Considerable labor can then be saved (compared to the more general problem described above) since now only vector-matrix rather than matrix-matrix operations are required. The scheme is then

(3*a*) $B^1 = A[I;]$

(3*b*) $B^k = \vee / B^{k-1} \wedge A$ $k \geqslant 2$

or in expanded form

(3*c*) $B^k[L] = \vee / B^{k-1} \wedge A[;L]$ $1 \leqslant L \leqslant N_Q$

Once again the OR of the *B* vectors up to B^k will specify the states reachable from state *I* by sequences of length *k* or less.

A somewhat different solution of the reachability problem is as follows. Let

$S_i =$ any subset of the states of an FSM that we desire to serve as starting states

$G_k(S_i) =$ the set of states reachable from any state of S_i by an input sequence of length 1; thus, $G_1(S_i)$ is easily obtained from a state diagram or a transition table

A recursion scheme for $G_k(S_i)$ is then

(4a) $G_0(S_i) = S_i$

(4b) $G_k(S_i) = G_1(G_{k-1}(S_i))$ $1 \leqslant k \leqslant m$

where m, the upper limit on k, is the smallest integer for which

(5) $G_{m+1}(S_i) = G_m(S_i)$

This last condition states the following: suppose we have a list of all states reachable from states S_i by input sequences of length m or less. If, when we permit the input sequence to become one longer, we find that no *new* states can be reached, new states are not reachable by sequences of *any* length longer than m. This can be proved by induction as follows:

$$G_{m+1} = G_1(G_m(S_i))\qquad \text{by Eq. (4b)}$$
$$G_{m+2} = G_1(G_{m+1}(S_i))\qquad \text{by Eq. (4b)}$$

since

$$G_{m+1} = G_m\qquad\qquad \text{by Eq. (5)}$$

substitution into the right side of the G_{m+2} equation gives

$$G_{m+2} = G_1(G_m(S_i))$$

since the right side is identical with G_{m+1} as given above, $G_{m+2} = G_{m+1}$. Hence by induction, once $G_m = G_{m+1}$, $G_{m+1} = G_m$ for all i. This last result may be extended to a fundamental theorem.

T2:   Given an FSM having n states, if any specified state is reachable from any other specified state, it will be reachable by some input sequence of length at most $n-1$.

The proof of this theorem follows from the discussion just above since the recursion of Eqs. (4) and hence length of input sequence can progress only as long as there is at least one new state added to the list in each recursion step. Since there are only n states in all, there can be at most $n-1$ steps beyond the initial state.

7.4   PERIODIC BEHAVIOR OF FINITE-STATE MACHINES

One fundamental property of an FSM is that if the *same* input symbol is applied repetitively, the output sequence will become periodic; the first period starts after no more than n input symbols have been applied, and the period is at most n symbols long. More generally:

T1: Let an n-state FSM be supplied an input sequence that is periodic with length p. The output sequence must ultimately become periodic with period at most np.

7.5 STATE EQUIVALENCE

It will be convenient to use the notation M/q for the words "machine M starting in state q."

The definition of *two equivalent states* follows.

D1: State q_1 of machine M_1 and state q_2 of machine M_2 are said to be *equivalent* if M_1/q_1 and M_2/q_2 supplied with the same input sequence yield identical output sequences and this property holds true for *any* input sequence. States that are not equivalent are said to be *distinguishable*. The two machines M_1 and M_2 may be the same.

This definition asserts that two states are distinguishable (not equivalent) only if there is some input sequence which when applied with the machine in one of the states will yield an output sequence differing from that resulting when the same sequence is applied to the machine in the other state.

The input sequences under which two states are judged equivalent (or distinguishable) must be of *any* length, no matter how long. A related idea is *k-equivalence*, defined as follows.

D2: State q_1 of machine M_1 and state q_2 of machine M_2 are said to be *k-equivalent* if for each possible input sequence k symbols long M_1/q_1 and M_2/q_2 yield identical output sequences. Two states not k-equivalent are said to be *k-distinguishable*.

It follows immediately from definition 2 that two states that are k-equivalent are m-equivalent for all $m \leqslant k$. Also, two states are equivalent (see definition 1) if they are k-equivalent for all k.

7.6 STATE MINIMIZATION†

Although the cost and complexity of an FSM depends on many factors, all else being equal, it is reasonable to suppose that reducing the number of states will also reduce the cost. The main purpose of this section is to develop an algorithm for converting the transition table for any given FSM M_1 to a transition table for

†This section is somewhat difficult and may be omitted without losing continuity.

another FSM M_2 which will exhibit the same I/O behavior as M_1 but have as few states as possible.

To begin, we define what is meant by the equivalence of two machines. This definition uses the idea of equivalent states defined earlier.

D1: Two machines are *equivalent* if for each state of the first there is an equivalent state of the second and for each state of the second there is an equivalent state of the first.

The state-minimization problem can then be stated as follows. Given a machine M_1, derive a machine M_2 equivalent to M_1 with as few states as possible. Although the minimum possible number of states to realize a given machine is a single number, there may be several equivalent minimal machines. The algorithm for state minimization will now be explained. The reader is

	0		1	
A	B	0	C	0
B	C	0	E	0
C	A	1	F	0
D	G	0	F	0
E	F	0	G	0
F	D	1	C	0
G	C	0	B	0

(*a*) Original.

	0		1	
D	G	0	F	0
G	F	0	G	0
F	D	1	F	0

(*b*)

	0		1	
D	E	0	F	0
E	F	0	E	0
F	D	1	F	0

(*c*)

(*b*) and (*c*) Two reduced machines.

Start: Obtain partition P_1 (each state subset has same inputs and outputs)

$P_1 = (A,B,D,E,G)\ (C,F)$

To obtain partition P_2:

1. Partition subset (A,B,D,E,G):
   (A) (B)
   (A,D) (B)
   (A,D) (B,E)
   (A,D) (B,E,G)

2. Partition subset (C,F):
   (C,F)

3. Hence $P_2 = (A,D)\ (B,E,G)\ (C,F)$

To obtain partition P_3:

1. Partition subset (A,D):
   (A,D)

2. Partition subset (B,E,G):
   (B,E)
   (B,E,G)

3. Partition subset (C,F):
   (C,F)

4. Hence $P_3 = (A,D)\ (B,E,G)\ (C,F)$

Since $P_3 = P_2$ reduction steps are complete. A reduced machine consists of one state from each subset of the last partition. See (*b*) or (*c*).

Fig. 7.6.1 Example of state reduction.

advised to follow the discussion with an example (see Fig. 7.6.1). The process consists of deriving a succession of state partitions P_1, P_2 ..., where each partition is a list of state subsets (groupings) such that all states in a subset are k-equivalent and all states are included (once) in the list of subsets. Partition P_k is derived from partition P_{k-1} and the transition table, as will now be explained:

1. Construct a *partition P_1* of states, i.e., a list of subsets such that each state is in only one subset and all states in a subset are 1-equivalent. This is done by placing into each subset of P_1 all states (row headings) of the transition table that have the same input and output symbols.
2. Partition P_2 is next derived from P_1 and the transition table as follows. Place each state in a subset of the new partition P_2 only if all other states in this subset correspond to the same output symbols and have successor states that are in the same subset of partition P_1. When all states have been considered using this rule, the set of state subsets so constructed is the partition P_2.
3. In a similar manner, partition P_3 is constructed from partition P_2, etc., until $P_{k+1} = P_k$. After this point no further partitioning is possible. Each state subset is then an equivalence set so only one state from each subset is required and all other states in the subset can be replaced with the selected state. Thus we select one state from each state subset from the final partition.
4. The transition table for the minimized machine is constructed as follows:
   a. Copy those rows of the original state table having row headings equal to the selected states.
   b. Replace each nonselected state symbol in this new table by the selected state symbol of its subset.

7.7 HOMING AND DIAGNOSIS EXPERIMENTS

The process of applying controlled input sequences to an FSM and observing its outputs is called an *experiment*. Experiments may be divided into two broad categories:

1. *Preset Experiments*   The input sequence is completely determined in advance and is not changed once the experiment starts
2. *Adaptive Experiments*   The input sequence is altered during the experiment based on observed (sensed) results

Preset experiments tend to be somewhat easier to implement but lack the potential for efficiency (e.g., measured by length of input sequence to achieve a desired result) available from the adaptive type of experiment.

Another issue in the classification of experiments is the number of copies of the machine that is assumed available to the experimenter. This multiplicity is important because in many experiments the initial state of the machine at the start of the experiment is unknown, so that there is no way to reset the machine to the starting state after an experiment begins, say for the purpose of investigating a new input sequence.

Two important types of experiments are:

1. *Diagnosing Experiment* Given a machine *M* including its transition table. At the start of the experiment it is in some one of its states. Design an experiment to determine this state.
2. *Homing Experiment* Given a machine *M* including its transition table. Find an input sequence that will take the machine from its (unknown) initial state to a specified final state.

Every diagnosing experiment is also a homing experiment.

7.8 SEQUENTIAL-CIRCUIT APPLICATIONS OF FSM MODELS

The properties of the FSM model have thus far been described in an abstract manner. In the next few sections this theory is applied to the design of illustrative circuits of the type found in computer systems. Since computers usually operate using binary signal levels, the inputs and outputs of the FSM (circuits) will use the alphabet 0, 1. The state of the FSM will be held in some configuration of elementary storage circuits called *flip-flops,* each capable of storing 1 bit. It will therefore be convenient to represent the state of a circuit as a bit vector Q, where $Q[I]$ is the state of flip-flop I.

One class of sequential circuits is called *synchronous;* the outputs of all such circuits are considered effective only at certain definite intervals marked by pulses spaced equally in time and generated by a *clock* circuit. The clock, in effect, implements a kind of ternary (three-valued) logic even though the actual circuitry is two-level, because at points in time when the clock signal is 0, the circuit outputs are treated as *not sensed* or null. This is an alternative to the actual circuit values of 1 or 0. Another way of saying this is that a *zero* value on a clock line is used to obtain the desired logical value of *null* by mapping the null state into 0 state.

A clock signal is generally derived from a central source and is a "clean" electric waveform. These signals perform the desirable function of pulse shaping since most important signals are ANDed with a clock signal. The output from such an AND circuit will be a clean waveform because of the clock, even though the other waveform may be sloppy, say, because of its traversal through several stages of logic circuitry. This pulse-regeneration function can be an important factor in circuit reliability. The central source of clock signals is also an economical way of generating signals to sequence events in the machine. For this

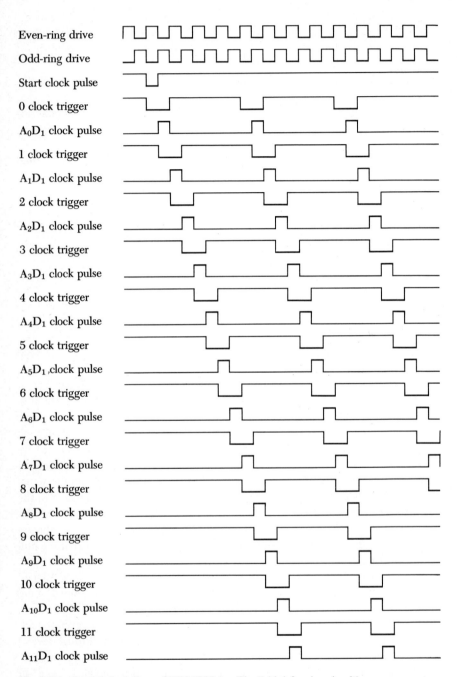

Fig. 7.8.1   Central clock lines of IBM 7090 (see Fig. 7.11.1 for ring circuit).

reason, a clock generally consists of a set of lines (typically from 4 to 40 lines). Each line carries a waveform of repetitive pulses or gates, but the waveforms of different clock lines are offset in time. To illustrate, the clock signals of the IBM 7090 are shown in Fig. 7.8.1. There are 11 basic clock lines, each accompanied by a pseudocomplement line.

Another class of circuits, called *asynchronous,* does not require a clock. Each circuit event initiates its successor(s). Asynchronous circuits are potentially faster than synchronous circuits because they need not wait for a clock pulse for the flow of signals. On the other hand, asynchronous circuits must face the problem of representing the null logical state without the help of a clock. This can be done in several ways. For example, each logic variable can be represented by two lines in an arrangement called a *double rail.* The two lines can have four combinations of values; two of these correspond to 0, 1 values for the variable and one of the others represents the null state.

Most computers use synchronous circuits because of ease of design, high reliability, and economy. With care in the choice of the clock rate, the speed potential of most logic circuitry can be utilized in synchronous circuits.

The choice between synchronous and asynchronous circuits need not be made strictly— a combination of both is feasible. Typically, the synchronous circuits are used within rather large units of the machine, e.g., the memory and processor; but communication between the units is done by request and response, an asynchronous technique.

In the remainder of this chapter, unless otherwise noted, we shall assume synchronous circuits.

7.9 FLIP-FLOPS AND REGISTERS

The most elementary sequential circuit called a *flip-flop* is one capable of two states. The several types of flip-flops differ in the way the circuit is induced to change from one state to another. The state variable will be noted by Q. This will also denote an output of the flip-flop. In some cases a complement output is also provided.

An RS flip-flop has an R (reset) input terminal which if 1 sets Q to 0 and an S (set) input terminal which if 1 sets Q to 1. The symbol and truth table for the RS flip-flop are given in Fig. 7.9.1a. This truth table is a way to give the state transition function

$$(1) \qquad Q' \leftarrow F(X,Q)$$

where for this case $X \equiv R, S$. To avoid confusion on the truth tables, the result state is shown with a prime Q'. Also notice the "don't care" condition in the truth table for the case where both R and S are 1.

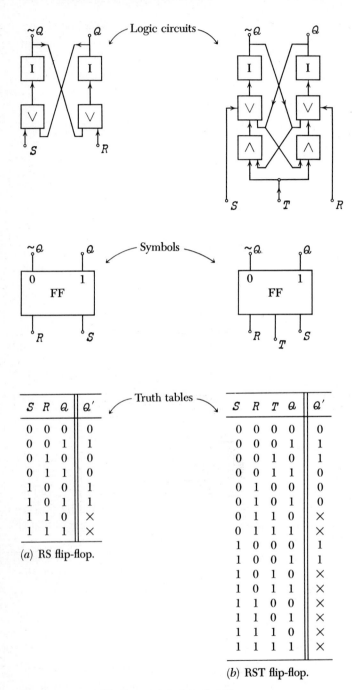

Fig. 7.9.1   Some flip-flops and their truth tables.

Another type of input to a flip-flop is called the T or *trigger* type. When the T terminal is set to 1, the state w *changes* to the complement of its present value. Strictly speaking, the T input would produce a continuous alternation of states for the duration of its value of 1. However, we consider that only a single transition is produced by any one setting of a T input. A flip-flop combining the inputs of R, S, T is called an RST *flip-flop*. Its truth table and circuit are shown in Fig. 7.9.1b. The circuit may be considered as an RS flip-flop with additional pulse-steering input logic to implement the T function.

Another common type of flip-flop, called JK, is similar to the RST in function but instead of a separate T input terminal, the function of state complementation is performed when both the R and S inputs are 1.

The three flip-flop types discussed thus far do not exhaust the possibilities. Common sets of flip-flop types used in the IBM Solid Logic Technology (SLT) circuits are shown in Fig. 7.9.2. Each type is shown in a block form and is defined by a truth table and then by an equation derived from the truth table.

The *polarity-hold* flip-flop has two inputs called *data* and *control*. When the control line is 0, the circuit retains its current state; when the control input becomes 1, the state assumes the value on the data-input line.

Unfortunately, terminology for flip-flops is very nonuniform. The reader will encounter many alternative names for flip-flops in the literature.

A *register* is a collection of flip-flops used for storing the binary-encoded representation of a number or some other collection of bits. Registers supply temporary fast-access storage for data and addresses to storage as well as control information.

Consider the logic for respecification of the state of a register composed of RS flip-flops by a set of incoming lines X. Functionally, the operation is

(2) $Q \leftarrow X$

However, the details require specification of how X and a clock line $C[0]$ are connected to the R and S terminals of the flip-flops. This may be done in two basic ways. In the first, the clock line is ANDed with X to feed the S terminals and with $\sim X$ to feed the R terminals, that is,

(3) $S \leftarrow X \wedge C[0]$
       $R \leftarrow (\sim X) \wedge C[0]$

The second method respecifies the register state in two clock steps: first the register is set to 0, then only the S terminals are fed by X lines; i.e.,

(4) $R \leftarrow (\rho R) \rho C[0]$
       $S \leftarrow X \wedge C[1]$

The second method is cheaper in circuitry but more expensive in time.

Type	IBM-SLT designation	Symbol	Truth table					Equations

RS flip-flop — Flip-flop

Symbol: Set — *FF* — Q[0]; Clear — Q[1]

S	C	Q[0]	Q'[0]	Q[1]
0	0	0	0	1
0	0	1	1	0
0	1	0	0	1
0	1	1	0	1
1	0	0	1	0
1	0	1	1	0
1	1	0	1	0 } ?
1	1	1	1	0

Equations:
$$Q'[0] \leftarrow S \vee Q[0] \wedge {\sim} C$$
$$Q[1] \leftarrow {\sim} Q'[0]$$

RS flip-flop — Flip-latch

Symbol: Set — *FL* — Q[0]; Clear — Q[1]

S	C	Q[0]	Q'[0]	Q[1]
0	0	0	0	1
0	0	1	1	0
0	1	0	0	1
0	1	1	0	1
1	0	0	1	0
1	0	1	1	0
1	1	0	1	1 } ?
1	1	1	1	1

Equations:
$$Q'[0] \leftarrow S \vee Q[0] \wedge {\sim} C$$
$$Q[1] \leftarrow ({\sim} Q'[0]) \vee S \wedge C$$

RT flip-flop — Flip-flop

Symbol: Comp. / C — *FF* — Q[0]; Clear / R — Q[1]

C	R	Q[0]	Q'[0]	Q[1]
0	0	0	0	1
0	0	1	1	0
0	1	0	0	1
0	1	1	0	1
1	0	0	1	0
1	0	1	0	1
1	1	0	0	1 } ?
1	1	1	0	1

Equations:
$$Q'[0] \leftarrow ({\sim} R) \wedge C \neq Q[0]$$
$$Q[1] \leftarrow ({\sim} Q'[0]) \vee C \wedge R$$

Polarity hold flip-flop — Polarity hold

Symbol: Data / D — *PH* — Q[0]; Control / C

D	C	Q[0]	Q'[0]
0	0	0	0
0	0	1	1
0	1	0	0
0	1	1	0
1	0	0	0
1	0	1	1
1	1	0	1
1	1	1	1

Equations:
$$Q'[0] \leftarrow (D \wedge C) \vee Q[0] \wedge {\sim} C$$

Notes: } ? Denotes specific assignment to yield equations shown.

⌐ Denotes normally complement output.

Fig. 7.9.2 Examples of logic blocks for flip-flops.

A shift register is a device that can move a bit pattern to the left or right. Positions at the end which are vacated are usually filled with either 0s or input from some standard source. The function of the 0-fill shift register for right shift by 1 position may be expressed as

(5) $X \leftarrow 0, ^{-}1 \downarrow X$

Shift registers are important circuits for the following reasons:

1. A shift left by one place is equivalent to multiplying the binary number represented by the bits by 2. Similarly a shift right by one position is equivalent to division by 2.
2. A shift register is capable of translating a serial representation of information into a parallel representation, or vice versa.

In this discussion we first consider a circuit for right shift by one position (similar principles apply to left shift; multiple position shift will be considered later). Right shift by one position could be performed by moving each bit one position to the right starting with the one at the far right. It will not do to effect all these transfers at exactly the same instant since then there would be ambiguity as to which value (the earlier or later) was actually moved to the adjacent position. Nevertheless it is important to seek a scheme which does not require one clock interval to move each bit one position.

Figure 7.9.3 shows a circuit for shifting a register one position right in one clock interval. Since all cells are identical except for slight differences at the ends, only one typical cell is shown. The main idea of the circuit is to provide a delay D in each output and complement-output line and have the delayed outputs feed the RS terminals of the flip-flop immediately to the right. The delays, in effect, act as storage for the original register contents until the new contents are established. The shift clock pulse, applied in common to all delayed outputs, controls the set-reset of the register flip-flops. To work properly the delays D should be longer than the transition time of the flip-flops.

Shift by more than one position is usually done by a microsequence. To perform K shifts, for example, a shift counter is initially set to value K. The counter is tested for 0; if 0, shifting is complete. If the count is nonzero, it is decremented by 1 and a shift by one position is performed. The cycle is then repeated until a 0 count is obtained.

As mentioned earlier, one use of the shift counter is for serialization or deserialization. To understand this, it is important to recognize that information in a shift register exists in the parallel representation since each bit has its own space position. To convert this parallel representation into serial, it is only necessary to take a single line output from the rightmost stage and apply n shift

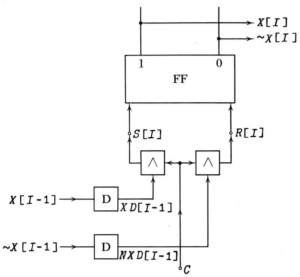

(a) One cell of shift register for right shift.

```
        ∇ K RSHIFT X                    ∇ RSHIFT1  X
    [1]   P←K                        [1]  XD←X
    [2]   T←∨/P                      [2]  NXD←~X
    [3]   TST:→(~T)/0                [3]  S←C∧0,⁻1↓XD
    [4]   RSHIFT1  X                 [4]  R←C∧1,⁻1↓NXD
    [5]   P←(6ρ2)T⁻1+2⊥P                 ∇
    [6]   →TST
          ∇
```

(b) Microprogram for right shift by *K* places (64-bit register).

Legend

$2 \perp K$	Number of places to be shifted.
$2 \perp P$	Remaining number of places.
X	Register outputs.
R,S	Reset, set terminals of register flip-flops.

Fig. 7.9.3 A shift register.

pulses to the register (*n* is the number of positions of the register). This will cause the register contents to appear in serial form (i.e., in time sequence) on the single output line.

Deserialization can also be done with a shift register. Now the input is a time sequence of bits on a single line; this line is fed into the leftmost end of the shift register (to the S' terminal of the flip-flop). After each bit appears at input, the contents of the shift register are shifted one position to the right. At the end of the shifting, the register contains the information which was originally in serial form in parallel form.

It should not be inferred from this discussion that a shift register is absolutely essential for performing serialization operations. For example, consider a single-bus circuit (Sec. 6.1) fed in parallel from a register holding information. If successive positions of the bus are fed successive clock pulses, the parallel input to the bus will appear at the single output line in time sequence, i.e., serially.

7.10 COUNTERS

An *n*-bit binary counter is a sequential circuit which has *n* state variables, 2^n states, and at least one input line called the COUNT input (P). Whenever a 1 appears on the COUNT line, the circuit progresses to the next state; the outputs are the state variables. Counters also often include other lines such as a single RESET line which, when set to 1, resets the counter (i.e., sets all bits) to 0 or to some standard configuration. Provision is sometimes made to set each bit position of the counter from some external source; this allows counting to proceed from any specified starting state. Counters may also be classified as UP or DOWN counters, depending on whether the state progression is up or down in binary sequence.

Counters are used to tally occurrences of events—often where there is some uncertainty in the times of their occurrence. They are widely used in instrumentation equipment, e.g., nuclear-particle counters, signal generators, analog-digital converters. In a computer, counters appear in various control functions such as controlling the number of shifts in multiplication or division or controlling the number of bytes transferred between storage and an external device. Counters are usually *not* used for addition of numbers because they cannot sum numbers which appear in the usual positional representation.

To design a counter to count from 0 to $C - 1$, where C is a power of 2, *n* states are required, where

(1) $n \equiv \log_2 C \equiv \rho Q$

Let Q be the state vector and also the outputs of the counter.

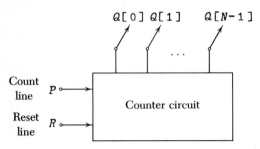

Count line P

Reset line R

Counter circuit

$Q[0]$ $Q[1]$ $Q[N-1]$

Fig. 7.10.1 A counter in block form.

Most binary counters count modulo 2^n; they develop the count of 0 as the successor to the full count. The count-up function may then be stated as

(2) $Q \leftarrow (N\rho 2)\top(2*N)|P+2\bot Q$

where N is given by Eq. (1) and P is the input signal line, which has a value of 1 only when the count is to be advanced.

To design a counter, consider the fundamental sequential-circuit equations. Since the state and output variables are identical.

(3) $Y \equiv Q$

For a counter, the transition equation

(4) $Q \leftarrow F(P,Q)$

may be given as a function-specification table where the input variable P and each possible state Q are listed as arguments and the corresponding next states Q' are listed in the function columns (Fig. 7.10.2).

If the counter is to be built using a certain type of flip-flop, the properties of the flip-flop should now be introduced into the design. Consider for example the RS flip-flop. Its state transition function and its inputs (R,S) are listed in *inverse* order:

Q	Q'	R	S
0	0	0	0
0	1	0	1
1	0	1	0
1	1	0	0

The counter design table can be completed using this table as follows: in the counter's function-specification table, select a value of $Q[I]$ and a corresponding $Q'[I]$ entry. These are used as arguments to the flip-flop state transition table to obtain values for $R[I]$ and $S[I]$, that is, the required inputs to the flip-flop I whose state transition will be $Q[I]$ to $Q'[I]$. These $R[I]$, $S[I]$ values are entered in the columns for these variables. By repeating this process, a table of R and S values can be constructed as shown in Fig. 7.10.2. Once the table is obtained, each R and S column can be treated as a truth vector with arguments taken from the Q,P part of the table. Logical equations can be set down from these, and the simplification techniques of Chap. 5 applied. The final logical equations can then be translated into logic circuits whose inputs are the Q variables and the outputs the R, S lines to feed the inputs to the flip-flops.

If the type of flip-flop is not RS but some other type, say RST, the P,Q,Q' remain as before. Now however a new flip-flop state table is needed. For the T flip-flop this table is:

Q	Q'	T
0	0	0
0	1	1
1	0	1
1	1	0

The process described earlier is now used as shown in Fig. 7.10.2b to obtain three T columns of the design table. These three functions can then be simplified to obtain the logic circuits to be placed between the flip-flops.

An N-stage binary counter can contain a maximum count of $2^N - 1$ and will reset to 0 at count 2^N. Thus the contents of the counter after c input pulses may be described as the residue of c modulo 2^N. If the counter is to count modulo K, where K is any integer, then the expression for count-up is

(5) $\qquad Q \leftarrow (N \rho 2) \top K | P + 2 \bot Q$

The counter must reset at the count of K where K may be any number specified in the design of the counter. A modulo-K counter may be designed by the general method detailed previously. However, it is instructive to consider another method.

To design a modulo-K counter, start with a binary counter, i.e., one that counts modulo 2^N where $N \equiv \lceil \log_2 K$. Now in the state progression, the count of K will appear at or before the count of 2^N. Since the counter is to reset at the count of K, arrange an AND *detector* circuit which will yield a 1 only when the count of K is reached; this circuit should give an output D where

$\qquad D \leftarrow \wedge / Q = (N \rho 2) \top K$

The line D should be connected (e.g., by an OR circuit) to the counter RESET line.

Counter-specification table   *R, S required values*

P	Q[0]	Q[1]	Q[2]	Q'[0]	Q'[1]	Q'[2]	R[0]	S[0]	R[1]	S[1]	R[2]	S[2]
1	0	0	0	0	0	1	0	0	0	0	0	1
1	0	0	1	0	1	0	0	0	0	1	1	0
1	0	1	0	0	1	1	0	0	0	0	0	1
1	0	1	1	1	0	0	0	1	1	0	1	0
1	1	0	0	1	0	1	0	0	0	0	0	1
1	1	0	1	1	1	0	0	0	0	1	1	0
1	1	1	0	1	1	1	0	0	0	0	0	1
1	1	1	1	0	0	0	1	0	1	0	1	0

R, S flip-flop table

Q	Q'	R	S
0	0	0	0
0	1	0	1
1	0	1	0
1	1	0	0

Logic equations (from R, S, Q columns):

$$R[2] \equiv Q[2] \wedge P \qquad R[1] \equiv Q[1] \wedge Q[2] \wedge P$$
$$S[2] \equiv (\sim Q[2]) \wedge P \qquad S[1] \equiv (\sim Q[1]) \wedge Q[2] \wedge P$$

$$R[0] \equiv Q[0] \wedge Q[1] \wedge Q[2] \wedge P$$
$$S[0] \equiv (\sim Q[0]) \wedge Q[1] \wedge Q[2] \wedge P$$

General equations $(N \equiv \rho Q)$:

$$R[N-1] \equiv Q[N-1] \wedge P \qquad R[I] \equiv Q[I] \wedge R[I+1]$$
$$S(N-1) \equiv (\sim Q[N-1]) \wedge P \qquad S[I] \equiv (\sim Q[I]) \wedge R[I+1]$$

(a) Design of 3-bit counter using RS flip-flops.

Fig. 7.10.2 Logic design of a counter using RS and T flip-flops.

Q	Q'	T
0	0	0
0	1	1
1	0	1
1	1	0

P	Q[0]	Q[1]	Q[2]	Q'[0]	Q'[1]	Q'[2]	T[0]	T[1]	T[2]
1	0	0	0	0	0	1	0	0	1
1	0	0	1	0	1	0	0	1	1
1	0	1	0	0	1	1	0	0	1
1	0	1	1	1	0	0	1	1	1
1	1	0	0	1	0	1	0	0	1
1	1	0	1	1	1	0	0	1	1
1	1	1	0	1	1	1	0	0	1
1	1	1	1	0	0	0	1	1	1

Logic equations (from Q, T columns):

$$T[2] \equiv P$$
$$T[1] \equiv Q[2] \wedge P$$
$$T[0] \equiv Q[1] \wedge Q[2] \wedge P$$

General equations ($N \equiv \rho P$):

$$T[N-1] \equiv P$$
$$T[I] \equiv Q[I+1] \wedge T[I+1]$$

(b) Design of 3-bit counter using T flip-flops.

Fig. 7.10.2 Logic design of a counter using RS and T flip-flops (continued).

7.11 ELECTRONIC STEPPING SWITCH: RING COUNTER

A common requirement in clock, control, and display circuits is for a
commutator, i.e., the electronic counterpart of the stepping switch. This circuit
has one input (to time the stepping) and several output lines, only one of which

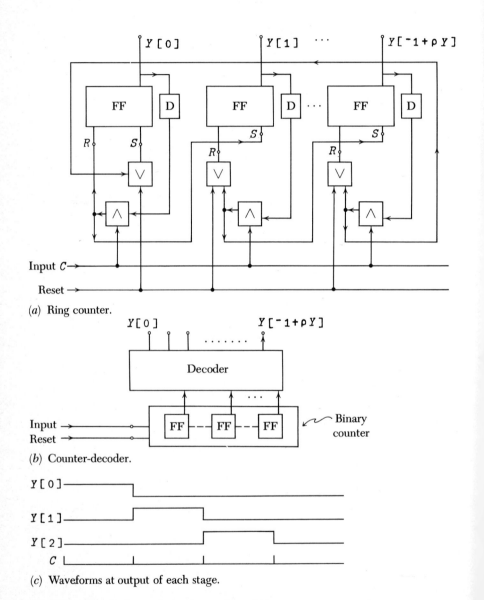

(a) Ring counter.

(b) Counter-decoder.

(c) Waveforms at output of each stage.

Fig. 7.11.1 Circuits for an electronic stepping switch.

is ON at any one time. As time progresses (as signaled by pulses on the single input line C), the lone ON signal steps from one output line to its successor; since the last stage feeds the first, after the last output is ON, the next state finds the first output ON; i.e., the states progress in a closed cycle.

There are at least two basic methods of implementing an electronic stepping switch. The first is a *ring counter* (Fig. 7.11.1*a*), which for N positions of output requires N flip-flops. In the reset condition, the leftmost bit is 1, the rest 0. In general, for bit I ON, since its flip-flop output is fed back through a delay (D) to its reset terminal, the next input pulse (C) will reset this flip-flop to 0. This reset signal is also fed to the S terminal of the next stage to turn it ON.

An alternative implementation of the stepping switch is to provide a counter whose outputs feed a decoder. The decoder has just the required property of 1-out-of-N output; the counter provides the necessary state transitions. The counter need have only $\lceil \log_2 N \rceil$ stages (instead of N for the ring counter). However, the economy is not as great as might appear at first glance because:

1. The decoder is costly.
2. The decoder outputs do not usually have as good drive properties as the flip-flop outputs of the ring counter.

A major use of 1-out-of-N stepping circuits is to obtain clock signals from a one-line oscillator source. A single central source of clock signals can be used to sequence events throughout a computer or a major part of a machine.

7.12 CONVERSION BETWEEN ANALOG AND DIGITAL REPRESENTATIONS

Modern data-processing systems are often applied to tasks like the control of chemical or other physical processes where some of the information sources do not supply ON-OFF signals of the type readily acceptable by the computer. A source that can assume a continuum of values will be called an *analog source.* Analog sources include the outputs of devices sensing temperature, pressure, velocity, and acceleration. The representation of the information from these sources is generally first converted to electrical form by devices called *transducers.* The analog transducer output is then *sampled* and *digitized.* The sampling refers to selecting a value at some point or area in time. It might appear that the finite digital representation of a value chosen from a continuum of possible values necessarily implies a loss of information. However, all sources contain an uncertainty in their values because of noise, drift, and the nature of the transducer process. Only the number of digits necessary to represent the value above this natural *quantizing increment* need be provided by the conversion process. The more precise analog transducers are capable of accuracy in the range of 0.01 to 0.1 percent of full scale. This corresponds to about 14 bits, not counting sign.

One form of analog-digital converter (Fig. 7.12.1) uses a linearly rising waveform or *ramp* as a reference in the conversion process. A *start* pulse sets a control flip-flop whose output (1) initiates generation of the ramp waveform and (2) opens a gate to admit regularly spaced clock pulses into the counter. Thus as the ramp waveform rises, the accumulation in the counter increases in proportion. The ramp and the input analog level are sent to an analog comparator (which can be a high-quality differencing circuit). The comparator includes a 0-detection circuit which generates an output pulse only when the ramp and input analog signal are equal. This output pulse is used to turn off the control flip-flop, thus resetting the ramp and blocking admission of further pulses to the counter. The counter contents then contain the converted value of the analog signal (possibly within a scale factor which is a function of the ramp slope).

The ramp-type converter is simple and can be made relatively cheap, but it contains several sources of imprecision. These include:

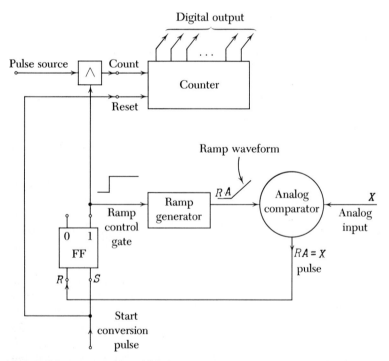

Fig. 7.12.1   Ramp-type analog/digital converter.

1. Nonlinearity and drift offset of the ramp
2. Nonuniformity of spacing in the pulse source
3. Resolution of the comparator and its freedom from displacement error

Of these, the first two are properties of the ramp-type converter; the comparator appears to be a fundamental unit in any type of converter.

The ramp converter also is basically a slow device, especially for large inputs.

Digital-to-analog conversion is the inverse of analog-to-digital conversion. Here we are presented with digital information, say in the form of a set of outputs of a register, and the problem is to convert this set to a voltage level proportional to the number in the register. This problem arises, for example, when an analog recording device such as a curve plotter which uses a servo for positioning is to be used to display the results of a digital data processor. Also, as will be seen later, the digital-analog converter may be used as the basis for a high-speed analog-digital converter.

One type of digital-analog converter uses a set of stable currents, each weighted in accordance with the digits of the number system used. Thus for a binary system the currents would be i, $2i$, $4i$, $8i$, etc. These currents are switched into an analog adder under the control of the state of the register. Analog addition and weighting of current values may be done with a resistor network or with resistors feeding an operational amplifier. Since the digital-analog converter does not require a comparator, it is much easier to design than the analog-digital converter.

As mentioned previously, the digital-analog converter can be used as the basis of an analog-digital converter. A common arrangement is shown in Fig. 7.12.2. The principle is to systematically cycle through the digit states of the register in the digital-analog converter, thus developing trial analog voltages. Each of these is compared with the input voltage whose conversion is desired, and as a result of the comparison a decision is reached whether to retain the latest trial increment. After all positions of the register have been tried and retained or rejected, the register contents is the digital form of the analog voltage. The process is equivalent to a binary search (see Chap. 4).

A clock-pulse generator is used to supply timing pulses for the trials; these are applied to the register inputs, the most significant digit position receiving the first clock pulse, etc. Each trial results in the addition of another current source to the analog adder in the digital-analog converter, so in this way we obtain a trial analog voltage. This is then compared with the input analog voltage (the comparison may be a subtraction of the voltage); if the trial results in a voltage larger than the input, the comparator and shaper circuit generate a pulse which is applied through an AND circuit to reset the proper stage of the register. The AND circuits select the proper stage since the other input is the delayed selection gate for the proper digit which was generated by the clock.

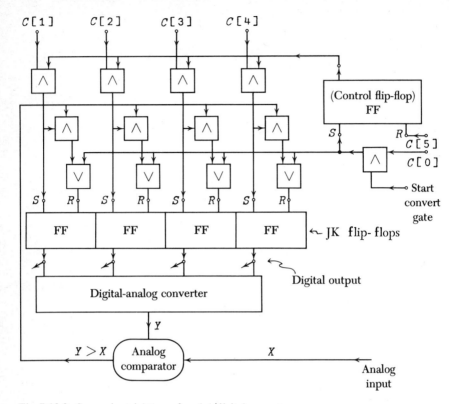

Fig. 7.12.2 Successive trial type of analog/digital converter.

It is seen that if the digital output is to have *n* bits, it takes *n* clock pulses to complete the conversion. This should be compared with 2^n pulses required in the system of the ramp converter discussed earlier. The increased speed of conversion is obtained at the expense of an increase in the amount of logic circuitry.

It should not be inferred that the converters discussed exhaust the types which have been developed. The examples given consisted of (1) a relatively economical circuit that is not inherently fast and (2) a fast, expensive, and more accurate type.

7.13 CATHODE-RAY DISPLAY SYSTEMS

One type of analog-digital and digital-analog complex of great interest in computer systems is the cathode-ray-tube (CRT) display. This includes a CRT that is much like a television picture tube with similar circuit facilities for:

1. Moving the electron beam striking the screen to any desired position by means of signals sent to magnetic deflection circuits
2. Controlling the energy of the beam so that the point where it strikes the screen appears light or dark

In many computer display systems, the "pictures" to be painted on the screen are composed of certain standard shapes like straight lines and circles. This can significantly reduce the data rate required from the computer since it need only send the few parameters of each such shape to the display electronics; the latter derives the detailed waveforms to the tube-deflection and intensity circuits. Some display devices include "character-generator" electronics so that the computer need only specify a print character (say as an 8-bit byte) and the display device will generate the signals to display it.

One fundamental issue in the design of display systems is how the storage for the display information should be supplied. The possibilities include:

1. Storage tube
2. Computer's main storage
3. Buffer storage in the display device (or sometimes shared by several devices)

The storage tube is a special type of display tube that holds its image indefinitely until changed. Cases 2 and 3 imply a tube that does not, so a persistent image can be sustained only by supplying its signals repetitively at a high enough rate to avoid flicker of the image to the eye. If the storage used to refresh the display is simply a part of computer storage, this is economical in storage cost but requires a high-speed data link and control electronics at the computer end. Supplying storage at the display end has dual advantages and disadvantages. Most systems, especially those where the display is, say, miles from the computer, use method 3. CRT displays are very convenient for rapidly displaying pages of printed text and graphical information such as curves, blueprint-type drawings and three-dimensional pictures. One disadvantage is the lack of hard copy of the images, although of course photographs can always be made of the screen. Also, some systems include typewriter and plotter devices that can be directed to accept the information on the screen to produce a permanent record.

A CRT display itself is an output device. Most displays are accompanied by keyboards like those on a typewriter that permit the user to enter character data. A most interesting input feature available in some display systems is the *light pen*, a device permitting the user to supply man-generated *input* information to both a display system and computer storage. The light pen is a photocell connected by wire to the computer (via appropriate electronics). The user can place the pen at some point on the display image. The photocell picks up the light from the point on the image when that point is being displayed; this sends a pulse to the computer. Since the image itself is being generated by the display electronics, it can correlate the time of the received light-pen pulse with the pen's position on the display. In this way, the user communicates to the computer a desired position on the display. This simple, fundamental capability gives the user a remarkably convenient way of interacting with display information. For example, the program may display a "menu" of possible actions or requests for programs. By placing his light pen over the desired item on the menu, he can select a program or display without any keying.

The light pen also enables the user to trace a curve on the screen and at the same time to enter a representation of the curve into computer storage, where it can be used as input data to programs. This is done by the display supplying, say, a small circle on the screen; as the user traces his curve, the computer senses where the pen cuts the circle, then moves the center to that point for the next increment of the curve. Thus, the circle follows the pen.

A device that provides the same function as the light pen is the supersonic pen. Here, the pen device held by the user generates a supersonic signal which is sensed by microphones distributed along the X and Y coordinates of the display. By measuring the time delay to reach the microphones, the circuitry can determine the coordinates of the pen position and convert them into numbers, which are sent to computer memory or used to control the display.

PROBLEMS

7.1 Write a quadruple list for a Turing machine which yields a 1 if some given number is odd and a 0 if it is even.

7.2 Write a Turing machine quadruple list to operate on a string of N 1s to produce a string of 0,1 values that is the usual binary representation of N. Start with a tape arranged as follows (for $N = 5$).

BBBS11111S

The strategy is to start at the rightmost S and replace the first 1 and from there every other 1 by say an X until the left S is reached. If the leftmost remaining 1 has been replaced by an X, the first B encountered is replaced by a 1, otherwise by 0. This process is repeated developing the next B value, etc., until there are no more 1s. The B string is then the desired binary representation of N.

7.3 Given the two FSMs

	0		1	
A	B	0	D	0
B	E	1	D	0
C	E	0	D	0
D	A	1	B	0
E	A	0	C	1

FSM 1

FSM2

a) Draw the state diagram for FSM 1.
b) Construct the transition table for FSM 2.

7.4 Suppose that a string of all 1s are supplied to FSM1. Give the trace table for one cycle of repetition.

7.5 Construct an FSM state diagram and transition table that gives a 1 output only for the string 0 followed by exactly three successive 1s.

7.6 Repeat Prob. 7.5 when the 1 output is to appear whenever the current and two previous inputs are 1.

7.7 In many communication systems, a stream of input symbols is to be simply routed to the output until a delimiter symbol, say *, is encountered. Although this would seem to rule out the use of * as a data symbol, a simple procedure permits * as a data symbol by requiring it to be given twice in succession (the reader will recognize this scheme for the quote mark for APL character vectors discussed in Chap. 2). Design an FSM:

a) Input alphabet A,B,C,*
b) Output alphabet A,B,C,*,∅   (∅ means null symbol)
c) State alphabet S1,S2, etc.

The output stream is to be the same as the input stream with the restriction noted. Include a START and STOP state.

7.8 *a*) Write a program that accepts a transition table (say as a character matrix) and any input string and prints a trace table (see text).
b) Test your program using at least the cases of Probs. 7.5 and 7.6.
c) Verify that the FSM does not change if the rows of the transition table are interchanged (except the first row).

7.9 Design a 3-bit full-binary counter with all the following features. Show a circuit and equations. Use polarity-hold flip-flops.

a) A single reset line to set the counter to 0
b) A count-start line to control inputs
c) Lines to set the counter to any value from 0 to 7
d) An output line which signals a counter state of 0

7.10 Design a 3-bit binary counter capable of counting either up or down depending on a control signal c. Include lines for setting the counter to any arbitrary value prior to count-start. Use RST flip-flops. The design must include equations for the r, s, t inputs to all flip-flops.

7.11 Design a counter whose outputs in response to successive ADVANCE pulses are

$$4, 17, 3, 4, 17, 3, 4, 17, 3, \ldots$$

7.12 Design a circuit to generate the sequence of Prob. 7.11 assuming three clock lines are available.

7.13 Design a recognizer circuit, i.e., a circuit which delivers a 1 output if 4-bit binary encodings of any of the numbers 9, 12, 6, 7, 8 are received. Assume the input bits appear on a single line in time sequence, low-order bit first. A clock source c synchronized with the input bits may also be assumed as available. Give equations of inputs to all flip-flops.

REFERENCES

1. Davis, M. (ed.): "The Undecidable: Basic Papers on Undecidable Propositions, Unsolvable Problems and Computable Functions," p. 115, Raven Press, New York, 1965. (Contains a reprint of Turing's original paper on the Turing machine, first published in 1936.)
2. Gill, A.: "Introduction to the Theory of Finite-state Machines," McGraw-Hill Book Company, New York, 1962.
3. Hennie, F. C.: "Finite-state Models for Logical Machines," John Wiley & Sons, Inc., New York, 1968.
4. Minsky, M.: "Computation: Finite and Infinite Machines," Prentice-Hall Inc., Englewood Cliffs, N.J., 1967.
5. Phister, M.: "Logical Design of Digital Computers," p. 117, John Wiley & Sons, Inc., New York, 1958.

8

Number Representations and Arithmetic Operations

Numerical or other types of information are usually represented internally in a data-processing system by finite-length strings of two-valued signals (bits); these signal values will be denoted by 0 and 1; respectively. The two-valued nature of the elementary unit of representation is due to the fact that technology presently yields the most reliable device operation when these devices need distinguish only between the minimum number of states—two. Although the translation of all numbers or other symbols into this binary-encoded form is not difficult (as will be seen presently) it does represent a tiresome chore for people. Fortunately, most modern systems perform this job of symbol translation automatically, in the computer-language translators. As a result, for example, most users need not be proficient in or even understand the binary number system. (This is not true of machine designers or people who program in assembly language.)

A somewhat more fundamental property of computer arithmetic is that it deals entirely with number representations of finite extent; i.e., it is basically finite-integer arithmetic. This has great theoretical and practical implications. Theoretically it means that most of the results of mathematics must be applied with caution since they often were derived assuming infinite (or at least indefinite) precision. It also means that fractions must be represented as integers and mixed numbers must be expressed as integer pairs. Although many modern machines include the ability to manipulate integer pairs representing mixed numbers or numbers expressed in floating-point notation, it is well to keep in mind that internally the machine usually performs only integer arithmetic.

In this chapter the problem of representing numbers by symbol strings, especially of the 0, 1 type, will be discussed. The first part deals with converting representations of a given number from one form to another. The latter sections deal with the elementary arithmetic operations in the binary number systems, including some commonly used algorithms for addition, subtraction, multiplication, and division. Finally, principles of some methods of checking and correcting corrupted binary-symbol strings are described.

A word is in order about the notation used in this chapter. As elsewhere in this book, mathematical notation with the usual precedence assigned to the various operators will be used in derivations and formulas and the APL language will be used in programs. Unless otherwise stated, indexing will use the 0-origin scheme.

8.1 POSITIONAL NUMBER SYSTEMS

Most common number systems represent an integer n as a string of integer elements called *digits*. A digit is an integer restricted in value to a definite range 0 through $r - 1$. Each digit is given a distinct symbol; a system with r symbols is said to be of radix r. Our everyday arithmetic and number representation uses radix 10.

The string of digits representing an integer is understood to be combined by weighting each digit by a power of the radix and then summing these weighted values. Thus in our usual decimal notation

$$(1) \qquad 3856 \equiv 3 \times 10^3 + 8 \times 10^2 + 5 \times 10^1 + 6 \times 10^0$$

In general an m-digit number with digits d in radix r means

$$(2) \qquad r \perp d \equiv d_0 r^{m-1} + d_1 r^{m-2} + d_i r^{m-i-1} + \cdots + d_{m-1}$$

where $m \equiv$ number of digits
$r \equiv$ radix
$d \equiv$ vector of digits; d_0 is the high-order digit, d_{m-1} is the low-order digit
$r^{m-i-1} \equiv$ weight given to position i, that is, to digit d_i

Notice that Eq. (2) states that the value represented by a digit string d is obtained by evaluating a polynomial in r with coefficients d.

It is most important to distinguish between a number and its representation as a digit string. In our notation a number will be written without commas separating the digits; such a symbol will be understood to represent the value of the number in the ordinary sense. Thus by convention the following are equivalent

$$10 \perp 3,8,9,7,2 \equiv 38972$$

More generally, to specify that a digit string, say 2,8,9, is to represent a number in radix r, say $r \equiv 12$, we write

$$12 \perp 2,8,9 \equiv 2 \times 12^2 + 8 \times 12^1 + 9 \equiv 393$$

In other notation systems this is sometimes written $(289)_{12} \equiv 393$.

There are at least two methods of performing the operations indicated by

(3) $N \leftarrow R \perp D$

The first uses a table in which a vector of weights W is set down as r^{p-1}, r^{p-2}, r^{p-3}, ..., r, 1, where $p \equiv \rho D \equiv \rho W$. Under each power of r is placed an element of the digit representation D. The value N is then

(4) $N \leftarrow W + . \times D$

that is, each weight is multiplied by the corresponding digit and the weighted digits are then summed.

EXAMPLE: Find the value for the digit string 1,2,3,7 interpreted as an octal (radix 8) number.

SOLUTION:

(5) $N \leftarrow 8 \perp (1,2,3,7)$
        $W \equiv 512,64,8,1$
        $D \equiv 1,2,3,7$
        $W \times D \equiv 512,128,24,7$
        $N \equiv W + . \times D \equiv + / W \times D \equiv 671$

The weighted-digit method is useful for numbers containing a few digits. For the more general case, the base value may be obtained using the polynomial nature of the function as indicated in Eq. (2). The polynomial can be evaluated with the fewest operations by the method of nesting. This subject was covered in Chap. 2 and applied to the base-value operation in Sec. 2.5. To help recall the process, it will be applied to the octal digit string of Eq. (5).

EXAMPLE: Find N in Eq. (5).

SOLUTION:

$$N \equiv 7+8(3+8(2+8(1)))$$

Evaluating the expression right to left:

$$N \equiv 7+8(3+80)$$
$$\equiv 7+8(83)=7+664$$
$$\equiv 671$$

Noninteger numbers are conventionally represented in two parts, an integer part and a fraction part. Each part separately constitutes a digit string. Fractions are represented by introducing weights that are negative powers of the radix. The fraction and integer parts are included in the representation of a mixed number. The property of implied weights may be retained by providing a separator, usually a period, between the positions for which the weight is $r^0 \equiv 1$ and r^{-1}. Thus, for example, in ordinary notation

$$31.416 \equiv 3 \times 10^1 + 1 \times 10^0 + 4 \times 10^{-1} + 1 \times 10^{-2} + 6 \times 10^{-3}$$

It can be shown that any rational number (a number that can be expressed as the quotient of two integers) will always have repeating cycles of digits to the right after some finite number of positions of the representation of the fraction part. For some radices, the repeating digits will be all 0s for some fractions. For example, the representation of the fraction $\frac{1}{3}$ in the ordinary decimal radix system is

$$0.333333 \cdots$$

In the radix-3 number system, $\frac{1}{3}$ is represented by

$$0.100000 \cdots \quad \text{or} \quad 0.1$$

Radix values of particular interest in computer work are radix 10, since this is the common scheme used by human beings, and radix 2 (binary), because the simplicity and reliability of two-state devices make it most convenient for machine arithmetic to use binary. Two other systems closely related to binary are octal (radix 8) and hexadecimal (radix 16). The close relation of these systems to binary is due to the fact that 8 and 16 are powers of 2. In any radix system of radix r, r symbols for digits are required. For the octal system it is natural to use the familiar integer symbols $0, 1, 2, \ldots, 7$. For the hexadecimal (base-16) system, 16 symbols are required. The first 10 use the familiar integers; for the last six, letters are used. Thus the digits of a hexadecimal number use the following representations:

Decimal: 0 1 2 3 4 5 6 7 8 9 10 11 12 13 14 15
Hex: 0 1 2 3 4 5 6 7 8 9 A   B   C   D   E   F

As mentioned earlier, numbers expressed in binary are easily expressed in octal or hex since the latter radices are powers of 2. A simple analysis with Eq. (2) shows the rule for this type of conversion to be as follows: to convert a binary number to an octal number, group the bits of the binary number by 3-bit groups starting from the right, and then express each 3-bit group as an octal digit. For example, the base-8 representation of a binary number may be obtained as follows:

$$(2\rho 8)\top 2\bot 1,1,0,1,0,0\equiv 6,4$$

Similarly, conversion of binary to hexadecimal is done by grouping the binary digits by fours starting from the right and expressing each of these in hex. A complete APL expression for converting from a binary-digit string to a dense hexadecimal representation is illustrated by

$$\texttt{'0123456789}ABCDEF\texttt{'}[(3\rho 16)\top 2\bot 1,1,0,1,0,0,1,0,0,1,0,1]\equiv D25$$

Conversions from octal or hexadecimal back to binary can be done by converting each digit separately to binary and catenating the resultant bit strings.

8.2 CONVERSION FROM ONE RADIX REPRESENTATION TO ANOTHER

The first question that may well be asked is: How many digits d are required in a system of radix r to represent a number requiring D digits with some other radix R? A D-digit number of radix R can represent a number no larger than

(1) $R^D - 1$

Similarly, in radix r, d digits can represent a number no larger than

(2) $r^d - 1$

To represent the *same* largest number

(3) $r^d - 1 \approx R^D - 1$

where the wavy line indicates rough equality since for a given R, D, r there may be no exact integer solution for d. Solving Eq. (3) for r^d and R^D much greater than 1,

$$d \, \log_r r \doteq D \log_r R$$

or

(4) $$d \doteq \lceil D \log_r R$$

For example, to represent a 31-bit binary number requires d decimal digits obtained by substituting into Eq. (4) ($D \equiv 31, r \equiv 10, R \equiv 2$):

$$d \equiv \lceil 31 \log_{10} 2 \equiv \lceil 31(0.301) \equiv 10$$

The main problem of this section is how to express a number as a k-digit string representation for *any* specified radix. We assume positive integers only. In our notation the problem is to derive a detailed procedure to find D from N and R to satisfy the statement

(5) $$D \leftarrow (K\rho R) \top N$$

It is important to understand that a number has definite value no matter what radix system is used to represent it.

To make the procedure concrete, take the problem of expressing the number 86 in binary ($r \equiv 2$). Then Eq. (2) of the previous section gives as the form of representation

(6) $$n \equiv 86 \equiv d_0 2^6 + d_1 2^5 + d_2 2^4 + d_3 2^3 + d_4 2^2 + d_5 2^1 + d_6$$

The fact that seven binary digits are required may be verified using Eq. (4). The problem now is to find the seven values of d_i. Note that by definition of a digit, all d_i must be less than 2. To find the d_i, we make use of the fact that n is considered a polynomial containing the powers of 2 as weights. Because of this, division of n by 2 is seen to produce a quotient made up of a weighted sum of all digits but the last; each weight is the original weight divided by 2. Since d_6, the rightmost (low-order) digit of n, is less than 2 and has a weight of 1, this digit will be the *remainder* of the division. In summary, to find the rightmost digit of the converted number, divide by the radix; the remainder is the desired digit. Now note from Eq. (6) that the quotient of the division has a weight of 1 in *its* rightmost position. The digit in this position is the second digit (from the right) of the original number. Division of the quotient by the radix will yield as the remainder the second digit of the converted number. It is evident that this process may be continued until all the digits of the binary number are found. To show the details for $(7\rho 2)\top 86$

Division	Quotient	Remainder
86 ÷ 2	43	0 (low-order digit)
43 ÷ 2	21	1
21 ÷ 2	10	1
10 ÷ 2	5	0
5 ÷ 2	2	1
2 ÷ 2	1	0
1 ÷ 2	0	1 (high-order digit)

Binary representation of 86 is then 1,0,1,0,1,1,0.

Conversion of a fraction can be done by successive multiplication by the radix. To understand the procedure assume a fraction presented in a system of radix r as a radix point followed by digits. The digits f_i are understood to multiply weights which are negative powers of the radix; i.e., the fraction n may be written

$$(7) \quad n \equiv f_0 r^{-1} + f_1 r^{-2} + f_2 r^{-3} + \cdots + f_i r^{-(i+1)} + \cdots$$

The problem at hand is to find the f_i. Each of the f_i may be calculated successively starting with f_0. To obtain f_0, multiply n by r. The resulting number will have f_0 as its integer part; this is the high-order digit of the result fraction. The sum of the remaining terms constitutes a fraction. However, multiplication of this fraction by r will yield f_1 as the integer part (as well as a fraction part). Continuation of this process will yield the elements of f as far as desired.

EXAMPLE: Convert decimal fraction 0.321 into a binary fraction.
SOLUTION:

Multiplication	Integer part	Fraction part
0.321 × 2 ≡ 0.642	0	0.642
0.642 × 2 ≡ 1.284	1	0.284
0.284 × 2 ≡ 0.568	0	0.568
0.568 × 2 ≡ 1.136	1	0.136
0.136 × 2 ≡ 0.272	0	0.272
0.272 × 2 ≡ 0.544	0	0.544
0.544 × 2 ≡ 1.088	1	0.088

Thus the binary fraction equivalent to 0.321 is 0.0101001 to seven binary places. Conversion of a mixed number can be done by converting integer and fraction part separately or by multiplying the number by r^p ($p \equiv$ desired number of places after the decimal point), rounding the result to the nearest integer, then converting the integer to the radix-r representation. The rightmost p digits (elements) of the result constitute the fraction part, the remaining digits the integer part.

Thus far the problem of expressing a number as a digit string in any radix system has been discussed. A somewhat more general problem is that of converting one representation to another, i.e., expressing the digit string d representing some number in radix r to the n-digit string c representing the same number in radix q. In APL, the problem can be stated as

(8) $C \leftarrow (N\rho Q) \top R \bot D$

If this expression is read properly from right to left, the elementary operations (all previously described) are suggested. First the D representation is used to

Example:

Express the hex representation 4, C, 2 as a base-5 representation.
First the tableau to obtain the number being represented:

Weight	256	16	1
Digits	4	C	2
Products	1024	192	2

Number $\equiv$ 1218

Representation of 1218 in base 5:

	Quotient	Remainder
1218 ÷ 5 $\equiv$	243	3
243 ÷ 5 $\equiv$	48	3
48 ÷ 5 $\equiv$	9	3
9 ÷ 5 $\equiv$	1	4
1 ÷ 5 $\equiv$	0	1

Answer: 1,4,3,3,3

Check (for last part only):

Weights	625	125	25	5	1
Digits	1	4	3	3	3
Products	625	500	75	15	3

Sum $\equiv$ 1218

Fig. 8.2.1 Conversion from radix 16 to radix 5.

obtain a number; this can be done with a digit-weight tableau as described earlier. Then the number is represented in radix Q. This process was described in the previous portions of this section. An example is given in Fig. 8.2.1.

8.3 BINARY-DECIMAL CONVERSIONS

Consider a computer with only a binary arithmetic unit. Since man-generated input is decimal, machine hardware, possibly in conjunction with a program subroutine, must be provided to perform decimal-binary conversion on input information and binary-decimal conversion for output.

First take the problem of decimal-binary conversion. Consider a decimal number 385. The radix-10 representation is the digit vector 3,8,5.

<table>
<tr><td colspan="3" align="center">*Table 1*</td><td colspan="3" align="center">*Table 2*</td></tr>
<tr><td>*Arg*</td><td>*Function*
(octal)</td><td>*Function*
(decimal)</td><td>*Arg*</td><td>*Function*
(octal)</td><td>*Function*
(decimal)</td></tr>
<tr><td>0</td><td>0000</td><td>0</td><td>0</td><td>0000</td><td>00</td></tr>
<tr><td>1</td><td>0001</td><td>1</td><td>1</td><td>0012</td><td>10</td></tr>
<tr><td>2</td><td>0002</td><td>2</td><td>2</td><td>0024</td><td>20</td></tr>
<tr><td>3</td><td>0003</td><td>3</td><td>3</td><td>0036</td><td>30</td></tr>
<tr><td>4</td><td>0004</td><td>4</td><td>4</td><td>0050</td><td>40</td></tr>
<tr><td>5</td><td>0005</td><td>5</td><td>5</td><td>0062</td><td>50</td></tr>
<tr><td>6</td><td>0006</td><td>6</td><td>6</td><td>0074</td><td>60</td></tr>
<tr><td>7</td><td>0007</td><td>7</td><td>7</td><td>0106</td><td>70</td></tr>
<tr><td>8</td><td>0010</td><td>8</td><td>8</td><td>0120</td><td>80</td></tr>
<tr><td>9</td><td>0011</td><td>9</td><td>9</td><td>0132</td><td>90</td></tr>
</table>

<table>
<tr><td colspan="3" align="center">*Table 3*</td></tr>
<tr><td>*Arg*</td><td>*Function*
(octal)</td><td>*Function*
(decimal)</td></tr>
<tr><td>0</td><td>0000</td><td>000</td></tr>
<tr><td>1</td><td>0144</td><td>100</td></tr>
<tr><td>2</td><td>0310</td><td>200</td></tr>
<tr><td>3</td><td>0454</td><td>300</td></tr>
<tr><td>4</td><td>0620</td><td>400</td></tr>
<tr><td>5</td><td>0764</td><td>500</td></tr>
<tr><td>6</td><td>1130</td><td>600</td></tr>
<tr><td>7</td><td>1174</td><td>700</td></tr>
<tr><td>8</td><td>1440</td><td>800</td></tr>
<tr><td>9</td><td>1604</td><td>900</td></tr>
</table>

Fig. 8.3.1 **Tables for BCD–binary (octal) conversion.**

Within the machine, each decimal digit is usually *encoded* into 4 or more bits, i.e., signals each of which can be only in a 0 or 1 state. One such encoding, called *binary coded decimal* (BCD) or *8-4-2-1 code,* encodes each decimal digit into its binary equivalent. Notice that although the number 385 then appears as a string of bits, this string is *not* the same as the number 385 expressed in binary radix. To emphasize this point, we show both cases.

    0011 1000 0101   BCD for 385
    0001 1000 0001   binary for 385

Returning to the problem of decimal-binary conversion, it might be thought that we can divide the decimal number by 2 successively as described earlier, but this is meaningful only if the arithmetic unit is capable of treating the digit encodings as decimal digits; i.e., if the arithmetic unit is capable of decimal arithmetic. If only binary arithmetic is available, another method must be used.

Figure 8.3.1 shows three tables, each containing 10 binary numbers as function values. These as well as the arguments would in actuality be in binary but are shown in decimal as well as octal (base 8) for readability. It is seen that

```
      ∇ BCDTOBIN
[1]     B←(16)ρ0
[2]     'ENTER 4 BCD DIGITS(16 BITS)'
[3]     D←□
[4]     K←(6ρ2)T4
[5]  LP:B←((ρB)ρ2)T(2⊥B)+2⊥4↑D
[6]     →(0=∨/K←(6ρ2)T¯1+2⊥K)/END
[7]     B←((ρB)ρ2)T(2⊥B)+2⊥(2↑B),2ρ0
[8]     B←(1↓B),0
[9]     D←(4↓D),4ρ0
[10]    →LP
[11] END:'THE BINARY REPRESENTATION IS:'
[12]    □←B
      ∇
```

```
      BCDTOBIN
ENTER 4 BCD DIGITS(16 BITS)
□:
      0 0 1 0 0 0 1 1 1 0 0 0 0 1 0 1
THE BINARY REPRESENTATION IS:
0 0 0 0 1 0 0 1 0 1 0 1 0 0 0 1
```

(*a*) BCD to binary conversion

Fig. 8.3.2 Conversion algorithm with binary arithmetic.

```
     ∇ BINTOBCD
[1]    'ENTER 16 BIT BINARY NUMBER:'
[2]    B←□
[3]    D←16ρ0
[4]    K←(6ρ2)⊤4
[5] LP:R←(4ρ2)⊤10|2⊥B
[6]    B←((ρB)ρ2)⊤⌊(2⊥B)÷10
[7]    D←(4ρ0),⁻4↓D
[8]    D←D∨R,12ρ0
[9]    K←(6ρ2)⊤⁻1+2⊥K
[10]   →(0≠∨/K)/LP
[11]   'THE BCD REPRESENTATION IS:'
[12]   □←D
     ∇


     BINTOBCD
ENTER 16 BIT BINARY NUMBER:
□:
      0 0 1 0 0 0 1 0 0 0 0 0 1 1 0 0
THE BCD REPRESENTATION IS:
1 0 0 0 0 1 1 1 0 0 0 1 0 1 1 0
```

(*b*) Binary to BCD conversion

Legend

	0-origin indexing
D	BCD representation (bit vector)
B	Binary representation (bit vector)
K	Shift counter

Fig. 8.3.2 Conversion algorithm with binary arithmetic (Continued).

Table 1 contains the numbers 0 to 9; Table 2 contains 0 10, 20, 30, etc., through 90; Table 3 contains 0, 100, 200, 300, etc., through 900. The conversion procedure consists of using each BCD digit as an argument to one of the tables; the value obtained is then added to the accumulated result held in an accumulator register. Starting with accumulator≡0:

1. The rightmost digit to be converted is used as an argument to Table 1 and the function value there is added to the accumulator.
2. The second digit from the right is used as an argument to Table 2, and the function found there is added to the accumulator.

3. The process of accessing successive tables and accumulating the values found continues for each digit to be converted.
4. After digits have been treated as described above, the accumulator contains the desired number.

An alternative approach to using tables for decimal-to-binary conversion is to add the 4 bits of each BCD digit into the four low-order positions of the accumulated binary result. After each such addition, the accumulated binary result is multiplied by 10. This can be done by actually multiplying by the constant "10" stored in binary form, or else by shifting the accumulated result left by two places (thus multiplying by 4), then adding the preshifted value (thus obtaining five times the preshifted value), then shifting left by one position to finally complete multiplication by 10. A procedure using the above principles is shown in Fig. 8.3.2.

Conversion of a binary number to decimal (BCD) can be done in a straightforward manner in a binary machine by dividing by the binary representation of 10; the remainder is the low-order BCD digit. The quotient is then subjected to the same treatment to obtain the second BCD digit, and so on. By appropriate shifting and OR operations, the successive BCD digits can be packed into a single computer word and later sent to a printer or punched card or other I/O device.

8.4 SUBTRACTION OF POSITIVE INTEGERS WITH COMPLEMENT ARITHMETIC

The familiar "borrow" method of subtraction is unsuitable for automatic machines because a borrow may propagate through all positions of a number, thus necessitating expensive circuits. Instead, using the idea of the *complement,* it is possible to reduce a problem of subtraction to two simpler problems, complementation and addition. Since circuits for addition must be present anyway, the only additional problem presented by subtraction is complementation. Subtraction is important not only in addition and subtraction of signed numbers but also in comparison operations.

The method will first be shown without detailed explanation for an example of subtraction of decimal numbers. Then, the principles will be developed in general for any radix.

Take for example the problem:

    3587   Minuend (a)
  − 1976   Subtrahend (s)

The first step is to find the 9s complement of the subtrahend 1976. This is defined as subtracting 1976 from $10^4 - 1 \equiv 9999$.

$$\begin{array}{r} 9999 \\ {}^{-}\underline{1976} \\ 8023 \end{array} \equiv \text{9s complement of } 1976$$

Notice this does *not* require a borrow. Now we *add* the minuend to this number

$$\begin{array}{r} 3587 \\ {}^{+}\underline{8023} \\ 1\ 1610 \end{array}$$

↑_____ Overflow digit for "end-around" addition

Notice the overflow 1, which will always be present if the difference of the original numbers is positive. The overflow 1 is itself set to 0 and a 1 added to the result

$$\begin{array}{r} 1610 \\ {}^{+}\underline{\quad 1} \\ 1611 \end{array}$$

This is the final answer.

A general theory of these operations for any radix r will now be presented. The $r - 1$ complement of an m-digit number n in radix r will be denoted by n'. It is obtained by subtracting n from $r^m - 1$

(1) $n' \equiv (r^m - 1) - n$

Now consider $r^m - 1$. r^m is a number written as the digit 1 followed by m 0s. $r^m - 1$ is composed of identical digits; each is $r - 1$. Subtraction of n from this will never require a borrow. Thus, obtaining the $r - 1$ complement of a number requires subtraction but never requires a borrow.

EXAMPLE: Decimal radix. Find 9s complement of 3804.

SOLUTION: Since $m \equiv 4$, $r^4 - 1 \equiv 10,000 - 1 \equiv 9999$. The 9s complement of 3804 is then

$$\begin{array}{r} 9999 \\ {}^{-}\underline{3804} \\ 6195 \end{array}$$

Now suppose we desire the difference $a - s$ between two numbers a and s. Throughout this discussion we assume a and s are positive and are represented with the same number of digits m. Consider the expression

(2) $e \equiv a + (r^m - 1 - s)$

e is thus the sum of a number a and the complement of s. Now the desired difference d can be written in terms of e:

(3) $d \equiv a - s \equiv e - (r^m - 1) \equiv (r^m - 1 - s) + a - (r^m - 1)$

The expression on the right is arranged to show the order of operations, which is:

1. Complement the subtrahend s; that is, perform $r^m - 1 - s$.
2. Add the minuend a to the complemented subtrahend.
3. Subtract $r^m - 1$.

Although the last operation might appear to be difficult, a little thought will show that r^m is simply a 1 in the "overflow" position on the left of the m-digit sum number. This is easy to subtract (by discarding). The rest of step 3 requires subtraction of -1, that is, the addition of 1.

Since the result of a subtraction may be positive or negative, it is important to see how the process indicates the sign of the result. To understand this, Eq. (2) is rearranged slightly:

(2a) $e \equiv r^m - 1 + (a - s)$

The sign of $d \equiv a - s$ is determined by the three cases:

$a > s$ $a - s$ is positive
$a < s$ $a - s$ is negative
$a \equiv s$ $a - s$ is 0

The nature of e for these cases can be understood when it is recalled that $r^m - 1$ is the largest m-digit number possible in radix r. Thus Eq. (2a) shows that a positive difference $a - s$ will produce an overflow 1 in the m-digit representation of e. Also a negative or 0 difference $a - s$ will subtract its magnitude from $r^m - 1$, thus yielding a 0 overflow. In short, the presence of a 1 or 0 overflow after the addition of minuend to the complement of the subtrahend signals a positive or negative result, respectively. Furthermore, for the case of $a - s$ negative, Eq. (2a) shows that e is the complement of the magnitude of the difference.

In summary, to subtract two positive integers having the same number of digits, add the minuend to the $r - 1$ complement of the subtrahend. If a 1 appears in the overflow position of the sum, the desired difference is positive and is obtained by discarding the overflow 1 and adding a 1 to the sum. If a 1 does not appear in the overflow position, this signifies that the result is negative or 0 and appears as the complement of the magnitude of the difference, i.e., the difference, in complement representation.

The above process was described in general terms and hence applies to any radix. To illustrate the procedures, Fig. 8.4.1 shows examples for binary and decimal subtractions for cases where the results are positive and negative.

It is important to note the ease of finding the 1s complement of a number in the binary number system. This requires subtraction of the number from 1111111 · · · 1, which is simply the digit by complement; i.e., all 1s are changed to 0s, all 0s to 1s. Since the bits of the number to be complemented usually come from a register with normal and complement outputs both available, the complementation-addition process simply involves routing the complement outputs of the subtrahend register together with the minuend to the adder.

For the case where the difference is negative, no end-around appears, and the difference appears in complement form. This may be stored directly, or else the complement form may be complemented to give a "true" representation.

Another type of complement operation is called the *radix complement*. The radix complement of an m-digit number n in radix r is defined by

$$r^m - n \equiv (r^m - n - 1) + 1 \qquad (4)$$

The form on the right shows that the radix complement of a number can be obtained by adding 1 to the $r - 1$ complement of the number.

```
  0 | 3 5 8 7     0 | 3 5 8 7
- 0 | 1 9 7 6   + 0 | 8 0 2 3
  --+--------   ----+--------
    |             1 | 1 6 1 0
                            1
                    ---------
                    +1 6 1 1     Result (3587 - 1976)

                                 (Recomplement)
  0 | 1 9 7 6     0 | 1 9 7 6     9 9 9 9
- 0 | 3 5 8 7   + 0 | 6 4 1 2     8 3 8 8
  --+--------   ----+--------
    |             0 | 8 3 8 8   - 1 6 1 1  <- Result (1976 - 3587)
```

(*a*) Illustrations of subtraction with 9s complements ($r \equiv 10$).

```
  0 | 1 1 1 0 1  (29)10     0 | 1 1 1 0 1
- 0 | 0 1 1 1 0  (14)10   + 0 | 1 0 0 0 1
  --+----------           ----+----------
    |                       1 | 0 1 1 1 0
                                        1
                          ----+----------
                            0 | 0 1 1 1 1  <- Result (29 - 14)

  0 | 0 1 1 1 0    (14)10     0 | 0 1 1 1 0         | 1 1 1 1 1
- 0 | 1 1 1 0 1  - (29)10   + 0 | 0 0 0 1 0         | 1 0 0 0 0
  --+----------             ----+----------         +----------
    |                         0 | 1 0 0 0 0    1    | 0 1 1 1 1  <- Result (14 - 29)
```

(*b*) Illustrations of subtraction with 1s complements ($r \equiv 2$).

Fig. 8.4.1 Examples of subtraction using $r - 1$ complements.

Consider the problem of subtraction $a - s$ using the radix complement of the subtrahend. Thus, in a manner analogous to the development given above,

(5) $d \equiv a - s$

(6) $e \equiv a + r^m - s \equiv (a - s) + r^m$

Now for numbers m digits in length, r^m is a 1 in the overflow position to the left, followed by all 0 digits to the right. If $a - s$ is positive, the expression for e shows it to consist of the desired difference in the rightmost m positions, but there is also present an overflow 1 to the left. On the other hand, if $a - s$ is negative, the result is the magnitude of the difference in complement form. In summary then, for a and s positive numbers, addition of a to the radix complement of s gives the true difference if the difference is positive (together with a 1 in the overflow position); if the difference is negative, the overflow 1 does not appear and the result appears in radix-complement form.

EXAMPLE: Radix-2 (binary) system.

    110101   (53 in radix 10)
    $-$ 011011   (27 in radix 10)

First find 1s complement of subtrahend and add this plus 1 to the minuend.

    110101
    100100
         1
    ————————
    1 011010   (26 in radix 10)

The overflow 1 indicates a positive result; hence it is in true form.

Unlike the 1s-complement scheme, end-around addition of 1 is *not* required, thus saving another possible addition operation. The addition of 1 required to obtain the 2s complement from the 1s complement is done as part of the normal addition.

There are three common methods of representing *signed* binary numbers; in all cases a positive sign is 0, a negative sign 1.

1. Signed true (signed magnitude)
2. Signed 1s complement
3. Signed 2s complement

A summary of these three is given in the chart of Fig. 8.4.2. A 3-bit example (including sign) shows the possible bit combinations and their

(BIT-STRING)	SIGNED TRUE	1-S SIGNED COMPLEMENT	2-S SIGNED COMPLEMENT
← X →			
0 1 1	+3	+3	+3
0 1 0	+2	+2	+2
0 0 1	+1	+1	+1
0 0 0	+0	+0	+0
1 0 0	-0	-3	-4
1 0 1	-1	-2	-3
1 1 0	-2	-1	-2
1 1 1	-3	-0	-1
N	$(1,\bar{1})[X[0]]\times2\perp1\downarrow X$	$(2\perp X)-X[0]\times(2*\rho X)-1$	$(2\perp X)-X[0]\times2*\rho X$
X	$(N<0),((\bar{1}+\rho X)\rho2)\top|N$	$(N<0)\neq((\rho X)\rho2)\top|N$	$(N<0)\neq((\rho X)\rho2)\top|N+1\times(N<0)$
MOST POSITIVE REPRESENTATION	$(2*\bar{1}+\rho X)-1$ $(\bar{1}+\rho X)\rho1$	$(2*\bar{1}+\rho X)-1$ $(\bar{1}+\rho X)\rho1$	$(2*\bar{1}+\rho X)-1$ $(\bar{1}+\rho X)\rho1$
MOST NEGATIVE REPRESENTATION	$-(2*\bar{1}+\rho X)-1$ $(\rho X)\rho1$	$-(2*\bar{1}+\rho X)-1$ $1,(\bar{1}+\rho X)\rho0$	$-2*\bar{1}+\rho X$ $1,(\bar{1}+\rho X)\rho0$
+ ZERO	$(\rho X)\rho0$	$(\rho X)\rho0$	$(\rho X)\rho0$
- ZERO	$1,(\bar{1}+\rho X)\rho0$	$(\rho X)\rho1$	NONE
SHIFT LEFT (K PLACES)	$X[0],((K+1)\downarrow X),K\rho0$	$X[0],((K+1)\downarrow X),K\rho X[0]$	$X[0],((K+1)\downarrow X),K\rho0$
SHIFT RIGHT (K PLACES)	$X[0],(K\rho0),(-K)\downarrow1\uparrow X$	$X[0],(K\rho X[0]),(-K)\downarrow1\uparrow X$	$X[0],(K\rho X[0]),(-K)\downarrow1\uparrow X$

Fig. 8.4.2 Three types of representation of signed binary numbers.

interpretations. All three representations are identical for positive numbers. The signed true and signed 1s-complement representation have two bit strings which represent 0 (+ 0 and – 0). This can be troublesome to programmers who often require a rigid distinction between a negative number and 0. The chart gives general expressions for converting any bit string in any specified representation to a number value (X to N) and vice versa (N to X). Expressions are also given for the limiting values of numbers (0, most positive, most negative) available in each system. Finally, expressions for shifting rules are also stated. Left shift of a true number by k places is equivalent to multiplication by r^k (provided no significant digits are lost on the left). Similarly, right shift is equivalent to division by r^k (with the low-order k places of the original number lost). What are the rules for shifting numbers in the system where signed complemented representation is used for negative numbers? In the shift operation, two suboperations are carried out:

Addition: $a + s$

Case ① $|a| + |s|$
     ② $|a| + -|s|$
     ③ $-|a| + |s| \rightarrow -(|a| - |s|) \rightarrow -②$
     ④ $-|a| + -|s| \rightarrow -(|a| + |s|) \rightarrow -①$

Subtraction: $a - s$

Case ⑤ $|a| - |s| \rightarrow ②$
     ⑥ $|a| - -|s| \rightarrow |a| + |s| \rightarrow ①$
     ⑦ $-|a| - |s| \rightarrow -(|a| + |s|) \rightarrow -①$
     ⑧ $-|a| - -|s| \rightarrow -(|a| - |s|) \rightarrow -②$

Summary

Case	p	a	s	c	r
①	+	+	+	0	0
②	+	+	–	1	0
③	+	–	+	1	1
④	+	–	–	0	1
⑤	–	+	+	1	0
⑥	–	+	–	0	0
⑦	–	–	+	0	1
⑧	–	–	–	1	1

	Notation
p	Operator sign: + addition – subtraction
c	Complement s control: $c \equiv 1$ complement s $c \equiv 0$ no complement s
r	Negate-result control: $r \equiv 1$ negate $r \equiv 0$ do not negate

Fig. 8.5.1   A complement sign control method.

1. The digits are moved.

2. Each vacated position is filled with some digit. The digit used for *fill* is 0 for positive numbers; for negative numbers it is given by:

Operation	Radix complement	Radix-1 complement
Left shift	0 fill	(radix-1) fill
Right shift	(radix-1) fill	(radix-1) fill

In the radix-complement system, 0 should be used for the + sign, 1 for the – sign. Then the fill for right shift is seen to be the sign digit (for radix 2).

It is quite feasible to use several different representations of signed numbers in different portions of the same computer. For example, the storage may use only signed true representation, but the arithmetic unit may perform its arithmetic in signed 1s-complement representation. In this case the machine must automatically change each negative number to the signed 1s complement before each arithmetic operation and back to signed true before storage of each result. Other combinations of representation are also quite common.

8.5 SIGN CONTROL FOR ADDITION AND SUBTRACTION

Automatic control of the result sign is essential in computer arithmetic. If the signed-true-number representation scheme is used, the sign as well as the ordering of certain operations can be determined as shown in Fig. 8.5.1. There are three signs involved: the sign of each number and the sign of the operator. There are then eight sign combinations; all are displayed in truth-table form. They are seen to reduce to essentially two cases: addition or subtraction of magnitudes with possible negation of the result. The circuitry is simplified by the fact that for the operations $a + s$ if complementation is required, it will be of s, never of a.

If the numbers are represented in the signed 2s-complement system, it can be shown that if the sign bit is treated the same as any other bit in the addition (subtraction), the resultant sign bit will be correct (the reader should convince himself of this by a few examples).

Since computer numbers usually have some fixed number of bits, it is possible for the result to be larger than can be represented by the number of bits available. This is called *overflow*. When it occurs, a signal should be sent to the program, usually through the mechanism of the program interrupt (see Chaps. 9 and 10). In the case of signed 2s-complement number representation, an overflow condition during addition/subtraction is detected as follows: *An overflow exists if the carry signal out of the sign position is different from the carry signal into the sign position.*

8.6 SERIAL AND PARALLEL REPRESENTATIONS OF NUMBERS

Consider a positive integer expressed in the binary-radix system. Since a computer internally processes only electric signals, the 0 or 1 state for each binary digit must be represented by a two-valued electric signal which must appear on some wire within the computer. A most important design consideration is whether each bit is to be represented by a physically distinct wire (line) or whether all bits of a number are to timeshare a single line by being sent to the line in time sequence. The first method of one line per bit is called *parallel* representation; the second method is called *serial* representation. In comparing the two representations, as was done in Chap. 1, it is found that the serial scheme is economical in circuitry since only a single line (and associated circuitry) is required. On the other hand, the serial circuit is slow since the bits must wait their turn to be routed to the single line. In practice, the equipment

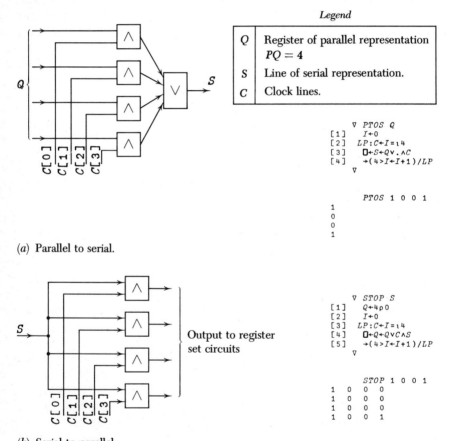

Legend

Q	Register of parallel representation $PQ = 4$
S	Line of serial representation.
C	Clock lines.

```
      ∇ PTOS Q
[1]      I←0
[2]    LP:C←I=ι4
[3]      □←S←Qv.∧C
[4]      →(4>I←I+1)/LP
      ∇
```

```
PTOS 1 0 0 1

1
0
0
1
```

(*a*) Parallel to serial.

Output to register set circuits

```
      ∇ STOP S
[1]      Q←4ρ0
[2]      I←0
[3]    LP:C←I=ι4
[4]      □←Q←QvC∧S
[5]      →(4>I←I+1)/LP
      ∇
```

```
STOP 1 0 0 1

1 0 0 0
1 0 0 0
1 0 0 0
1 0 0 1
```

(*b*) Serial to parallel.

Fig. 8.6.1   Parallel-serial conversion circuits timed by clock lines c.

savings of the serial system may be considerable, but somewhat less than one might expect because of the cost of the circuits to sequence the bits.

The economy advantage of the serial representation and the speed advantage of the parallel method are often combined in a serial-parallel arrangement. For example, addition may be performed on two 32-bit numbers by routing each of them in groups (bytes) of 8 bits to an adder circuit capable of adding 8-bit numbers. (Provision is made to store any carry which results in the high-order position of the adder and enter it into the addition of the next byte.) A faster (but more expensive) scheme would partition the 32-bit number into two 16-bit groups and use a 16-bit adder.

The above example suggests that there are degrees of seriality and parallelism. It is quite feasible to use different bit widths for paths, adders, registers, etc., within the same system. If such a mixed scheme is used, it will of course be necessary to provide circuits at appropriate points to translate between serial and parallel representations. Although such translation circuits are not obtained without cost, substantial savings in overall costs are possible by judicious choice of serial and parallel configurations.

Another point worth noting is that decisions on serial versus parallel representations are, to a large extent, implementation choices which may strongly affect cost-performance (speed) but which need not strongly affect the architecture of the system, i.e., the logical appearance of the system to the user or programmer.

Although the above discussion is in terms of numbers representation, similar considerations apply to other types of information such as the instructions and control bits.

The serial-parallel interplay possibilities also appear in the organization of storage devices. For example, most magnetic-tape drives use a parallel-by-bit, serial-by-byte (character) representation. Typically, the tape read/write station handles, say, 7 bits of information at each tape position. This parallel-serial scheme increases the data rate by a factor of 7 over a strictly serial-by-bit method, and this is done without increase in tape speed or density. The same principle is often applied to other serial-access devices such as magnetic drums and disks. By access to several tracks in parallel, these devices can approach in data rate nonmechanical storage such as magnetic-core storage. (Random access on serial-storage devices is generally much slower than magnetic-core storage, but this is an independent parameter in characterizing a storage device.)

8.7 SERIAL COMPLEMENTER CIRCUITS

A serial 1s complementer circuit routes the input stream to the output either directly or else through a NOT (complement) circuit. Which path is taken depends upon *true/complement* control gates t and c (see Fig. 8.7.1a).

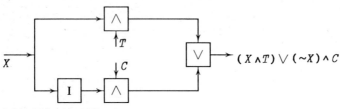

$$(X \wedge T) \vee (\sim X) \wedge C$$

(*a*) Serial 1s complementer.

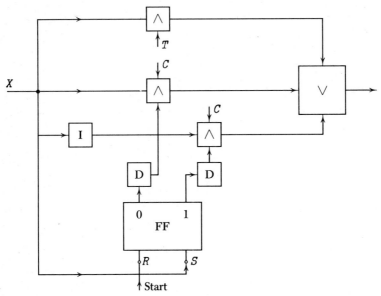

(*b*) Serial 2s complementer.

Note: T and C denote control gates for true or complement outputs.

Fig. 8.7.1 Serial complement circuits.

A serial 2s complementer (Fig. 8.7.1*b*) can be designed based on the fact that the 2s complement of a binary number can be obtained by inspecting the bits in turn (from low to high order) and copying 0 bits into the output (low to high order) until the first 1 bit is encountered. This bit is also copied into the output, but all succeeding input bits are inverted to produce corresponding output bits. The justification of this method of 2s complementation follows from the fact that a string of rightmost 0 bits will, upon 1s complementation, yield a string of 1 bits. If 1 is added into the low order of such a string (to obtain the 2s complement from the 1s complement), the string of 1 bits will become a string of 0 bits. These may be supplied by the input stream itself. Just after a 1 is encountered in the input stream, the string of 0 bits is broken and successive bits are inverted to obtain the outputs.

The circuit to perform the above transformation contains a flip-flop which "remembers" whether the initial string of 0s has passed or not; this flip-flop is initially set OFF at start-up and is set ON by the first 1 which appears in the input stream.

8.8 SERIAL BINARY ADDITION

A serial-by-bit binary adder may be built with a 1-bit full-adder circuit, a flip-flop for storing a single carry signal, and some control logic (Fig. 8.8.1). The two numbers to be added are presented to the adder input terminals as two

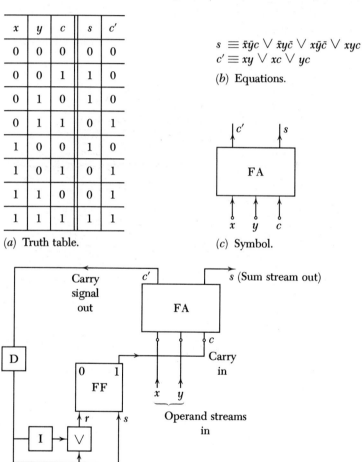

x	y	c	s	c'
0	0	0	0	0
0	0	1	1	0
0	1	0	1	0
0	1	1	0	1
1	0	0	1	0
1	0	1	0	1
1	1	0	0	1
1	1	1	1	1

(*a*) Truth table.

$$s \equiv \bar{x}\bar{y}c \vee \bar{x}y\bar{c} \vee x\bar{y}\bar{c} \vee xyc$$
$$c' \equiv xy \vee xc \vee yc$$

(*b*) Equations.

(*c*) Symbol.

(*d*) Serial adder.

Fig. 8.8.1 One-bit serial adder.

streams of bits synchronized in time; i.e., corresponding bits appear at the same time. The bits in the streams appear from low to high order as time progresses. The streams may originate from a drum's READ head or from a delay line.

Since an adder is a combinational circuit, it contains no storage. One of the outputs is the sum bit, which can be stored in the same medium as the input stream. The other output of the 2-bit adder is the *carry*, which is stored in a simple flip-flop to supply the carry-in to the adder for the next input bit pair.

A complete addition circuit must be able to handle signed numbers and both subtraction and addition. The routing of the serial representations of the numbers through complementer circuits depends on the signs of the numbers; in most serial-by-bit systems, the rightmost bit, which is the first to arrive, is the sign bit. The signs of the two operands and the sign of the operation then set up complement and other controls for execution of the operation on signed numbers.

8.9 DESIGN OF PARALLEL BINARY ADDERS

A parallel binary adder is a circuit which accepts $2n$ input lines, n lines for each of two binary number representations, and produces n output signals representing the sum of the two numbers. The two input bit strings are called x and y and the sum string is called s. The parallel adder is fed all elements of x and y at the same time, and after circuit delays are over, the correct s signals are available (say, for routing to a register) all at the same time.

A simple approach to parallel adder design is to design n 1-bit full adders and interconnect them as shown in Fig. 8.9.1. For position i (starting with $i \equiv 0$ from the left and increasing to the right), the equations for the sum s_i and carry-out, c_i, are the same as for the 1-bit adder considered in the last section except for the subscripting

(1) $s_i \equiv \bar{x}_i\bar{y}_ic_{i+1} \vee \bar{x}_iy_i\bar{c}_{i+1} \vee x_i\bar{y}_i\bar{c}_{i+1} \vee x_iy_ic_{i+1}$

(2) $c_i \equiv x_iy \vee x_ic_{i+1} \vee y_ic_{i+1}$

It is often convenient to rearrange Eq. (2) using Boolean algebra and some renaming as follows in Eq. (3):

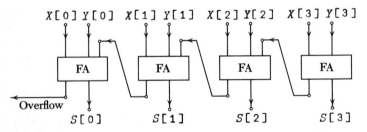

Fig. 8.9.1 **Ripple carry connection of full adders.**

(3)　　$g_i \equiv x_i y_i$

(4)　　$p_i \equiv x_i \vee y_i$

(5)　　$c_i \equiv g_i \vee p_i c_{i+1}$

The functions g_i and p_i are sometimes called *carry generate* and *carry propagate,* respectively, since when g_i is 1, a carry is generated in position i and sent to position $i - 1$, while if p_i is 1, a carry into position i will propagate out of position i. Equation (5) is of course simply another way of writing the carry equation of Eq. (2). Equation (5) may be used successively to obtain an equation for carry-out for any position in terms only of the adder input lines x and y. For example, for a 2-bit adder, we use Eq. (5) twice as follows:

(6)　　$c_0 \equiv g_0 \vee p_0 c_1$

(7)　　$c_1 \equiv g_1 \vee p_1 c_2$

Substituting Eq. (7) into Eq. (6)

(8)　　$c_0 \equiv g_0 \vee p_0(g_1 \vee p_1 c_2) \equiv g_0 \vee p_0(g_1)$

The last expression assumes that $c_2 \equiv 0$; that is, there is no carry into the lowest-order position.

It is instructive to consider a 4-bit adder, in which case the corresponding equation for the carry-out of the leftmost position is

(9)　　$c_0 \equiv g_0 \vee p_0(g_1 \vee p_1(g_2 \vee p_2 g_3))$

When Eq. (9) is read from the right and the groups with the c_i are identified, Eq. (9) can be implemented by connecting the carry-out of each position to the carry-in of the next higher-order position. Such a circuit, shown in Fig. 8.9.1, requires two circuit levels per position or $2n - 1$ circuit levels in cascade from lowest- to highest-order carry positions. In the worst case, typified by x all 1s and y all 0s except for a rightmost 1, the carry generated in the lowest-order position must be propagated through all $2n - 1$ levels before the correct sum appears at s. For other numbers, fewer levels may be traversed before the correct sum is obtained. However, there are no simple methods for detection of completion of carry, although at least one scheme has been proposed to take advantage of early detection of actual carry completion (see Richards, 1955). Most circuits do not use the s output until the time for worst-case carry-propagation delay is over.

The adder is a most important circuit determining the speed of arithmetic operations because it is used in addition, subtraction, multiplication, division, comparison, and other operations. Obtaining high adder speed is an important objective in high-speed machines. Of course one approach is to use faster circuits; however, for circuits of a given speed much can be done to trade off speed for cost, fan-in, and fan-out. For given circuits, the speed of the adder is determined by the number of circuit levels to develop the high-order carry. The simple connection of n 1-bit full adders, called a *ripple-carry* circuit, requires $2n - 1$ circuit levels.

Is it possible to reduce the number of circuit levels for carry propagation over the ripple-carry circuit, and if so, how? That the possibility exists is easily established because, as was shown in Chap. 5, *any* logic function can be obtained with two levels as a (simplified) canonical form. For example, consider the high-order carry for the 4-bit adder given in Eq. (9). By expanding the expression using the distributive law of AND over OR, the parentheses can be removed to obtain

$$(10) \quad c_0 \equiv g_0 \lor p_0 g_1 \lor p_0 p_1 g_2 \lor p_0 p_1 p_2 g_3$$

Direct implementation of this circuit requires two levels and a cost of 13. To this we must add one level for obtaining the g's and p's from x and y, Eqs. (3) and (4), and a cost of 14 for these circuits to obtain a total cost of 27 and three circuit levels. The cost is only slightly more than the cost of 26 for the slower ripple-carry circuit that required seven levels. However, the three-level circuit requires a fan-in of four compared with two for the ripple circuit.

The expanded form of the carry equation typified by Eq. (10) can be used to design an adder having any specified number of bits n and using circuits with a specified fan-in f. Consider the design of the carry circuits of an 8-bit adder using logic blocks with a fan-in of three as shown in Fig. 8.9.2. Such a design is called a *look-ahead* carry circuit. The expression for c_0 is set down as a series of triangular patterns partitioned into lined figures. Each triangle shows all terms available after some logic level. Each lined figure represents the result of AND and OR operations of the terms contained within the figure, horizontal distance denotes AND, vertical distance OR. Thus part (*a*) of the figure shows that all p's and g's are available after the first logic level. In the second level, the logic blocks with fan-in of three are used to obtain groups of terms as indicated. After level 3 all AND terms are available as well as the result of the OR of the topmost three AND terms. After four levels, only two terms remain for OR operations. The final OR operation, and hence c_0, is obtained after the fifth level.

An upper bound for L, the number of levels required for carry-handling for an n-bit adder using logic blocks with fan-in f, is obtained by noting that the longest AND term as well as all intermediate AND terms require $\lceil \log_f n \rceil$ levels for AND

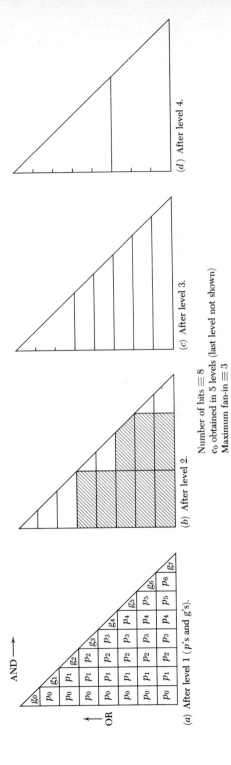

Number of bits $\equiv 8$
c_0 obtained in 5 levels (last level not shown)
Maximum fan-in $\equiv 3$

Fig. 8.9.2   Triangle diagrams for look-ahead carry logic.

operations; there are n such AND terms which can be ORed with f-input circuits in $\lceil \log_f n$ levels for OR operations. To these we add one level to obtain p and g, giving

(11) $L \equiv 1 + 2 \lceil \log_f n$

Equation (11) is an upper bound since it did not take into account the opportunity to do some OR operations at the same time as AND operations, as indicated in Fig. 8.9.2.

Some design procedures to achieve fast parallel addition are summarized in Fig. 8.9.3.

It is quite feasible to apply the look-ahead carry design to groups of bits of an adder rather than the adder as a whole. This results in a compromise between speed, cost, and fan-in. For example, a 32-bit adder can be partitioned into eight groups of 4 bits per group. Each group is designed for three levels to obtain carry-out from the group. A total of 24 levels is therefore required instead of 63 for the ripple circuit.

To summarize the adder-design principles, for high-speed arithmetic operations it pays to invest in high-speed adder circuitry. High-speed parallel addition with a given technology requires fast carry logic which implies a small number of logic levels for handling the longest carry propagation. All carries can be obtained for any number of positions in only two levels, but such a circuit for reasonably large n is expensive and has high fan-in requirements. A design procedure for use with logic blocks of a specified fan-in has been given. The procedure indicates

Type	Number of levels	Cost	Fan-in
Ripple	$2n - 1$	$8n - 6$	3
Look-ahead	3	$\dfrac{n(n+11) - 6}{2}$	n
Look-ahead with fan-in restrictions	$1 + 2 \times \lceil \log_f n$†	Formula not available	f

Notes:

† Upper bound.
$n \equiv$ No bits in addition.
$f \equiv$ Fan-in of logic blocks.

Fig. 8.9.3   High-order-carry circuit summary.

the trade-off possible between number of levels, fan-in, and cost. The idea of look-ahead carry circuitry may be applied to groups of bits to compromise speed with cost and fan-in.

8.10 SERIAL-BY-BYTE ADDITION

As indicated earlier, it is not necessary for the adder or other processing circuits to be as wide as the data being processed. Figure 8.10.1 shows a diagram of a 1-byte adder that adds numbers n bits wide. Each of the registers holding the numbers feeds a byte-selector circuit; this selects a single byte at a time to be routed to the ADDER input. The sum byte is sent to a byte-distributor circuit, which gates the result byte to the proper positions of the register z. Another result of a byte addition is a carry signal; this is saved in a flip-flop and introduced into the next byte addition. The selector-distribution circuits may be physically controlled by clock lines.

8.11 DECIMAL ADDITION IN A BINARY ADDER

Two numbers represented in the 8,4,2,1 BCD code can be added using the circuitry of a binary adder, provided certain correction operations are done. To simplify the description, we assume that the adder and the BCD representations are fully parallel; this is by no means essential, and the techniques of serial-by-byte addition are entirely feasible.

The basic problem in adding BCD representations of numbers is handling the carries from each digit. One method is to translate digits that generate carries to hexadecimal, where the carries can be handled easily by the binary adder. This translation is done by adding one of the BCD strings to the BCD representation of 6666 · · · 6. Note that this addition in itself will never result in a carry-out from a 4-bit group since the BCD representation must be less than 10 in each digit position. The result of the addition thus far is then added to the BCD representation of the other operand. Carry-out signals are kept as a vector c of the carries resulting at the output of each digit (every fourth bit). Now these carries are the carries that would have resulted from decimal addition. If there is a carry-out signal of 1 from a given digit position, the sum digit is correct since the above process mapped sum digits 10 or over to sum digits 16 or over. If, however, there is not a carry-out from a given digit position, this signifies an excess of 6 for that position, and 6 must be subtracted from that position. The subtraction of 6 from all such positions is the final correction operation.

∇ A BINADD B
[1]   S←((N+1)ρ2)⊤C+(2⊥A)+2⊥B
∇

(a) Adder function.

∇ Z←X BINADDER Y
[1]   'ENTER NO. OF BITS PER BYTE:'
[2]   N←□
[3]   J←ρY
[4]   Z←Jρ0
[5]   TC←C←0
[6]   LP:J←J-N
[7]   P←J+ιN
[8]   TC←TC+1
[9]   X[P] BINADD Y[P]
[10]   C←S[0]
[11]   Z[P]←(-N)↑S
[12]   →(J>0)/LP
[13]   'NO. OF ADDER USES=';TC
[14]   'SUM:'
∇

ENTER 1 1 1 0 0 0 BINADDER 1 1 0 0 0 1
ENTER NO. OF BITS PER BYTE:
□:
      2

NO. OF ADDER USES=3
SUM:
1 0 1 0 0 1

(b) Byte-by-byte addition.

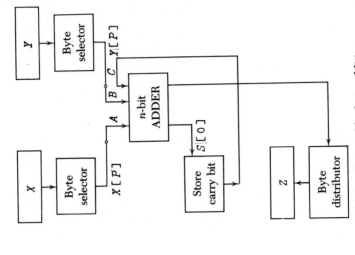

(c) Flow for serial-by-byte addition.

Fig. 8.10.1 Addition of binary numbers by byte.

```
      ∇ A←X BINADD32 Y
[1]      A←(32ρ2)⊤(2⊥X)+2⊥Y
[2]      'THE THIRTY-TWO BIT BINARY RESULT IS:'
      ∇


      1 1 0 0 1 1 0 0 1 1 BINADD32 1 0 0 0 0 0 0 1 1 1
THE THIRTY-TWO BIT BINARY RESULT IS:
0 0 0 0 0 0 0 0 0 0 0 0 0 0 0 0 0 0 0 0 0 0 0 1 0 1 0 0 1 1 1 0 1 0
```

(*a*) Binary addition (32 bits).

```
      ∇ A←X BCDADD Y
[1]      A←(32ρ2)⊤(2⊥X)+2⊥(32ρ2)⊤16⊥6×8ρ1
[2]      C←(((8ρ16)⊤2⊥A)+(8ρ16)⊤2⊥Y)≥16
[3]      A←(32ρ2)⊤16⊥((8ρ16)⊤(2⊥A)+2⊥Y)-(~C)×6
[4]      'THE THIRTY-TWO BIT BCD RESULT IS:'
      ∇


      0 1 1 0 0 0 1 0 0 1 0 0 1 0 0 0 BCDADD 0 0 0 1 0 0 1 0 1 0 0 1 1 0 0 0
THE THIRTY-TWO BIT BCD RESULT IS:
0 0 0 0 0 0 0 0 0 0 0 0 0 0 0 0 0 1 1 1 0 1 0 1 0 1 0 0 0 0 1 1 0
```

(*b*) Addition of BCD representations in binary adder with corrections.

Example:

$$
\begin{array}{r}
2\ 9\ 4\ 7 \\
+\ \underline{1\ 4\ 3\ 8} \\
4\ 3\ 8\ 5
\end{array}
$$ Original problem

Initial correction   *Addition*   *Final correction*

$$
\begin{array}{r}
1\ 4\ 3\ 8 \\
+\ \underline{6\ 6\ 6\ 6} \\
7\ A\ 9\ E
\end{array}
\qquad
\begin{array}{r}
7\ A\ 9\ E \\
+\ \underline{2\ 9\ 4\ 7} \\
A\ 3\ E\ 5 \\
c\equiv 0\ 1\ 0\ 1
\end{array}
\qquad
\begin{array}{r}
A\ 3\ E\ 5 \\
-\ \underline{6\quad 6\quad} \\
4\ 3\ 8\ 5
\end{array}
$$ Answer

(*c*) Example—all arithmetic in hexadecimal.

Legend

	0-origin indexing
X,Y	Two BCD representations $PX\equiv PY\equiv 32$
C	Digit–carry vector $PC\equiv 8\equiv 32\div 4$
A	BCD sum

Fig. 8.11.1 BCD addition in a binary adder.

8.12 BINARY MULTIPLICATION

In principle the usual method of multiplying two binary numbers in a computer is similar to the method used with pencil and paper; i.e., a succession of product-sum operations as follows:

1. The multiplicand is multiplied by the rightmost digit of the multiplier. With binary numbers, since the multiplier digit can only be 0 or 1, the product is either 0 or the multiplicand itself.
2. The result of the multiplication described above is added to the high-order positions of the partial product.
3. The partial product (representation) is shifted one position to the right. The multiplier is shifted one position to the right. A tally is kept of the number of shifts made.
4. If the number of shifts made is equal to the number of digits in the multiplier, the multiplication is complete. Otherwise, the entire cycle of steps 1 through 4 is repeated.

The procedure can easily be mechanized by providing an accumulator register A, set initially to 0, and a multiplier register Q, which initially holds the multiplier. The addition of successive multiplicands into the partial product need only take place in the accumulator. Both accumulator and multiplier registers can be shifted as *one long* register. Note that the control of whether to add the multiplicand to the accumulator or not depends only on the rightmost bit of the multiplier at any one step. The result of multiplication is a double-length product that may either be stored in two storage cells or rounded and stored in one cell.

EXAMPLE:

$$1 \quad 1 \quad 0 \quad \text{multiplicand}$$
$$1 \quad 0 \quad 1 \quad \text{multiplier}$$

A	Q	Remarks
0 0 0	1 0 1	Initial state
1 1 0	1 0 1	After addition of $Q[2] \times$ multiplicand
0 1 1	0 1 0	Shift right
0 1 1	0 1 0	After addition of $Q[2] \times$ multiplicand
0 0 1	1 0 1	Shift right
1 1 1	1 0 1	After addition of $Q[2] \times$ multiplicand
0 1 1	1 1 0	Shift right (complete)

Since only one bit of the multiplier is used at any one time, the method is applicable to the case where the multiplier is available serially by bit; but the multiplicand is available in parallel form. The multiplier stream is applied on a single line to AND-gate the multiplicand into one side of a parallel adder. The other side of the adder circuit is fed the high-order bits of the partial product. This is derived by offsetting the previous adder output one position to the right (thus giving a right shift). The rightmost bit of the offset is a bit of the product; after all multiplier bits have appeared, the lower half of the product has been obtained in serial form. The rest of the product is available in parallel form at the adder output; it may be serialized by *run-out* through the adder.

A generalization of the above process again assumes that the multiplicand is available in parallel form but that the multiplier appears in parallel-serial form, e.g., two bits at a time. The basic idea is to simultaneously generate all four possible products of the multiplicand and 2-bit numbers and then use the

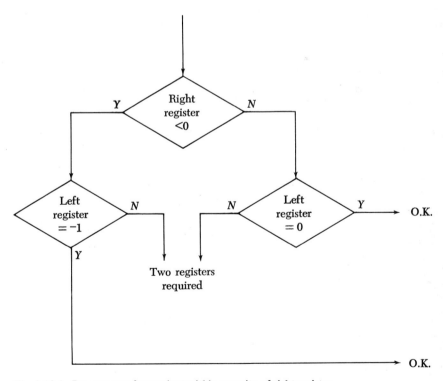

Fig. 8.12.1 Program test for product within capacity of right register.

current 2 bits of the multiplier to select (say, with a decoder circuit) one of these for addition to the partial product. The partial product is then offset two positions to the right, thus yielding at the rightmost end two bits of the desired product. This process is repeated using the next 2 high-order bits of the multiplier, etc., until all multiplier bits have been used. The necessary simultaneous multiplication by 00,01,10,11 is simply mechanized by respectively copying 0, copying the multiplicand, copying the multiplicand offset left by one position or addition of the last two cases. The idea can be extended to even higher-speed multiplication by handling more than 2 multiplier bits at one time, but the circuit costs increase.

The result of multiplying two m-bit numbers (not counting signs) is a number that can require up to $2m$ bits, i.e., two words. Both these words can be stored, used as a dividend in division, or used in double-precision arithmetic operations. Yet it is often the case that the product "fits" into the low-order single word of the register pair Q. A test for this is shown in Fig. 8.12.1. If the test succeeds, the product can be stored in a single word of storage.

8.13 SPEEDING UP PARALLEL MULTIPLICATION

Since multiplication is performed with addition and shifting operations, any increase in speed of these can contribute to faster multiplication.

Multiplication speed can be improved with little increase in circuit complexity by skipping the ADD cycle whenever a 0 multiplier bit is encountered (since this merely omits the addition of 0 to the partial sum). Thus ADD cycles are taken only for 1 bits in the multiplier. If this method is used, the time to execute multiplication is not a fixed constant but depends on the data being multiplied. This is one reason why multiplication execution times are often given for maximum, minimum, and average cases.

Since multiplication requires summing several numbers, an economy in time is possible for the overall carry propagation as compared with the sum of carry propagation times for individual additions. To understand how this economy is obtained, consider the example of Fig. 8.13.1 for decimal radix (for ease of reading). Addition is done in each cycle on three numbers— the partial sum, one of the numbers to be added, and a carry number derived from the previous addition. The addition in a given cycle treats each digit independent of all others—although a carry is obtained in each digit position in the usual way. This carry is *not* immediately applied to the next higher order; instead it is *saved* or stored in a form suitable for addition in the next cycle. Note that no carry propagation takes place in any addition but the last. Using the carry-save principle, multiplication time is determined by the time for carry propagation for a single addition and the delay for shift logic and single digit addition.

```
0294
0148
0744
0293
0466
────
1945
```

(*a*) An original problem of summing several numbers.

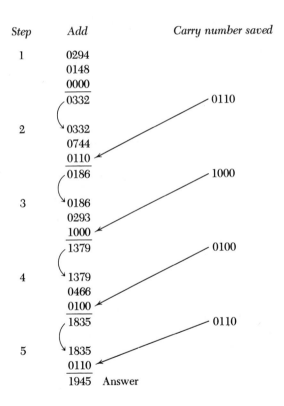

Step	Add	Carry number saved
1	0294 0148 0000 → 0332	0110
2	0332 0744 0110 → 0186	1000
3	0186 0293 1000 → 1379	0100
4	1379 0466 0100 → 1835	0110
5	1835 0110 → 1945 Answer	

(*b*) Example in decimal radix of carry-save principle.

Fig. 8.13.1 Carry-save principle.

```
       ∇ S ZEROSKIP Q
[1]      B←ρQ
[2]      A←Bρ0
[3]      'ENTER NO. OF BITS IN SHIFT COUNTER:'
[4]      K←((M←□)ρ2)⊤B
[5]   LP:→(0=Q[B-1])/GR
[6]      A←(Bρ2)⊤(2⊥A)+2⊥S
[7]   GR:Q←(¯1↑A),¯1↓Q
[8]      A←0,¯1↓A
[9]      K←(Mρ2)⊤¯1+2⊥K
[10]     →(0≠∨/K)/LP
[11]     'THE RESULT IS:'
[12]     A;'   ';Q
       ∇
```

```
       1 1 0 0 1 ZEROSKIP 1 0 0 0 1
ENTER NO. OF BITS IN SHIFT COUNTER:
□:
       8
THE RESULT IS:
0  1  1  0  1  0  1  0  0  1
```

(*a*) Zero-skip.

```
       ∇ S CARRYSAVE Q
[1]      B←ρQ
[2]      C←A←Bρ0
[3]      'ENTER NO. OF BITS IN SHIFT COUNTER:'
[4]      K←((M←□)ρ2)⊤B
[5]   LP:T←A≠(S∧Q[B-1])≠C
[6]      C←(A∧C)∨(A∨C)∧(S∧Q[B-1])
[7]      A←T
[8]      Q←(¯1↑A),¯1↓Q
[9]      A←0,¯1↓A
[10]     K←(Mρ2)⊤¯1+2⊥K
[11]     →(0≠∨/K)/LP
[12]     'THE RESULT IS:'
[13]     A←(Bρ2)⊤(2⊥A)+2⊥C;'   ';Q
       ∇
```

```
       1 1 0 0 1 CARRYSAVE 1 0 0 0 1
ENTER NO. OF BITS IN SHIFT COUNTER:
□:
       8
THE RESULT IS:
0  1  1  0  1  0  1  0  0  1
```

(*b*) Carry save.

Fig. 8.13.2 Two algorithms for fast binary multiplication.

Legend

	0-origin indexing
B	No. of bits in multiplier
K	Counter of remaining shifts
Q	Register originally holding multiplier (right register)
S	Register originally holding multiplicand
A	Accumulator (left register)
C	Carry register

Fig. 8.13.2 Two algorithms for fast binary multiplication (Continued).

8.14 DIVISION PRINCIPLES

A formal definition of division is:

Given: an integer d called the *dividend* and a nonzero integer v called the *divisor*. Either or both may be negative. Find two integers q and a called the *quotient* and *remainder*, respectively, that satisfy all the relations:

(1) $d \equiv (q \times v) + a$

(2) $(\mid a \mid) < \mid v$

From these, the rules for determining the signs for quotient and remainder are deduced to be:

1. If the signs of d and v are alike, the sign of q is positive; otherwise it is negative.
2. The sign of the remainder is the same as the sign of the dividend d.

Division methods are usually categorized as *restoring* or *nonrestoring*. In the restoring method, the divisor is successively subtracted from the high-order positions of the dividend; the result replaces the dividend. The quotient is increased by 1 for each successful subtraction, i.e., for each subtraction yielding a positive result. When a negative result of subtraction is obtained, an *overdraw* is said to exist and the current dividend is restored by adding the divisor to it. The dividend and quotient are then both shifted left one position and the process is repeated. In any one cycle (between shifts) the count of successful subtractions must be less than the radix and hence can be stored in the rightmost position of the quotient register. Figure 8.14.1 shows an example in radix 10. Note that at the start of division, the dividend may be a double-length number stored with its high-order part in the accumulator D, its low-order part in the quotient register Q. The D register includes an extra leftmost digit position. At

$1976 \div 94$

D	Q	Comments
0001	976	Initial
		Subtract 94 from $10 \perp D$; (overdraw)—restore
0019	760	Shift left
		Subtract (overdraw)—restore
0197	600	Shift left
0103	601	Subtract; add 1 to Q
0009	602	Subtract; add 1 to Q
		Subtract (overdraw)—restore
0096	020	Shift left
0002	021	Subtract; add 1 to Q
		Subtract (overdraw)—restore

Quotient in Q, remainder in D

Fig. 8.14.1   Restoring-division principle.

the start it is essential that the divisor be larger in magnitude than the portion of the dividend in the accumulator. This ensures that the first subtraction will not be successful thus resulting in a left shift. This provides the rightmost digit of the quotient register as a place for storing the tally of the number of successful subtractions in the next cycle. In this way, one digit of the quotient is developed in the rightmost position of Q between any two successive shifts. After ρQ shifts and associated subtractions, the division is complete; the quotient is in the Q register, and the remainder is in the D register.

The major step of the restoring method of division is subtraction of the divisor v from the high-order $m + 1$ positions of the partial remainder d. The subtraction when done with radix-complement arithmetic may be expressed as

(3) $D \leftarrow D + ((-V) + R*M + 1) \times R*M$

If the result represents a positive number, $d \geqslant r^{1 + 2 \times m}$; that is, a 1 overflow will appear as discussed previously for radix-complement subtraction. For this case a 1 is added to the quotient, and the process is repeated until a negative value of d is indicated (by a d value less than $r^{1 + 2 \times m}$). When this occurs, an overdraw is said to exist. The overdraw is restored by adding the divisor (as usual, to the high-order positions) of the partial remainder.

(4) $D \leftarrow D + V \times R*M$

The partial remainder and quotient are then multiplied by the radix; this is easily done by shifting the representations left one position. The radix complement is then added:

```
      ∇ D RESTOREDIV V
[1]    'ENTER RADIX OF SYSTEM:'
[2]    R←▯
[3]    Q←0
[4]    'ENTER NO. OF DIGITS IN DIVISOR:'
[5]    K←M←▯
[6]   LP:D←R×D
[7]   HH:D←D+((-V)+R*M+1)×R*M
[8]    →(D<R*1+2×M)/GR
[9]    Q←Q+1
[10]   D←D-R*1+2×M
[11]   →HH
[12]  GR:D←D-((-V)+R*M+1)×R*M
[13]   →(0=K←K-1)/END
[14]   Q←R×Q
[15]   →LP
[16] END:'QUOTIENT: ';Q;'    ';'REMAINDER: ';⌊D×R*(-M)
      ∇
```

      1976 RESTOREDIV 94
ENTER RADIX OF SYSTEM:
▯:

      10
ENTER NO. OF DIGITS IN DIVISOR:
▯:

      2
QUOTIENT: 21   REMAINDER: 2

Legend

K	Count of shifts remaining
Q	Quotient
D	Dividend and partial remainder
V	Divisor

Example: 7 ÷ 2
         M ≡ 4

		K	Comments
(5ρ2)⊤2	0 0 0 1 0		
(5ρ2)⊤32-2	1 1 1 1 0	4	Start
(9ρ2)⊤7	0 0 0 0 0 0 1 1 1		
	0 0 0 0 0 1 1 1 0	3	Shift left
	1 1 1 1 0		Add complement V
	1 1 1 1 0		Sum (overdraw)
	0 0 0 1 0		Restore (add V)
	0 0 0 0 0		Sum
	0 0 0 0 1 1 1 0 0	2	Shift left
	1 1 1 1 0		Add complement V
	1 1 1 1 1		Sum (overdraw)
	0 0 0 1 0		Restore (add V)
	0 0 0 0 1		Sum
	0 0 0 1 1 1 0 0 0	1	Shift left
	1 1 1 1 0		Add complement V
①	0 0 0 0 1		Sum
	0 0 0 0 1 1 0 0 1		Update Q
	0 0 0 1 1 0 0 1 0	0	Shift left
	1 1 1 1 0		Add complement V
①	0 0 0 0 1		Sum
	0 0 0 0 1 0 0 1 1		Update Q

Fig. 8.14.2 General restoring algorithm for division showing a radix-2 example.

```
       ∇ D NONRESTOREDIV V
[1]      Q←S←0
[2]      'ENTER NO. OF DIGITS IN DIVISOR:'
[3]      K←M←□
[4]      MS←V,(-V)+2*M+1
[5]      D←D+((-V)+2*M+1)×2*M
[6]  LP:→(K=0)/END
[7]      K←K-1
[8]      Q←2×Q
[9]      D←(2*1+2×M)|2×D
[10]     D←D+MS[S]×2*M
[11]     S←D≥2*1+2×M
[12]     Q←Q+S
[13]     D←D-S×2*1+2×M
[14]     →LP
[15] END:D←((2*M)|(~S)×V)+D×2*-M
[16]     'QUOTIENT: ';Q;'    ';'REMAINDER: ';D
       ∇
```

```
       39 NONRESTOREDIV 4
ENTER NO. OF DIGITS IN DIVISOR:
□:
       6
QUOTIENT: 9    REMAINDER: 3
```

Example: $39 \div 4$
$m \equiv 6$
$(7\rho 2)\tau 4 \equiv 0\ 0\ 0\ 0\ 1\ 0\ 0$
$(7\rho 2)\tau(2*7)-V \equiv 1\ 1\ 1\ 1\ 1\ 0\ 0$ (2s complement of 4)

		k	s	Comments
$(13\rho 2)\tau D \equiv (13\rho 2)\tau 39 \equiv 0\ 0\ 0\ 0\ 0\ 0\ 0$	1 0 0 1 1 1	6	0	Start
1 1 1 1 1 0 0				Add (124) ≡ compl. of 4
1 1 1 1 1 0 0				Sum
1 1 1 1 0 0 1	0 0 1 1 1 0	5	0	Shift left
0 0 0 0 1 0 0				Add 4
1 1 1 1 1 0 1				Sum
1 1 1 1 0 1 0	0 1 1 1 0 0	4	0	Shift left
0 0 0 0 1 0 0				Add 4
1 1 1 1 1 1 0				Sum
1 1 1 1 1 0 0	1 1 1 0 0 0	3	0	Shift left
0 0 0 0 1 0 0				Add 4
① 0 0 0 0 0 0 0				Sum
0 0 0 0 0 0 0	1 1 1 0 0 1	3	1	Update

Fig. 8.14.3   Nonrestoring binary division with 2s complements.

0 0 0 0 0 0 1	1 1 0 0 1 0	2	1	Shift left
1 1 1 1 1 0 0				Add 124
1 1 1 1 1 0 1				Sum
1 1 1 1 0 1 1	1 0 0 1 0 0	1	0	Shift left
0 0 0 0 1 0 0				Add 4
1 1 1 1 1 1 1				Sum
1 1 1 1 1 1 1	0 0 1 0 0 0	0	0	Shift left
0 0 0 0 1 0 0				Add
① 0 0 0 0 0 1 1				Sum
0 0 0 0 0 1 1	0 0 1 0 0 1	0	1	Update

Legend

K	Count of shifts remaining
Q	Quotient
D	Dividend and partial remainder
V	Divisor

Fig. 8.14.3 Nonrestoring binary division with 2s complements (Continued).

(5) $D \leftarrow R \times D$ (multiplication by R or shift)

(6) $D \leftarrow D + ((-V) + R*M+1) \times R*M$

From the above equations, it is seen that the restoring method requires an addition operation to restore each overdraw besides the complement additions required for subtraction. For decimal radix, overdraw may be expected for about 18 percent of the additions (assuming all digits are equally likely). For binary representation the fraction of additions required for overdraw will be much worse since all digits are only two-valued. One simple method to reduce restore additions is to recognize that when a nonoverdraw subtraction takes place, the next subtraction is certain to be an overdraw; it is not performed and the algorithm proceeds directly to the shift (multiplication by 2). One algorithm embodying these principles is shown in Fig. 8.14.2.

The time required for restore-addition operations may be eliminated entirely by a *nonrestoring* algorithm, as shown below for binary radix. The basis of the procedure may be understood by observing that Eqs. (4) to (6) require two additions as done in the restoring algorithm, but only one addition if Eq. (4) is substituted into (5) and (5) then into (6). After algebraic rearrangement,

(7) $D \leftarrow (R \times D) + (V \times (R-1) \times R*M) + R*1 + 2 \times M$

For binary radix $R \equiv 2$ and this simplifies to

(8) $D \leftarrow (2 \times D) + (V \times 2*M) + 2*1 + 2 \times M$

or to the successive statements

(9a) $D \leftarrow 2 \times D$

(9b) $D \leftarrow D + V \times 2 * M$

Here the rightmost term of Eq. (7) has been discarded as an overflow. Equation (9) indicates that when a negative partial remainder is encountered, if this is shifted left one position and then added to the divisor, the process of restoration *and* subsequent addition is in effect accomplished with a single shift-addition. An algorithm based on this idea is Fig. 8.14.3. Line 10 is the key statement; to the high-order $m + 1$ positions of d is added either the $(m + 1)$-digit divisor or its 2s complement, depending upon s. The value of s can be only 1 or 0, depending (in effect) on the sign of d prior to the shift. If the last digit of the quotient is a 1, the remainder appears in the proper form. If, however, the last digit of the quotient is 0, a final correction of adding the divisor to the partial remainder must be performed.

8.15 FLOATING-POINT NUMBER REPRESENTATION

In the early days of machine computation it was noticed that a good deal of effort was being consumed in scaling tests and operations to maintain significance of numbers appearing during computation. In time, a rather standard set of scaling procedures (subroutines) began to emerge, and it became natural to seek to improve execution speed and save program storage by including these in the hardware repertoire of machine instructions. As will be seen later, floating-point operations are not an unmixed blessing; however, they are very valuable because they simplify programming and increase computation speed, especially in a majority of scientific problems where the range of numbers is very wide and not predictable in advance.

Normalized floating-point notation is a variant of *scientific* notation, whereby a number is represented in two parts; the first part contains all the significant digits in a number of very restricted range; the second part consists of a scale factor, which is usually a power of 10. In one common system of this kind, the following examples may be given:

$$32487.2256 \leftrightarrow 3.24872256 \times 10^4$$
$$0.0004523 \leftrightarrow 4.523 \times 10^{-4}$$

The first part of the number is thus forced to be 0 or a magnitude between 1 and 10. This representation is said to be *normalized*. In some notation systems, the first part of the number must be a fraction less than 1 but greater than 0.1. A floating-point number may be represented on paper as

(1) $n \equiv f \times r^e$

where f = signed fraction in some implied radix system

$\quad$ r = radix of scale factor

$\quad$ e = exponent of scale factor

Often, but not always, the radix of the scale factor and the fraction are the same. For implementation reasons, the exponent e is often given in a somewhat indirect form called the *characteristic c,* which is simply a *biased* exponent,

(2) $\quad c \equiv e + b$

where the bias b is a fixed constant. Using the characteristic rather than the exponent directly results in exponent information always represented as a positive integer even when the exponent is negative.

A floating-point number is then typically represented by an integer *pair c, f,* where c is the characteristic and f is a (signed) fraction. One example in some decimal computers or programming systems uses an excess-50 characteristic.

$$0.3972 \times 10^2 \leftrightarrow 52.3972 \quad \text{or} \quad c,f \equiv 52, 0.3972$$
$$-0.3972 \times 10^{-4} \leftrightarrow -46.3972 \quad \text{or} \quad c,f \equiv 46, -0.3972$$

where the double arrow denotes "is represented by."

In the internal machine representation of a floating-point number, some binary representation of the sign, characteristic, and fraction are packed into a contiguous string of bits. A typical example is that used in the IBM System/360 machines, as shown in Fig. 8.15.1. Two lengths are provided, one called the floating-point *word* comprises 32 bits, the other called the floating-point *double word* comprises 64 bits. In both cases the leftmost bit is the sign and the next 7 bits are the characteristic in excess-64 form. The remainder of the word or double word comprises the fraction (24 or 56 bits). The fraction uses the signed true representation and is best considered as binary coded hexadecimal. The exponent, obtained by decreasing the characteristic by the bias of 64, is considered as a power of 16 in forming the scale factor.

To illustrate some of the principles of floating-point arithmetic, an algorithm for floating-point addition and subtraction for any radix r is shown in Fig. 8.15.2. The argument operands are assumed available in normalized form, and the result (omitting the exceptional cases) is also normalized. Since a step-by-step description is given and should be followed with an example, only general comments will be made here. At first glance some of the operations might look a bit difficult to mechanize until it is recalled that multiplication or division by the radix is simply a left or right shift, and a test for the fraction $\geq r^{-1}$ may be done by testing the leftmost digit of the representation of the fraction for 0.

An algorithm again applicable to any radix r is shown for floating-point multiplication in Fig. 8.15.3. This program uses the same symbols as Fig. 8.15.2.

```
     01    78              31
X [ s  |  c  |  f(24 bits)  ]        Floating-point word (32 bits)
```

```
     01    78                       63
X [ s | c |       f(56 bits)        ]    Floating-point double
                                         word (64 bits)
```

Bits	Meaning	Symbol	Expression
0	Sign	+, −	$X[0]$
1–7	Characteristic	c	$2\perp{}^-7\uparrow8\uparrow X$
8–31	Fraction	f	$(2\downarrow8\downarrow X)\times16\star{}^-6$
8–63	Fraction	f	$(2\downarrow8\downarrow X)\times16\star{}^-14$

Example conversion: Express − 181.214 *as floating-point word:*
181 in hexadecimal: B5
0.214 in hexadecimal: 0.36C9 (4 places)
Characteristic: 66 or 42 in hexadecimal
Add 8 to leftmost characteristic digit (for minus sign): C2
Answer as a hexadecimal-string: C2B536C9
Answer as a bit-string: $X \equiv 11000010101101010011011011001001$

Fig. 8.15.1   IBM System/360 floating-point ADD/SUBTRACT in radix R.

```
       ∇  A FLOAT B
[1]       'ENTER RADIX OF SYSTEM:'
[2]       R←□
[3]       'ENTER MAXIMUM VALUE OF CHARACTERISTIC:'
[4]       K←□
[5]       C←F←3ρ0
[6]       C[0]←⌊A
[7]       C[1]←⌊B
[8]       F[0]←A-C[0]
[9]       F[1]←B-C[1]
[10]      D←C[1]-C[0]
[11]      X←D<0
[12]      F[X]←F[X]×R⋆-|D
[13]      'FOR ADDITION,ENTER ADD;FOR SUBTRACTION,ENTER SUB'
[14]      →(∧/'ADD'=XXX←□)/AD
[15]      →(0=0×F[2]←F[0]-F[1])/AD1
[16]   AD:F[2]←F[0]+F[1]
[17]  AD1:C[2]←C[~X]
[18]      →(1≤|F[2])/LP
[19]      →(0≠|F[2])/GR
[20]      →(0=C[2]←0)/END
[21]   GR:→((R⋆-1)≤|F[2])/END
[22]      →(0>C[2]←C[2]-1)/UF
[23]      →(0=0×F[2]←F[2]×R)/GR
[24]   LP:→(K<C[2]←C[2]+1)/OF
[25]      F[2]←F[2]×R⋆-1
[26]  END:'RESULT:     ';C[2]+F[2]
[27]      →0
[28]   UF:'UNDERFLOW CONDITION HAS BEEN RAISED'
[29]      →0
[30]   OF:'OVERFLOW CONDITION HAS BEEN RAISED'
       ∇
```

Fig. 8.15.2   Normalized floating-point ADD/SUBTRACT in radix R.

```
        67.4536 FLOAT 65.8796
ENTER RADIX OF SYSTEM:
□:
        10
ENTER MAXIMUM VALUE OF CHARACTERISTIC:
□:
        99
FOR ADDITION,ENTER ADD;FOR SUBTRACTION,ENTER SUB
ADD
RESULT:  67.462396


        67.4536 FLOAT 65.8796
ENTER RADIX OF SYSTEM:
□:
        10
ENTER MAXIMUM VALUE OF CHARACTERISTIC:
□:
        99
FOR ADDITION,ENTER ADD;FOR SUBTRACTION,ENTER SUB
SUB
RESULT:  67.444804
```

Step	Description
1–9	Enter values; separate characteristics and fractions
10	Obtain D, difference in characteristics
11	Obtain X, identifier of fraction to be shifted
12	Shift fraction of smaller number right $\lvert D$ places
13–16	Specify ADD or SUBtract; add/subtract fractions
17	Set result characteristic to larger characteristic
18	Go to LP if result fraction $\geqslant 1$
19	Go to GR if result fraction $\neq 0$
20	Result fraction = 0; set characteristic to 0; go to END
21	GR test for normalized fraction; if yes, go to END
22	Decrease characteristic by 1; go to UF if less than 0
23	Shift fraction left; go to GR
24	LP: increase characteristic by 1; if larger than maximum, go to OF
25	shift result fraction right by one position
26–30	Normal end, overflow and underflow exits

Notes:

1. Steps 19 to 25 normalize a number and may be used for prenormalization.
2. Programs assume arithmetic in radix R.

Legend

0-origin indexing	
$C[0],C[1],C[2]$	Characteristics of arguments and result
$F[0],F[1],F[2]$	Fractions of arguments and result
K	Largest possible characteristic
R	Radix of number system

Fig. 8.15.2 Normalized floating-point ADD/SUBTRACT in radix R. (Continued).

```
     ∇ A MULTFLOAT B
[1]    'ENTER RADIX OF SYSTEM:'
[2]    R←□
[3]    'ENTER MAXIMUM VALUE OF CHARACTERISTIC'
[4]    K←□
[5]    C←F←3ρ0
[6]    C[0]←⌊A
[7]    C[1]←⌊B
[8]    F[0]←A-C[0]
[9]    F[1]←B-C[1]
[10]   F[2]←F[0]×F[1]
[11]   →(0=F[2])/ZERO
[12]   C[2]←C[0]+C[1]
[13]   →(C[2]≥3×(K+1)÷2)/OF
[14]   →(C[2]<(K+1)÷2)/UF
[15]   C[2]←⌈C[2]-(K+1)÷2
[16] LP:→(F[2]>R*¯1)/END
[17]   →(C[2]=0)/UF
[18]   F[2]←R×F[2]
[19]   →(0=0×C[2]←C[2]-1)/LP
[20] ZERO:C[2]←0
[21] END:'RESULT:    ';C[2]+F[2]
[22]   →0
[23] UF:'UNDERFLOW CONDITION HAS BEEN RAISED'
[24]   →0
[25] OF:'OVERFLOW CONDITION HAS BEEN RAISED'
     ∇
```

```
      72.4526 MULTFLOAT 59.7831
ENTER RADIX OF SYSTEM:
□:
      10
ENTER MAXIMUM VALUE OF CHARACTERISTIC
□:
      99
RESULT:    81.35443106
```

Step	Description
1–9	Enter values, separate characteristics, fractions
10	Multiply fractions
11	Branch if result = 0
12	Add argument characteristics
13	Test for result characteristic too large
14	Test for result characteristic too small
15	Subtract excess bias
16	*LP*: If fraction is normalized go to *END*
17	Go to *UF* if characteristic = 0
18	Multiply fraction by R
19	Decrease characteristic by 1; go to *LP*
20–25	Normal end, underflow and overflow exits

Note: See Fig. 8.15.2 for legend.

Fig. 8.15.3 Normalized floating-point multiplication.

As mentioned earlier, the purpose of floating-point operations is to facilitate automatic scaling operations. One criticism of this approach is that every word requires the same number of bits for the characteristic, leaving fewer bits for the significant digits of the number. To some extent this issue is academic since most modern computers provide both fixed- and floating-point arithmetic. A more serious concern is the possible loss of precision in the automatic shifting operations, without the programmer's being aware of this loss. Some systems notify the programmer of such loss, and he is free to respond in any way he chooses by a *fix* routine. Despite the real difficulties only mentioned here, automatic floating-point arithmetic is standard equipment on most large computers and is offered as an option on many small systems.

8.16 ENCODING

The encoding of each decimal digit into the direct 4-bit BCD representation is an important example of the general problem of symbol representation and translation. One simple but important class of representation problem may be stated abstractly as follows: given an alphabet of symbols A, translate each element of A into a distinct element of another alphabet C. This type of encoding is called *simple substitution* or *one for one*. Clearly all that is required is a correspondence table containing A as the arguments and C as the function. The table may also be used in the opposite direction. A precise procedure for translating a given symbol belonging to A is to compare the symbol with each element of A, and when the match is found, extract the corresponding element from C. The process may be formalized by saying that the encoded value of X is Y according to

$$Y \leftarrow (A = X)/C$$

A slightly more general version of this problem allows the encoding to be a matrix such as a bit matrix C, where each element of A corresponds to a row vector of C. A few of the many encodings of the decimal digits into bit strings are shown in Fig. 8.16.1; each code is given as a bit matrix C. One class of codes, illustrated by the common BCD code, is called *weighted* because each bit position carries an implied weight. However, a code need not be weighted, although arithmetic operations are facilitated with weighted codes. For arithmetic operations, one important property is self-complementation. This refers to certain codes (e.g., the excess-3 code) with the characteristic that if the representation of any digit is inverted bit by bit, the result is the representation

Digit	BCD(8,4,2,1)	Excess-3	Biquinary	2-out-of-5	Reflected gray
0	0000	0011	0100001	00011	0000
1	0001	0100	0100010	00101	0001
2	0010	0101	0100100	00110	0011
3	0011	0110	0101000	01001	0010
4	0100	0111	0110000	01010	0110
5	0101	1000	1000001	01100	0111
6	0110	1001	1000010	10001	0101
7	0111	1010	1000100	10010	0100
8	1000	1011	1001000	10100	1100
9	1001	1100	1010000	11000	1101
	C	C	C	C	C

Notes:

1. A weighted code is one for which a weight vector W exists such that

$\iota 10 \equiv C+.\times W$

2. A 9s self-complementing code is one for which

$C[I;]\equiv\sim C[9-I;]$

3. A Gray code is one for which

$(+/C[I;]\neq C[I+1;])\equiv 1$ for $0\le I<(\rho C)[1]$

Fig. 8.16.1 Some common decimal codes.

of 9 minus the original digit. Since the subtraction of a digit from 9 is a basic operation in handling signed numbers, self-complementing codes are convenient for arithmetic operations.

The biquinary and 2-out-of-5 codes have the property that each representation contains exactly 2 bits that are 1; the rest are 0. This fact makes it relatively easy to provide checking of numbers.

A Gray code is a code with the property that if the code rows are listed in the order of the numbers they represent, two adjacent rows of code bits differ in exactly one bit position. Gray codes are important in certain types of analog-digital converters of the mechanical type to overcome ambiguities that may otherwise appear due to the mechanization of conversion. The particular Gray code listed is called a *reflected* code because its rows are symmetrical about the dashed line, except for the leftmost bit. This n-bit Gray code C may be converted to the usual binary code B by the following equations (as usual, the leftmost bit is in position 0):

(1) $B[0] \equiv C[0]$

(2) $B[J+1] \equiv (B[J] \neq C[J+1]) \equiv (B[J] \wedge \sim C[J+1]) \vee (\sim B[J]) \wedge C[J+1]$
    ·for $0 < J < (\rho C)[2]$

The encoding of more comprehensive alphabets than the decimal digits is essential not only for nonarithmetic data processing but also because all modern source languages permit the user to give alphanumeric names to data and program references. This establishes the necessity for some means of encoding in devices that directly feed the system as well as within the central processing and internal storage of the machine. Thus the problem of encoding arises in the design and use of punched-card, typewriter, printer, and other I/O devices.

The standard IBM punched card used in the conventional manner is considered to contain 80 characters, each of which is encoded into a hole–no-hole configuration in one column of the card. The hole positions of the columns are traditionally designated as 12, 11, 0, 1, 2, 3, 4, 5, 6, 7, 8, 9 from the top to the bottom of the card held horizontally. Although in principle the availability of 12 positions in a column would allow a representation of up to 2^{12}, or 4096, symbols, typically only a small fraction of these combinations are needed and most card codes use at most two or three holes per column.

Card Code	Printer Graphics	Internal Representation	Card Code	Printer Graphics	Internal Representation
	blank	01000000	11,1	J	11010001
12,8,3	. (period)	01001011	11,2	K	11010010
12,8,4	<	01001100	11,3	L	11010011
12,8,5	(	01001101	11,4	M	11010100
12,8,6	+	01001110	11,5	N	11010101
12	&	01010000	11,6	O	11010110
11,8,3	$	01011011	11,7	P	11010111
11,8,4	*	01011100	11,8	Q	11011000
11,8,5	)	01011101	11,9	R	11011001
11	-	01100000	0,2	S	11100010
0,1	/	01100001	0,3	T	11100011
0,8,3	,	01101011	0,4	U	11100100
0,8,4	%	01101100	0,5	V	11100101
8,3	#	01111011	0,6	W	11100110
8,4	@	01111100	0,7	X	11100111
8,5	' (quote)	01111101	0,8	Y	11101000
8,6	=	01111110	0,9	Z	11101001
12,1	A	11000001	0	0	11110000
12,2	B	11000010	1	1	11110001
12,3	C	11000011	2	2	11110010
12,4	D	11000100	3	3	11110011
12,5	E	11000101	4	4	11110100
12,6	F	11000110	5	5	11110101
12,7	G	11000111	6	6	11110110
12,8	H	11001000	7	7	11110111
12,9	I	11001001	8	8	11111000
			9	9	11111001

Fig. 8.16.2 IBM System/360 card, internal and graphic representations.

One important example of a card code is that used by the FORTRAN language; see Chap. 1 for a card image showing the entire FORTRAN alphabet. Another example is the card-encoding, graphics, and internal-bit representations used by the IBM System/360. This code is a subset of a more comprehensive alphabet of 256 characters called the *Extended-binary-coded-decimal Interchange Code* (EBCDIC) (see Fig. 8.16.2).

8.17 ENCODING FOR COMPACTION

All the codes discussed thus far used the same number of bits to encode each symbol. Another class of codes does not have this requirement, and by permitting frequently occurring symbols to be encoded into short bit strings, a worthwhile reduction can be achieved in the number of bits required to store or transmit a given text. This idea is used, for example, in the Morse telegraphic code.

One formal procedure for encoding according to the above principle is called the *Shannon-Fano code*. To design such a code it is first necessary to specify the expected frequency of appearance for each symbol in the alphabet. Frequencies can be obtained by counting appearances of each alphabet symbol in several long samples of representative texts. After the frequencies have been obtained, the symbol alphabet and corresponding frequencies are listed in order of decreasing frequency. The encoding process may then begin by dividing the ordered list into two lists such that as nearly as possible each list contains symbols whose frequencies sum to half the total. A 1 is assigned to the code of all symbols in the first sublist, a 0 to those of the second. The process then continues on each of the sublists. As the encoding proceeds, sublists containing only one symbol will be encountered; encoding of such a symbol is then complete. The encoding is complete when all symbols have been encoded. A simple example is given below. A chart of observed symbol frequencies and the results of an encoding for the English alphabet is given in Fig. 8.17.1.

EXAMPLE:

Symbol	Frequency	Encoding
A	0.35	1 1
B	0.25	1 0
Q	0.18	0 1
R	0.15	0 0 1
M	0.07	0 0 0

The average number of bits in the code is 2.22.

SYMBOL	RELATIVE APPEARANCE	SHANNON-FANO CODE
A	0.0583	1010
B	0.0115	000001
C	0.0198	001001
D	0.0288	00111
E	0.0936	110
F	0.0189	001000
G	0.0138	000010
H	0.0424	0101
I	0.0522	1000
J	0.0007	0000000001
K	0.0044	00000001
L	0.0291	01000
M	0.0180	000111
N	0.0521	0111
O	0.0573	1001
P	0.0138	000011
Q	0.0007	0000000010
R	0.0439	01100
S	0.0467	01101
T	0.0723	1011
U	0.0207	00101
V	0.0075	0000001
W	0.0159	000110
X	0.0012	0000000011
Y	0.0149	000101
Z	0.0005	0000000000
⊥	0.1688	111
.	0.0319	01001
,	0.0145	000100
⌊	0.0232	001101
⌈	0.0226	001100

MEAN NO. OF BITS IN CODE: 4.3712

⊥:BLANK
⌊:LOWERCASE SHIFT
⌈:UPPERCASE SHIFT

Fig. 8.17.1 Letter frequencies and encoding of sample English text.
Note: Data of relative appearances for 144,604 characters of Teletype text taken by J. M.Keehan.

8.18 ERROR DETECTION

The minimum number of bits required to distinguish among N symbols is

(1) $b \equiv \lceil \log_2 N$

Each symbol can be represented (encoded) as a bit vector; these bit vectors are binary integers. The dimension of a bit vector is b. More generally, each symbol can be encoded into any number of bits (but we assume the same number for all symbols in the set). A listing of these bit vectors constitutes a bit matrix which is called a *code*. Each row vector of the code is called a *code point*, since it may be considered to represent a point in a space of b dimensions where each bit value gives a distance along a coordinate axis. If the number of bits used in the encoding is larger than the minimum necessary [see Eq. (1) for this minimum] then the redundancy in the code can be used to achieve useful error detection and/or correction properties.

In order to systematize thinking about error-detection codes, consider the following definitions:

1. Two code points are said to be *distance d* from each other if changes in d positions of one code point will produce the other.
2. A code is said to be a *distance-d code* if the minimum distance between any two of its points is d.

11011	1101101
10001	0010101
01110	1011010
00000	0000000
Distance-2	Distance-3
code	code

To design a code capable of detecting e errors, the basic requirement is that each code point be such that any combination of bit changes (0 to 1 or 1 to 0) in up to e positions will not yield a bit pattern which is another code point. Thus the encoding must be chosen such that there is a separation or distance between code points sufficient to ensure that the corruption of a code point at least to some limit by noise or equipment failure will produce a code point not a member of the code. The receiver then need only be designed to distinguish code points which are or are not in the code.

A code designed to detect up to e errors must therefore be at least a distance-d code where

(2) $d \equiv e + 1$

Suppose it is desired to derive a distance-d code with code points containing n bits. How many such code points are there? A general recursion formula for the largest number of such code points n bits long and distance d apart derived by Hamming is as follows:

(3) $B(n,1) \equiv 2^n$

(4) $B(n,2) \equiv 2n-1$

(5) $B(n, 2k-1) \equiv 2m$ where $m \equiv \llcorner n - \log_2 \left[1 + \sum_{j=1}^{k-1} C(n,j) \right]$

(6) $B(n, 2k) \equiv B(n-1, 2k-1)$

A very common scheme for single-error detection is the parity-check method. It provides a simple way of constructing a distance-2 code for any number of bits and a simple way of detecting the code points. A parity-check code is shown for the 10 decimal digit symbols. The encoding is seen to consist of the usual BCD code as the leftmost 4 bits and a single *check bit* to the right.

The check bit is determined from the other bits in the construction of the code by taking the modulo-2 sum of the rest of the bits in each row. In a 0-origin indexing system:

(7) $X[;4] \leftarrow 2 | +/4 \uparrow X$

	X	
	0123	4
0	0000	0
1	0001	1
2	0010	1
3	0011	0
4	0100	1
5	0101	0
6	0110	0
7	0111	1
8	1000	1
9	1001	0

Fig. 8.18.1 Parity-checked BCD code.

Another way of stating this is to say that the parity bit is set to 1 or 0 in such a way that the total number of 1 bits is an even number in each row. Yet another viewpoint is that the parity bit is obtained by an EXCLUSIVE-OR or NOT-EQUAL operation on the other bits in the row.

(8) $X[;4] \leftarrow \neq /4 \uparrow X$

The above relations specify how the parity bit is determined (at the transmitter). Detection of a bit vector Y containing a parity bit determined as above consists in determining whether the number of 1 bits in Y is even (no error) or odd (error).

8.19 SINGLE-ERROR CORRECTION OVER
A SET OF BINARY NUMBERS

A simple scheme to provide *correction* of a single error in a set of numbers is to consider the set of numbers as a bit matrix; each row is a single number (encoded in binary). Append to each number a parity-check bit as described above. Also, append to each column a parity-check bit. The numbers thus encoded are then transmitted. At the receiver, the usual parity check is made for each row and each column. Any single error will produce a parity error on the row and column in which it occurs; this provides the information necessary to locate and correct the error bit (by inverting it).

Somewhat the same process is used for error detection in many magnetic-tape devices (see Chap. 3). A parity-check bit is appended to each byte across the width of the tape, and a parity-check byte (1 bit per column) is written as a "longitudinal" check at the end of the record.

8.20 SINGLE-ERROR CORRECTION OF
EACH CODE POINT: HAMMING CODE

A single-error-correcting code is one which will not only detect a single error in a code point but will also locate the bit in error. Once located, the bit error is easily corrected by complementation.

Consider the construction of a code which requires n information bits. The Hamming single-error correction requires k additional bits. k must be chosen so that the additional bits can point to any bit in the $n + k$ bits constituting a code point (since any of these may be in error). There must also be one other combination of the k bits to indicate no error. These conditions require

(1) $2^k \geqslant n + k + 1$

Several values of n and k are tabulated in Fig. 8.20.1.

Construction of a single-error-correcting code will be illustrated with an example of $n \equiv 4$. Equation (1) (or Fig. 8.20.1) shows that a value for k of 3 must be used. The problem now is to describe a method of specifying how values for each of the 3 extra bits are to be specified and where these bits are to be located in a code point (see Fig. 8.20.2).

Each of the 3 check bits is determined by making a parity check over a *set* of certain bit positions of the 7 bits constituting the code point. In this example there are three such sets; each set includes one-half of the position numbers. To see how the particular position numbers constituting each set is derived, consider the three sets of 3-bit numbers shown. In each set one bit position (shown with

Information bits n	Extra bits k
1	2
2	3
3	3
4	3
5	4
6	4
7	4
8	4
16	5
32	6
64	7

Fig. 8.20.1 **Table of the smallest k for $2^k \geqslant n + k + 1$.**

arrow) is fixed with the bit value set of 1. The other positions are permitted to take on all combinations of values. This process generates the numbers shown.

Having derived the sets of position numbers corresponding to each check bit, it remains to assign check bits and data bits to the positions in the code. The process can be systematized by noticing that the first number derived from each set appears only in that set. It is most convenient to assign the first number of each set as a check position. Thus for example, the bit in position 4 will be used to record the parity of bit positions 5, 6, 7.

To derive a code point for a given bit position, the information bits are first entered in the usual way except that care must be taken to skip over bit positions used for the check bits. Then, each check bit is determined by performing the parity check over the positions specified for the set corresponding to the check bit.

EXAMPLE: Correction of error.

```
                            1 2 3 4 5 6 7     Bit position
                              X   X X X
Correct (BDC) 9:1,0,0,1—encoded   0 0 1 1 0 0 1
Corrupted      9 encoded          0 1 1 1 0 0 1
   Check bits: 4,5,6,7    0XX
               2,3,6,7    X1X
               1,3,5,7    XX0
   Check bits: 0 1 0—bit no. 2 is in error!
```

	↓	1 2 3 4 5 6 7	Bit position
Group A	001 1 011 3 101 5 111 7	*p* X X X	
Group B	↓ 010 2 011 3 110 6 111 7	*p* X X X	
Group C	↓ 100 4 101 5 110 6 111 7	*p* X X X	

Fig. 8.20.2 Bit sets for parity check in an error-correcting code.

The receiver performs the parity checks in a manner similar to that de-
cribed above. When the 3 parity check bits are determined, there are two
cases:

1. The calculated check bits are all 0; this means the code point is not in error.
2. The calculated check bits are not all 0; in this case, consider these 3 bits (in
the example above) as a binary number; its value is the position number of
the bit in error.

Notice that the parity check groups include the check-bit positions;
i.e., the check bits are themselves included in the check-correction
process.

PROBLEMS

8.1 Convert the following binary numbers to decimal:

a) 11011001
b) .110101
c) 1011.00110

8.2 Convert the following decimal numbers to octal:

a) 2579
b) 347.956
c) 0.0572

8.3 *a)* Convert the numbers of 7.2 to hexadecimal (base 16).

  b) Convert the numbers of 7.2 to binary.

8.4 Convert the following BCD integer to hexadecimal:

0011100100100111

8.5 Write a program for the table-look-up method of BCD-binary conversion described in the text. Assume the tables are stored contiguously as the vector T. Include a specification of T.

8.6 *a)* Trace the BCD-to-binary program of the text for D corresponding to 75 and B having 8 bits.

  b) Trace the binary-to-BCD program of the text for B corresponding to 75 and D having 8 bits.

8.7 Subtract using 10s-complement arithmetic:

  a) $947 - 285$
  b) $285 - 947$
  c) $256 - 89$
  d) $24.87 - 196$

Hint: Give careful attention to the number of digits and their alignment:

8.8 Repeat all parts of Prob. 8.7 using 9s-complement arithmetic.

8.9 This problem illustrates an important property of 2s-complement arithmetic. The bit string representing a number in 2s-complement form including the sign bit (whose 0 value denotes + and 1 value denotes −) can be handled in addition operations as if the number were unsigned and the result including sign will be correct. Verify this for the following cases using 6-bit representations including sign:

  a) $14 + 9$
  b) $14 + (-9)$
  c) $(-14) + 9$
  d) $(-14) + (-9)$

8.10 Design a minimum-level carry look-ahead adder for 10-bit operands using AND circuits with fan-in of 3 and OR circuits with fan-in of 3.

a) How many levels are required?
b) Show the triangle design.
c) Write equations for c_0 and c_1 showing the inputs to blocks by parentheses grouping.
d) Draw the circuit for c_0.

8.11 Using binary arithmetic and 9-bit registers, show multiplication steps for:

a) 19×12
b) 19×-12 (Assume signed 2s-complement representation for original negative numbers.)

8.12 Show the steps in binary division for the problem $19 \div 13$:

a) Using the restoring algorithm
b) Using the nonrestoring algorithm

8.13 Consider multiplication of numbers in a system which uses signed radix-complement representation of negative numbers. Assume operands are *n* digits long. Prove that a correct multiplication can be done *without* any complementation provided the result contains no more than *n* digits.

8.14 Given the hexadecimal integer

B24A9DE3

Interpret this as a floating-point number in System/360 format, and write the equivalent number in the usual decimal notation.

8.15 Represent the decimal number 287.92 as a System/360 normalized floating-point word. Express the answer as a hexadecimal integer.

8.16 Analyze the program for floating-point addition using for example data:

$$r \equiv 10$$
$$k \equiv 99$$

First operand:	$c_1 \equiv 52$	$f_1 \equiv 0.724521$
Second operand:	$c_2 \equiv 48$	$f_2 \equiv 0.192346$

a) Give the result of the addition program.
b) Express the result in the normal scientific notation.

8.17 Using the data in the previous problem, obtain the result for multiplication of the two numbers.

8.18 Given a normalized decimal floating-point representation with 8-digit fraction, and a 2-digit excess-50 characteristic, express the following:

a) 397.682
b) 0.00472
c) 3.426×10^{-14}
d) The most negative number
e) The smallest nonzero fraction

8.19 How many check bits are required for a single-error-correcting code if the number of information bits is 36?

8.20 Construct a single-error-correcting code which includes 6 information bits. Give your answer as the position of each check bit and the positions checked by it. Also give at least two examples of code points as encoded and corrupted by one error. Show in each case how the error would be corrected.

8.21 The following represents received bit strings for a single-error-correcting code containing 8 information bits. For each, give the position (if any) that is in error and give the corrected bit string:

a) 1 0 1 1 1 1 0 1 0 1 1 0
b) 1 0 0 1 1 1 0 0 0 1 1 0

8.22 *a)* Select a sample of text from any source containing at least 500 words and construct a frequency-of-character table. Include entries for space and punctuation but disregard capitalization.
b) Using the table constructed in (*a*), construct a Shannon-Fano code.
c) Give the average number of bits per character encoding.

8.23 Write a program to generate the positions of the check bits for an *m*-bit Hamming code.

REFERENCES

1. Buchholz, W.: "Planning a Computer System," McGraw-Hill Company, New York, 1962.

2. Carr, J. W., III: Error Analysis in Floating Point Arithmetic, *Commun. ACM,* May 1959, pp. 10–15.

3. Gilchrist, B., J. H. Promerene, and S. Y. Wong: Fast Carry Logic for Digital Computers, *IRE Trans. Electron. Comput.,* December 1955, pp. 113–136.

4. Hamming, R. W.: Error Detecting and Error Correcting Codes, *Bell Sys. Tech. J.,* vol. 29, pp. 147–160 (April 1950).

5. Lehman, M., and N. Burla: Skip Techniques for High-speed Carry Propagation in Binary Arithmetic Units, *IRE Trans.,* vol. PGEC EC-10, no. 4, pp. 691–968 (December 1951).

6. MacSorley, O. L.: High Speed Arithmetic in Binary Computers, *Proc. IRE,* vol. 49, no. 1, pp. 67–91 (January 1961).

7. Metropolis, N., and R. L. Ashenhurst: Significant Digit Arithmetic, *IRE Trans. Electron. Comput.,* December 1958, pp. 256–267.

8. Richards, R. K.: "Arithmetic Operation in Digital Computers," D. Van Nostrand Company, Inc., Princeton, N.J., 1955.

9. Robertson, J. E.: A New Class of Digital Division Methods, *IRE Trans. Electron. Comput.,* September 1958, pp. 218–222.

10. Sklansky, J.: Conditional-sum Addition Logic, *IRE Trans.,* vol. PGEC EC-9, No. 2, pp. 226–231 (June 1960).

11. Weinberger, A., and J. L. Smith: A One-microsecond Adder Using One-megacycle Circuitry, *IRE Trans. Electron. Comput.,* June 1956, pp. 65–73.

12. White, G. S.: Coded Decimal Number System for Digital Computers, *Proc. IRE,* October 1953, pp. 1450–1452.

9

Computer Architecture and Microprogramming

The word "architecture" usually means the functional appearance of the system to its users. Architecture, which is user- and specification-oriented, should be contrasted with *implementation,* which is concerned with the design of efficient real objects like circuits and programs that give actual form to the architecture specifications. Because there are several classes of users, it is meaningful to speak of several kinds of architecture. For example, to those who program in machine (assembler) language or who write system programs like compilers and operating systems, machine architecture is of primary interest. On the other hand, to those who program in a high-level language, like FORTRAN or PL/I, machine architecture is likely to be less important than the architecture of the language.

This chapter is primarily concerned with machine architecture, particularly considerations such as how the machine gets started, how the addresses to instructions and data are specified, how various data types like words and variable-length byte strings are described, and what machine features are necessary and desirable to an operating-system program that automatically manages machine and program resources. Wherever possible, various alternatives for a given feature will be compared for advantages and disadvantages. Examples to illustrate principles will be given in the form of APL functional microprograms for a simple hypothetical machine and also from current or recent actual systems.

Although functional microprograms in APL are very valuable in describing what a machine is to do, i.e., its architecture, they are not suitable for directly describing the physical implementation such as the data-flow structure or the form of machine controls in most common use, *microprogrammed* control. The latter part of this chapter discusses this subject.

One of the key considerations in selecting an equipment feature is how frequently it can be expected to be used. This is true for several reasons. First, machine circuitry is expensive and usually cannot be justified for an operation which will be executed only rarely. Second, it is quite feasible and often advisable to include complex operations in the programming system rather than to build them into the machine. This not only improves equipment economy but also makes it relatively easy to introduce changes in the feature, since a program can usually be changed more economically than a circuit. Program (as opposed to equipment) implementation achieves these advantages at the expense of execution time and the storage necessary to hold the programs.

As technology develops, the fraction of total system cost due to programming is increasing relative to the cost of equipment. This is perhaps not always obvious to the user since manufacturers traditionally allocate most charges to equipment although they supply expensive programs as well. (Ultimately, of course, the user pays all costs.) As usual, the economic facts of cost distribution greatly influence architecture and design decisions. For example, it may well be unwise to omit certain features to economize on hardware if the machine will then require much greater programming effort to be competitive.

A most important factor in machine architecture is the recognition of the increasingly important role of the high-level languages as the principal medium of user-system interaction. This makes designers turn their attention to features that facilitate the operations used in compilers or those that are likely to be valuable to the object instructions produced by a compiler.

To an increasing extent, machine architecture reflects the results of careful study and observation of certain salient features of programs. For example, it has been noticed that most programs exhibit the property of *locality of reference;* i.e., over a time interval spanning several instruction executions, references to storage for program and data tend to cluster in localized areas of storage. This property suggests that highest speed of reference and access may be necessary only to a relatively small area of storage. Of course the system must be able to address larger storage also but not necessarily at the highest speeds.

9.1 INITIAL PROGRAM LOAD AND INSTRUCTION SEQUENCING

To illustrate some fundamental principles, consider Fig. 9.1.1, which describes some properties of a simple 32-bit machine with an instruction format specifying an OP code giving the operation to be performed, usually on data in a machine

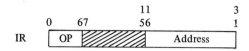

OP code for branching: 000XXXX where XXXX specifies condition
to be tested

```
     ∇IPL
[1]  M[ι20;]←CARD
[2]  P←16ρ0
[3]  IFETCH
     ∇
```

(*a*) IPL (initiated by pressing button).

```
     ∇IFETCH
[1]  FTCH:A←P
[2]  S←M[2⊥A;]
[3]  IR←S
[4]  P←(16ρ2)⊤(ρM)[1]|1+2⊥P
[5]  →(∧/~3↑IR)/TST
[6]  EXECUTE
[7]  →FTCH
[8]  TST:T←C[2⊥4↑3↓IR]
[9]  P←(T∧¯16↑IR)∨(~T)∧P
[10] →FTCH
     ∇
```

(*b*) Instruction fetch and branching.

Legend

	0-origin indexing
A	Storage address register
P	Program counter
M	Main storage; *M[I;]* is word *I*
S	Storage register
IR	Instruction register
C	Condition triggers

Fig. 9.1.1   Functional microprogram for IPL, instruction fetching.

register, and a word in main storage at the location specified by ADDRESS. In
the present discussion we are interested *not* in the data-manipulation operations
(see Chap. 8) but in how the machine proceeds from one instruction to the next.
However, it will be necessary to assume something about how the machine
receives information from the outside world. Specifically, we assume that one of

the OP codes, called READ, works as follows: it causes the next punched card in the reader hopper to be read; i.e., the holes in each card column are translated into 8 bits (say according to the card code of Fig. 8.16.2). Thus, four columns are packed into a 32-bit word and hence one entire card is sent to 20 successive words starting at the location given by the ADDRESS part of the instruction.

Suppose now we wish to start the machine cold, i.e., with nothing meaningful in its memory. "Starting" means initiating program execution, but on what program? If we have a particular machine program as a deck of punched cards in the card-reader hopper, it might appear that the machine should now be able to start on this program. However, this is not so since a machine instruction can read only one card; a sequence of instructions, i.e., a program is needed to bring the information on our program cards into storage. Such a program (not detailed here) is called a *loader*. A loader can read our program in, but how is the loader program itself to be read into storage? Note that the card deck in the hopper now consists of the loader-program cards followed by our problem program. A loader program is initiated by a process that is essential to any machine called IPL (*i*nitial *p*rogram *l*oad) or sometimes *cold start*. A functional microprogram for IPL is given in Fig. 9.1.1*a*, and the physical implementation is a sequential circuit that is part of the machine. The process starts when the user presses the IPL console button, which results in the reading of one card of data into 20 words of storage, starting at location 0, followed by the program counter being set to 0 and the start of instruction sequencing. The first instruction to be executed will then be the one at location 0, i.e., the first one read by IPL, which we have arranged to be the first instruction of our loader program. This first word is followed by 19 others of the image of the first card of the loader. These usually contain enough READ instructions to enter the rest of the loader program, which is then capable of reading any other program that follows. This simple but remarkable process is called *bootstrapping* and is typical of machine start-up (there are of course many variations).

The IPL microprogram calls IFETCH which is responsible for all instruction fetching, updating of the program counter, and testing for branching. The branching mechanism in this machine is as follows (see Fig. 9.1.1*b*): a flip-flop is set to 1 whenever a condition that can be tested for a branch occurs in the machine's registers (like a specified register being all 0 or negative). These conditions, called vector C, are combined with certain bits of the OP code when the current instruction is BRANCH-ON-CONDITION, and if the tested condition is 1, the branch is taken by replacing the program counter P by the ADDRESS part of the instruction.

For instructions other than BRANCH-ON-CONDITION, the IFETCH microprogram calls the EXECUTION function (not detailed here) which implements all other machine instructions.

Some of the parameters of the instruction sequencing control are summarized in Fig. 9.1.2. In most machines, the next instruction is obtained by advance of a

Normal sequencing
  Explicit: Next instruction location specified in each instruction (used on drum machines to minimize access delay)
  Implicit: Advance a program counter
Conditions tested
  1. Arithmetic conditions

$$\text{Primitive} \begin{cases} = & \rightarrow T[0] \\ > & \rightarrow T[1] \end{cases}$$

$$\begin{array}{c}\text{Derived} \\ \text{from} \\ \text{primitive}\end{array} \begin{cases} \neq & \rightarrow \sim T[0] \\ \leq & \rightarrow \sim T[1] \\ \geq & \rightarrow T[0]\,\vee\,T[1] \\ < & \rightarrow \sim T[0]\,\vee\,T[1] \end{cases}$$

  2. I/O or other indicator bits
  3. Condition flip-flops T set automatically or by a COMPARE instruction
     Sometimes test turns trigger off
     Test specified in OP code of branch or explicitly
Branch location
  Explicitly specified
  Implicit: Skipping-on condition, return from subroutine
EXECUTE instruction
  Address part of instruction (not program counter) specifies next instruction location
  Control returns to program counter after execution of a single instruction
Interrupts (traps)
  Forced program branch when certain conditions occur

Fig. 9.1.2 Instruction sequence classification.

program counter. This implicit address calculation conserves bits which would otherwise be needed in an explicit next-instruction scheme. The latter is, however, often employed in computers with serial-access storage (e.g., drum) so that programs can be written to place the instructions in the store in such a way that rotational delays are reduced to a minimum.

All stored-program computers provide a means for branching. An unconditional branch may be considered as a special case of a conditional branch.

The branching process involves two ideas: (1) a test on some condition and (2) replacement of the program counter from the instruction register if the condition is met. Usually, for arithmetic-comparison tests, comparison is actually done by subtraction. Two primitive results, e.g., *equal* and *greater than,* suffice to derive four others by simple logic as shown.

The condition to be tested may be specified in the machine's OP code, and the branch address held in the address part of the same instruction. This method is common for branch-on-accumulator-sign or index-register-contents-zero in a single-address system. In a two-address system without implicitly addressed registers, the test and branch operations are usually done in two distinct instructions.

Where address bits are scarce, as in the IBM 7090 COMPARE-ACCUMULA-TOR-TO-STORAGE instruction, the branch location may be implicit: if the condition is satisfied, the machine skips the next instruction; otherwise the next instruction is taken in sequence.

The EXECUTE type of instruction is a means of specifying a single instruction to be executed without disturbing normal sequencing. The address part of an EXECUTE instruction is in effect used as a temporary program counter. The instruction specified is fetched and executed; control then returns to the normal program counter. The EXECUTE instruction is useful for writing routines wherein one instruction sequence controls the execution of another. It is also valuable in lieu of indirect addressing.

The simple machine of Fig. 9.1.1 is unbearably primitive by modern standards. For example, to program even a simple loop that marches through a vector, successive addresses are required but obtainable only by the program modifying the address part of one of its own instructions. This is tedious to program (and hence error-prone) and slow in execution. By using indirect addressing or indexing (see below), instruction modification can be avoided. Also, our primitive machine recognizes only words as data. Access to character strings (bytes) is possible but only by several programmed references per string, possibly combined with shifting of bytes in the machine registers to separate them. In the next few sections we investigate some architecture features to handle variable-length structures and also considerations in choosing the size of fixed-length words.

9.2 CHOICE OF RADIX AND LENGTH OF INFORMATION UNITS

Of the many options in machine design, surely one of the most fundamental is the choice of radix. In practice, modern computers most commonly use the radix-2 (binary) system for storage and number representation. The motivation is primarily reliability of device operation. It is of interest to investigate other radix possibilities with the following simple model. Let

$C \equiv$ cost of representing a number
$N \equiv$ maximum number value to be represented
$m \equiv$ number of digits in N
$R \equiv$ radix
$k \equiv$ proportionality constant

Assume the cost is proportional to both m and R

$$C \equiv kmR$$

also

$$N \equiv R^m - 1 \approx R^m$$

Substituting for m gives

$$C = \frac{kR \log_e N}{\log_e R}$$

For a given N, we seek that value of R that minimizes C. This is obtained by setting to 0 the derivative of C with respect to R. The result shows that the optimum radix is e, the base of natural logarithms.

$$R_{opt} = 2.718 \cdots$$

Radix 2 is thus not much different from the optimum, and the cost difference is relatively slight (about 6 percent).

Although the irreducible unit of information is the single bit, it is common practice to group bits into larger units and define the operations to take place on those. Most modern systems define at least two data units—one called a *character* or *byte* comprising (typically) 4 to 8 bits, which is used to represent a single decimal digit or alphabetic or special character; the other is a *word* composed of a bit string that is typically some binary encoding of a signed number. Particular methods of encoding are discussed in detail in Chap. 8. Although two types of data unit are a practical minimum, many machines use more types; e.g., the IBM System/360 includes eight kinds of data.

The choice of data types, especially their lengths, has a profound effect on storage efficiency and processing and I/O speed. This is because for a given amount of storage, the larger the unit of information chosen for a data or instruction type, the fewer units can be stored. The number of bits in a data unit influences the speed of the system, since for given widths of paths and processing circuits the smaller the data unit, the more data units that can be handled at one time. For example, consider the choice of word length of data. The greater the length, the greater the precision of the number being represented. This favorable aspect is, however, offset by the observation that for a given total storage capacity in bits, the longer the word , the fewer the number of words. As another example, consider the choice of a byte size for a magnetic-tape device capable of 8-bit parallel transmission. If the byte size is chosen as 8 bits, a rich character set (256 elements in the alphabet) can be accommodated; but the data rate in bytes per second is half of that possible with the same device if a 4-bit byte is adopted. If most of the system work were to be on decimal digits (as opposed to alphanumeric characters) the 4-bit byte might well be favored. For manipulation of alphanumeric or binary data, the 8-bit byte would be more suitable. In some systems both schemes are offered.

One choice that deserves attention is the length of the fixed-point data word. An important consideration here is that its length in bits should be an integer multiple of the number of bits in the byte since this facilitates dense storage of bytes into words. Another consideration is that fixed-point data are often used for addressing—the data word should not be smaller than the address length. It may, however, be larger (and often is). All else being equal, the length of the fixed-point word should be as short as possible for storage-capacity and speed reasons. But how short can this be? The word length in scientific calculations should be sufficient to include the "natural precision" of the original data but must be greater than this to allow for loss of precision in the operations performed in executing the program. In general, the longer the computation, the greater the loss of precision; or to put it the other way round, longer word lengths should be used for problems with longer computations. Some quantitative basis for this qualitative statement has been reported by Neumann and Goldstine for the problem of inverting matrices. Although this is only one type of problem, it is a common and nontrivial one in scientific computation. To maintain reasonable precision in matrix inversion, the following inequality should hold:

(1) $n < 0.15 \ r^{s \div 4}$

where $n \equiv$ dimension of matrix
$r \equiv$ radix of the number system
$s \equiv$ number of bits in word

EXAMPLE: What is the minimum word length for a binary machine required to invert a 72×72 matrix?
SOLUTION: Here

$$n \equiv 72$$
$$r \equiv 2$$
$$72 \equiv 0.15 \times 2^{s \div 4}$$

or

$$480 \equiv 2^{s \div 4}$$
$$s \equiv \lceil \ 4 \log_2 480 \equiv 36 \text{ bits}$$

(Notice that a 36-bit word will, however, accommodate a matrix as large as 77×77.)

Another consideration in data-word length is compatibility with the instruction length. Equal data and instruction length is tempting partly because both normally share the same storage device and instructions are often treated as data, e.g., in moving operations. Many systems impose this property, but there is a trend toward better satisfying the distinct requirements of data and instruction length.

The length of operand may be fixed, e.g., at one word, in which case it is built into the machine's controls and does not require specification by the user. A few fixed lengths may be provided for storage efficiency—each instruction typically implies the length of the operand.

To conserve storage where widely varying operand lengths are expected, as in many business data-processing problems, a variable operand length may be permitted. In these variable-yield-length systems, the address specifies the beginning of the operand, which for numbers may be the high- or low-order digit; often the ability to specify either is included in the same system. Text material in the Western nations is normally handled left-to-right; moving operations including I/O are provided for this direction. Arithmetic operations, on the other hand, proceed most simply from the low- to high-order digits, which in the usual number systems is set down from right to left.

The length (in bytes) of variable-length operands may be specified in at least the following ways:

1. Within the instruction
2. By a register specified by an instruction
3. By a delimiter embedded in the data
    a. A separate bit or bits in every byte denoting possible end-of-field
    b. A reserved byte denoting end-of-field

The first method is used in the IBM System/360 and has the advantage of separation of control from data, as is the case with other data types. It has the disadvantage that only relatively short lengths (256 bytes maximum) can be specified, otherwise the instruction becomes excessively large, with the attendant storage and time inefficiencies. The second method is used in the XDS Sigma 7 and IBM System/370 systems; since the register capacity is large, very long field lengths are possible with only a few bits required in the instruction to reference the register specifying the length. However, this method requires use of a valuable register as well as the expenditure of space and time for the instruction to load it with the desired length. Method *3a* was used in the IBM 1401 and 1620 systems and was generalized somewhat in the Honeywell H200 system, where two bits called *item* and *word* marks were used per byte. Instructions were able to manipulate each kind of field. Method *3a* is rather wasteful of bits since every byte in storage must have a delimiter bit although very few of these are actually used as delimiters in any given program. Method *3b* avoids this waste by using a byte *value* (often called a record or group mark) as a delimiter only where needed. For example, if 6-bit bytes are used, a 64-byte alphabet can be represented. But suppose that only a 56-character set is required. Then one of the eight unused byte combinations can be used as a record mark. Since the record-mark byte appears only where a delimiter is actually required, it tends to be storage efficient. However, this scheme has one serious defect not shared by method *3a*: since one bit combination is reserved for control purposes (end-of-field), it cannot be used as data. Hence dense binary data cannot be processed using the record-mark scheme as the only type of delimiter. Although none of the above schemes for variable field length is without its disadvantage, most modern systems favor methods 1 or 2.

9.3 SOME FUNDAMENTAL OBJECTIVES IN ADDRESS-SYSTEM DESIGN

Most computer instructions include a reference to at least one operand. Since the amount of storage, hence the number of operands, is very large, it might seem that a large number of address bits would be required in every instruction. Fortunately, this is not essential because implicit addressing and a hierarchal structure of address context can keep the number of address bits within any given context small (or at least moderate). Of course, the minimum number of bits to address n words is ultimately the same whether done in one stage or in a hierarchy of stages; what is gained in a hierarchal structure is the smaller number of bits required in the most frequently executed instructions. A short instruction length has two beneficial effects: (1) it reduces the space required to store instructions, and (2) for a storage with a given bandwidth or flow rate (in bits per unit time) the shorter the instruction, the larger the number of instructions that can be fetched per second.

Much of the rationale for address-system design follows from two rather general properties which have been observed in a large variety of programs. These can be stated only qualitatively because the extent to which they appear varies from problem to problem as well as with system properties.

1. The number of written (or explicit) addresses is far fewer than the number of executed *effective* addresses because most effective addresses are computed *from* the explicit addresses. Often, some of this computation is implicitly specified in a process called *indexing.*

2. Over reasonably long sequences of executed effective addresses, most programs exhibit a *locality of reference;* i.e., their effective addresses tend to dwell in a relatively few localized areas of storage.

Design of an addressing system can take advantage of the first property by providing instructions that need only reference the few explicit address parameters rather than supply the long effective addresses directly. This is typically done in a two-step *indirect* addressing scheme that specifies a short *address* in the instruction; but the quantity at this address is *not* the operand, it is the long storage address of the operand. Indirect addressing can be slow unless the long address is held in a fast-access storage device (commonly called an *index* or *base register*).

The second property of executed address patterns, called *locality of reference,* is illustrated by repeated execution of a short program loop or by successive reference to elements of an array. Since locality of reference implies many references to the same locations, the system can execute programs by first moving the soon-to-be-used information into a local context; the high frequency of subsequent references need only refer to this smaller context.

In other words, a section of the program or data is first *set up* in a local context by either moving data or establishing pointers; the frequent subsequent references need only be to the small local context. By implementing the local context as a small fast-access storage, often called *registers,* not only is the speed of instruction flow improved as discussed earlier, but most executed data references will also be faster. Thus, from this viewpoint, a *set of registers* spurs the user to specify to the machine those operands that he expects to be currently referenced with a high frequency, at least for each local section of the program. Of course, instructions to change context are also provided, but these are often less space- and time-efficient than those addressing only the local context.

The reader is encouraged to examine machine architecture features described below such as indirect addressing, push-down stores, and management of transmission between main processor storage and auxiliary storage as applications of the above principles.

9.4 ADDRESSING MODES (IMMEDIATE, DIRECT, INDIRECT)

A simple but widely used addressing scheme considers storage to be composed of cells each having the same number of bits. A cell is called a *word.* Addressing is initiated by routing the address to the storage address register together with a control signal specifying READ or WRITE. In the latter case, the data to be entered into storage are also routed to the storage data-in register. In any case the storage unit itself uses the address to make selection of the desired cell and transmits data between this cell and the storage data register. The details of this entire process are automatic from the programmer's viewpoint.

Assume for illustration the simple 32-bit machine of Sec. 9.1 and focus attention on how a word is obtained (Fig. 9.4.1). The instruction about to be executed is assumed to be available in the instruction register IR. The addressing is discussed only for the case of obtaining an operand for the register called S (32 bits long).

For *immediate* (or sometimes *literal*) addressing, the operand is taken as the

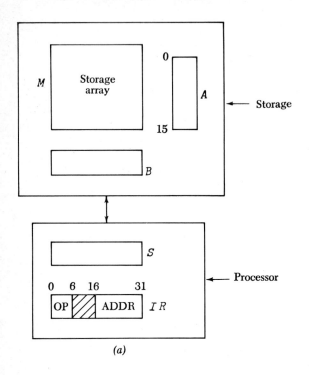

(a)

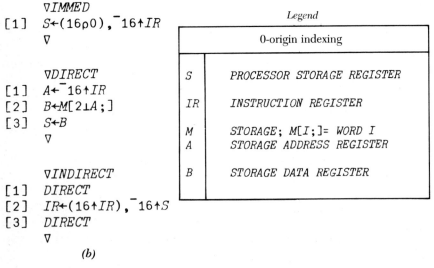

(b)

Fig. 9.4.1 Three common addressing types.

address part of the instruction itself. Access consists of routing the rightmost 16 bits of IR to the data register of the processor S. Since S is assumed in this example to be 32 bits long, the bits from IR are routed to the low-order positions and the rest of S is filled with 0s.

The second type of addressing is called *direct* or *normal* addressing. The rightmost 16 bits of the instruction are sent to the memory address register A, and the word specified by A is fetched to the processor storage register S. Direct addressing is the most essential of the three types under discussion; many machines allow only direct addressing.

In the third type of addressing, called *indirect* addressing, the address part of the instruction is first used to fetch a word from storage in the same way as in direct addressing. Now, however, the rightmost 16 bits of the word thus obtained are routed to replace the address part of the instruction register. The system now behaves as if it had just obtained the instruction; i.e., the address is used as for direct addressing. Although indirect addressing may appear at first glance to be a strange operation, it is a very convenient feature to the programmer. To understand this, it should be recalled that a direct address is a *name* of an operand. An address in an instruction used as an indirect address therefore specifies the name of another name. One use of indirect addressing is to process operands whose names are specified by other names. Indirect addressing, when used in conjunction with normal addressing, allows for convenient manipulation of names. Here a name may be treated as an operand in a normal addressing operation. Subsequent indirect addressing using the name encounters a modified *name* (address). The alternative method of performing this same function, without indirect addressing, is to modify program instructions in storage—a rather awkward procedure fraught with initialization-error possibilities.

A somewhat different use of indirect addressing is to improve the instruction information rate from a memory of given bandwidth (access rate in bits per second). Here the basis of comparison is a conventional direct-addressing system. The instruction rate can be improved by allowing most instruction types to have short addresses. This of course confines such instructions to a restricted area of storage for direct addressing. However, indirect addressing may also be specified; the address thus accessed may be a long address which can refer to the rest of storage. Such a scheme allows a short instruction length and hence a possible high instruction fetch rate for many instruction types. Constants or data already in the directly addressable area are accessed with no time penalty. For access out of the restricted area of direct addressing, the cost of the extra memory cycle for indirect addressing must be paid. Note that such a system makes use of the fact that the number of *program addresses* is usually far smaller than the number of effective addresses (since most *effective addresses* are calculated from program addresses and constants by indexing operations). The relatively few program addresses can usually fit in the restricted storage area.

9.5 ADDRESS MODIFICATION: INDEXING

In early simple machine designs it was found that a very frequent programming operation was the updating of addresses, e.g., for access to arrays. It was clear that speed could be considerably improved by circuitry that would automati-

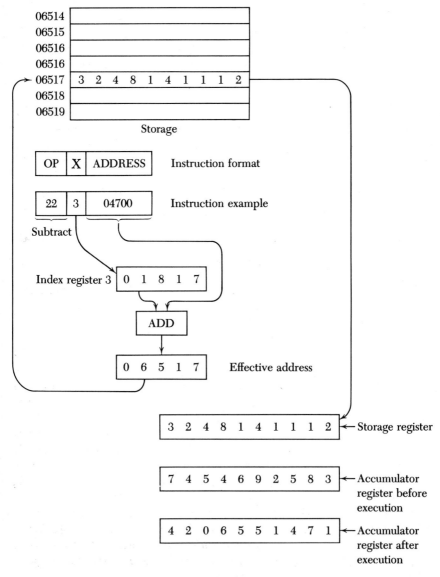

Fig. 9.5.1 Example of indexed subtraction instruction.

cally perform this function without program steps. To obtain the maximum speed advantage, it is desirable that a storage cycle not be required for reference to an address parameter. This suggests one or more registers for holding address parameters and an *implicit* operation (e.g., addition) when these registers are referenced. Indexing may be viewed as a type of indirect addressing with an implicit operation on the address. In a single-address system, for example, each instruction may specify an index register as well as an address. The address is added to the index register contents to form the *effective* address (Fig. 9.5.1). In most machines, this disappears after it is used and is replaced by the next effective address.

Some systems permit the program counter to be used as an index register as well. This facilitates relocation of programs.

The address addition required by indexing generally uses the same adder circuits that are used for data addition. Indexing thus requires data paths from the index registers to the adder and from the adder to the storage-address register. Where circuit economy is important, some benefit from index registers is possible, even if the registers are physically in storage. In this case economy with moderate speed is the objective; the cost of the hardware index register is saved at the expense of a memory cycle. Aside from data paths, index registers have other effects on computer organization. For example, more instructions are required in the machine's repertoire for loading and storing the registers; instruction bits are required to designate the registers.

9.6 BINDING TIME AND RELOCATABILITY

In every system, problem-oriented names of information objects must be translated into physical memory addresses. This translation process is done in a variety of ways; the particular way a given system *binds* names to addresses can give significant insight into the nature of a system. Generally speaking, the later the final binding time, the more adaptable the system to actual storage needs and last-moment changes in these needs. For example, an interpreter-translator binds its names very late (at the moment of each statement execution), while the simplest kind of compiler system discussed in Chap. 3 binds all names to addresses before loading or executing any statement. The flexibility of late binding is often offset, at least in part, by its cost in time (as in the interpreter) or hardware (see below).

An important impetus to a two-stage binding scheme is that most programs are written as a collection of smaller programs and subroutines. Often some of these modules will be used in several programs. Examples include floating-point arithmetic (if the computer lacks the hardware), mathematical functions, I/O handling programs, as well as entire subroutine and user libraries. Modern programming systems permit all subprograms to be compiled only once each with its address origin at 0. Before a program composed of several such object programs is run, they must be linked together; i.e., their references to each other must be resolved by relocating the common address origins to distinct starting locations and then reflecting these origins in the places they are referenced in the programs. This binding is usually done by a *linkage-editor program.*

Thus far, we have been considering only a single program (job) in main storage at a time. Modern systems often permit several programs to share main storage concurrently. Furthermore, the particular area where a program is to reside is usually not known until the moment the program is to be loaded into main storage. The ability to locate a program in various places in storage is called *relocatability* and may be accomplished with either hardware or software. The software-only solution requires the user to follow certain conventions in writing his program to permit the compiler-link-editor to indicate to a loader which object words are addresses so that these can be modified to reflect the origin for loading the program. Such a scheme, usually called *static* relocation, is used in the IBM System/360.

Another method does not require an address-processing loader but instead uses one (or more) hardware base registers. In its simplest form, requiring the program and data to be contiguous in storage, every *executed* processor address is added to the contents of the register to finally bind the program address to memory location. Register relocation is *dynamic* since its very late binding permits the system to move a program to a different physical origin (and change the base register). Relocation registers have been used on CDC, UNIVAC, and PDP computers.

A much more general scheme of dynamic relocation is used in the Burroughs 5500/6500/7500 systems. Programs are modularized into natural *segments;* each is separately relocatable with its own origin. Since there are now several relocation base "registers," this is economically supplied (at some expense in speed) by indirect addressing to a table of segment *descriptors* that hold the segment relocation information.

Another scheme of dynamic relocation is used in so-called *paging* systems, which in effect automatically partitions programs and data into fixed-size units called *pages* and a separate relocation origin is supplied (by hardware) for each page. Further discussion of this interesting and profound idea, used in the IBM S/370, the GE 645, and some RCA systems, is outside the scope of this book.

9.7 FEATURES OF AN ADDRESSING SYSTEM

A number of considerations must be given careful attention when designing the addressing system of a computer. Figure 9.7.1 lists some of these factors. Many computer systems combine several features in each category.

Types of explicit addresses
   Immediate (literal)
   Direct
   Indirect
Number of addresses per instruction
   0. Implicit addresses (machine registers, e.g., push-down)
   1. One explicit and one implicit
   2. Two explicit addresses

      $R \leftarrow A+B$ (result sent to register R)
      $A \leftarrow A+B$ (result replaces one operand)

   3. Two operands and a result specified explicitly

      $C \leftarrow A+B$

Resolution of the addresses
   To the bit
   To the byte
   To the word
Length of addressed operand
   Implicit (fixed at one word)
   Variable field length (VFL)
      Length specified explicitly in each instruction
      Length specified by a register
      Length specified by delimiter marks associated with data
         Reserved-bit delimiter(s) (field or word mark)
         Reserved-bit configuration (record or group mark)
      Direction of processing
         Right-to-left for arithmetic processing
         Left-to-right for moving
         Right-to-left for moving

Fig. 9.7.1 Some features and options in addressing.

A NO ADDRESS instruction can refer either to no operands or to implicit operands. Examples of the first type are instructions for NO OPERATION and HALT. The second type may be illustrated by many instruction codes in a machine with a push-down store. The top levels of the push-down are assumed to contain the current operands (see Sec. 9.8).

Single-address instructions can often be described as "1 + 0" address; i.e., one explicit and one implicit operand are specified. For example, an ADD instruction in a single-address system specifies addition on a specified operand with a second implied operand in an accumulator register. The use of an implied address like an accumulator saves instruction bits (for an explicit address) and results in higher instruction access rate (since fewer instruction bits need be fetched from storage). Also, if the implied operand is held in a fast register, data-access rate is increased over a system with a two-address structure, since access to the implied operand does not require a memory cycle. Single-address systems are particularly attractive with highly parallel data-flow structures using very few central registers.

The multiple-address, especially two-address, scheme has found wide application in machines oriented to variable-field-length (VFL) operands. Such machines are often (but not necessarily) designed with serial-by-character data-flow structures. The VFL (rather than fixed data-word length) data structure does not lend itself to easy implementation with a highly parallel processor data flow because large registers would be required to hold intermediate data results. Without a central data register to serve as an implied address, the single-address approach loses much of its rationale.

In a two-address system, it is natural for one address to specify FROM and the other TO locations for data movement. For transformation operations, the two addresses usually specify two operands. The result may be stored in a register (in which case the result address is implicit), or, more commonly, the result replaces one of the operands in storage.

In both cases a third *explicit* address for the result operand is not required.

In many serial two-address VFL machines the transformations on the addressed operands are overlapped with the storage access so that with the simple transformations, e.g., addition of numbers with like signs, the execution time depends entirely on the number of storage cycles required for access and storing of operands. (See Chap. 6 sections on core storage and overlap.)

The instruction rate and instruction storage efficiency of the implied-operand idea of the single-address instruction can be largely retained, and yet the programming simplicity of the two-address structure can also be kept by a modified two-address scheme wherein one address specifies a location in storage while the other specifies one of a few fast-access central registers. The fact that only a few (say, 16) central registers need be specified by one of the addresses means that only a few instruction bits are required for this purpose. The success of such a system depends upon the program containing redundant storage references (as most programs do); i.e., the number of distinct addresses in the written program is considerably less than the number of *effective* addresses which must appear eventually in the address register. Moreover, the redundancy of address references is usually local; i.e., there is a high probability of recurrent references to the same locations in a short succession of instructions. Unless this is true, many instructions will have to be executed solely in loading and storing the registers.

The category "resolution of the addressed operand" refers to the fineness to which the beginning of the oprand may be specified. Address resolution is a parameter independent of the length of the operand, although a frequent restriction is that the length of the operand must be a multiple of the resolution. If only a single resolution is required throughout the machine, this can be implicit; otherwise the resolution must be specified, say, in the instruction

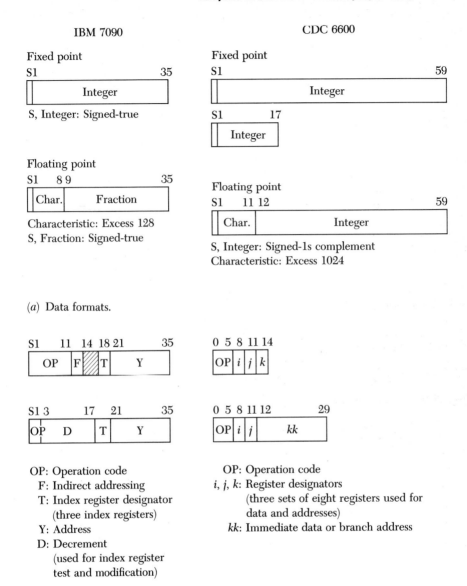

(*a*) Data formats.

OP: Operation code
  F: Indirect addressing
  T: Index register designator
    (three index registers)
  Y: Address
  D: Decrement
    (used for index register
    test and modification)

  OP: Operation code
  i, j, k: Register designators
    (three sets of eight registers used for
    data and addresses)
  kk: Immediate data or branch address

(*b*) Instructions.

Fig. 9.7.2 Major CPU formats of IBM 7090 and CDC 6600 computers.

operation code. High resolution (the highest is to the individual bit) is desirable from a programming viewpoint but is expensive in address bits. High resolution increases the storage required for the program (which includes all addresses) and, if the address is specified in the instruction, lengthens the instruction. One technique to resolve this dichotomy of objectives is to provide a hierarchy of address resolutions. For example, to reference information held in large-capacity auxiliary storage, the address resolution is typically one track or sector comprising hundreds of characters. This rather coarse resolution is used primarily to move *blocks* of information into (and out of) processor storage. Once the information is in processor storage, a finer resolution (to the byte or character) may be specified. Since most of the executed references are to process storage, this approach results in high address resolution for the most frequent references.

Another parameter of an addressing system is the address radix. Here it should be recognized that addressing is not simply an access operation; it also performs an important type of transformation. A good general rule is that all data-bit combinations should also be valid in addresses. This ensures that any data may be used as an address argument. The use of the binary radix in addressing satisfies this rule and has other advantages as well, including economy of bits and ease of performing simple arithmetic, e.g., shifting to obtain division or multiplication by 2.

Figure 9.7.2 shows formats for two computers designed primarily for scientific applications. Both use fixed-length data words, but each 7090 instruction also requires a full storage word; the 6600 achieves a high instruction rate by packing up to four instructions per storage word. This is done by making storage addressing indirect through sets of eight registers, thus requiring only 3 instruction bits per address. The 7090 programmer is little concerned with address context since each instruction can directly reach any storage word. The 6600 programmer or programming system must segment problem contexts to map address parameters into the available registers. Change of context is facilitated by an instruction that swaps all the 6600's CPU registers with an area of storage in a single operation.

9.8 PUSH-DOWN STORAGE, OR STACK

An important illustration of implicit addressing is the control of a logical structure called a *push-down store,* or LIFO (last in, first out) list, or *stack.* An address specifies a storage location as a source/destination of data to/from the top of a list of contiguous storage words. Operations implicitly reference the operand(s) at the top of the list, and the result operand replaces the operand(s) at the top of the list. The structure thus behaves as if an entered item "pushed down" the other items. When an operation is performed, the result replaces one

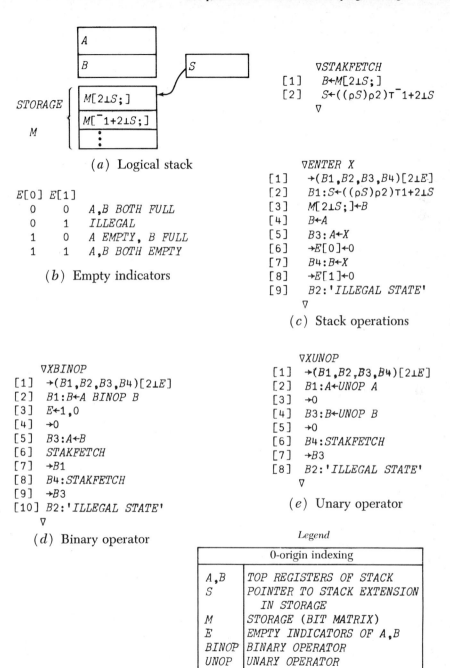

(a) Logical stack

```
∇STAKFETCH
[1]    B←M[2⊥S;]
[2]    S←((ρS)ρ2)⊤¯1+2⊥S
   ∇
```

E[0] E[1]

0	0	A,B BOTH FULL
0	1	ILLEGAL
1	0	A EMPTY, B FULL
1	1	A,B BOTH EMPTY

(b) Empty indicators

```
∇ENTER X
[1]    →(B1,B2,B3,B4)[2⊥E]
[2]    B1:S←((ρS)ρ2)⊤1+2⊥E
[3]    M[2⊥S;]←B
[4]    B←A
[5]    B3:A←X
[6]    →E[0]←0
[7]    B4:B←X
[8]    →E[1]←0
[9]    B2:'ILLEGAL STATE'
   ∇
```

(c) Stack operations

```
∇XBINOP
[1]    →(B1,B2,B3,B4)[2⊥E]
[2]    B1:B←A BINOP B
[3]    E←1,0
[4]    →0
[5]    B3:A←B
[6]    STAKFETCH
[7]    →B1
[8]    B4:STAKFETCH
[9]    →B3
[10]   B2:'ILLEGAL STATE'
   ∇
```

(d) Binary operator

```
∇XUNOP
[1]    →(B1,B2,B3,B4)[2⊥E]
[2]    B1:A←UNOP A
[3]    →0
[4]    B3:B←UNOP B
[5]    →0
[6]    B4:STAKFETCH
[7]    →B3
[8]    B2:'ILLEGAL STATE'
   ∇
```

(e) Unary operator

Legend

0-origin indexing	
A,B	TOP REGISTERS OF STACK
S	POINTER TO STACK EXTENSION IN STORAGE
M	STORAGE (BIT MATRIX)
E	EMPTY INDICATORS OF A,B
BINOP	BINARY OPERATOR
UNOP	UNARY OPERATOR

Fig. 9.8.1 Control of a push-down store (stack).

of the top two operands (at least for binary operators); the list is, as it were, pushed up one position. The push-down structure is important in many types of compilers (see Chap. 3 on Polish notation and recursive functions).

Machines using the stack idea are the Burroughs Corporation's B5500/6500/7500. The following description of internal operations is indicative of those required in a stack-storage machine.

Figure 9.8.1 refers to a structure consisting of two registers A and B which constitute the top two cells of the stack and a register S which contains the location in storage of the next cell in the stack. In other words, our logical push-down store has its top two cells implemented in registers (since these are the most active cells); the rest of the stack is in storage. This mechanization permits a size of push-down store that can be very large without many expensive registers. Furthermore, the internal operations to be described can make this mixed nature of the implementation invisible to the users. This is done by automatically moving information between the cell whose address is given by S and the A and B registers. Information is moved between the A, B registers also; this movement is much faster than movement between registers and storage.

Two indicators $E[1,2]$ are used to specify whether the A, B registers, respectively, contain information or not. These *empty* indicators can have a total of four states; these are listed for reference purposes (see Fig. 9.8.1).

The operations described as microprograms specify how an entry is made to the stack and how operations obtain operands. Depending upon the state of the empty indicators and the type of operation (binary or unary), it is seen that an operation may require either zero, one, or two references to storage to perform an operation. This number may be reduced on the average by increasing the number of registers used to implement the top cells of the stack. For example, in the B6500/7500 machines the top of stack has four registers. This can lead to significant speed increase because most activity involves the top members of the stack.

9.9 OPERATING SYSTEMS: ESSENTIAL HARDWARE REQUIREMENTS

A computer system is often best considered as a service facility for processing *jobs,* which are defined as named units of work, each logically independent of any other. Although by definition there is no problem dependency between jobs, they often compete for common resources (storage and other devices as well as programs such as compilers). A vital part of the operating system called variously the monitor, supervisor, executive, or master, is responsible for deciding which requesting job should receive the services of requested resources.

In making its allocation decisions, the supervisor typically attempts to *overlap-process,* i.e., keep several resources working productively on different parts of different jobs. Figure 9.9.1 shows an extremely simple example of two jobs, each with an input, compute, and output phase, as they might be processed (1) in pure sequence (no overlap) and (2) with overlap. The two methods are evaluated with respect to (1) throughput H = no. of jobs processed per total elapsed time and (2) utilization fractions of each resource. On both measures, overlap is seen to be advantageous.

Perhaps the simplest but very important instance of overlap is SPOOLing (simultaneous peripheral operations on-line). I/O and compute are done concurrently on different jobs as follows (see Fig. 9.9.2):

1. An incoming job (as a deck of punched cards) is read by the card reader, and this information is moved to an area of disk storage called SYSIN.
2. A job is assigned to the processor for computing from the SYSIN disk area. Results are stored back on the disk in the SYSOUT area.
3. Information is sent to the printer from the SYSOUT disk area.

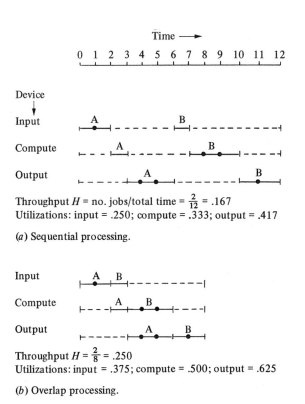

Throughput H = no. jobs/total time = $\frac{2}{12}$ = .167
Utilizations: input = .250; compute = .333; output = .417

(*a*) Sequential processing.

Throughput $H = \frac{2}{8}$ = .250
Utilizations: input = .375; compute = .500; output = .625

(*b*) Overlap processing.

Fig. 9.9.1 Sequential and overlap processing of jobs A and B.

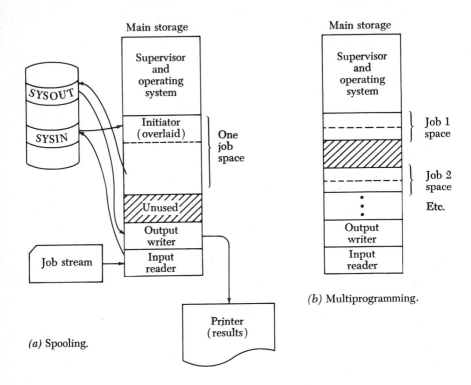

(a) Spooling.

(b) Multiprogramming.

Fig. 9.9.2   Spooling and multiprogramming use of main store.

This use of the disk as a large buffer for card reader, printer, and CPU permits the system supervisor program to overlap several jobs with reasonable concurrency provided the jobs use resources equally on the average (but not necessarily in the particular). Since the data paths of most computers require all information moved from one device to another to pass through main storage, SPOOLing is seen to require at least four areas of main storage, including one for the supervisor. In more sophisticated systems even more jobs can be held in main storage concurrently. A system that space-shares its main storage is said to be *multiprogrammed.*

The timesharing and space sharing of resources among independent jobs which by definition cannot know of each other's existence indicates the need for a scheme where all jobs and all devices report changes in their resource states, such as operation completion and error conditions, to the supervisor program. Also, only the supervisor can be entitled to allocate resources to jobs, at least in the simplest kind of control scheme, which will be assumed from now on.

Because it receives all resource reports, the supervisor is the logical place to accumulate resource-use data for accounting, billing, and system-improvement purposes.

We now give a brief list of certain essential functions which require operations to be done at such high speeds that hardware is necessary for their efficient implementation by supervisor programs:

1. Clocks
   a. Time-of-day
   b. Interval timers
   Both are typically registers that can be set and read by program and are automatically updated by circuitry at regular intervals to record the passage of time. The first is incremented; the interval timer is decremented, and when zero is reached, it generates an interrupt request.
2. Interrupt Automatic monitoring of the occurrence of certain events and forcing the system to enter the supervisor program to respond to them.
3. Storage protection Prevention of one program's unauthorized access to another's storage area.
4. Privileged mode To ensure that certain critical instructions used to select and start devices, to control the interrupt and storage-protect mechanisms can be executed only by the supervisor program (never by problem programs).

Much of the remainder of this chapter is devoted to discussing these features.

9.10 STORAGE PROTECTION AND PRIVILEGED MODE

The ease of changing stored information is a major positive feature of modern data processing. This same property can also be a source of difficulty especially under program-error or equipment-error conditions. Various provisions are made to protect selected stored information from replacement, i.e., destruction. For example, most tape systems include a *file-protect* ring, which can be manually placed on or off each tape reel. In IBM systems, when the ring is off, the tape drive will not execute a signal to WRITE on the tape. i.e., the tape is protected against writing. Storage protection for tape and disk as well as other auxiliary storage devices are quite commonly supplied in modern systems.

The problem of storage protection in main storage is somewhat more difficult, partly because any added equipment associated with fast storage is likely to be expensive and because efficient use of processor storage does not permit a single fixed area of storage to be protected. Storage is generally restructured by each program into read and write areas, and these may change within a program as the execution progresses.

The major impetus for storage protection arises in multiprogram sharing of processor storage. The main requirement here is that while one program is being executed, no operation arising in that program should ever result in write operations in an area currently belonging to another program. If protection is to be absolutely complete, the problem has no program solution since some program(s) must control the protection mechanism and an error in such a program could void the protection system whatever its details. For this reason, among others, multiprogrammed or shared systems make a dichotomy among programs. In its simplest but quite practical form, one program called a *supervisor* or *control* or *monitor* program is responsible for assignment of *all* physical facilities to programs. The supervisor (program) is written by the most experienced and able programmers available; every effort is made to keep it completely error free. We shall assume it to be error free unless otherwise noted. The other side of the program dichotomy is the set of *problem* programs—these are the programs that perform the user's work. The supervisor program is responsible for resolving all points of conflict between problem programs and common facilities, including requests for I/O devices, auxiliary or main storage, and the processor unit or units. Access to common programs as well as equipment is also coordinated by the supervisor. The supervisor controls the set-up of the storage-protect mechanism, which is, after all, but one component of system facilities. In its simplest form, store-protect control uses a single register which specifies the extent, i.e., the number of words, in the currently running program. Each program-effective address (i.e., the effective address before possible relocation) is checked against the extent register; if it is less than the extent, the storage access is permitted; if not, the access is suppressed and the supervisor is signaled via the interrupt system (see Sec. 9.11).

An alternative to the single extent register is to consider storage to be partitioned into rather small fixed blocks (e.g., of 256 words each) and to assign a *protection tag* to each. The tag assignments are held in some storage device changeable only by the supervisor. Each processor or channel includes a protection-key register, whose contents specify the (single) tag for storage references. The protection key is modifiable only by the supervisor program and will be changed, when the processor is switched from one program to another. Each reference to storage is accompanied by a match-check of the protection key and the storage tag; if these do not agree, then the access may be suppressed. The tag-key method is more expensive than the extent-register scheme, but it does not restrict all the current protected storage to one set of contiguous storage locations.

In some systems, storage protection may be applied only to WRITE references; in others both READ and WRITE references may be protected.

An error-free supervisor program controlling *all* device assignments, and hence the storage protection mechanism, can go a long way in permitting multiprogram or shared use of a system. Yet there is a logical gap remaining in our story; the machine hardware must, in some way, be "aware" of whether the supervisor program or a problem program is executing a critical control instruction. This is essential since otherwise deliberate or accidental problem-program instructions could modify the relocation or extent registers with logically disastrous consequences. To prevent this, machines intended for shared operation usually include a feature called by different names, which we shall call the *privileged mode*. During privileged-mode operation all instructions including those controlling selections and protection will be executed normally. When not in the privileged mode, the machine will not execute these system-control instructions. Naturally, the machine is in the privileged mode when executing certain parts of the supervisor program.

The machine enters and leaves the privileged mode in a variety of ways. Entry to the mode is usually in response to most (but not necessarily all) interrupt conditions or attempts to execute privileged-mode instructions when not in the privileged mode. A specific instruction may also be provided to permit a problem program to *call* the supervisor. The essential requirement is that the transition from problem to supervisor mode always must be accompanied by a program branch to a part of the supervisor which can determine the action to be taken.

To summarize: multiprogrammed, or shared, use of a system is often organized as a single supervisor program and several problem programs. The supervisor is carefully designed and programmed. It allocates all machine facilities to problem programs and responds to most exceptional conditions such as those detected and signaled by machine interrupt. The machine architecture and hardware recognizes the privileged or problem mode; any critical selection or control instruction encountered in the current program can thus be recognized as being due to the supervisor program or illegally to a problem program.

A system utilizing a supervisor program has great potential for economical operation of systems since it opens the possibility of shared use of expensive centralized equipment. The management of allocation of system resources, including common programs (i.e., compilers, subroutines), as well as equipment hinges on the success of the supervisor program. To the system user, the supervisor program appears almost like a part of the equipment. It is often designed, delivered, and maintained by the system manufacturer.

9.11 PROGRAM INTERRUPT

It has already been described how a program can branch based on explicit tests of data or index conditions. Now it is often most desirable to give a computer system the ability to respond to stimuli other than those generated by current internal computer operations. This is especially necessary in real-time systems but is also important in the control of I/O devices whose long access times are to be overlapped with computation. In all these cases, while one program may have initiated certain operations which will require ultimate attention by a program, the computer processor is to be employed in the intervening indefinite interval on a logically independent routine. In other words, the processor hardware is to be timeshared by two programs. To make this sharing possible, the logical dependencies within a program must be preserved even though an indefinite time interval may elapse between execution of parts of the program. A sound approach to program-machine organization for this type of operation may be described as follows: A program is viewed as a collection of instructions and data which mostly resides in a "dormant" state in storage. During execution, parts of the program "come alive" by being moved from storage to the processor registers. During such a phase of the program, the processor state is also part of the program state. If a program is to be interrupted—in order to allow another program access to the processor—the program which is interrupted must have its state preserved in order that it can be resumed later with no loss of its logical structure. The system must also be capable of resetting a processor state previously stored.

One example of the nature and benefit of program interruption is the *interval timer.* This provides a word in storage (or a processor register) which can

Requests for interrupt
    Request register R
Program control over granting request
    Enable flip-flop E
    Selective mask over requests M
Interrupt flip-flop
    $T \leftarrow C[0] \wedge E \wedge M . \wedge R$
    $C[0]$=clock pulse after instruction execution is complete
If $T=1$, store interrupt state
    Store program counter (location may depend on R)
    Store R and M
    $E \leftarrow 0$
Force a branch
    Location may depend on R
After interrupt system must be able to:
    1. Store remainder of processor state (registers, etc.)
    2. Load processor state for new program from storage
    3. Access to R,M to fully decode interrupt cause
    4. Set control over M,E

Fig. 9.11.1 Simple multiple request interrupt system.

Legend

∇INTPROC
[1] T←E∧M∨.∧R
[2] →T/PRI
[3] FTCH:IR←M[2⊥P;]
[4] →0
[5] PRI:N←(M∧R)ι1
[6] R[N]←0
[7] E←0
[8] M[0;]←(16ρ0),P
[9] M[1;]←(32ρ2)⊤N
[10] P←M[2;]
[11] →FTCH
∇

0-origin indexing	
E	Enable flip-flop
R	Interrupt requests
M	Interrupt masks
IR	Instruction register
P	Program counter
M	Storage as a bit matrix
	M[I;]=word I

Step	Explanation
1	Set T to 1 only if interrupts are enabled and some unmasked request is *ON*
2	Branch to *PRI* (step 5) if $T=1$
3,4	No interrupt; fetch instruction and exit
5	Specify N the leftmost unmasked request identifier
6	Reset request flip-flop
7	Disable further interrupt response
8	Store program counter in memory word 0
9	Store request identifier (cause) in memory word 1
10	Set program counter from memory word 2
11	Branch to *FTCH*

Fig. 9.11.2 Functional microprogram for interrupt.

be set by a program to any desired value. At regular intervals (say 100 μsec) the computer hardware automatically decrements this storage word value by 1 and then tests the resulting value for 0. If it is nonzero, normal execution proceeds. If 0, the timer interval originally specified by the program has elapsed and the program currently being executed is interrupted, i.e., the processor is switched to another routine. In this way, the system can be given a sense of real time.

An event which may initiate an interrupt will be called an interrupt request; each request may set a flip-flop which is considered an element of a request flip-flop vector R. Examples of events which may set an element of R are the interval timer (discussed above) and completion of transmission by an I/O device or an external signal. A functional description of a typical way to respond to interrupts is shown in Fig. 9.11.2.

Once the interrupt requests have been stored, it is necessary to provide control over when any given request or combination of requests should indeed result in an interrupt. This must be carefully considered not only because competing requests must be resolved but also because the processor program which is to be interrupted must be capable of being "saved" for continuation later. In most systems, response to an interrupt is controlled by a program mask scheme. Often this is done on two levels for programming convenience and response speed:

1. Enabling (or disabling) of *all* interrupts
2. Selective masking of interrupt requests

Assuming that the system is "enabled" and that a given request is not masked (inhibited), the interrupt is now effective after completion of the current instruction execution. Interrupt response almost always is limited to the end of the instruction; otherwise the storage of the machine state would be much more expensive in time and equipment. At that time, the processor must be able to:

1. Store the state of the processor so that the program being interrupted can be resumed later
2. Branch to the new routine

The primary component of the state of the interrupted program is the program counter. Most interrupt systems store this register automatically. In some systems indicators and even index registers may also be stored automatically. In other systems storage of these components of the processor state is done by program instructions in the new routine. It is during this latter process that it is awkward for the system to respond to another interrupt. This is one of the primary reasons for the enable (and disable) facility mentioned earlier. In most cases, the interrupt response mechanism is automatically disabled just after the program counter is stored. It is subsequently enabled by the new routine after the state of the processor has been stored.

The branch to the new routine, which is usually the supervisor program, constitutes a partial decoding of the cause of the interrupt. Thus there may be several branch locations, one for each interrupt cause. On the other hand, a minimum of one branch location for all interrupt causes is also feasible, provided that the specific cause of the interrupt is stored where program instructions can determine its nature. This can be done by storing the request and mask vectors (or equivalent information). In practice a compromise between the two extremes is usually made.

Eventually, the system will probably return to the program which was interrupted. This requires that the system be capable of restoring the processor state saved by the interrupt routine. It is thus necessary to provide paths between all program-accessible processor registers (and indicators), storage, and instructions for moving the relevant information along these paths.

9.12 INPUT/OUTPUT CONTROL

A description of some typical types of auxiliary storage I/O devices will be found in Chap. 4. The present discussion is concerned with the various ways in which stored program control is exerted on the devices.

The problems of input and output are very similar; to be concise, all descriptions will be in terms of input, i.e., transfer of information from an external device to processor storage.

As usual there are only a few philosophies used in I/O systems, but a myriad of variations of these appear when details are studied of specific systems.

Any I/O control system must make provisions for:

1. Selection of a particular I/O device for transmission (of the many that may be physically connected to the system).
2. The type of operation—READ, WRITE, SPACE, etc.
3. Definition of the area on the external device *from* which the information is to be selected.
4. Definition of the area in processor storage *to* which the information is to be sent.
5. Action to be taken when transmission is complete.
6. Sense of the state of the I/O device and system in order that the other operations may be done in an orderly manner. For example, the state normally includes indication of whether the device is idle or busy with an ongoing operation, whether its check circuits have detected an error or not.

Perhaps the simplest overall philosophy of implementing these operations is to consider them as CPU functions. The processor instruction set is extended to include selection, operation, and sensing operations and movement of data. Record definition may be done by the usual addressing facilities available in the instruction set. Such an approach is typified by the *copy loop,* wherein successive records are read by a READ instruction included in an ordinary program loop. Within the loop, the destination address is advanced and the count of number of words to completion or test of search argument against key-field is made. If the device is of the sequential-access type, the READ operation implies "the next record" on tape or cards; there is no need for the program to define the source area on the device.

The copy-loop idea has the advantage of simplicity and economy since much use is made of CPU facilities already required such as loop control and index advance—only the minimum of additional control is required (READ, WRITE, CONTROL instructions). Another advantage of the copy-loop method is that the full logical power of the CPU instruction set is available to define source and destination areas or to test for search argument properties. The copy-loop method was almost universally used in early systems. In more recent systems it is not nearly so prevalent. To understand why, it is necessary to recall that, especially in large systems, I/O transmissions are usually slow compared with the speeds of processor storage. If the system were to perform I/O instructions in the same way as any other instructions, i.e., in strict sequence, the bandwidth (flow rate) of processor storage would be largely wasted during I/O transmission. It is therefore most desirable that the program be permitted to proceed after initiating an I/O operation. Now this can be done (and is done) even with the copy-loop method of control. However there is a fundamental difficulty; many I/O devices deliver their information at a steady flow rate (or else long access delays may be involved). The device must transmit its current data to the processor within a definite time limit or else the flow will cause an *overrun*, i.e., loss of information. This means that the control of transmission must take place within definite time constraints. With the copy-loop philosophy, this imposes a limitation on the number and type of instructions that can appear in the loop.

One cure for the above difficulty is to permit an I/O instruction to define transmission of a *block* of information and supply circuitry to automatically step the address for storage and count-to-completion of transmission. The circuitry is simplified if the record area in processor storage is contiguous since then successive addresses can be computed by counting. This block-transmit method can be implemented by ordinary CPU instructions. However, once an I/O transmission is initiated, the CPU program advances to the next instruction while the transmission is in process. During transmission, the I/O control circuits will "steal" processor storage cycles as needed to store the incoming informa-tion. For slow transmissions, this will occur only infrequently—the CPU program execution proceeds concurrently and is only occasionally delayed slightly to permit a storage cycle for I/O activity. The idea may be extended to permit several I/O devices and the CPU to proceed concurrently (see Chap. 4).

The block-transmission idea may be generalized and even greater possibilities for overlap of CPU and I/O operations obtained by defining an I/O control device here to be called a *channel*. A channel may best be viewed as a primitive stored-program computer whose instruction set is specialized to control transmission between I/O devices and processor storage. Many devices may be physically connected to one channel, but only one device can be controlled by a channel at one time. To avoid confusion in terminology, instructions executed by a channel will be called *commands* or *control words*. Naturally, a channel contains a command counter analogous to the CPU program counter. The command counter is a register containing the location of the next command. It is typically stepped to point to the next command after each command is fetched. A command usually specifies an operation and the record definition of a contiguous area in processor storage. It may also specify, often by indirect addressing, the selected area on the device or other control information.

Another type of information included in commands is the action to be taken after completion of the command. Typical actions are to proceed to the next command whose location is specified by the command-location counter or interrupt the CPU program (to notify it of completion of an I/O operation).

In most channel-organized systems, only a CPU instruction can start a channel executing its program. CPU instructions also are provided to stop channel operations and test channel status to aid decision making on initiating channel activity. These are the principal mechanisms of CPU-to-channel communication. The channel in turn typically communicates with the CPU by interrupt or by setting an indicator which can be tested by a CPU instruction.

The above brief sketch of the principles of channel control will be detailed further for a specific system in Chap. 10.

A somewhat different philosophy of I/O control is used in the Control Data Corporation's 6000 series of large computers. Here, the logical power of the channel is extended to include the facilities of a full-fledged small stored-program computer (which is technically a general-purpose computer). Each of these *peripheral processors* (PP) includes its own modest-size storage for holding its programs and for holding the transmitted data. The PP instruction set includes a block-transmission instruction which can move a block of information between PP storage and main storage. The PP's are capable of controlling not only transmission but searching and editing functions as well. They also are suited to executing the supervisor program: in fact, primary control of the system, i.e., the privileged mode resides with PP's. Thus the PP's have sole access to storage-protect and relocation control registers and a PP instruction must start each new CPU program.

9.13 MICROPROGRAMMING: PURPOSES AND PRINCIPLES

Each machine instruction, such as ADD, MULTIPLY, or BRANCH-ON-CONDITION, requires a *sequence* of switching-gating operations in the machine's data-flow structure, and some of these are conditional on the outcome of previous results. The process of interpretation and execution of a single machine instruction may then be considered as a kind of interpreter program called a *microprogram*. Microprograms are executed in a *host* machine; this is the name that will be given to the collection of primitive machine resources such as the data-flow structure, hardware registers, and the storage for the micro-programs. The host machine should be distinguished from the logical machine (here called simply the machine), by which we mean the machine as seen by its machine-language programmers.

Each microinstruction specifies a sequence of information movements in the host-machine data flow. The microinstructions are stored in a *control store* (CS). In most computers built before 1964 or so, the control store was *not* a recognizable single hardware device; the storage of microsequencing information was distributed in many places in the machine. More recently, most computers are organized so that the CS is a specific storage device and the term "microprogrammed machine" has come to apply only to such systems.

The CS usually has two registers by which it communicates with the rest of the machine: a data register (CSDR) and an address register (CSAR). In many systems, the machine is to have only a very few instruction sets (sometimes only one). In such cases, since the microprograms will not be changed frequently, a CS device can often be built at lowest cost by making it read-only (it is then called a *read-only store* or ROS). Such a device can be read at high electronic speeds as required to implement the microprogram but requires slow mechanical operations (usually at the factory) for changing its contents. Most IBM System/360 models use a ROS although the Mod 85 and the Mod 25 use a writable control store.

Microprogramming as a method and technology of organizing the control of a computer has a number of advantages.

1. Control functions are systematized into a kind of programming discipline rather than a problem in logical design.
2. Introducing modified or new machine features is simplified, e.g., changing existing instructions, adding new ones, or building new interfaces between the computer and external devices.
3. Two or more sets of microprograms can make the same host machine appear at different times as two different logical machines. Typically, one of the machines is a recent model which makes best use of the host-machine facilities while the second one is an earlier machine for which many programs are available.
4. Microprogramming gives its users direct access to the hardware resources of the machine. This has considerable potential for speed improvement if microprograms are tailored to specific applications or classes of applications.

The cost of the microprogramming organization is usually not justified if only a single simple instruction set is desired. In this case direct-circuit implementation of machine controls is likely to be cheaper than a CS device and its associated registers. However, for more than one instruction set or for a single rather complex set of instructions, the investment in the control store is often justified.

From a speed viewpoint, the highest-speed machines usually cannot be built with the delays inherent in a CS-organized control scheme. However, where the speed of the CS itself is not limiting, microprograms for parts of application or systems programs can result in appreciable speed improvement. A few words of caution are in order. Microprogramming is still done within the constraints of the host machine's (1) data flow and register structure, (2) switching-circuit speeds, and (3) the speed of the main store from which instructions and data must still flow. How much speed improvement can be obtained is also determined to some extent by judicious choice of the parts of a program to be microcoded. Since microprogramming is usually exceedingly tedious and difficult and the CS capacity limited, it usually pays to microcode only the very frequently used portions of programs. To identify them requires careful analysis of the executed program, preferably with a program trace. Not much data have been published showing program activity, even in very popular programs such as compilers or the code produced by compilers. Intuitively, operations like conversion of data types, indexing, list processing, and string-manipulation primitives seem likely candidates. Direct implementation of high-level languages has also been suggested; decisions of this kind must depend on the nature of the languages. For example, a language like FORTRAN, which is designed with a compiler translator in mind, would not seem to offer as great a potential for speed improvement as a more sophisticated language like APL, which was designed for an interpretive translator.

To date microprogramming seems to have demonstrated its value in providing a method of implementing complex instruction sets on small machines, thus permitting the great advantages of program compatibility to be realized over a whole range of machine sizes. It has also proved its worth in *emulation,* or the use of microprogramming (sometimes combined with systems programming) to give the user a reasonably efficient implementation of two or more instruction sets. Other uses which should be easy to justify are the complex functions, e.g., square root and trigonometric and Fourier analysis, where they can be shown to be frequent or critical computations.

9.14 MICROPROGRAMMING: AN EXAMPLE CONFIGURATION

To illustrate some of the principles of microprogram organization of machine controls, we consider a simple hypothetical machine quite similar to the structure used in the IBM System/360/370 (especially Mod 50).

The architecture of the example machine is indicated by the instruction format of the IR register (Fig. 9.14.1), whose bit groups have the following meanings:

OP	Bits 3–7	Operation code
I	Bit 2	Indirect addressing
R	Bits 8–11	One of 16 registers (usually for data)
X	Bits 12–15	One of 16 registers (same set as R but only right 16 bits are used as index)
A	Bits 16–31	Address

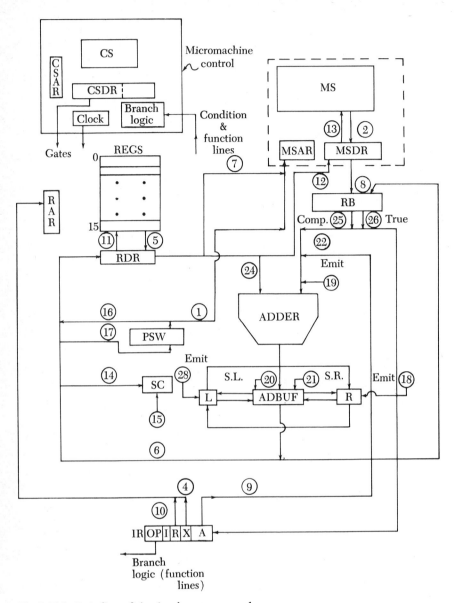

Fig. 9.14.1 Data flow of simple microprogrammed processor.

Most of the functions of instruction processing (instruction fetching, branch testing, indexing, and indirect addressing) have been discussed in this chapter; arithmetic operations were covered in Chap. 8. It is our present objective to get some feeling for how these can be implemented with a microprogrammed structure. We shall stop short of actually writing microprograms, since this is tedious, is different for each structure, and requires a specialized language.

Figure 9.14.1 shows a 32-bit-wide data flow of our machine which is seen to have the following resources:

1. ADDER   A combinational parallel adder circuit
2. ADBUF   Buffer register for adder output augmented by two bits (L,R). L,ADBUF,R may be shifted left or right in end-around fashion
3. IR   Instruction register holding the current instruction
4. REGS   A small fast store holding 16 general registers; selection of one of these is done via RAR (4 bits), and the selected register is sent to register RDR
5. RB   A data buffer register
6. SC   A shift counter
7. PSW   Program status word (32 bits) of which the rightmost 16 is the program counter
8. MS   Main storage with its address register (MSAR) and data register (MSDR)
9. Micromachine control (see Fig. 9.14.2 for detail)
   a. Control store (CS) with its address and data registers
   b. Microprogram branch logic; branches are determined in part by CSDR bits and in part by the state of selected bits in the data flow
   c. Gate lines from decoded bit groups of CSDR
   d. Clock lines to time gates

At various points in the data flow we see circled numbers indicating points where, at appropriate clock times, gate signals supplied by CSDR will cause information to move. For example, to fetch an instruction, the sequence of gate openings is:

PSW → MSAR	Gate 1
MEMORY ACCESS	
MSDR → RB	Gate 8
RB → R	Gate 25,3

The step MEMORY ACCESS involves only appropriate clock signals, not microprogram steps (this permits access to be made concurrently with routings in the data flow).

The upper left of Fig. 9.14.1 may be understood to be a primitive computer itself (a machine inside the machine!). Its instructions are the microinstructions

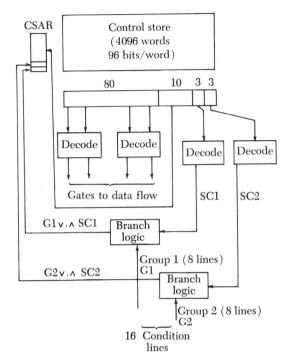

(a) Micromachine detail.

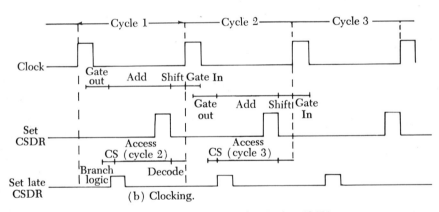

(b) Clocking.

Fig. 9.14.2 Micromachine control and clocking. (After Tucker, 1967.)

held in CS, and it obtains *its* data from the machine registers, condition lines, and flip-flops. The micromachine is shown in some detail in Fig. 9.14.2. The CSDR is not only the CS data register; it is also the micromachine instruction register, and hence its bit groupings say much about microinstruction meanings. These may be classified into four classes:

1. Gating signals which after decoding are sent to control the numbered points in the data flow
2. Emit signals which send bits to various flip-flops and registers
3. Next microinstruction address (fixed part)
4. Next microinstruction address (condition/function selectors)

The first two of these may be considered as essentially one class. We only remark that the grouping of CSDR bits to feed a given gates decoder is done so that no two output lines from the same decoder need be 1 at the same time. The last two categories refer to how *branching* is done in the microprogram. This may be described as follows:

1. The CSAR is not only the CS address register; it is also the micromachine program counter; i.e., it holds the location of the next microinstruction.
2. The 12 CSAR bits are determined as follows:
   a. 10 (or 6) bits are from CSDR, i.e., the current microinstruction.
   b. 2 bits are from two groups of branch conditions.

As a result of *2a,* every microinstruction contains the address of a set of four contiguous words in CS where the next microinstruction is located. One of these four is chosen by selected condition lines or flip-flops in the data flow (like adder overflow, sign bits of two registers alike, etc.). Since each of the two condition bits for CSAR is selected in a similar way, we describe only one. Typically, the bit selected is one of eight conditions; the chosen one is specified by a 3-bit condition-selector field in the microinstruction (CSDR). In other words, the final selection of the next microprogram word is done by selecting one condition each from two 8-bit groups.

Sometimes a 4-way branch choice as described above does not suffice. In such cases, a 64-way branch is provided by permitting 4 additional bits from the data flow to replace 4 of the CSDR-supplied bits in CSAR.

From what has been said thus far it might seem that a microinstruction can control only one gating at a time. This is not necessary since several CSDR fields can open several gates concurrently, which is desirable to achieve overlapped operations. However, it makes microprogramming resemble multiprocessing with its complexities of coordinating concurrent sequences.

Thus far, only microprogrammed control of CPU instructions has been discussed. Microprogramming can also be used to control I/O operations. One

approach applicable in small systems where economy is a paramount consideration is to have I/O control use the same registers as the CPU and also share its
micromachine. During I/O operations, the CPU resources then become a channel
(controller) rather than CPU, and CPU operations are not possible.

In larger systems like the IBM System/360 Mod 50, whose CPU structure
resembles Fig. 9.14.1 I/O and CPU operations can proceed concurrently except
for short periods of I/O sharing of the CPU. Each Mod 50 selector channel has
its own control circuitry for accumulating bytes from the I/O device into a
one-word (4-byte) buffer register. During accumulation of bytes into a word,
CPU and I/O control proceed independently. When an I/O word is available, it is
moved to main storage using CPU registers and microprogram control. The main
data-flow connection required is a path from the channel to the ADBUF register
of Fig. 9.14.1 Control of moving the word into storage is done by taking a
micromachine interrupt, whereby the CSAR is saved in a temporary register, the
microprogram enters "I/O mode" to move the incoming word (for input
operation) from ADBUF to main storage. CSAR is then restored, and CPU
microsequencing mode is resumed. (For more details see Husson, 1970.)

9.15   A SIMPLE MACHINE

An outline of the architecture and design of a simple, binary fixed-word
computer called SIMP/I will be presented to link together many of the principles
discussed in this and previous chapters. SIMP/I architecture is similar to the
IBM System/360 as far as internal operation on integers are concerned. However,
our example machine has very primitive I/O logic and no interrupt system.

The machine consists of the following resources:

1. A punched-card reader/punch
2. A printer
3. Main storage
4. Arithmetic-logic unit (ALU)

The information unit is a 32-bit word that can represent an instruction or data as
an integer in the signed 2s-complement form.

The architecture of the machine includes the following registers available to
the programmer:

1. A Program Status Word (PSW)

CC		Instruction address

The leftmost 2 bits are the *condition code* (CC) and are used to record the out-come of several instruction types. The CC is tested to make branching decisions. The rightmost 16 bits are the instruction address (program counter).

2. **Sixteen General Registers (32 Bits Each)** These registers are used as source/destination of data and also as index registers.

The instruction word is composed of several bit groups shown here as they appear in the instruction register. See Fig. 9.14.1 for the data-flow structure of SIMP/I.

```
               11    11           3
  0 1 2 3   78  12    56          1
IR O T I   OP   R1   X2   Address
```

Bit	Meaning
0	Always 0
1	Trace ON/OFF (used for debugging)
2	Indirect addressing (ON/OFF)
3–7	Operation code
8–11	One of the 16 general registers or branch mask
12–15	One of 16 general registers used for indexing
16–31	Address

Since most instructions reference main storage, an effective address must be computed. This is done by adding the rightmost 16 bits of the register specified by the X2 field and the 16-bit address field. If R denotes the registers as a bit matrix, where register I is row I, then the *effective address* EA (as a number) may be expressed as the APL sequence

$$[1]\ X2 \leftarrow {}^{-}4 \uparrow {}^{-}16 \downarrow IR$$
$$[2]\ ADR \leftarrow 2 \perp {}^{-}16 \uparrow IR$$
$$[3]\ EA \leftarrow ADR + 2 \perp {}^{-}16 \uparrow R[2 \perp X2;\,] \wedge \vee / X2$$

Addressing can proceed farther if bit 2 is 1, indicating indirect addressing. In this case, the rightmost 20 bits of the word at the effective address are routed to the corresponding positions of IR, and addressing is resumed. Thus the process specifies a new index register as well as address part of the instruction.

The arithmetic and Boolean instructions obtain and return operands as indicated in the following pseudo-APL statement:

$$R[R1;\,] \leftarrow R[R1;\,] o M[EA;\,]$$

Thus the $R1$ field of the instruction specifies a register that contributes an operand and also receives the result; the other operand is obtained at the effective address in main storage.

The multiplication and division instructions (MUL,DIV) as well as the long left and right shifts (LLSL,LRSL) involve a register pair, as required for example to hold the product or dividend. Such a pair are always in neighboring registers and always in the order even - odd. With this rule, the programmer states the even register, and the machine determines the next higher-numbered register by ORing a 1 into the $R1$ field (this saves a trip through the ADDER).

Figure 9.15.1 lists the instruction set for SIMP/I. Functionally the instructions may be considered in classes:

1. *Arithmetic*   ADD,SUB,MUL,DIV,COM,COML
2. *Boolean*   AND, EXR,OR
3. *Load and Store*   LOD,STO,LDA
4. *Shift*   LLSL,LRSL,SLSL,SRSL
5. *Sequence Control and Branching*   BAL,BC,HLT
6. *Input/Output*   RDX,RDA,WRX,WRA

Most of the arithmetic operations have been discussed in Chap. 8, and the reader is encouraged to try his hand at describing them in APL and also microprograms using the structure of Fig. 9.14.1. The two *compare* instructions (COM,COML) compare the word in register R1 with the word in storage, and the condition code is set to record the outcome of the comparison. The COM instruction treats both words as 32-bit signed integers, while COML (Compare-logical) treats them as 32-bit *un*signed integers. COML is therefore valuable for comparing characters as they appear packed into words, where the leftmost bit does not have the meaning of a sign bit. Note that several other instructions besides the compares also set the condition code.

The Boolean instructions AND,OR, and EXR (exclusive OR) each consider the two operand words as 32-bit vectors.

The load-and-store instructions (LOD,STO) move a word from/to main storage to/from a general register. The load-address (LDA) instruction clears the R1 register to 0 and then places the effective address into the rightmost 16 bits of this register.

The shift instructions shift either one register right or left by an amount equal to the effective address (SRSL,SLSL), or else this is done to two adjacent registers considered as a single long one. In all cases, vacated positions are filled with zeros.

The sequence-control instructions include the halt (HLT), which stops the machine's instruction sequencing. The BAL (branch-and-link) instruction is intended for subroutine linking and saves the PSW in the R1 register and then branches to the effective address. The BC instruction (branch on condition) is really several instructions since the R1 field is used as a "mask" to specify a condition to be tested; if the condition exists, the branch is to be taken. The condition itself is recorded (from a previous operation like a COM or COML) in

| | | 11 | 11 | 3 |
| 0 1 2 | 78 | 12 | 56 | 1 |

| O | T | I OP | R1 | X2 | Address | Instruction format |

Symbolic	Hexa	Word description	Condition code			
			0	1	2	3
ADD	01	Add	0	<0	>0	0vflo
AND	0D	And	0	≠0	—	—
BAL	11	Branch and link	—	—	—	—
BC	10	Branch on condition	—	—	—	—
COM	0C	Compare (register with storage)	EQ	LOW	HIGH	—
COML	18	Compare logical (unsigned 32 bits)	EQ	LOW	HIGH	—
DIV	04	Divide	0	≠0	—	—
EXR	0F	Exclusive OR	—	—	—	—
HLT	12	Halt	—	—	—	—
LDA	0A	Load address	—	—	—	—
LLSL	07	Long left-shift logical	—	—	—	—
LOD	09	Load (storage to register)	—	—	—	—
LRSL	08	Long right-shift logical	—	—	—	—
MUL	03	Multiply	—	—	—	—
OR	0E	OR	0	≠0	—	—
RDA	13	Read alphanumerically (20 words)	—	—	—	—
RDX	14	Read hexadecimally (10 words)	—	—	—	—
SLSL	05	Short left-shift logical	—	—	—	—
SRSL	06	Short right-shift logical	—	—	—	—
STO	0B	Store (register to storage)	—	—	—	—
SUB	02	Subtract	0	<0	>0	0vflo
WRX	15	Write alphanumerically (20 words)	—	—	—	—
WRX	16	Write hexadecimally (10 words)	—	—	—	—

Pseudo OP codes symbolic	Word description	Mask (hexa)
BE	Branch on equal	8
BL	Branch on less than	4
BH	Branch on high	2
BNH	Branch on not high (less than or equal)	D
BNL	Branch on not low (less than or greater)	B
BNE	Branch not equal	7
NOP	No operation	0
B	Branch unconditionally	F

Assembler statements

OP	Parameter	Word description
DC	N	Define unsigned integer constant N
DS	N	Define (reserve) next N words of storage
DORG	N	Define origin: set storage allocation counter to N
DTON		Set trace bit ON (=1) for following instructions
DTOF		Set trace bit OFF (=0) for following instructions
END		Delimiter for end-of-source program
*		An asterisk in column 1 indicates a comment

Fig. 9.15.1 SIMP/I Instruction set.

the two CC bits of the PSW. Branching is determined as follows; the two CC bits are used as a selector of one of the R1 bits, and if this bit is 1, the branch is taken; otherwise it is not. Note that as special cases R1 of 0 means no operation, and R1 of 15, that is, all 1s, specifies *un*conditional branch. R1 fields of 1000, 0100, and 0010 specify less-than, equal, and greater-than conditions, respectively. Also an R1 field of 1100 denotes a condition of less or equal (and similarly for other combinations). Since it is tedious for the programmer to remember these encodings of conditions, he may use abbreviations like BL, BE, BNH for branch less, branch equal or branch not high, etc. These designations are simply pseudomachine operations available in the assembler language. The assembler translator will compile any of these into a BC instruction with the proper R1 field.

The I/O instructions move card-image information between 10 or 20 contiguous main-storage words and a punched card or printed line. The R1 field of these instructions do not specify a register; instead they designate the I/O device as follows:

0   Card reader
1   Card punch
0   Printer

The RDA instruction interprets each card column as an 8-bit byte according to the card code given in Fig. 8.16.2. Four bytes are packed into a word, and hence the 80-byte card image is sent to 20 words starting at the one located at the effective address. The WRA instruction moves 20 words to the printed line (and advances the carriage to the next line).

The RDX and WRX instructions are intended for the simplest conversions between card-punch or print-character and binary (actually hexadecimal) encodings. The character alphabet is 0 through F; any other character, including blank, is interpreted as 0. Since each character is represented by 4 bits, eight card columns fill one word. A single RDX instruction reads 80 card columns into 10 contiguous words starting at the one specified by the effective address. WRX prints 80 hexa characters from 10 words in main storage. Since a single I/O instruction reads/prints only a single card or line, a program loop is usually required to read a deck of cards or print several lines.

SIMP/I is started by an IPL procedure as described in Sec. 9.1.

An assembler language and translator can be constructed using principles discussed in Sec. 3.3. The symbolic machine OP codes, pseudo OP codes, and assembler instructions are listed in Fig. 9.15.1. The form of a statement in the language is

Label   OP R1,ADDRESS,X2,I,T

The label means the name of the statement and is not required although every name used in the program must appear as a label exactly once. The R1 and X2 fields are integers from 0 through 15 and refer to general registers. The ADDRESS part is either a name or one of the simple expressions of the type shown below. The I indicates indirect addressing, and the T the trace bit. If any field is omitted, a default value of 0 is supplied automatically.

Example statements:

ADD 2,JOE,5,1,1	Indexing, indirect addressing, trace
SUB 2,JOE	No indexing, no indirect addressing, no trace
ADD 2,JOE+1,,1	Address 1 higher than JOE, trace
BL 0,*-4	Branch to "here minus" 4 words

Figure 9.15.2 shows a simple program to read and print cards. Also shown are the hexadecimal card images produced by the assembler (at the bottom). These

```
SIMP/I  APL ASSEMBLER
••••PASS 1••••


•••SYMBOL TABLE•••
NAME     ADDR.
 REP      0066
 FINI     006B
 BUF      006C
•••END OF FIRST PASS•••


••••SECOND PASS•••
••••••SOURCE STATEMENT•••••••••••• ADDR   INSTRUC.
(001)*PROGRAM TO READ AND PRINT CARDS
(002)*FIRST CARD OF DECK MUST BE A DELIMITER LIKE ZZZZ
(003)*LAST CARD MUST ALSO BE THE SAME DELIMITER
(004)      RDA 0,BUF        0064   1300006C
(005)      LOD 1,BUF        0065   0910006C
(006)REP   RDA 0,BUF        0066   1300006C
(007)      COML1,BUF        0067   1810006C
(008)      BE  0,FINI       0068   1080006B
(009)      WRA 0,BUF        0069   1500006C
(010)      B   0,REP        006A   10F00066
(011)FINI  HLT              006B   12000000
(012)BUF   DS  20           006C
(013)      END
•••END OF ASSEMBLY•••
NO. OF SIMP/I STORAGE WORDS REQUIRED= 28
CARD IMAGES: LOADER FIRST 3 CARDS
1400000A1400001414000017091000170510001006100010092000170520000C0620001C0B200016
0C20001510810000092000140932001708310000C2000161080000201100014012000141010F0000D
000000001000000000000000000
001800641300006C0910006C1300006C1810006C1080006B1500006C10F0006612000000
00200064
```

Fig. 9.15.2 SIMP/I assembler-language programs.

begin with a three-card bootstrap loader followed by the object cards in a format expected by this particular loader:

Column	Meaning
1–3	Card sequence number
4	Number of instructions on the card
5–8	Address of first instruction
9–80	Up to nine instructions

9.16 SUMMARY

Many of the architecture and design considerations in computer engineering have been discussed in this chapter. These include start-up (IPL), instruction sequencing, and how information is located (addressed) by the instructions. A judicious path through the maze of possible design choices can be found only if the designer has a good understanding not only of the possible options but also of the ways the machine uses its resources, especially main storage. Of special significance is the frequency-of-use pattern of storage reference and the idea of *locality,* i.e., the tendency of programs to dwell in small parts of the total store for relatively long periods of time.

Because of the nature of storage technology, most systems consist of a storage hierarchy (main store, disk, drum, tape, etc.). Such devices are slow compared to logic speeds, and the physical nature of many of these devices requires that access to them be controlled by a different mechanism than reference to main storage. This is the reason for specialized processors called *channels.*

Many modern systems run under an operating-system program; it manages all system resources for a stream of jobs that constitutes the workload of the system. Several hardware features are necessary for efficient operation of an operating system, especially one that multiprograms, i.e., permits several programs to share the machine's resources concurrently.

Microprogramming implementation of machine controls has proved an excellent way to provide extensive instruction sets on small machines so that it is now practical to make them program-compatible with larger machines. It also permits one machine to emulate another with reasonable efficiency, thus giving a desirable insulation of most users from changes in circuit technology. Specialized instructions and control of I/O devices are also feasible using microprogramming.

Some of the above considerations and a feel for machine programming can be obtained with a simple example machine like SIMP/I. The reader is urged to write assembler-language programs for this machine and explore construction of a machine simulator on both the functional level (using APL) and the microprogram level (see the problems).

PROBLEMS

9.1 Using the Neumann-Goldstine criterion, what is the largest matrix that should be inverted in a machine with the following:

a) A 32-bit fixed-point word?
b) A 32-bit floating-point word with 24-bit fraction, 8-bit sign and characteristic?

9.2 Name and describe the system feature most convenient for:

a) Specifying a constant for use by a single instruction
b) Changing a data value referenced in several places in a program
c) Changing a name appearing several places in a program
d) Using a data value to choose one of several branch locations

9.3 Consider the principle of locality of reference in the following situations, and briefly state your estimate of the relative extent to which the principle is satisfied. Assume all vector arrays are stored in contiguous storage cells and all examples use vector (not matrix) arrays. Chapter 3 may be consulted for details of specific algorithms.

a) Addition of two vectors
b) Inner product of two vectors
c) Binary search for match of an argument with an element of an ordered list
d) Search for match in an *m*-category list

9.4 In a certain machine designed for variable-field operands, a choice is to be made between specifying end of field by a length in the instruction or by a bit in every byte. Processor storage is to have 100,000 bytes.

a) Assuming BCD encoding, how many bits are required for length information in the instruction if instruction specification of field length is used?
b) How many field-mark bits are required in storage if the field-mark method is selected?
c) List other considerations besides number of bits for length specification in making the choice.

9.5 A certain computer is to have an instruction to compare a specified operand x against specified upper and lower limit values u, b and set indicators to indicate the outcome of the comparison. Enumerate the five possible outcomes of such a comparison.

9.6 Given: a push-down store as described in the text. Assume registers as follows:

$2{\perp}A{\equiv}056$
$2{\perp}B{\equiv}029$
$2{\perp}S{\equiv}394$
$2{\perp}M[394;]{\equiv}087$
$2{\perp}M[393;]{\equiv}044$

a) Show the state of the above after an ADD operation is performed. How many storage references are required?
b) After the ADD operation of part (*a*), suppose another ADD is to follow immediately; how many storage references are required?
c) If, after the ADD of part (*a*), an entry is made to the push-down list, how many storage references are required?

9.7 Discuss briefly the nature of the problem of permitting interrupts to be effective before completion of an instruction. Include the important factors of where such a feature may be needed and the nature of the cost to supply it.

9.8 Compare static and dynamic relocation with respect to:

a) Software properties
b) Required hardware (be specific)
c) Time for relocation (all in a clump or every reference)

9.9 Given a stream of n jobs with execution times given by vector X. If the first job starts at time $T0$:

a) Write an expression for the throughput in terms of n, $T0$, and X.
b) Consider the stream for which $T0{\equiv}0$; $X{\equiv}1,8,2,2,4$. Compute the throughput.
c) For the stream of (*b*) compute the elapsed time for each job. What is the *average* elapsed (response) time for this stream
d) Consider the same job times as in (*b*) only now reorder the jobs in ascending time order. Compute throughput and average response time. Compare with values obtained with (*b*) and (*c*). What do you conclude about the sensitivities of throughput and response time to job ordering?

9.10 List the four major hardware features found in most multiprogramming systems.

9.11 Using the example data-flow structure of Fig. 9.14.1, specify micro-sequenced (gate openings) for the following instructions (assume effective address is available in register ADBUF).

a) Store a register in memory
b) Store the PSW into register I and branch (BRANCH-AND-LINK)

9.12 Write a SIMP/I assembler-language program that reads a deck of alpha-numeric cards preceded by a control card, prints these cards, then sorts their images in main storage and prints the sorted images. Sort decisions are to be made using only columns 1 through 00*nn,* where *nn* are two hexadecimal digits specified in columns 3 and 4 of the control card. *Suggestions:* (1) use the bubble-sort algorithm as the basis of your program; (2) use the COML instruction for comparison of words in the sort field.

9.13 One way to understand the significance of various architecture features is to try programming and performance measurement on a machine without the features. Write two programs for the sort of Prob. 9.12 as follows:

a) Assume that only registers 0 and 1 are available and that these cannot be used for indexing. *Hint:* Use indirect addressing to simulate the index registers.
b) Assume the same as (*a*) except now indirect addressing is not available. *Hint:* This will require the program to modify the address part of instructions.

9.14 This is a project. Write a functional simulator for SIMP/1 in APL (or some other language). Include provisions for counting execution of each instruction type. Implement and trace bit as follows: if the bit is 1 in any instruction, print the PSW and 16 registers (in hexadecimal) after the instruction is executed.

REFERENCES

1. Beckman, F. S., F. P. Brooks, and W. J. Lawless, Jr.: Developments in the Logical Organization of Computer Arithmetic and Control Units, *Proc. IRE,* vol. 49, no. 1 (January 1961).
2. Bell, C. G., and A. Newell: "Computer Structures: Readings and Examples," McGraw-Hill Book Company, New York, 1971. (Contains extensive bibliography.)

3. Bock, R. V.: An Interrupt Control for the B5000 Data Processing System, *AFIPS Conf. Proc.,* 1963, pp. 229–241.

4. Buchholz, W.: "Planning a Computer System," McGraw-Hill Book Company, New York, 1962.

5. Burks, A. W., H. H. Goldstine, and J. von Neumann: Preliminary Discussion of the Logical Design of an Electronic Computing Instrument, Institute for Advanced Study, pt. I, June 28, 1946.

6. Burroughs Corp.: "B6500/7500 Information Systems Characteristics Manual   No. AA950739," Detroit, Mich. 1968.

7. Casale, C. T.: Planning the 3600, *Proc. AFIPS Fall Jt. Comput. Conf.,* 1962, pp. 73–85.

8. Clayton, B. B., E. K. Dorff, and R. E. Fagen: An Operating System and Programming Systems for the 6600, *Proc. AFIPS Fall Jt. Comput. Conf.,* 1964, vol. 26, pt. II.

9. Denning, P. J.: Virtual Memory, *ACM Comput. Surv.* vol. 2, no. 3 (September 1970).

10. Denning, P. J.: Third Generation Computing Systems, *ACM Comput. Surv.,* vol. 3, no. 4 (December 1971).

11. Dennis, J. B.: Segmentation and the Design of Multiprogrammed Computer Systems, *J. ACM,* vol. 12, no. 4, pp. 589–602 (October 1965).

12. Frankel, S. P.: The Logical Design of a Simple General Purpose Computer, *IRE Trans. Electron. Comput.,* March 1957.

13. Graselli, A.: The Design of Program-modifiable Microprogrammed Control Units, *IEEE Trans. Electron. Comput.,* vol. EC-11, pp. 336–339 (June 1962).

14. Green, J.: Microprogramming. Emulators and Programming Languages, *Commun. ACM,* vol. 9, no. 3, pp. 230–232 (March 1966).

15. Herwitz, P. S., and J. H. Pomerene: The Harvest System, *WJCC Proc.,* 1960, pp. 23–32.

16. S. S. Husson: "Microprogramming Principles and Practice," Prentice Hall Inc., Englewood Cliffs, N.J., 1970.

17. IBM Corporation: "A Guide to the IBM System/370 Model 155 (GC 20-1729)," White Plains, N.Y., 1970.

18. IBM Corporation: "IBM System/370 Principles of Operation (GA   22-7000)," White Plains, N.Y., 1970.

19. Illinois, University of: On the Design of a Very High Speed Computer, *Rept.* 80, 1957.

20. Kilburn, T., R. B. Payne, and D. J. Howarth: The ATLAS Supervisor, *Proc. East. Jt. Comput. Conf.,* 1961, pp. 279–294.

21. Kinslow, H. A.: The time-sharing Monitor System, *Proc. Fall Jt. Comput. Conf.,* 1964.

22. McCormack, M. A., T. T. Schansman, and K. K. Womack: 1401 Compatibility Feature on the IBM System/360 Model 30, *Comm. ACM,* vol. 8, no. 12 (December 1965).

23. Neumann, J. von, and H. H. Goldstine: Numerical Inverting of Matrices of High Order, *Bull. Am. Math. Soc.,* November 1947.

24. Rosin, R. F.: Contemporary Concepts of Microprogramming and Emulation, *ACM Comput. Surv.,* vol. 1, no. 4, pp. 197–212 (December 1969).

25. Thompson, R. N., and J. A. Wilkinson: The D 825 Automatic Operating and Scheduling Program, *AFIPS Conf. Proc.,* 1963, pp. 41–50.

26. Thornton, J. E.: Parallel Operation in the Control Data 6600, *AFIPS Proc. Fall Jt. Comput. Conf.,* 1964, vol. 26, pt. II.

27. Tucker, S. G.: Emulation of Large Systems, *Commun. ACM,* vol. 8, no. 12, pp. 753–761 (December 1965).

28. Tucker, S. G.: Microprogram Control for System/360, *IBM Syst. J,* vol. 6, no. 4, p. 222 (1967).

29. Wilkes, M. V.: Microprogramming, *Proc. East. Jt. Comput. Conf.,* December 1958.

10

The IBM System/360 and System/370

It is axiomatic in systems work that the whole of a system is something more than the sum of its parts; i.e., although it is an aggregate of parts, it has a behavior distinct from that deducible from even a thorough knowledge of the parts alone. For this reason, it is essential that any treatment of systems include not only descriptions and analyses of parts but also a consideration of one or more entire systems. Since most interesting systems are complex, the size of the description can be kept reasonable only by giving it in enough detail to display essentials or to impart insight into "what to look for," so that the reader can fill in detail according to his specific purposes.

In this chapter the IBM System/360 and System/370 will be described. Since the objectives are to illustrate principles discussed in previous chapters and to impart understanding not only of this particular system but of data-processing machines in general, we shall stop short of complete detail, say, on the level required to actually program the machine (such detail may be obtained from the manufacturer).

Specific planning for System/360 began in late 1961. A single architecture implemented by six models was announced in the spring of 1964. Deliveries began one year later.

In the following five years, several other models appeared, including the small Mods 20 and 25, the intermediate Mod 44, and the medium to large 65 and 75 (which replaced the originally announced models 60, 62, and 70, which were never produced). At the high-performance end there are Mod 85 and Mod 91.

Finally, we must mention the Mod 67, which is a Mod 65 fitted with a set of hardware features such as dynamic relocation registers, intended for use by a virtual-storage operating system. Although several programming systems using this principle were developed and used (TSS and CP/67 by IBM and MTS by the University of Michigan), none had achieved widespread acceptance. Virtual-storage operating systems for System/370 were announced by IBM in 1972.

The years 1965 to 1970 saw considerable adoption of the System/360 architecture, accompanied by a very great investment in programming. Concurrently, progress in technology was bringing monolithic circuits and memories to practical maturity with its low cost, high speed, and improved reliability. These facts help explain why IBM's successor generation to System/360, the System/370, maintains the 360 architecture and hence complete program compatibility (although some rather minor additions were made) while the *internal* organization of the new models often differs significantly from that used in System/360.

Uniform architecture among models means that they all handle identical data representations and can have the same instruction repertoire. Machine-language programs are therefore compatible among the models, although memory capacity and I/O configuration also influence the degree of actual program compatibility which can be realized. Compatibility among the models reduces the cost of developing compilers and monitor programs. More direct savings also accrue to the customer, who often must run the same program on a variety of system sizes, e.g., when he expands his facilities to include a larger system.

The decision to adhere strictly to uniform architecture over all models profoundly influenced many design decisions. For example, to be performance-competitive, the large machines had to have a rich instruction repertoire, which implied complex and expensive control hardware. The small machines had to have the same repertoire yet be low in price. To solve this paradox, a new technology (at least to IBM) and a new type of organization of machine controls were developed. In all but the largest models, internal control sequences are stored as microprograms in a fast but relatively cheap read-only storage (ROS) instead of being generated by expensive transistor logic circuits. Also, control logic is systematized, simplifying design and maintenance.

The control-storage implementation of machine control logic makes feasible the *emulator,* i.e., a set of alternative and additional microprograms designed to enable System/360/370 to execute programs written for other machines such as the IBM 1401. Such emulators ease the programming costs to the customer in his long-term reprogramming.

Although all models have the same architecture, the speed of any given model is determined by its particular hardware organization and component speeds. The primary factor in obtaining increased speed in the larger systems is the increased use of parallel memory and data-flow structures. The larger models also employ interleaved access to multiple storage units and overlap between more parts of instruction execution.

The principle of uniform architecture also applies to the I/O part of the system. An I/O *channel* is a logical entity that controls transmission of information between processor storage and an external device. The transmission is under stored program control by the channel. Such a program is logically independent from, and hence can be overlapped with, the CPU program. A channel program can communicate with a CPU program by means of the interrupt system and the mechanism of initiation of a channel program. CPU instructions may sense, initiate, or halt channel activity. Implementations of the channels differ among processor models. In the smaller systems there is a good deal of sharing of circuitry and ROS between the channel and the processor. In the larger models these logically distinct units are closer to being physically distinct. High-speed devices are controlled by a type of implementation called a *selector* channel. Another type of channel implementation, called the *multiplexor* channel, is designed to interleave control of several low-speed devices by having a high multiplicity of logical channels timeshare one common set of channel control circuits. A multiplexor channel can also be operated as a single selector channel.

System/360 architecture makes specific provisions to aid automatic control of the equipment by a supervisor program. For example, certain instructions are *privileged* and can be executed only when the machine is in the privileged mode. These instructions select all I/O devices, initiate channel programs, and control the interrupt and storage-protection parts of the system. The privileged mode is essential to multiprogramming, including multiple remote users sharing the system under control of a supervisor program, as in a timesharing system.

10.1   DATA REPRESENTATIONS

The smallest unit of data addressable by an instruction is the 8-bit byte. Although each 8-bit storage byte is accompanied by a parity bit for checking, to the user the word "byte" denotes an 8-bit quantity in System/360 unless otherwise stated. One 8-bit byte may represent any one of the following: one alphanumeric character, two binary-coded-decimal (BCD) digits, one decimal digit in zoned format, 8 bits of logical (Boolean) data, a portion of a fixed-point or floating-point word. The size of the byte was chosen as 8 bits primarily to accommodate an extended character set (up to 256 characters may be represented). For storing a single BCD digit, an 8-bit byte is wasteful since only 4 bits are required. A packed-decimal representation is therefore provided that packs two BCD digits into an 8-bit byte.

Once the 8-bit byte was selected, for the reasons noted above, it was desirable for

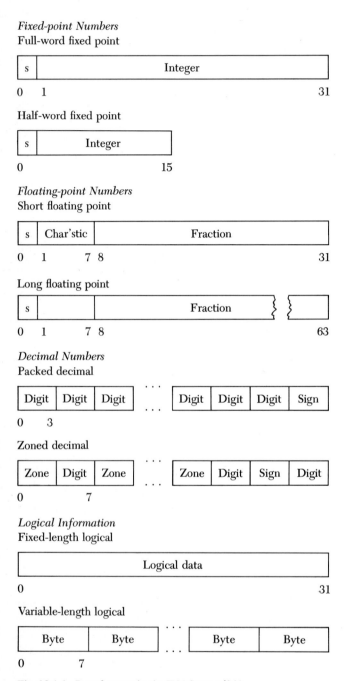

Fixed-point Numbers
Full-word fixed point

Half-word fixed point

Floating-point Numbers
Short floating point

Long floating point

Decimal Numbers
Packed decimal

Zoned decimal

Logical Information
Fixed-length logical

Variable-length logical

Fig. 10.1.1 Data formats in the IBM System/360.

uniformity and simplicity of the addressing structure that larger data units be an integral numbers of bytes. Ability to specify any length of operand (in bytes), at least to some limit, leads to storage economy and programming simplicity for manipulating bit or character strings (e.g., for editing) and decimal numbers such as are encountered in commercial data processing.

In commercial data processing, the variable-length feature is valuable because numbers of many different lengths are encountered, although the lengths are known in advance. For these reasons, instructions to manipulate logical operands may specify variable lengths from 1 to 256 bytes; BCD operands may be specified in lengths of 2 to 32 digits (including 1 sign digit). Since it is not feasible to provide registers for variable-length operands, all instructions of this type obtain operands and return results to storage.

The binary radix is most desirable for addressing because of its storage efficiency and high resolution. Once binary addressing is adopted, binary fixed-point arithmetic is essential for address arithmetic. It is also valuable for data representation and manipulation. For addressing purposes, the fixed-length data unit(s) must be an integral number of bytes, i.e., a multiple of 8 bits. A 2-byte (16-bit or *half-word*) data unit is provided for limited-precision work where storage efficiency is paramount, as in many data-reduction and process-control applications. A major early decision in System/360 architecture was to enable most instructions to uniformly address a large storage of about 4 million fixed-point words. To provide reasonable precision, a word would have to be from 3 to 6 bytes long. This meant that the 4 million words of storage required 12 to 24 million bytes, which in turn required an address of 24 or 25 bits. To obtain, in a simple way, full arithmetic power in manipulating addresses, it is desirable to use common arithmetic conventions for both data and address modification. A fixed-point data unit of at least 24 bits was therefore indicated. This length, however, was judged insufficient for precision of data; the next multiple of 8 bits is 32 bits. This length (four bytes) appeared to be the best compromise between storage efficiency and necessary fixed-point precision. A 32-bit (4-byte) quantity is called, in System/360, a *word.*

By 1961, when System/360 was in the planning stage, floating-point arithmetic was an established means for representing numbers of a wide and uncertain range, as is commonly encountered in scientific problems. In choosing lengths of floating-point operands, the first constraint was imposed by addressing—the length must be a multiple of 8 bits. A dichotomy between a short length for maximum storage efficiency and a long length for best precision usually exists in such a choice. Thus, instead of a single length, two lengths were selected: a 32-bit (4-byte) word and a 64-bit (8-byte) double word. All floating-point instructions may specify either length of operand. (The 56-bit fraction part of the long floating-point word will also satisfy most requirements for fixed-point numbers longer than 31 bits.)

As indicated above, both decimal and binary representations and associated instructions are provided in System/360. Decimal arithmetic is especially useful where there is relatively little internal computation per I/O operation (this is typical of many commercial problems). In the contrary case full logical power is obtainable only with logical operations and binary arithmetic. Accordingly, System/360 includes instructions to convert decimal data to binary, and vice versa.

To summarize the results of the above discussion of System/360 data representations, the basic addressable unit of data is the 8-bit byte accompanied by 1 parity-check bit.

Fixed-point binary data are available in two lengths, half word and word (2 or 4 bytes). In each case the representation is binary signed 2s complement.

Floating-point data may be represented in a short 4-byte form or a long 8-byte form. Both forms use a 7-bit characteristic which is interpreted as an excess-64 exponent of 16. The range of the normalized floating-point numbers corresponds to

$$10^{-78} < n < 10^{75}$$

The fraction is represented in signed true form. The short and long floating-point numbers differ only in the length of their fractions, these being 24 and 56 respectively (see Fig. 8.15.1).

A decimal operand may be represented as a variable-length number in packed form, in which case two BCD digits are packed into each byte with the sign of the number being the rightmost half byte. In the zoned decimal representation, a full 8-bit byte is used to represent each decimal digit. Instructions are provided to convert binary and zoned decimal to packed decimal and packed decimal to binary. Decimal arithmetic is provided only on packed decimal operands.

Logical data may be represented in either fixed-length form, in which case it comprises 4 bytes (a word), or else by a variable number of 8-bit bytes.

10.2 REGISTERS AND ADDRESSING

The architecture includes the following registers, which may be referenced by an instruction:

1. Sixteen general registers, each 32 bits, used to hold operands or addresses. Certain 4-bit fields in the instruction, yielding a number from 0 to 15, refer to registers. Sometimes a single reference implies a reference to an even-odd pair of registers.

2. Four floating-point registers, each 64 bits. Certain 4-bit fields in certain instructions, yielding an even number, refer to floating-point registers.

Since the same registers may be used for either addressing information or for data, the manner of reference is specified in the *format* of the instruction. There are five instruction formats which differ in the way in which the bits of the instruction are interpreted to produce the effective addresses. The next section discusses these in some detail; the present discussion confines attention to some general properties of the addressing system.

All addresses are binary numbers.

An effective address specifies the location of a byte in storage; this is the first byte of the operand. For fixed-length operands, length of the operand is implicit in the instruction operation code. In these cases the effective address must be a multiple of the operand length (in bytes). Variable-length operands may also be specified with certain operations; the length is then specified explicitly in the instruction.

An effective address to storage is *not* normally given in the instruction directly. It is automatically computed by adding the contents of a register specified by 4 bits in the instruction to a 12-bit *displacement* field extracted from the instruction. The contribution taken from the register is always its rightmost 24 bits; hence up to 2^{24} (about 16 million) bytes may be addressed even though only 16 instruction bits are used for specifying the address. (One class of instruction also specifies a second register to contribute to the sum which produces the effective address.)

Most instructions specify an operation and two addresses, called the first and second addresses. The operands at the first and second addresses are combined per the instruction operation; the result operand replaces the first operand.

Except in the case of program branching, successive instruction addresses are obtained by updating (incrementing) a program counter. Since an instruction may be 2, 4, or 6 bytes in length, the updating is by one of these numbers as specified in the operation code of each instruction. At instruction fetch, the program counter must contain an even number. In System/360, the program counter is considered as only one component of the processor state; this state is called the *program status word* (PSW) and comprises 64 bits. The PSW includes all the status information about the CPU necessary to capture the state of a program if it is interrupted. In addition to the program counter, the PSW includes the mask bits for the interrupt system, condition code, address protection key, and instruction-length code and contains space for automatic storage of interrupt status bits. Half of the PSW is accessible, at least for modification, only to privileged instructions; the other half is available to the programmer. The PSW is automatically loaded and stored as a single unit during interrupt procedures.

Storage protection, standard on models 50 and higher and optional on the others, is intended to allow a supervisor program to control the areas of storage which can be modified by other programs (an optional feature can also control

Legend

0-origin indexing

I	Instruction bit matrix $\rho I \equiv 3,16$
A	Vector of addresses $\rho A \equiv 3$
R	General registers
	$\rho R \equiv 16,32$
L	Vector of field lengths $\rho L \equiv 3$
F	Floating-point registers
	$\rho F \equiv 4,64$
M	Storage-matrix of bits
	$\rho M \equiv 8$
	$M[AT;] \equiv 1$ byte (row AT of M)
	$M[AT+\iota N;] \equiv N$-successive bytes, the first is $M[AT;]$
F	Format designator
	0–RR
	1–RX
	2–RS
	3–SS
	4–SI

```
    ∇EFFADR F
[1]    →(RR,RX,RS,SS,SI)[F]
[2]    RR:A[2]←2⊥¯4↑I[0;]
[3]    →A1
[4]    RS:A[3]←2⊥¯4↑I[0;]
[5]    J←0
[6]    →A2
[7]    RX:J←J←2⊥(0≠2⊥¯4↑I[0;])∧R[2⊥¯4↑I[0;]]
[8]    A2:A[2]←(2*24)|J+(2⊥¯12↑I[1;])+2⊥(0≠2⊥14↑I[1;])∧R[2⊥14↑I[1;];]
[9]    A1:A[1]←2⊥¯8↑I[0;]
[10]   →0
[11]   SS:L←(2⊥¯8↑I[0;]),(2⊥¯8↑I[0;]),2⊥¯4↑I[0;]
[12]   A[2]←(2*24)|(2⊥¯12↑I[2;])+2⊥(0≠2⊥14↑I[2;])∧R[2⊥14↑I[2;];]
[13]   A[1]←(2*24)|(2⊥¯12↑I[1;])+2⊥(0≠2⊥14↑I[1;])∧R[2⊥14↑I[1;];]
    ∇
```

(a) Effective address (see Ref. [1])

Addressing rules:

1. All storage addressing is to the byte.
2. Instruction address must be even. Instruction length 2, 4, 6.
3. Data address must be multiple of length (except VFL).
4. If rules 1 to 3 are violated, a "specification" interrupt-request is generated.

Operand type	No. bytes	No. bits
Byte	1	8
Half-word	2	16
Full-word	4	32
Double word	8	64
VFL	1–256	8–2048

Format diagram header: $I[0;]$ | $I[1;]$ | $I[2;]$ with bit positions 0 7 11 12 15 | 0 4 15 | 0 14 15

Format	Fields	Representative operations	Remarks
RR	OP code | R1 | R2	$R[A[1];]\leftarrow R[A[1];]\circledcirc R[A[2];]$ $F[A[1]\div2;]\leftarrow F[A[1]\div2;]\circledcirc F[A[2]\div2;]$	Register-register operations
RX	OP code | R1 | X2 | B2 | D2	$R[A[1];]\leftarrow R[A[1];]\circledcirc M[A[2]]+\iota N;$ $F[A[1]\div2;]\leftarrow F[A[1]\div2;]\circledcirc M[A[2]]+\iota N;$	$N\equiv2,4$ in most cases (half or full word) .... $N\equiv4,8$ for floating point
RS	OP code | R1 | R3 | B2 | D2	$R[A[1];]\leftarrow(S\rho0),(-S+64|A[2])\uparrow R[A[1];]$ $R[A[1];]\leftarrow(S\uparrow R[A[1]),(S+64|A[2])\rho0$ *LOGICAL RIGHT AND LEFT SHIFT*	Arithmetic shifts; logical shifts One register or an even-odd numbered pair Load and store multiple registers
SI	OP code | 12 | B1 | D1	$M[A[1];]\leftarrow M[A[1];]\circledcirc{}^{-}8\uparrow[0;]$	Storage and immediate operand 1-byte data
SS	OP code | L1 | L2 | B1 | D1 | B2 | D2	$M[LT;]\leftarrow M[LT\leftarrow A[1]+\iota1+L[0];]\circledcirc M[A[2]+\iota1+L[0];]$	VFL—storage-storage operands; up to 256 bytes

(b) Formats.

Fig. 10.3.1 S/360 addressing rules and instruction formats.

READ access as well as WRITE access). Each block of 2^{11} (2048) bytes may be assigned a 4-bit protection tag by a privileged instruction. These tags are kept in a special tag memory. A 4-bit *protection key* is included in the PSW; this designates the tag corresponding to storage blocks which are currently legally accessible. Assuming, for illustration, both read and write protection, each effective address to storage results in a match test between the protection key and the tag; if these do not match, the access is not made and the program may be interrupted.† Each channel has a *channel status word* (CSW) which is the analog of the PSW and includes its own protection key. The use of the tag principle allows a program to occupy noncontiguous space in storage; this facilitates segmentation and relocation of segments of programs under dynamic conditions.

Certain operations are automatically monitored for invalidity by the machine and if detected can signal the program by interrupt. In the addressing system, there are two types of these *exceptions*. An address exception occurs if any effective address is outside of the range of available storage for the particular machine. A specification exception occurs for a variety of reasons. These include an odd-numbered effective address to an instruction or a reference to a fixed-length operand in storage which is not a multiple of its length.

10.3 INSTRUCTION FORMATS

An instruction may comprise one, two, or three half words (2, 4, or 6 bytes) corresponding to 16, 32, or 48 bits, respectively.

An instruction is in one of five formats; these differ in the way the effective address(es) are determined from the instruction bits. An *effectice address* specifies an operand by giving the number of a general or floating-point register or a storage location of the operand (see Fig. 10.3.1).

In all formats the first instruction byte specifies the operation code. The leftmost 2 bits of this byte specify the instruction as RR, RX, RS or SI, SS format. In these designations R denotes *register,* X denotes *index,* I denotes *immediate,* and S denotes *storage.* The 2 format bits imply the length of the instruction.

In all instructions of more than one half word, the second and third half words are each composed of a 4-bit portion specifying a general register used as a base address and a 12-bit portion used as an unsigned increment (displacement) to the base address. (Reference to the base or index register numbered 0 signals no

---

†An exception to the match requirement of key and tag is when the key bits are all 0. In this case all tags are considered to match. Thus the supervisor (0-key) can access all areas.

RR Format

xxxx	BRANCHING AND STATUS SWITCHING 0000xxxx		FIXED-POINT FULL WORD AND LOGICAL 0001xxxx		FLOATING-POINT LONG 0010xxxx		FLOATING-POINT SHORT 0011xxxx	
0000			LPR	LOAD POSITIVE	LPDR	LOAD POSITIVE	LPER	LOAD POSITIVE
0001			LNR	LOAD NEGATIVE	LNDR	LOAD NEGATIVE	LNER	LOAD NEGATIVE
0010			LTR	LOAD AND TEST	LTDR	LOAD AND TEST	LTER	LOAD AND TEST
0011			LCR	LOAD COMPLEMENT	LCDR	LOAD COMPLEMENT	LCER	LOAD COMPLEMENT
0100	SPM	SET PROGRAM MASK	NR	AND	HDR	HALVE	HER	HALVE
0101	BALR	BRANCH AND LINK	CLR	COMPARE LOGICAL				
0110	BCTR	BRANCH ON COUNT	OR	OR				
0111	BCR	BRANCH/CONDITION	XR	EXCLUSIVE OR				
1000	SSK	SET KEY	LR	LOAD	LDR	LOAD	LER	LOAD
1001	ISK	INSERT KEY	CR	COMPARE	CDR	COMPARE	CER	COMPARE
1010	SVC	SUPERVISOR CALL	AR	ADD	ADR	ADD N	ALR	ADD N
1011			SR	SUBTRACT	SDR	SUBTRACT N	SER	SUBTRACT N
1100			MR	MULTIPLY	MDR	MULTIPLY	MER	MULTIPLY
1101			DR	DIVIDE	DDR	DIVIDE	DER	DIVIDE
1110			ALR	ADD LOGICAL	AWR	ADD U	AUR	ADD U
1111			SLR	SUBTRACT LOGICAL	SWR	SUBTRACT U	SUR	SUBTRACT U

RX Format

xxxx	FIXED-POINT HALF WORD AND BRANCHING 0100xxxx		FIXED-POINT FULL WORD AND LOGICAL 0101xxxx		FLOATING-POINT LONG 0110xxxx		FLOATING-POINT SHORT 0111xxxx	
0000	STH	STORE	ST	STORE	STD	STORE	STE	STORE
0001	LA	LOAD ADDRESS						
0010	STC	STORE CHARACTER						
0011	IC	INSERT CHARACTER						
0100	EX	EXECUTE	N	AND				
0101	BAL	BRANCH AND LINK	CL	COMPARE LOGICAL				
0110	BCT	BRANCH ON COUNT	O	OR				
0111	BC	BRANCH/CONDITION	X	EXCLUSIVE OR				
1000	LH	LOAD	L	LOAD	LD	LOAD	LE	LOAD
1001	CH	COMPARE	C	COMPARE	CD	COMPARE	CE	COMPARE
1010	AH	ADD	A	ADD	AD	ADD N	AE	ADD N
1011	SH	SUBTRACT	S	SUBTRACT	SD	SUBTRACT N	SE	SUBTRACT N
1100	MH	MULTIPLY	M	MULTIPLY	MD	MULTIPLY	ME	MULTIPLY
1101			D	DIVIDE	DD	DIVIDE	DE	DIVIDE
1110	CVD	CONVERT-DECIMAL	AL	ADD LOGICAL	AW	ADD U	AU	ADD U
1111	CVB	CONVERT-BINARY	SL	SUBTRACT LOGICAL	SW	SUBTRACT U	SU	SUBTRACT U

RS, SI Format

xxxx	BRANCHING STATUS SWITCHING AND SHIFTING 1000xxxx		FIXED-POINT LOGICAL AND INPUT/OUTPUT 1001xxxx		1010xxxx	1011xxxx
0000	SSM	SET SYSTEM MASK	STM	STORE MULTIPLE		
0001			TM	TEST UNDER MASK		
0010	LPSW	LOAD PSW	MVI	MOVE		
0011		DIAGNOSE	TS	TEST AND SET		
0100	WRD	WRITE DIRECT	NI	AND		
0101	RDD	READ DIRECT	CLI	COMPARE LOGICAL		
0110	BXH	BRANCH/HIGH	OI	OR		
0111	BXLE	BRANCH/LOW-EQUAL	XI	EXCLUSIVE OR		
1000	SRL	SHIFT RIGHT SL	LM	LOAD MULTIPLE		
1001	SLL	SHIFT LEFT SL				
1010	SRA	SHIFT RIGHT S				
1011	SLA	SHIFT LEFT S				
1100	SRDL	SHIFT RIGHT DL	SIO	START I/O		
1101	SLDL	SHIFT LEFT DL	TIO	TEST I/O		
1110	SRDA	SHIFT RIGHT D	HIO	HALT I/O		
1111	SLDA	SHIFT LEFT D	TCH	TEST CHANNEL		

SS Format

xxxx	1100xxxx	LOGICAL 1101xxxx		1110xxxx	DECIMAL 1111xxxx	
0000						
0001		MVN	MOVE NUMERIC		MVO	MOVE WITH OFFSET
0010		MVC	MOVE		PACK	PACK
0011		MVZ	MOVE ZONE		UNPK	UNPACK
0100		NC	AND			
0101		CLC	COMPARE LOGICAL			
0110		OC	OR			
0111		XC	EXCLUSIVE OR			
1000					ZAP	ZERO AND ADD
1001					CP	COMPARE
1010					AP	ADD
1011					SP	SUBTRACT
1100		TR	TRANSLATE		MP	MULTIPLY
1101		TRT	TRANSLATE AND TEST		DP	DIVIDE
1110		ED	EDIT			
1111		EDMK	EDIT AND MARK			

NOTE: N = NORMALIZED   DL = DOUBLE LOGICAL   S = SINGLE
       SL = SINGLE LOGICAL   U = UNNORMALIZED   D = DOUBLE

Fig. 10.3.2 S/360 operation codes.

register used.) Parts of the instruction are labeled R, X, D, or L followed by a number designating the first or second operand. In most instructions two addresses are specified; the first address is also the address of the result. In the RR, RX, and RS formats the first operand is contained in a register. In the RR format the second operand is also contained in a register; in the RX format the second operand is obtained from storage with the X2 field specifying a register for indexing; i.e., its contents are added to the contents of the register specified by the B2 field and to the D2 displacement to form the effective address. In the SI format the first operand (and hence the result) is a byte in storage; the second operand is *immediate,* i.e., is extracted from the second byte of the instruction itself. The SS format specifies a variable number of bytes in storage-storage operations. For logical operations both operand lengths are the same, and 8 instruction bits are used to specify the length as a number of bytes *beyond* the addressed byte. For packed decimal instructions the length is given separately for each operand; each 8-bit byte is then considered as two 4-bit digits. Maximum variable lengths are therefore 256 bytes for logical data and 32 digits (16 bytes) for decimal data. System/370 permits longer fields (see Sec. 10.8).

Figure 10.3.2 shows mnemonics and the assignment of operation code bits to all instructions.

10.4 BRANCH-TYPE INSTRUCTIONS

As in most computers, a program counter is maintained to "point" to the storage location of the next instruction. In System/360, the 24 bits of the program counter are the rightmost 24 bits of a 64-byte logical register called the program status word (PSW) P. The *condition code* (CC) consists of bits 34, 35 of the PSW; these are set implicitly in most data-manipulation instructions to indicate some property of the result. COMPARE instructions explicitly specify a test on data or status and record the outcome in the CC. For example, a COMPARE instruction can specify comparison of two operands with the CC set as follows:

> 0,0   If both operands are equal
> 0,1   If the first operand is low
> 1,0   If the first operand is high

Branch-on-condition instructions test the condition code and replace the program-counter contents or not, as the condition is or is not satisfied. Bits 8 to 11 of such an instruction are a "mask" in which the programmer specifies the desired condition-code state for branching. One of these bits is selected by the condition code. In the microprogram description of Fig. 10.4.1 this is shown by step 2, which determines the integer J as a number between 8 and 11, depending on the CC $P[34,35]$; J is then used to select a bit in the mask field of the first half word of the instruction $I[0;J]$ for test. If the mask bit thus selected is zero, there is no replacement of the program counter $P[40+\iota24]$; otherwise it is replaced by the branch location. Steps 5 and 7 show the replacement for the RR and RX format versions of the instruction. In the case of the RX type of BOC instruction, the program counter is replaced by the address $A[2]$ which is computed in the usual way for RX format instructions. Two special cases of BOC are mask bits all 0 and all 1s. These yield a no-operation and unconditional branch, respectively.

BRANCH-AND-LINK (BAL or BALR) instructions are intended to facilitate subroutine control. There are two versions, one in the RX and the other in the RR format. In both cases the rightmost 32 bits of the PSW which contains the program counter are stored in a specified register, and the program branches by having its program counter replaced as described above. Notice that this instruction "saves," in a specified register, not only the program counter but also the program (interrupt) mask, condition code, and instruction-length code.

The branch-on-count instruction is a composite operation that decreases the contents of a specified register by 1 and then tests the result for 0. If the register contents are 0, the program branches to the second effective address $A[2]$; otherwise the program continues in sequence. The instruction may be specified in the RR or RX formats, which differ only in the manner of determining $A[2]$.

More powerful register update-test-branch facility is provided in the complementary instructions BRANCH ON INDEX HIGH (BXH) and BRANCH ON INDEX LOW/EQUAL (BXLE). In these instructions, which are in the RS format, a sum is formed of the contents of two registers; this sum is compared with the contents of one of the registers (or the one numbered one higher), and a program branch is taken to the second address if the condition specified in the operation code is satisfied. Finally, the sum of the registers obtained before comparison replaces the register specified by the first address. Notice that the sum of the registers is compared with the original contents of the comparand register; if this register is the same as the one eventually receiving the sum, the initial value is used in comparison. The process is described in the microprogram which shows the register sum developed as the variable K in line 1; the register designator $A[3]$ is then replaced by the nearest odd integer equal to or larger than itself (line 2). Line 3 is the main control point in this microprogram: it specifies a selection of the next microstatement as $B1$ or $B2$, the selection depending on both the instruction type (U) corresponding to BXH or BXLE and whether the register sum K is larger than the contents of the comparand register. Step 6 is selected if the condition for a branch is satisfied; the mechanism of the branch consists of replacing the rightmost 24 bits of the PSW by $A[2]$. The final step of the program, whether the branch is taken or not, is the replacement of the register $A[1]$ by the sum K.

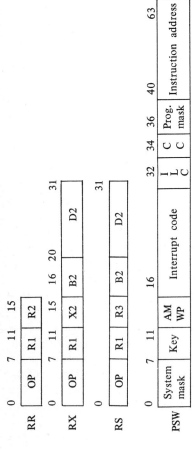

(a) Formats of branch instructions and PSW.

```
     ∇BOC I
[1]  →(TST,SEL)[I]
[2]  TST:J←8+2⊥P[34,35]
[3]  →(0=I[0;J])/0
[4]  SEL:→(B1,B2)[F]
[5]  B1:P[40+⍳24]←((A[2]≠0)∧¯24↑R[A[2];])∨(A[2]=0)∧¯24↑P
[6]  →0
[7]  B2:P[40+⍳24]←(24⍴0)⊤A[2]
     ∇
```

(b) Branch on condition (BC, BCR).

```
     ∇BCTBCTR
[1]  R[A[1];]←(32⍴2)⊤¯1+2⊥R[A[1];]
[2]  →(0=∨/R[A[1];])/0
[3]  BOC 1
     ∇
```

(c) Branch on count (BCT, BCTR).

```
         ∇BX
[1]   K←2⊥R[A[1];]+2⊥R[A[3];]
[2]   A[3]←A[3]+~I[0;15]
[3]   →(B1,B2)[U=K>2⊥R[A[3];]]
[4]   B1:R[A[1];]←(32ρ0)⊤K
[5]   →0
[6]   B2:P[40+ι24]←(24ρ2)⊤A[2]
[7]   →B1
         ∇
```

(d) Branch on index high (BXH) or on index low/equal (BXLE).

```
         ∇BAL
[1]   R[A[1];]←⁻32↑P
[2]   BOC 1
         ∇
```

(e) Branch and link (BAL, BALR).

Note: Programs (c) and (d) are only valid for R[I;] representing a nonnegative value.

Legend

0-origin indexing	
P	Program status word
	$2\bot P[34,35]\equiv$ condition code
I	Instruction bits, each row of I is a half word
	$PI\equiv3,16$
R	General registers $\rho R\equiv16,32$
A[1,2,3]	Effective addresses (see Fig. 10.3.1)
F	Format indicator; $F\equiv0\rightarrow RR;F\equiv1\rightarrow RX$
U	Instruction indicator
	$U\equiv1\rightarrow BXH;U\equiv0\rightarrow BXLE$

Fig. 10.4.1 Branch-type instructions.

10.5 OTHER INTERESTING INSTRUCTIONS

Figure 10.5.1 describes several instructions by functional microprograms. Two of these are used to load or store any set of contiguously numbered registers (LOAD, STORE, MULTIPLE).

The TRANSLATE instruction treats a field of up to 256 bytes as a set of byte arguments to another field; the byte-by-byte look-up results in byte-by-byte replacement of the argument field. Another instruction also including successive look-ups byte-by-byte is TRANSLATE-AND-TEST. Here each byte of the first field is used as an argument to the second field, but now the result byte is tested for 0. If 0 (i.e., all bits are 0), the next argument byte is taken and the process continues. When a nonzero function byte is encountered, this signals instruction end. The address of the argument byte is stored in register 1, the function byte is stored in the rightmost 8 bits of register 2. The condition code ($P[34,35]$) is set to indicate the conditions under which the instruction end was reached. A condition code of 0 is set if the process reached the last argument byte in the field and only then encountered a function byte of 0. If the first nonzero function byte is encountered before the last look-up, the condition code is set to 1; otherwise it is set to 2.

10.6 INTERRUPT PRINCIPLES

The purpose of the program-interruption facility is to provide automatic (hardware) monitoring of certain exceptional conditions and, when they arise, to force the CPU to gracefully switch its facilities from whatever program is currently active to a new program responsive in some way to the detected condition. The interruption mechanism facilitates the sharing of the CPU and certain common programs by several logically independent programs. It also improves the response time to detected exceptional conditions since these are monitored by fast circuitry instead of by program test (as in a noninterrupt system). Examples of interrupt-request conditions include end-of-transmission of an I/O device, interval-timer-contents-are-0, overflow conditions in processing, execution of a SUPERVISOR CALL instruction.

Program interrupt, whose major effect is forcing a program branch, should not be confused with break-in or cycle-stealing, where an I/O channel or other external unit may force a pause in processing while one or more memory cycles are taken for data transmission or control. In this case, although there is often delay in processing due to *memory interference,* this delay imposes no logical problem for the programmer. Most problem programmers are shielded from detailed interrupt-system control by the supervisor program or other parts of the operating system. On the other hand, people engaged in design of operating systems or control programs must thoroughly understand the interrupt system.

```
     ∇LMSTM  I                              ∇TR
[1]  AT←A[2]                          [1]  A[0]←(2*24)|A[1]+L[0]
[2]  RT←A[1]                          [2]  MEM:M[A[1];]←M[A[2]+2⊥M[A[1];];]
[3]  BT:→(B1,B2)[I]                   [3]  →(A[1]=A[0])/0
[4]  B1:R[RT;]←,M[AT+ι4;]             [4]  A[1]←(2*24)|1+A[1]
[5]  →TST                             [5]  →MEM
[6]  B2:M[AT+ι4;]←(4,8)ρR[RT;]              ∇
[7]  TST:→(RT=A[3])/0
[8]  RT←16|RT+1                        (b) Translate (TR).
[9]  AT←(2*24)|AT+4
[10] →BT
     ∇
```

```
     0        8    12    16   20           31
RS   | OP     | R1 | R3 | B2 | D2          |
```

(a) LOAD/STORE MULTIPLE (LM,STM).

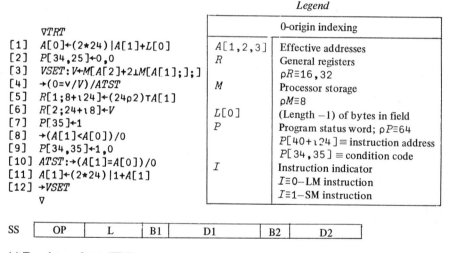

Legend

```
     ∇TRT
[1]  A[0]←(2*24)|A[1]+L[0]
[2]  P[34,25]←0,0
[3]  VSET:V←M[A[2]+2⊥M[A[1];];]
[4]  →(0=V/V)/ATST
[5]  R[1;8+ι24]←(24ρ2)TA[1]
[6]  R[2;24+ι8]←V
[7]  P[35]←1
[8]  →(A[1]<A[0])/0
[9]  P[34,35]←1,0
[10] ATST:→(A[1]=A[0])/0
[11] A[1]←(2*24)|1+A[1]
[12] →VSET
     ∇
```

	0-origin indexing
A[1,2,3]	Effective addresses
R	General registers
	ρR≡16,32
M	Processor storage
	ρM≡8
L[0]	(Length −1) of bytes in field
P	Program status word; ρP≡64
	P[40+ι24] ≡ instruction address
	P[34,35] ≡ condition code
I	Instruction indicator
	I≡0−LM instruction
	I≡1−SM instruction

```
SS   | OP     | L    | B1 | D1       | B2 | D2      |
```

(c) Translate and test (TRT).

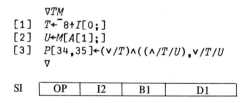

```
     ∇TM
[1]  T←¯8+I[0;]
[2]  U←M[A[1];]
[3]  P[34,35]←(V/T)∧((∧/T/U),V/T/U
     ∇
```

```
SI   | OP    | I2  | B1 |    D1    |
```

(d) Test-under mask (TM).

Fig. 10.5.1 Some S/360 instructions.

Address	Length	Purpose
0 0000 0000	Double word	Initial program loading PSW
8 0000 1000	Double word	Initial program loading CCW1
16 0001 0000	Double word	Initial program loading CCW2
24 0001 1000	Double word	External old PSW
32 0010 0000	Double word	Supervisor call old PSW
40 0010 1000	Double word	Program old PSW
48 0011 0000	Double word	Machine check old PSW
56 0011 1000	Double word	Input/output old PSW
64 0100 0000	Double word	Channel status word
72 0100 1000	Word	Channel address word
76 0100 1100	Word	Unused
80 0101 0000	Word	Timer
84 0101 0100	Word	Unused
88 0101 1000	Double word	External new PSW
96 0110 0000	Double word	Supervisor call new PSW
104 0110 1000	Double word	Program new PSW
112 0111 0000	Double word	Machine check new PSW
120 0111 1000	Double word	Input/output new PSW
128 1000 0000		Diagnostic scan-out area†

†The size of the diagnostic scan-out area depends upon the particular system's CPU and I/O channels.

(a) Permanent storage assignments.

System mask		Key	AMWP	Interruption code
0	7 8	11 12	15 16	31

ILC	CC	Program mask	Instruction address
32	33 34 35 36	39 40	63

0–7	System mask	14	Wait state (W)
0	Multiplexor channel mask	15	Problem state (P)
1	Selector channel 1 mask	16–31	Interruption code
2	Selector channel 2 mask	32–33	Instruction length code (ILC)
3	Selector channel 3 mask	34–35	Condition code (CC)
4	Selector channel 4 mask	36–39	Program mask
5	Selector channel 5 mask	36	Fixed-point overflow mask
6	Selector channel 6 mask	37	Decimal overflow mask
7	External mask	38	Exponent underflow mask
8–11	Protection key	39	Significance mask
12	ASCII mode (A)	40–63	Instruction address
13	Machine check mask (M)		

(b) Program-status word format.

Fig. 10.6.1 Fixed address assignments and interruption codes for S/360.

Source identification	Interruption code PSW bits 16–31	Mask bits	ILC set	Execution
Input/Output (old PSW 56, new PSW 120, priority 4)				
Multiplexor channel	00000000 aaaaaaaa	0	X	Complete
Selector channel 1	00000001 aaaaaaaa	1	X	Complete
Selector channel 2	00000010 aaaaaaaa	2	X	Complete
Selector channel 3	00000011 aaaaaaaa	3	X	Complete
Selector channel 4	00000100 aaaaaaaa	4	X	Complete
Selector channel 5	00000101 aaaaaaaa	5	X	Complete
Selector channel 6	00000110 aaaaaaaa	6	X	Complete
Program (old PSW 40, new PSW 104, priority 2)				
Operation	00000000 00000001		1,2,3	Suppress
Privileged operation	00000000 00000010		1,2	Suppress
Execute	00000000 00000011		2	Suppress
Protection	00000000 00000100		0,2,3	Supress/ Terminate
Addressing	00000000 00000101		0,1,2,3	Suppress/ Terminate
Specification	00000000 00000110		1,2,3	Suppress
Data	00000000 00000111		2,3	Terminate
Fixed-point overflow	00000000 00001000	36	1,2	Complete
Fixed-point divide	00000000 00001001		1,2	Suppress/ Complete
Decimal overflow	00000000 00001010	37	3	Complete
Decimal divide	00000000 00001011		3	Suppress
Exponent overflow	00000000 00001100		1,2	Terminate
Exponent underflow	00000000 00001101	38	1,2	Complete
Significance	00000000 00001110	39	1,2	Complete
Floating-point divide	00000000 00001111		1,2	Suppress
Supervisor Call (old PSW 32, new PSW 96, priority 2)				
Instruction bits	00000000 rrrrrrrr		1	Complete
External (old PSW 24, new PSW 88, priority 3)				
External signal 1	00000000 xxxxxxx1	7	X	Complete
External signal 2	00000000 xxxxxx1x	7	X	Complete
External signal 3	00000000 xxxxx1xx	7	X	Complete
External signal 4	00000000 xxxx1xxx	7	X	Complete
External signal 5	00000000 xxx1xxxx	7	X	Complete
External signal 6	00000000 xx1xxxxx	7	X	Complete
Interrupt key	00000000 x1xxxxxx	7	X	Complete
Timer	00000000 1xxxxxxx	7	X	Complete
Machine Check (old PSW 48, new PSW 112, priority 1)				
Machine malfunction	00000000 00000000	13	X	Terminate

Notes:
a = device address bits; r = bits of R_1 and R_2 field of SUPERVISOR CALL; X = unpredictable.

(c) Interrupt-cause and mask codes.

Fig. 10.6.1 Fixed address assignments and interruption codes for S/360 (Continued).

Knowledge of the interrupt system is also essential for programs which are time-dependent.

It is well to recall the notion of the *program state.* At any given time, a program may be inactive, in which case its state is entirely contained in machine storage, or else it may be active, in which case part of the state is in storage and part is in machine registers and indicators. It is meaningful to talk only about interruption of an active program. Since the time of interrupt request is not known in advance, an interrupt system must be capable, at any interrupt-recognition time, of saving (storing) the processor part of the active program state in order to properly resume execution of this program later. To simplify the circuitry for state storage, most systems only respond to interrupt request at certain microintervals, e.g., after the end of an instruction. For interrupts due to exceptional conditions in the processor, such conditions may force end of instruction. Some of the processor-state storage is left for machine instructions. For example, there is no automatic storage of the 16 general registers; these can, however, be stored with a single instruction.

Important state information is grouped into a 64-bit register, called the *program status word* (PSW). Twenty-four bits of the PSW serve as the program counter, which contains the location of the next instruction. Other bits of the PSW include the *condition code, storage-protect key, interrupt masks,* and 16-bit positions, called the *interruption code,* where the machine can automatically record the identification of the source of an interrupt. This recording supplies subsequent routines with information about the source of interrupt so that appropriate response can be made (see Fig. 10.6.1).

The system may contain a large number of primitive lines, each of which can signal for an eventual interrupt request. To handle these in a systematic and economical manner, the primitive request lines are in effect grouped into 32 sets; each set, called a *mask group,* feeds a group line. For example, all control units on a given channel are a mask group and feed one of the 32 group lines. Corresponding to each mask-group line, there is a mask bit furnished either from the PSW mask fields or else a constant 1 (signifying not masked). The masking mechanism is provided to allow privileged instructions to control which interrupt requests may indeed initiate the interrupt procedure. Four mask bits, called program mask, supplied by the PSW, apply to interrupt requests from the processor which arise when a result of processing is out of range. Another set of 8 PSW mask bits, called *system mask,* can mask any combination of the seven I/O channels or the set of eight external lines considered as a single group. Another bit of the system mask applies to all monitored machine-malfunction conditions. In summary, program control may be exerted on 13 of the 32 interrupt group lines; the other 19 lines, all pertaining to processor invalidities, are always masked ON.

For reasons of hardware economy and simplicity of programming interrupt control, the 32 mask-group lines are further multiplexed into five *levels* called *input/output, program, supervisor call, external,* and *machine check.* A pair of 64-bit PSW images is provided at fixed locations in lower core storage for *each* level. One member of each pair is called old-PSW, the other is called new-PSW. (Normally, the supervisor program will supply new-PSW's.) The primary action at interrupt is selection of one of the levels which is ON, then storage of the request identification which initiated this level in the interruption code bits of the PSW, then storage of the PSW into core storage at the location of the old-PSW for this level, and then replacement of the PSW from the new-PSW in core storage. Selection of a level for this treatment is always in the order: machine check, program, supervisor call, external, and I/O. After each PSW storage and fetch, the levels are searched again in this order. This means that several unmasked requests belonging to the highest ON level will be serviced before any of the next level are considered.

Let us now consider in more detail how the system can resolve concurrent interrupt requests. In general, it is possible for more than one interrupt request to be ON at the same time, even in the same mask group. In such cases, the machine has a built-in selection procedure at the various levels of grouping to decide which of the competing requests shall be treated first. Starting at the primitive request points, one of several ON requests belonging to a single group is selected. For I/O and external signals, the priority is according to the order of connection of the device control unit to the channel. Some control over this may be exerted when the devices are installed. In the case of the program level, one of the (possibly) competing requests is selected at random.

It is recalled from our earlier description that the selected group requests are then combined with their mask bits, and these are multiplexed to the five interrupt-level lines. Since in general more than one level line may be ON at the same time, a first decision procedure is used to select the one which will be serviced first. This is done according to the priority scheme described earlier; i.e., in order of their being recognized: machine check, supervisor call or program, external, I/O. Recognition of a given level results in reset of the device-request line which is being serviced, recording of request identification in the PSW interruption code and storing of the PSW as an old-PSW and refilling the PSW from a new-PSW. After such a sequence, the machine will seek the next waiting request in the highest priority level. In this way, several PSW's may be fetched and stored successively. Notice, however, each new-PSW will in general contain its own mask.

By proper control of new-PSW masks, the supervisor program can ensure that channel interrupt requests ON simultaneously are not lost. For example, if each new-PSW masks out previously serviced levels, including its own, in one store-fetch PSW sequence, no new-PSW interruption code will be replaced by another. An exception to this rule would appear to be the case where several of the permanently masked-ON requests of the program level are ON. However, interrupt requests of the program level are not held beyond recognition of a single member of this level; i.e., after a pending condition is selected (at random) for the program level, all requests for this level are set OFF. Thus, for this mask configuration, after handling at most one interrupt at each level, the supervisor starts CPU execution with the instruction at the address specified in the last PSW fetched. The routine thus entered can move the old-PSWs with their identification of request sources out of the fixed PSW image area. By loading new mask information, the supervisor can then reenable the interrupt system to service other requests not serviced on the previous pass.

10.7 CHANNELS AND CHANNEL LOGIC

The subject of auxiliary storage and I/O may be considered to have three aspects. First there are the properties of the devices. This was discussed in Chap. 4 for some typical devices. The second aspect is the manner in which the devices are logically connected to the rest of the system. Finally there is the logical appearance of the devices to the users of the system. These latter two subjects will be discussed below for System/360.

I/O devices are connected directly to control circuitry called *control units* (Fig. 10.7.1). These contain the mechanisms for addressing the recorded information as well as buffer circuitry for accumulating bits into an 8-bit byte en route between the access mechanism and the CPU. A single control unit may serve several modules of similar devices. To the programmer, the control unit and device are practically indistinguishable and will be so considered in this discussion, at least with respect to program control. Each control unit connects to a *channel* via a set of functionally standardized lines called the *I/O interface*. These include a 9-bit path in each direction. Several control units may physically connect to the same channel. However, only one device may be controlled by a logical channel at one time. In many systems an optional provision is made to allow two channels to connect to the same control unit. With this feature, two

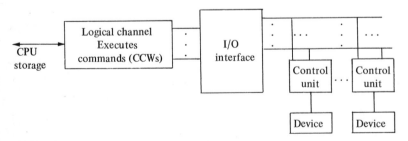

Fig. 10.7.1   Major logical parts of S/360 I/O subsystem.

channels, which may belong to different machines, can communicate with each other by access to a common storage device. Facing the CPU, each channel is connected (at least logically but not necessarily physically) to *main storage,* not the processing unit.

Program control of I/O devices resides with both the channels and the CPU. The basic idea is to give the CPU ultimate control by permitting only CPU privileged instructions to select channels and devices and to initiate channel activity (Fig. 10.7.2). Channels control details of transmission, including byte counting and address updating. The channel also often controls buffering, which on input is from the byte received from the interface lines to the number of bytes required by the memory for a single access cycle. This division of control responsibility allows full CPU stored-program control over gross features of I/O activity yet permits the autonomous channels to overlap long, slow I/O sequences with CPU processing.

A channel may best be viewed as a stored-program device with an instruction set highly specialized to control movement of information between I/O devices and processor storage (Fig. 10.7.3). To distinguish CPU instructions from those executed by the channels, the latter are called *commands* or *channel control words* (CCW). There are six types of CCW which differ in the operations they perform such as READ, WRITE, READ BACKWARD, SENSE, CONTROL, and TRANSFER-IN-CHANNEL. The primary functions of the first three types are self-explanatory. The SENSE command and TRANSFER-IN-CHANNEL will be discussed below. The CONTROL command in effect extends the command types to include other types of information which cannot fit into the 64-bit command format, e.g., the address of a record on a disk unit.

It was stated earlier that a channel is capable of stored-program control; i.e., it can access successive commands from storage (this is called *chaining*). To do this, each channel in effect contains a group of logical registers which is the analog of the CPU program status word; this is called a *channel status word* (CSW). The 64-bit CSW includes a pointer to the next CCW in storage following the one currently being executed.

Although the channel is logically autonomous from the CPU for detailed transmission operations, it is *slave* to the CPU program because only a CPU instruction (START I/O) can start a channel program and any channel program can be stopped by another instruction (HALT I/O). To aid decision making on initiation and termination of I/O activity, the CPU may sense the activity of a channel and device with the TEST I/O and TEST CHANNEL instructions. Finally, the device or channel can signal the CPU by requesting an interrupt.

I/O devices may differ significantly in the speed at which they accumulate or accept information. This speed is directly related to the required speed of the channel control functions since byte counting and address updating must be done for each byte (or small byte group) transferred. For low-speed devices these control functions can share common circuitry, and the channel's logical

1. All four I/O instructions only executed when machine is in privileged mode (PSW bit 15 ≡ 0)
2. All I/O instructions use SI format with effective address e determined as usual:

$$e \leftarrow (24\rho 2)\top(2\iota^{-}12\uparrow IR) + 2\iota(0 \neq 2\iota^{-}16\uparrow IR)\wedge R[2\iota^{-}16\uparrow IR;]$$

IR:

OP	B1	D1

bits: 0 7 | 15 19 | 31

3. Addressing, condition-code, and operation summary

Instruction	Channel	Subchannel	Device	Condition-code value				Operation summary
				0	1	2	3	
Test channel (TCH)	$2\iota^{-}11\uparrow E$	—	—	Available	Interrupt pending	Channel in burst mode	Channel/device not operational	Set condition code for channel status
Test I/O (TIO)		$2\iota 4^{-}8\uparrow E$	$2\iota^{-}4\uparrow E$	Available	CSW stored	Channel busy	Channel/device not operational	Set condition code for channel/device status
Start I/O (SIO)				I/O started	CSW stored	Channel busy		Send CAW at location 72 to channel to initiate channel program
Halt I/O (HIO)				Channel not working	CSW stored	Burst operation terminated		Terminate channel and device operation

4. Channel address word (CAW): 4 bytes at location 72

Prot key	0000	Command (CCW) address

bits: 0 3 | 7 8 | 31

5. Channel status word (CSW): one per channel; one image at location 64 for all channels

Prot key	0000	Command (CCW) address	Status	Count

bits: 0 3 | 7 8 | 31 | 47 | 63

6. Channel command word (CCW): One logical register per channel; program in storage

Operation	Data address	Flags	0000	Count

bits: 0 7 | 8 31 | 35 | 39 47 | 63

Fig. 10.7.2 Summary of S/360 instructions for I/O.

registers can reside in storage. Using this principle, it is possible to economically implement a large number of logical channels with a rather small amount of hardware. This arrangement is called the *multiplexor* channel. In some implementations of the multiplexor channel, not only several logical channels but also the CPU share common data paths and storage. The multiplexor channel is intended as an economical method of controlling a large number of low-speed devices such as card reader punches, printers, typewriters, and telephone lines. The multiplexor channel may also be used to control a single high-speed device; in this case it is said to be operating in the *burst* mode. The other implementation of the channel is called a *selector* channel. It generally contains its own physical control circuitry and is intended to control a single high-speed device at one time. From a programming viewpoint, all logical channels have a very similar appearance independent of whether they are (sub) channels of the multiplexor channel or selector channels.

Thus far only the main outlines of the I/O control have been sketched. More detail will now be given with the aid of charts that summarize various aspects of I/O control. These charts and the accompanying discussion are intended to convey principles and rationale for the system but are not intended to be complete, say, on the level required for programming. For such detail the programming manual "System/360 Principles of Operation" should be consulted.

The CPU may execute one of the four I/O instructions only if the machine is in the privileged mode (otherwise the instruction is not executed and an interrupt request is issued). All four I/O instructions use the SI instruction format and the effective address E (a 24-bit vector) is computed in the usual way for this format. The rightmost 11 bits of E specify the channel and device selected. In addition to their primary functions, all I/O instructions also result in setting of the condition code (CC) bits (bits 34 and 35) in the program status word. This CC setting is intended to convey the gross state of the channel and device (it is recalled that the CC may be tested by CPU instructions). Now when exceptional conditions exist in the channel or device, more detail is required for their identification than can be expressed in the 2 bits of CC. In these cases, a CC of 01 is entered, and detailed status is stored in the storage image for channel status words at storage location 64. Storage of a CSW in this image area may also be initiated by a channel as part of an interrupt response. Since there are several channels but only one CSW image, storage of a CSW due to interrupt is done only during response to interrupt. Since interrupt responses may be masked by (privileged) instructions, the CSW stored by an I/O instruction can be safeguarded against replacement until moved (copied) from location 64.

The primary function of the TCH and TIO instructions is storage of status in the PSW and possibly the CSW. The primary function of the START I/O (SIO) instruction is to start a channel program. Assuming the channel is available and

CONTROL-WORD FORMATS

Base and index registers:

/////	
0 7 8	31

0–7 Ignored
8–31 Base address or index

Program status word:

System mask	Key	AMWP	Interruption code
0 7 8	11 12	15 16	31

ILC	CC	Program mask	Instruction address
32 33 34	35 36	39 40	63

0–7	System mask
0	Multiplexor channel mask
1	Selector channel 1 mask
2	Selector channel 2 mask
3	Selector channel 3 mask
13	Machine check mask (M)
14	Wait state (W)
15	Problem state (P)
16–31	Interruption code
32–33	Instruction length code (ILC)
34–35	Condition code (CC)
36–39	Program mask

Command-code assignment:

Names

Write	CD CC SLI		PCI	MMMM	MM01
Read	CD CC SLI	SKIP	PCI	MMMM	MM10
Read Backward	CD CC SLI	SKIP	PCI	MMMM	1 100
Control	CD CC SLI		PCI	MMMM	MM11
Sense	CD CC SLI	SKIP	PCI	MMMM	0 100
Transfer in Channel				XXXX	1 000

CD = Chain data
CC = Chain command
SLI = Suppress length indication

SKIP = Skip
PCI = Program-controlled interrupt

Channel address word:

Key	0 0 0 0	Command address
0 3 4	7 8	31

0–3 Protection key
4–7 Zero
8–31 Command address

Channel status word:

Key	0 0 0 0	Command address
0 3 4	7 8	31

Status	Count
32 47 48	63

4	Selector channel 4 mask	
5	Selector channel 5 mask	
6	Selector channel 6 mask	
7	External mask	
8–11	Protection key	
12	ASCII mode (A)	

36	Fixed-point overflow mask
37	Decimal overflow mask
38	Exponent underflow mask
39	Significance mask
40–63	Instruction address

0–3	Protection key
4–7	Zero
8–31	Command address
32–47	Status
32	Attention
33	Status modifier
34	Control unit end
35	Busy
36	Channel end
37	Device end
38	Unit check
39	Unit exception

40	Program-controlled interruption
41	Incorrect length
42	Program check
43	Protection check
44	Channel data check
45	Channel control check
46	Interface control check
47	Chaining check
48–63	Count

Channel command word:

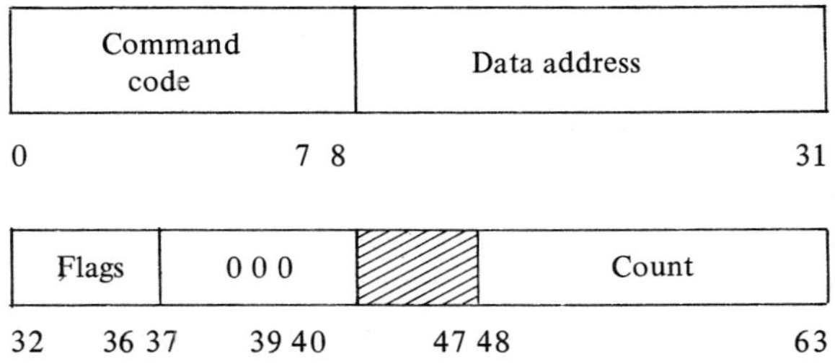

Command code	Data address
0 7 8	31

Flags	0 0 0	Count
32 36 37 39 40	47 48	63

0–7	Command code
8–31	Data address
32–36	Command flags
32	Chain data flag
33	Chain command flag
34	Suppress length indication flag
35	Skip flag
36	Program-controlled interruption flag
37–39	Zero
40–47	Ignored
48–63	Count

Fig. 10.7.3 S/360 Control words.

no unusual conditions, the SIO instruction results in 32 bits (4 bytes) of control information being sent to the selected channel's CSW. These 32 bits are called the CAW (channel address word) and are located starting at storage address 72. The CAW is identical in format to the first half of the CSW and hence specifies the storage protection key to be used for all channel accesses as well as the location of the first CCW (channel command word). This CCW is fetched from storage and sent to the channel's CCW register. (The command-address field of the CSW is advanced by 8 in anticipation of fetching the next CCW from storage after execution of the current CCW is complete.) The CCW just placed in the channel CCW register defines its function in its leftmost 8 bits. For transmission-type commands (READ, WRITE, READ BACKWARD) the direction of transmission is thereby defined, and the channel communicates with the device via the I/O interface and updates the CCW address and count field during transmission. Eventually transmission is completed, e.g., when the byte count reaches 0; at this point the action taken depends upon the flags portion of the CCW (Fig. 10.7.4). Three of these bits specify that either the next CCW is to be fetched (its address is specified in the CSW; this case is called *command chaining*) or else the next command is fetched except for the operation byte (which is

Name of flag bit	Abbreviation	Bit No. in CCW	Time of control	Meaning if bit $\equiv 1$
Chain data	CD	32	CCW count $\equiv 0$	Continue current operations but fetch new CCW (except for OP byte) from storage
Chain commands	CC	33	Control unit sends "End" and CD $\equiv 0$	Current operation terminated; fetch next CCW to start new operation
Suppress length indication	SLI	34	CCW count $\equiv 0$ or control unit end	Bit 41 of CSQ set to 1 if end of record of device is reached at a time other than count $\equiv 0$
Skip	SKIP	35	During input operations	Suppress transmission
Program-controlled interrupt	PCI	36	Just after CCW is accessed	Request CPU interrupt but channel executes command

Fig. 10.7.4   Principles of CCW flag bits.

Status-sensing mechanisms
1. Condition code (bits 34,35 of PSW)
    a. Set by SIO, TCH, TIO, HIO instructions
    b. One of three definite states recorded or else a fourth value indicating further status information in CSW image at storage location 64
2. Interruption-code (bits 16–31 of PSW)
    a. Identifies channel/device requesting interrupt
    b. Stored during interrupt response in old-PSW image for I/O interrupt at location 56
3. Channel status word (CSW) image (location 64)
    a. Includes identifier of condition
    b. Stored by TIO, SIO, HIO if certain exceptional conditions exist. Also stored as part of interrupt response
4. Command (CCW)-controlled storage of status
    a. Identifies a condition
    b. Stored by the channel command SENSE into storage specified in command. No interrupt involved (unless requested in CCW)

Initiation of channel operations
START I/O, a CPU instruction, selects channel and device
If no exceptional conditions, channel CSW register is loaded with address of first command from CAW (storage location 72)

Continuation of channel operation
After execution of a CCW is complete, bits in the *flags* field determine action taken as follows:
    a. Data chaining—fetch next CCW but retain current operation
    b. Command chaining—fetch next CCW, start new operation
TRANSFER-IN-CHANNEL command permits CCWs to be noncontiguous in storage

Termination of I/O operation (optional methods)
    a. End-of-transmission: interrupt
    b. Detection of error: interrupt
    c. HALT I/O (CPU instruction)

Fig. 10.7.5 Summary of I/O machine principles.

called *data chaining*). The ability to chain gives the channel stored-program facility. It permits the channel to control transmission between a device and noncontiguous blocks of storage. The channel program itself is also permitted to be noncontiguous by including one command-type TRANSFER-IN-CHANNEL which specifies an unconditional branch in the command program.

The CONTROL command allows a significant extension of command power by permitting specification of a storage area containing further control information such as the address of a record on a disk file. In general a control command results in no transmission of information except control information. In many cases all the control information (e.g., backspace tape) is contained in the operation part of the CCW. Where further control information must be accessed from storage, the location of this information is given in the data-address field of the CCW.

The SENSE command allows yet another means of storing status information, this time initiated by the channel program. The status stored may reflect various error conditions or the fact that manual intervention is required, e.g., a printer is out of paper. The status information is stored in main storage starting at the location specified by the data-address part of the CCW.

The subject of I/O control in System/360 is summarized in chart form in Fig. 10.7.5.

10.8 SYSTEM/360 IMPLEMENTATION SUMMARY

Some of the principal factors of the hardware implementations of the original-announcement models of the System/360 are summarized in Fig. 10.8.1. The category "relative speed" refers to internal speed neglecting I/O activity and was obtained by weighting each instruction execution time according to its frequency of appearance during the running of several typical programs (instruction-mix evaluation method).

Notice that the range of main storage cycles among the models is not particularly great; the larger systems achieve speed primarily by wider memory paths rather than by faster cycle time. Both width and cycle time may be combined into a single factor, the *memory bandwidth,* expressed, say, in kilobytes per second:

$$\text{MBW} \equiv \frac{\text{No. of bytes per access}}{\text{cycle time in milliseconds}}$$

Memory bandwidth is easy to compute and gives a rough way of comparing systems with similar architecture. It becomes less accurate for very small systems because some bandwidth is often used to implement indexing operations leaving less for data manipulation. For very large systems, main-storage bandwidth is also not too accurate a measure because a small, fast store is often interposed between main storage and the processor. Memory bandwidth must also be adjusted in the event a system contains interleaved memory access. In the case of two interleaved modules, the bandwidth is increased by about 1.4 (see Chap. 6).

The rest of the tabulation indicates the cost-performance trade-offs made by the implementations. The model 30 achieves economy by implementing general-purpose and floating-point registers in main storage technology and using an 8-bit memory and data structure. The model 40 uses a slower cycle for storage but has 16-bit paths and uses a fast local store to implement the registers. Path widths double from 16 to 32 bits to obtain the model 50 and become 64 bits for the model 65. Increased speed comes primarily from faster memory cycles and interleaving. Naturally, the faster the memory, the higher the circuit speeds and local storages that implement the registers. Other factors increasing

Model	Internal relative speed	Main storage				Controls		General-purpose and floating-point registers			Adder width	Circuit delay
		Cycle	Width	Interleave	Bandwidth	Type	Cycle	Type	Width	Cycle		
30	1	2.0	1	—	500	ROS	1.0	core	1	2.0	1	.030
40	3.5	2.5	2	—	800	ROS	0.625	core	2	1.25	1	.030
50	10	2.0	4	—	2,000	ROS	0.5	core	4	0.5	4	.030
65	30	0.75	8	2	14,933	ROS	0.2	circ	4	—	7	.010
75	45	0.75	8	2–4	21,300	circ	0.195	circ	4,8	—	8	.006
85	120	1.04	16	2–4	N.A.	circ	0.80	circ	8	—	8	.005
91	135–420	0.75	8	8–16	N.A.	circ	0.60	circ	8	—	8	.002

Notes:

1. All widths in bytes.
2. All cycle and delay times in microseconds (multiply by 1000 to get nanoseconds).
3. Storage bandwidths include a square-root factor for interleave (see Chap. 6).
4. ROS denotes "read-only storage"; circ denotes "logic circuitry."
5. Mod 85 includes 16- or 32-kilobyte "cache" memory (.080-μsec access).

Fig. 10.8.1 Summary of some IBM S/360 models.

performance are not indicated on the chart; these include more elaborate algorithms to implement the instructions especially those for floating-point arithmetic.

10.9 THE IBM SYSTEM/370: MOD 155 BUFFER STORAGE ORGANIZATION

The System/370 machines, which became available in 1970, feature fourth-generation technology in logic circuitry and memory, a more moderate but still significant improvement over System/360 in disk storage, and only relatively slight compatible changes in system architecture. Figure 10.9.1 summarizes major architecture improvements, including a time-of-day clock that is updated even when the machine stops (but not when power is removed) and several new instructions (among them ones to identify CPU and channel models, to move and compare very long byte strings, and to manipulate selected bytes in the general registers). Figure 10.9.2 briefly describes two new IBM disk devices available with System/370.

The monolithic technology may be appreciated from an example: in the Mod 135 the main memory is composed of monolithic silicon chips. Each chip,

I. Thirteen new instructions
  A. Move-compare up to 16 million storage bytes. Addresses and field lengths specified in two pairs of general registers. These instructions are interruptable.
      1. Compare-logical-long (CLCL).
      2. Move-long (MVCL).
  B. Compare-move selected bytes of general registers.
      1. Compare logical characters under mask (CLM).
      2. Insert characters under mask (ICM).
      3. Store characters under mask (STCM).
  C. Time-of-day clock; updated every 1 μsec as long as power is ON (capacity = 143 years).
      1. Set clock (SCK).
      2. Store clock (STCK).
  D. Shift and round decimal (SRP).
  E. CPU and channel model identification.
      1. Store CPU ID (STIDP).
      2. Store channel ID (STIDC).
  F. Start I/O fast release (SIOF).
  G. Load/store control registers (LCTL,STCTL).
II. Other
  A. Bit 12 of PSW = 1 no longer designates USASCII-8 code.
  B. Invalid decimal operands result in suppressed (not terminated) instruction.

Fig. 10.9.1 Highlights of S/370 architecture changes/additions from S/360. Does not include virtual storage features announced in 1972.

Model	2314	3330	2305
Technology	Disk	Disk	Fixed-head disk
Removable packs	Yes	Yes	No
Capacity per drive, megabytes	29.1	100	11.2
Capacity per eight drives, megabytes	233	800	
Head-access time, msec			
Maximum	130	55	0
Average	60	30	0
Average cylinder cycle	25	10	0
Maximum rotation delay, msec	25	16.7	10
Data transfer rate, kilobytes/sec	312	806	1500
Disks per pack	13	12	6
Recording surfaces per pack	20	19	12
Bytes per track	7294	13,030	14,660
Tracks per cylinder	20	19	
Cylinders per pack	200 (+ 3)	404 (+7)	

Fig. 10.9.2   Three disk storages for S/370.

manufactured by an automatic process, is less than $\frac{1}{8}$ inch square and holds 1440 components in 174 circuits. Functionally, this single chip constitutes 128 cells of storage and 46 supporting circuits.

Another interesting implementation feature is the writable control store (WCS) for holding microprograms in some models. WCS is used primarily for diagnostic microprograms and emulators; it is currently modifiable only by the manufacturer, not the programmer.

Some properties of three System/370 models are given in Fig. 10.9.3. In the larger Mods 155 and 165, high speed is attained by concurrent accesses to several interleaved main-storage modules and the use of a fast small buffer (cache) store. The buffer's job is to hold the currently most frequently accessed instructions

	S/360	S/370 model			
	50	135	145	155	165
Internal speed†	1	.35– .70	1.6	3.5–4	6–15
CPU cycle, nsec	500	275–1430	203–315	115	80
Width, bytes	4		4	4	8
Buffer store:					
Size, kilobytes	–	–	–	8	8 or 16
Access, nsec	–	–	–	230	160
Width, bytes	–	–	–	4	8
Main store:					
Technology	Core	Monolithic	Monolithic	Core	Core
Cycle, nsec	2000	770	540	2100	2000
Width, bytes	4	2	4	16	32
Interleave	–	–	–	4	4
Maximum size, kilobytes		256	500	2000	3000

† Estimated factors neglecting I/O operations.

Fig. 10.9.3   Four S/370 models (with S/360 Mod 50 for comparison).

and data so that most processor storage references will be from the buffer rather than the slower main store.

Since the buffer is purely an implementation device and has no user-architecture significance, it is made completely transparent to the programmer; the hardware *automatically* manages all information transfer between the main and buffer stores. This *virtual-storage principle* is essentially the same as that introduced on the rather large System/360 Mod 85. It is one example of the automatic methods for handling storage hierarchies that represent the current frontiers of machine and system organization. For this reason we now discuss the general principle in the context of CPU design and follow with a description of its use in the Mod 155.

To begin, refer to Fig. 10.9.4, the Mod 155 organization, which at this level of detail is indicative of most such designs. Assume that the buffer currently contains information from the active parts of main storage. All CPU storage addresses to main storage are checked for presence in the fast buffer. If found, access is rapid. If not, the system moves a block of information containing the referenced instruction or data from main storage to the buffer. If the buffer is full, one of its current blocks is overlaid (replaced). The block selected for replacement by the control circuits is typically the one least recently used (the LRU replacement algorithm). Because of good locality of reference in most programs (see Chap. 9), simulations show that most references (typically over 90 percent) will be found in the buffer. Store (as opposed to fetch) references by the processor are made to *both* the buffer and main storage (store through) with the result that information need never be moved back from the buffer to main storage. Although this would seem to slow the effective reference rate, in practice, this effect is small, partly because store references are relatively rare (20 percent of total is typical) and also because a store operation does not cause a processing delay unless an attempt is made to reference the same module before the write-access is completed. I/O channel references are typically handled as follows: incoming references check the buffer, and, if present, the information is entered in both buffer and main storage. Outgoing references need come only from main storage since the store-through principle ensures that the latest copy is in main store.

In a typical Mod 155, with 1000 kilobytes of main storage and 8 kilobytes of buffer, the processor will generate 20 significant bits of address for each reference, and this must be translated (mapped) into a 13-bit address to the buffer. Some details of this are shown in Fig. 10.9.5. First notice that the *main store* is considered to be composed of 256 rows of 128 blocks (columns) per row, 32 bytes per block. The *buffer* is considered as 2 rows, also of 128 blocks per row (also 32 bytes per block). Each column of main storage corresponds to

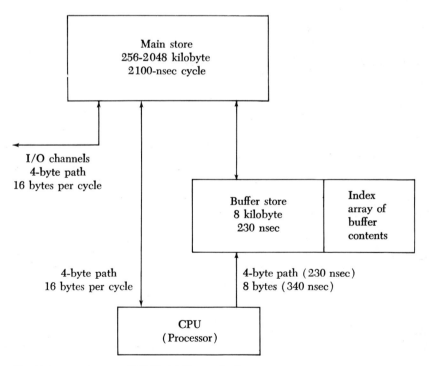

Fig. 10.9.4   IBM System/370 Mod 155 organization.

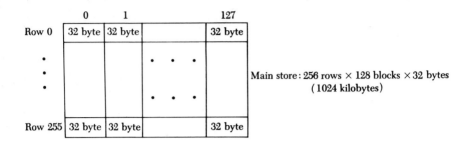

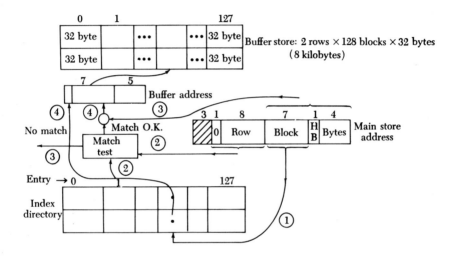

Notes: 1. Circled numbers indicate relative times during mapping.
2. Match test includes check of 2 validity bits in index for presence of data in buffer storage. No-match exit results in logic to replace a block in buffer with requested block of main store.
3. Since a block in column K of main store must be in column K of buffer, at most 2 blocks of any one main store column can be in buffer at once.

Fig. 10.9.5   Mapping main-store address into buffer address in Mod 155.

the same numbered column in the buffer. It follows that at most two blocks from each main-store column can be in the buffer at any one time. This restriction is the result of economy of the mapping scheme to be described. Simulation results are said to have demonstrated that statistically it will not degrade performance significantly. In any case, continuing with our description, Fig. 10.9.5 shows how the address transformation is performed. A buffer index store which has as many entries as buffer blocks holds the row numbers in main storage of the buffer blocks. The effective address, generated as usual in System/360/370 machines, is considered to be composed of several fields as shown. The block (column) field is used to address the index; the two index entries are then checked for match with the row part of the address (and validity bits). If the match is successful, the column number is used to access the buffer (together with the half-block and byte address that precisely locates the referenced byte or bytes). Not shown but also updated with each reference is an indicator of last reference for each block, used to decide which block (of two) is to be replaced when a replacement is necessary. At replacement time, although a block in the buffer is reserved, only a half block (16 bytes) is moved at once.

As indicated in the data-flow structure of Fig. 10.9.4, the I/O channels access main store and not the buffer. When the channel stores information in main storage, a check is made to see whether it is in the buffer. If not, there is no problem; if a copy is in the buffer, the validity bit of the associated block in the index is set to *invalid* so that buffer and main store will never logically have different data for the same block.

PROBLEMS

10.1 Which format(s) of System/360 instruction have the following properties?

  a) Two registers contribute to one effective address.

  b) Three operands may be specified.

  c) No operand memory cycle is required.

  d) Only 1 byte is processed.

  e) Used for composite index update, test, and branch instructions.

  f) Only format(s) applicable to floating-point instructions.

  g) Uses no registers for operands.

10.2 List the instruction bytes which, if present, have the same meaning in all formats.

10.3 Which operand types are subject to a System/360 COMPARE instruction?

10.4 List the instructions which change no data but only set the condition code. Give full name and mnemonic for each.

10.5 Is it possible to move an operand from a floating-point register to a general register with a single instruction?

10.6 In what way is reference to general register 0 different from reference to other registers?

10.7 State the general rule of validity which every effective address must satisfy when referencing a fixed-length operand of n bytes.

10.8 List the instructions (by name and mnemonic) in which an even-odd pair of registers is involved.

10.9 System/360 does not have an explicit NO OPERATION instruction. How can such an instruction be specified?

10.10 How many BCD digits result from a CONVERT BINARY TO DECIMAL instruction?

10.11 Can arithmetic be done directly on decimal numbers in the zoned format?

10.12 List all privileged System/360 instructions by name and mnemonic.

10.13 What part of the PSW can be modified by the problem programmer? List the fields by name.

10.14 *a*) How many distinct interrupt locations (levels) are there in System/360?
b) State three ways in which the system receives interrupt-identifier information.
c) State two ways in which the system-mask field can be respecified.

10.15 Explain (or speculate on) the reason for each System/370 feature that is new or improved over System/360 (see part I of Fig. 10.9.1).

10.16 In a buffer-backing store system like the Mod 155, suppose
$T_B \equiv$ buffer access time
$T_M \equiv$ main-store access time
$P_B \equiv$ "hit" probability of an access being found in buffer
a) Show that the mean (average) access time is
$$T_A \equiv T_B P_B + (1 - P_B) T_M$$
b) If the average access time is to be only twice the buffer access time for the Mod 155 (see Fig. 10.9.3), what must the hit probability be?

REFERENCES

1. Falkoff, A. D., K. E. Iverson, and E. Sussenguth: A Formal Description of System/360, *IBM Syst. J,* vol. 3, no. 3 (1964).

2. IBM Corporation: IBM System/360 Principles of Operation, IBM Form A22-6821, File no. S360-01, White Plains, N.Y.

3. IBM Corporation: A Guide to the IBM System/370 Model 155, no. GC20-1729, White Plains, N.Y.

4. IBM Corporation: IBM System/370 Principles of Operation, no. GA22-6962, White Plains, N.Y.

5. IBM Syst. J., vol. 3, no. 2 (1964). (Contains five articles on logical structure, implementations, processing unit-design considerations, channel-design considerations, and multisystem organization.)

6. Solomon, M. B., Jr.: Economies of Scale and the IBM System/360, *Commun. ACM,* vol. 9, no. 6, (June 1966).

11

Some Principles of Reliability Theory

Popular literature sometimes envisions a future society controlled by the computer. Although this may seem somewhat farfetched, as more of the complex and important problems used in decision making are committed to automatic processes, the computer's role shifts from solely data processing to vital control functions. It is then particularly essential that the computer system perform reliably. Complete breakdown of a system can be bad enough, especially in certain military or *real-time* cases; yet oddly enough, "slight" failures, especially of the intermittent type, can be worse! This is because high-speed processing can propagate a momentary or seemingly minor error very rapidly and in quite subtle ways throughout a computation, leading to wrong results easily accepted as correct. Good equipment and programming practice demand not only that careful attention be given to obtaining an error-free system initially, but also that certain types of errors in equipment and programs that may arise during the system's operational life be detected and corrected. However, there is a practical limit to the degree of error detection possible since the enormous processing capacity of a large computer makes it most difficult to check all results of a big problem. Insofar as we accept and are willing to act on incompletely verified computer results, the system exerts a real control on our behavior.

System reliability considerations must include the following:

1. Estimation of failure (or reliability)
2. Minimization of probability of failure

3. Detection of failure

4. Recovery from failure

All have important implications to the programming as well as to the equipment part of the system. However, the remainder of this chapter is concerned only with equipment reliability and particularly with the mathematical estimation of reliability of a system, given the reliability of its components based on a simple theoretical model of the failure properties of the system.

Reliability has been an essential consideration in computer planning from the earliest days of the electronic machines. Modern system design includes reliability considerations from device to system fabrication to programming. Examples include selection of the simplest and most reliable two-state operation of devices, worst-case design of circuits, parity checking in I/O, storage and data-flow paths, and more elaborate methods such as *echoing* and automatic retry on some mechanical devices. (Echoing is a technique of checking information entered into a device by copying it from that device and comparing this with the original.)

A computer system, of course, includes both equipment and programs. There is a maxim among programmers that states: There is no program which can be absolutely guaranteed to be error-free. Errors and measures to detect and correct errors can originate and be implemented in both hardware and software. For example, error-correcting codes have rarely been built into computer equipment, but programs for error correction have been designed and used. An error-correcting code is particularly valuable for intermittent single errors; for more stable failures, detection that a failure has occurred is usually by parity check or some other such circuit-monitoring device. Once a failure is detected, identifying its location in the machine is usually done by *diagnostic* programs supplied by the manufacturer and run by the repairman. These carefully designed programs feed exercise test patterns into different parts of the machine and compare the actual outputs with precomputed ones. In this way, the power of the stored program is brought to bear on the fault-location problem. Many systems run diagnostic programs routinely even when no errors have been encountered.

Like most other desirable commodities, reliability is costly; the most reliable system may not be the best practical system if the cost is too great. Naturally where national security, human life, or key operations of a firm depend critically on the system, a higher investment in reliability is wise, if not essential; One factor in deciding on the size of investment in reliability improvement is the estimated cost of failure to the users of the system.

Recently, the subject of reliability of general systems has become a full-fledged technical discipline, as evidenced by the appearance of textbooks, numerous technical papers, and professional organizations for workers in this field. A theory of reliability is developing which draws heavily on combinatorial mathematics, probability theory, and statistics. As in most theories, the mathematical techniques are applied to certain idealized models of the real world. In the rest of this chapter, one such model and its users are described.

11.1 DEFINITIONS AND SERIES-PARALLEL CONFIGURATIONS

Any well-defined part of a system that can be classified at all times as either working or else nonworking (failed) will be called a *component.* The *reliability* of a component will be defined as the probability that it will work (will not fail) over some specified time interval. If r is the reliability of a component, then $1 - r$ is the probability of failure (sometimes called the *unreliability*) of the component. A system consists of an interconnection of components. Notice that a system or subsystem is technically also a component. For this discussion, we are not interested directly in the physical interconnections but in a reliability structure which can often be represented as a networklike diagram that displays the behavior of the system from a reliability viewpoint. Two basic reliability structures, each containing n components, may be contrasted. The first, called a *series* system, has the property that if any one of its components fails, the system fails. An alternative statement is: A series structure is one so connected that all its components must work for the system to work. The reliability of the series structure is the *product* of its component reliabilities. In general, a reliability structure containing n components in series, the ith having reliability r_i will have a system reliability p:

$$(1) \qquad p \equiv \mathsf{X}/r \equiv \prod_{i \equiv 1}^{n} r_i$$

Equation (1) is shown in both our notation and the more common Π (for product) notation.

Another simple reliability structure is called *parallel* and has the property that the system fails only if *all* its components fail. In this case, the probability of failure of the system, equal to 1 minus the reliability of the system, is the product of the unreliabilities of the components.

$$(2) \qquad 1 - p \equiv \mathsf{X}/(1 - r)$$
$$p \equiv 1 - \mathsf{X}/(1 - r) \equiv 1 - \prod_{i \equiv 1}^{n} (1 - r_i)$$

Many system reliability structures can be considered to be composed of combinations of series and parallel substructures. The above fundamental relations are then applied to each such substructure until an expression is derived

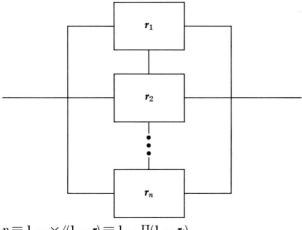

$p \equiv \times / r \equiv \prod_i r_i$

(a) Series reliability structure.

$p \equiv 1 - \times / (1 - r) \equiv 1 - \prod_i (1 - r_i)$

(b) Parallel reliability structure.

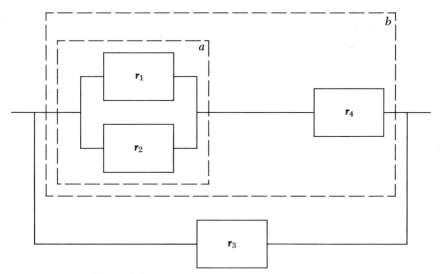

$a \equiv 1 - (1 - r_1)(1 - r_2); \; b \equiv r_4 a$
$p \equiv 1 - (1 - b)(1 - r_3) \equiv 1 - (1 - r_4 a)(1 - r_3)$
$\quad \equiv 1 - (1 - r_4(1 - (1 - r_1)(1 - r_2)))(1 - r_3)$

(c) A series-parallel reliability structure.

Fig. 11.1.1 Series-parallel structures.

for the system reliability in terms of the component reliability. An example is shown in Fig. 11.1.1*c* in step-by-step form. The reliability of the parallel substructure r_1, r_2 is called *a*; the expression for this is combined with r_4 to form the series substructure whose reliability is called *b*; finally *b* and r_3 are combined as a parallel structure to obtain the expression for *p*.

As another example, consider a computer system with the following component reliabilities:

One core storage unit with reliability r_1
One arithmetic unit with reliability r_2
Two disk file units each with reliability r_3
Three tape units each with reliability r_4

For this system to work, the core storage, arithmetic unit, at least one disk file, and at least two tape units must work. What is the reliability of the system? It should be clear that the reliability structure contains r_1 in series with r_2 and this in series with two r_3's in parallel. This substructure is in series with a substructure involving r_4. To derive the reliability representation for the 2-out-of-3-tapes specification, make an eight-row truth table representing the three tapes, place a 1 in the function column wherever the corresponding row has at least two 1s. These rows and their corresponding reliability expressions are

$$
\begin{aligned}
(3) \quad & 011 \rightarrow (1 - r_4)r_4 r_4 \equiv r_4{}^2 - r_4{}^3 \\
& 101 \rightarrow r_4(1 - r_4)r_4 \equiv r_4{}^2 - r_4{}^3 \\
& 110 \rightarrow r_4 r_4(1 - r_4) \equiv r_4{}^2 - r_4{}^3 \\
& 111 \rightarrow r_4 r_4 r_4 \equiv r_4{}^3
\end{aligned}
$$

The reliability of the tape part of the system is the sum of the above expressions:

$$
(4) \quad p \equiv 3r_4{}^2 - 2r_4{}^3
$$

This reliability should then be combined in series with the rest of the system as described earlier. The expression for total system reliability is then

$$
(5) \quad s \equiv r_1 r_2 (1 - (1 - r_3)^2) r_4{}^2 (3 - 2r_4)
$$

11.2   MORE GENERAL RELIABILITY STRUCTURES

Many reliability statements can be set down directly as a reliability structure network or as a truth table. Series and parallel parts may be expressed by some equations of the form of Eqs. (1) and (2), Sec. 11.1, respectively (or some combination of both). These as well as more general structures can be handled by truth table as indicated for the 2-out-of-3 cases of Eq. (3). It is also possible to obtain some relatively easy simplification of the reliability expression by a modification of a process like the Quine-McCluskey algorithm for circuit simplification (see Chap. 5), the main difference being that now a given minterm can be used no more than once in the simplification process.

11.3 COMPONENT VERSUS SYSTEM REDUNDANCY

Thus far only the reliability analysis problem, i.e., the computation of reliability of a given system, has been considered; the problem of improving reliability with specified components will now be explored.

If a system is specified with n components and the system has a reliability p, to improve the reliability it will usually be necessary to add components; the system then contains *redundancy*. In practice, the additional components may, with proper design, also be employed to increase performance. With such a system, highest performance (e.g., speed) is available when all components work. When failure occurs, at least up to some limiting number of components, the system suffers performance degradation, but it is still operational. Such a system is said to "fail softly."

Consider now an elementary question of how best to use a given amount of redundant equipment. If a system originally requires s components in series, each with reliability r, and we are willing to use ms components, there are two schemes that may be contrasted; these are called *component standby* and *system standby*. With component standby, each component is in parallel with $m-1$ components, and these parallel structures are connected in series. Reliability is then

$$(1) \qquad p \equiv (1 - (1 - r)^m)^s$$

With system standby, m systems are in parallel, and each is a copy of the original system containing s components in series. System reliability is

$$(2) \qquad p \equiv 1 - (1 - r^s)^m$$

It can be shown that for any reliability r and given values of s and m (amount of equipment) the component-standby scheme is at least as reliable as system standby. The component-standby system, however, requires more connections.

11.4 TIME-DEPENDENT RELIABILITY

Thus far, component reliability has been represented by the symbol r. In practice r will be a function of time. Theoretical models exist which are particularly suitable for deriving theoretical results and performing computations. Needless to say, the results from these models should be applied with caution to practical situations.

Before discussing a common analytic expression for $r(t)$, it is well to qualitatively consider a more practical case, as shown in Fig. 11.4.1. The shape of the curve is typical of vacuum-tube and many mechanical components. The curve has three regions: the first is called *burn-in* or *infant mortality,* which lasts from installation time to time t_1, after which there follows a period of constant failure rate to t_2, and finally there is the *wear-out* region. Although this function is fairly typical of many actual systems, it is difficult to represent analytically.

Consider the observation of a large number n_0 of identical components over a long time period. As time progresses, some components will fail, and hence the number surviving, n_s, will be a function of time. The reliability of the component at time t will be defined as the fraction of the original number that survive at time t:

$$(1a) \quad r(t) \equiv \frac{n_s(t)}{n_0}$$

Suppose that the components fail in such a way that in the interval from t to $t + dt$ the number that fail, dn_f, is proportional to the number surviving at the start of the interval and to the length of the interval

$$(1b) \quad dn_f \equiv an_s \, dt$$

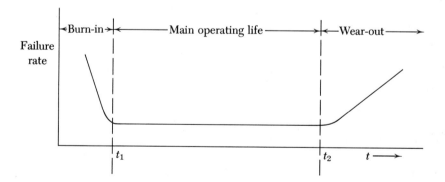

Fig. 11.4.1   Typical form of failure rate versus time.

Since $n_f \equiv n_0 - n_s$ and n_0 is independent of t, (1b) becomes

(1c) $- dn_s \equiv a n_s \, dt$

By (1a), $n_s \equiv n_0 r$, and (1c) can be written

(1d) $\dfrac{dr}{r} \equiv - a \, dt$

Integrating both sides and determining the integration constant with the condition $r(0) \equiv 1$, the exponential law is obtained:

(1e) $r(t) \equiv e^{-at}$

The reliability and failure densities are the derivatives of r and $1 - r$

(2a) $r' \equiv \dfrac{dr}{dt} \equiv - a e^{-at}$

(2b) $(1 - r)' \equiv a e^{-at}$

The *mean time to failure* (MTF) is the average over all time of the failure density

(3) $\text{MTF} \equiv \displaystyle\int_0^\infty t(1 - r)' \, dt$

using (2b) to find $(1 - r)'$

(4) $\text{MTF} \equiv \displaystyle\int_0^\infty t a e^{-at} \, dt$

Integrating by parts

(5) $\text{MTF} \equiv \dfrac{1}{a}$

For n identical components in *series*, exponential distribution of component reliability yields

(6) $p(t) \equiv [r(t)]^n \equiv e^{-nat}$

The mean time to failure of the system is then

(7) $\text{MTF} \equiv \dfrac{1}{na}$

From (5), this is seen to be $1/n$ times the mean time to failure of a single component.

More generally, if n components with nonidentical reliabilities are in series, the ith having a reliability r_i and a mean time to failure of $t_i \equiv 1 \div a_i$, Eq. (6) becomes a product, and for the exponential distribution, the sum of the a_i, appears in the exponent. For this more general case Eq. (7) becomes

$$(8) \qquad \text{MTF} \equiv 1 \div \sum_{i \equiv 1}^{n} a_i \equiv 1 \div +/a \equiv 1 \div +/1 \div t$$

The mean time to failure of a parallel system of identical components can be derived by a process similar to that for obtaining Eq. (7), although the algebraic manipulation is more involved. Using Eq. (2) of Sec. 11.1 and substituting into the definition of Eq. (3),

$$(9) \qquad \text{MTF} \equiv \frac{n}{a} \int_0^\infty at(1 - e^{-at})^{n-1} e^{-at} d(at)$$

Using the binomial expansion for the $1 - e^{-at}$ raised to the $(n - 1)$st power and then integrating and simplifying gives

$$(10) \qquad \text{MTF} \equiv \frac{1}{a} \sum_{j \equiv 1}^{n} (-1)^{j-1} \frac{C_j^n}{j}$$

where C_j^n is the binomial coefficient (number of combinations of n things taken j at a time). Equation (10) can be shown to simplify to

$$(11) \qquad \text{MTF} \equiv \frac{1}{a} \sum_{j \equiv 1}^{n} \frac{1}{j}$$

11.5   CONCLUDING REMARKS

The preceding sections have introduced the theory of reliability. Several assumptions were implicit in the mathematical models. A major one is that the failure properties of each component were independent of all others. Also, no account was taken of preventive and other types of maintenance and procedures for detection and replacement of defective components.

The assumption of exponential reliability dependence on time is important in theoretical work because it is convenient for mathematical treatment, especially in obtaining bounds on reliability improvement as a function of component configuration. The *exponential law* is equivalent to the assumption that the reliability for any given time interval is independent of the age of the component at the beginning of the interval. The reliability literature also treats distributions other than the exponential.

Early work of Neumann and Moore and Shannon established some theoretical methods of building reliable structures from unreliable components.

The theory of reliability is related to information theory, especially coding theory. There is strong evidence that these two disciplines will continue to influence each other productively.

PROBLEMS

11.1 A certain computer system can have the following types of units:

	Reliability
Arithmetic unit (AU)	0.95
Core storage module (CSM)	0.92
I/O channel (CH)	0.85
Disk file (DF)	0.80
Tape unit (TU)	0.80
Card reader/punch (CRP)	0.78

a) What is the reliability of a system consisting of one AU, two CSMs, two CHs, two TUs, one CRP? Assume all units must work for the system to work.

b) Repeat part (*a*), except now assume four TUs are present but that any two of these will suffice to keep the system working.

11.2 *a)* Repeat Prob. 11.1 but now assume two AUs are present only one of which need be working for the system to be working. Compare the reliability to that of Prob. 11.1.

b) If the improvement due to adding the additional AU is not great, discuss other factors that might still suggest a two-AU system.

11.3 Assume exponential forms for all reliability functions.

a) A system has a mean time to failure (MTF) of 14 hours. What is the probability that it will survive 3 hours?

b) What is the probability it will survive 14 hours?

11.4 Assume exponential reliability functions. If the MTF of a certain component is 100 hours, what is the MTF of:

a) Two components in parallel?
b) Four components in parallel?
c) Six components in parallel?

11.5 A certain computer is to contain 50,000 transistors and is to have a MTF of 50 hours. Assuming exponential distribution, what must be the MTF of each transistor?

11.6 *a*) Consider a component standby system with $n - 1$ components in standby, each containing a switch for connecting the standby component in the event of failure. Show that if r is the reliability of each component and w is the reliability of each switch, the system reliability is given by

$$p \equiv 1 - (1 - r)(1 - wr)^{n-1}$$

  b) Take $n \equiv 2$, plot a curve of p versus r for each $w \equiv 0.5, 0.8, 0.9, 0.95, 1$.
  c) Repeat (*b*) for $n \equiv 3, 4, 5$.

11.7 A certain circuit has 32 input lines and 16 output lines, which are the only logic connections to the outside world. Someone has suggested making an "exhaustive" test of the circuit by cycling all possible input vectors in all possible sequences of four per group. How many input vectors would actually be applied to perform this test? Assuming 100 nsec for each generation, how long would the test take?

REFERENCES

1. Barlow, R., and F. Proschan: "Mathematical Theory of Reliability," John Wiley & Sons, Inc., New York, 1965.
2. Bazovsky, I.: "Reliability Theory and Practice," Prentice-Hall, Inc., Englewood Cliffs, N.J., 1961.
3. Calabro, S. R.: "Reliability Principles and Practices," McGraw-Hill Book Company, New York, 1962.
4. Drenick, R. F.: The Failure Law of Complex Equipment, *J. Appl. Math.,* vol. 8, p. 680 (1960).
5. Feller, W.: "An Introduction to Probability Theory and Its Applications," vol. I, John Wiley & Sons, Inc., New York, 1957.
6. Flehinger, B. J., and P. A. Lewis: Two-parameter Lifetime Distributions for Reliability Studies of Renewal Processes, *IBM J. Res. Dev.,* vol. 3 (1959).

7. Moore, E. F., and C. E. Shannon: Reliable Circuits Using Less Reliable Elements, *J. Franklin Inst.,* vol. 262, pp. 191, 281 (September, October 1956).

8. Moskowitz, F., and J. B. McLean: Some Reliability Aspects of Systems Design, *IRE Trans. PGRQC,* vol. 8, no. 7 (1956).

9. Neumann, J. von: "Probabilistic Logics and the Synthesis of Reliable Organisms from Unreliable Components," Princeton University Press, Princeton, N.J., 1956.

10. Pierce, W. H.: "Failure-tolerant Computer Design," Academic Press Inc., New York, 1965.

11. Pieruschky, E.: "Principles of Reliability," Prentice-Hall, Inc., Englewood Cliffs, N.J., 1963.

12. Roberts, N. H.: "Mathematical Methods in Reliability Engineering," McGraw-Hill Book Company, New York, 1964.

Mathematical Constants in Radices 10, 8, and 16; Powers of 2

Mathematical constants in radices 10, 8, and 16

Constant	Radix 10 (decimal)	Radix 8 (octal)	Radix 16 (hexidecimal)
π	3.141592653589793	3.11037552421	3.243F6A89
π^{-1}	0.318309886183790	0.24276301556	0.517CC1B7
$\sqrt{\pi}$	1.772453850905516	1.61337611067	1.C5BF891C
$\ln \pi$	1.144729885849400	1.11206404435	1.250D048F
e	2.718281828459045	2.55760521305	2.B7E15163
e^{-1}	0.367879441171442	0.27426530661	0.5E2D58D9
$\sqrt{e}$	1.648721270700128	1.51411230704	1.A61298E2
$\log_{10} e$	0.434294481903252	0.33626754251	0.6F2DEC55
$\log_2 e$	1.442695040888963	1.34252166245	1.71547653
$\sqrt{10}$	3.162277660168379	3.12305407267	3.298B075C
$\sqrt{2}$	1.414213562373095	1.32404746320	1.6A09E668
$\ln 2$	0.693147180559945	0.54271027760	0.B17217F8
$\ln 10$	2.302585092994046	2.23273067355	2.4D763777
$\log_{10} 2$	0.301029995663981	0.23210115204	0.4D104D42

2^n	n	2^{-n}
1	0	1.0
2	1	0.5
4	2	0.25
8	3	0.125
16	4	0.062 5
32	5	0.031 25
64	6	0.015 625
128	7	0.007 812 5
256	8	0.003 906 25
512	9	0.001 953 125
1 024	10	0.000 976 562 5
2 048	11	0.000 488 281 25
4 096	12	0.000 244 140 625
8 192	13	0.000 122 070 312 5
16 384	14	0.000 061 035 156 25
32 768	15	0.000 030 517 578 125
65 536	16	0.000 015 258 789 062 5
131 072	17	0.000 007 629 394 531 25
262 144	18	0.000 003 814 697 265 625
524 288	19	0.000 001 907 348 632 812 5
1 048 576	20	0.000 000 953 674 316 406 25
2 097 152	21	0.000 000 476 837 158 203 125
4 194 304	22	0.000 000 238 418 579 101 562 5
8 388 608	23	0.000 000 119 209 289 550 781 25
16 777 216	24	0.000 000 059 604 644 775 390 625
33 554 432	25	0.000 000 029 802 322 387 695 312 5
67 108 864	26	0.000 000 014 901 161 193 847 656 25
134 217 728	27	0.000 000 007 450 580 596 923 828 125
268 435 456	28	0.000 000 003 725 290 298 461 914 062 5
536 870 912	29	0.000 000 001 862 645 149 230 957 031 25
1 073 741 824	30	0.000 000 000 931 322 574 615 478 515 625
2 147 433 648	31	0.000 000 000 465 661 287 307 739 257 812 5
4 294 967 296	32	0.000 000 000 232 830 643 653 869 628 906 25
8 589 934 592	33	0.000 000 000 116 415 321 826 934 814 453 125
17 179 869 184	34	0.000 000 000 058 207 660 913 467 407 226 562 5
34 359 738 368	35	0.000 000 000 029 103 830 456 733 703 613 281 25
68 719 476 736	36	0.000 000 000 014 551 915 228 366 851 806 640 625
137 438 953 472	37	0.000 000 000 007 275 957 614 183 425 903 320 312 5
274 877 906 944	38	0.000 000 000 003 637 978 807 091 712 951 660 156 25
549 755 813 888	39	0.000 000 000 001 818 989 403 545 856 475 830 078 125
1 099 511 627 776	40	0.000 000 000 000 909 494 701 772 928 237 915 039 062 5
2 199 023 255 552	41	0.000 000 000 000 454 747 350 886 464 118 957 519 531 25
4 398 046 511 104	42	0.000 000 000 000 227 373 675 443 232 059 478 759 765 625
8 796 093 022 208	43	0.000 000 000 000 113 686 837 721 616 029 739 379 882 812 5
17 592 186 044 416	44	0.000 000 000 000 056 843 418 860 808 014 869 689 941 406 25
35 184 372 088 832	45	0.000 000 000 000 028 421 709 430 404 007 434 844 970 703 125
70 368 744 177 664	46	0.000 000 000 000 014 210 854 715 202 003 717 422 485 351 562 5
140 737 488 355 328	47	0.000 000 000 000 007 105 427 357 601 001 858 711 242 675 781 25
281 474 976 710 656	48	0.000 000 000 000 003 552 713 678 800 500 929 355 621 337 890 625

Summary of Some Results in Combinatorial Analysis and Probability †

B.1 ARRANGEMENTS WITH AND WITHOUT REPLACEMENT

Consider a set of n objects numbered uniquely from 1 to n. A sequence of k selections (drawings) is to be made each of a single object, and after each such drawing the number of the selected item is to be recorded. Thus after k drawings, we have a sequence of k integers; each of the integers can have a value between 1 and n. We are interested in the number of possible sequences that can be formed under various rules of making selections and of counting sequences as distinct.

The first distinction in considering possible sequences is whether after a given object is drawn (and its identifying number recorded) it is returned to the set of eligible objects for subsequent drawings or not. If the object is returned, the drawings are said to take place *with replacement*. In this case, a sequence of k recordings can have the same integer appearing more than once; in fact it can have as many as k appearances of the same integer. In enumerating the sequences, the first element may be set down in n ways; with each of these the

†For more on these topics, see W. Feller, "An Introduction to Probability Theory and Its Applications," vol. I, 2d ed., John Wiley & Sons, Inc., New York, 1957, and J. Riordan, "An Introduction to Combinatorial Analysis," John Wiley & Sons, Inc., New York, 1958.

second may also be chosen in n ways so that there are n^2 sequences of length 2, n^3 sequences of length 3, and in general

(1) n^k

sequences of length k. A listing of all of these sequences is essentially the same as listing all possible representations of integers k digits long in a number system of radix n, the only difference being that we agreed to number the elements 1 to n, while the integers would show elements from 0 to $n - 1$.

Another rule of making drawings of k objects from n objects again selects an object from an eligible set of objects, but now, once an object is drawn and its number recorded, it is no longer eligible for drawing in the sequence. In other words, drawings to form a sequence are made *without replacement*. The first drawing is therefore made from n objects, the second from $n - 1$ objects, the third from $n - 2$ objects, etc. The number of possible sequences of length k that can be formed is called the number of *permutations* of n things taken k at a time and is given by

(2) $P(n,k) \equiv P_k{}^n \equiv n_k \equiv n(n - 1)(n - 2) \cdot \cdot \cdot (n - k + 1)$

where the symbols at the left are all used to denote the same function. $P(n,k)$ can also be expressed in terms of factorials:

(2a) $P(n,k) \equiv \dfrac{n!}{(n - k)!}$

A related function also resulting from drawings without replacement counts all sequences that contain the same elements only once; i.e., it does not include in the count any sequence that can be obtained from another by rearranging elements. This function is called the number of *combinations* of n things taken k at a time (without replacement). It is equal to the number of permutations divided by $k!$ since this latter number is the number of ways of arranging k things. This function together with some common notations for it is

(3) $C(n,k) \equiv C_k{}^n \equiv \dbinom{n}{k} \equiv \dfrac{P(n,k)}{k!} \equiv \dfrac{n!}{k!(n - k)!}$

$C(n,k)$ is sometimes called the binomial coefficient since it is the coefficient of the kth term in the expansion of $(x + y)^n$.

The entire discussion thus far will be illustrated with the following example. Given four objects from which sequences of two drawings are to be made so that $n \equiv 4, k \equiv 2$.

For the drawings, if made with replacement, there are, from Eq. (1), 4^2 sequences as follows:

```
1,1   2,1   3,1   4,1
1,2   2,2   3,2   4,2
1,3   2,3   3,3   4,3
1,4   2,4   3,4   4,4
```

For drawings without replacement, the number of permutations using Eq. (2a) is $4!/2! \equiv 12$ and are enumerated as

```
1,2√   2,1    3,1    4,1
1,3√   2,3√   3,2    4,2
1,4√   2,4√   3,4√   4,3
```

The number of combinations is given in Eq. (3) as $4!/2!2! \equiv 6$ and are shown checked.

Another type of combination reckoning may be identified with drawing k objects from n objects *with replacement*. Here a sequence may of course contain one or more elements more than once so that the number of these combinations is not C_k^n. Since we seek the number of combinations, we exclude rearrangements of all those that are included. For example, only one of the sequences

```
1,2,1,4
2,1,4,1
```

is counted. The number of combinations of this type is

$$(4) \qquad D(n,k) \equiv \frac{(n + k - 1)!}{k!(n - 1)!}$$

**B.2 THE BINOMIAL DISTRIBUTION
AND ITS POISSON APPROXIMATION**

Consider a sequence of trials, called Bernoulli trials, where in each trial there are only two possible outcomes called *success* and *failure*. Let the probability of success in a *single* trial be p and the probability of failure be $1 - p$. A trial may be identified with a drawing with replacement. The probability that in a sequence of n such trials there will be k successes is given by the binomial distribution:

(5) $\quad b(k,n,p) \equiv p^k(1-p)^{n-k}C(n,k)$

$$\equiv p^k(1-p)^{n-k}\frac{n!}{k!(n-k)!}$$

As with all probability functions

(6) $\quad \displaystyle\sum_{k=0}^{n} b(k,n,p) \equiv 1$

A special case of some interest is where $p \equiv \frac{1}{2}$. Then substituting Eq. (5) into (6)

(7) $\quad \displaystyle\sum_{k=0}^{n} C(n,k) \equiv 2^n$

Two important properties of the binomial distribution are the mean and the variance:

(8) $\quad \displaystyle\sum_{k=0}^{n} kb(k,n,p) \equiv np \qquad \text{(mean)}$

(9) $\quad \displaystyle\sum_{k=0}^{n} (k-np)^2 b(k,n,p) \equiv \sum_{k=0}^{n} (k^2 - (np)^2)b(k,n,p) \equiv np(1-p)$

$$\text{(variance)}$$

The second form of the variance may be obtained from the first by expanding the parenthesis term and using Eq. (6). Another useful form of Eq. (9) is

(10) $\quad \displaystyle\sum_{k=0}^{n} k^2 b(k,n,p) \equiv np(1+np-p)$

Consider now drawings made from a collection of $a + b$ objects of which a are of one type, say red balls, and b are of another type, black balls. If n drawings are made *with replacement,* the process can be identified with the Bernoulli trial model and the probability of drawing k red balls is given by the binomial distribution of Eq. (5) with

(11) $\quad p \equiv \dfrac{a}{a+b}$

If, however, the drawings are made *without replacement,* the probability of k successes is given by the *hypergeometric* distribution

$$(12) \quad h(k,n,a,b) \equiv \frac{C(a,k) \; C(b,n-k)}{C(a+b,n)}$$

When $a+b$ is large compared with n, the hypergeometric distribution approaches the binomial distribution since the lack of replacement will have only a slight influence on the result.

Returning to the binomial distribution of Eq. (5), this function is not particularly easy to compute or manipulate analytically. Under certain ranges of the variables, a more convenient form, called the Poisson distribution, is approximately equivalent. First, we define

$$(13) \quad \lambda \equiv pn$$

Then if

$$(14) \quad \lambda^2 \ll n$$

the binomial distribution may be approximated by the Poisson distribution

$$(15) \quad p(k,\lambda) \equiv e^{-\lambda} \frac{\lambda^k}{k!}$$

Of course the general properties stated for the binomial distribution of Eqs. (8) to (10) continue to apply, but in terms of λ they are

$$(16) \quad \sum_{k=0}^{n} k e^{-\lambda} \frac{\lambda^k}{k!} \equiv \lambda \quad (\text{mean})$$

$$(17) \quad \sum_{k=0}^{n} (k-\lambda)^2 e^{-\lambda} \frac{\lambda^k}{k!} \equiv \lambda(1-p) \equiv \lambda \quad (\text{variance})$$

$$(18) \quad \sum_{k=0}^{n} k^2 e^{-\lambda} \frac{\lambda^k}{k!} \equiv \lambda^2 + \lambda - \lambda p \equiv \lambda^2 + \lambda$$

Summary of some results from combinatorial analysis and probability theory

	Drawings with replacement	*Drawings without replacement*
Permutations of n things taken k at a time	n^k	$P(n,k) \equiv \dfrac{n!}{(n-k)!}$

← —— Example enumerations for $n \equiv 4$, $k \equiv 2$ —— →

1,1	2,1	3,1	4,1	1,2	2,1	3,1	4,1
1,2	2,2	3,2	4,2	1,3	2,3	3,2	4,2
1,3	2,3	3,3	4,3	1,4	2,4	3,4	4,3
1,4	2,4	3,4	4,4				

Combinations of n things taken k at a time	$D(n,k) \equiv \dfrac{(n+k-1)!}{k!(n-1)!}$	$C(n,k) \equiv \dfrac{n!}{k!(n-k)!}$

1,1	2,2	3,3	4.4	1,2	2,3	3,4
1,2	2,3	3,4		1,3	2,4	
1,3	2,4			1,4		
1,4						

Identity: $\displaystyle\sum_{k\equiv 0}^{n} C(n,k) \equiv 2^n$

Probability of k successes in n trials	Binomial distribution:	Hypergeometric distribution:

$$b(k,n,p) \equiv p^k(1-p)^{n-k}\,\frac{n!}{k!(n-k)!} \qquad h(k,n,a,b) \equiv \frac{C(a,k)C(b,n-k)}{C(a+b,n)}$$

$p \equiv$ probability of success in one trial

$a \equiv$ No. of red balls
$b \equiv$ No. of black balls

Properties of the binomial distribution:

$$\sum_{k\equiv 1}^{n} k\,b(k,n,p) \equiv np \qquad \text{mean}$$

$$\sum_{k\equiv 1}^{n} (k-(np))^2\,b(k,n,p) \equiv np(1-p) \qquad \text{variance}$$

$$\sum_{k\equiv 1}^{n} k^2\,b(k,n,p) \equiv np(1+np-p)$$

Poisson approximation (good if $p \ll 1$; $pn \equiv \lambda$; $\lambda^2 \ll n$):

$$b(k,n,p) \approx b(k,\lambda) \equiv \frac{e^{-\lambda}\lambda^k}{k!}$$

Index